MISERY BENEATH THE MIRACLE IN EAST ASIA

Studies of the Weatherhead East Asian Institute, Columbia University

The Studies of the Weatherhead East Asian Institute of Columbia University were inaugurated in 1962 to bring to a wider public the results of significant new research on modern and contemporary East Asia.

MISERY BENEATH THE MIRACLE IN EAST ASIA

Arvid J. Lukauskas
and Yumiko Shimabukuro

CORNELL UNIVERSITY PRESS   ITHACA AND LONDON

Copyright © 2024 by Cornell University

All rights reserved. Except for brief quotations in a review, this book, or parts thereof, must not be reproduced in any form without permission in writing from the publisher. For information, address Cornell University Press, Sage House, 512 East State Street, Ithaca, New York 14850. Visit our website at cornellpress.cornell.edu.

First published 2024 by Cornell University Press

Library of Congress Cataloging-in-Publication Data

Names: Lukauskas, Arvid John, author. | Shimabukuro, Yumiko, 1979- author.
Title: Misery beneath the miracle in East Asia / Arvid J. Lukauskas and Yumiko Shimabukuro.
Description: Ithaca : Cornell University Press, 2024. | Series: Studies of the Weatherhead East Asian Institute, Columbia University | Includes bibliographical references and index.
Identifiers: LCCN 2024024933 (print) | LCCN 2024024934 (ebook) | ISBN 9781501778735 (hardcover) | ISBN 9781501778742 (paperback) | ISBN 9781501778759 (epub) | ISBN 9781501778766 (pdf)
Subjects: LCSH: Social problems—Government policy—East Asia. | East Asia—Economic policy—Social aspects. | East Asia—Social conditions—21st century.
Classification: LCC HN720.5.A8 L85 2024 (print) | LCC HN720.5.A8 (ebook) | DDC 306.095—dc23/eng/20240709
LC record available at https://lccn.loc.gov/2024024933
LC ebook record available at https://lccn.loc.gov/2024024934

In memory of Rubee and Toto

Contents

Acknowledgments	ix
List of Abbreviations	xi
Introduction: Societies in Distress	1
1. The Promise and Perils of Productivism	11
2. Misery in the Golden Years: The Old Age Crisis in South Korea	51
3. Broken Promises: The Low Wage Crisis in High Performing Taiwan	74
4. Abused and Neglected: The Other Children's Welfare Crisis in Japan	100
5. In the Shadow of Victoria Peak: The Affordable Housing Crisis in Hong Kong	124
6. Left Behind: Misery beneath the Miracle in China	150
Conclusion: Lessons from East Asia and Advancing a New Research Agenda	179
Notes	201
Bibliography	251
Index	293

Acknowledgments

This book benefited tremendously from the research assistance and valuable insights of Ho Young Lee and Bingxing Zhou, both practitioners in the social sector. The reviewers of our manuscript helped make it so much better in every possible way. We were privileged to receive such incisive, encouraging, and incredibly thoughtful comments. We are indebted to the editorial committee of the Studies of the Weatherhead East Asian Institute and the entire team at Cornell University Press for bringing this project to fruition. No words can properly express our gratitude to Jim Lance, senior editor, for his counsel, patience, and vision. We extend special thanks to Ariana King for her skillful guidance from the start to the finish line. Finally, our heartfelt thanks to our families, friends, and colleagues, in particular, at the Picker Center for Executive Education, the Urban and Social Policy Program, and the Program in Economic Policy Management at the School of International and Public Affairs, for their unwavering support throughout.

Abbreviations

Organizations

ADB	Asian Development Bank
ILO	International Labour Organization
IMF	International Monetary Fund
OECD	Organization for Economic Co-operation and Development

General Terms

AI	Artificial intelligence
ALMPs	Active labor market policies
BLSP	Basic Livelihood Security Program
BOAI	Basic Old Age Insurance
BOAP	Basic Old-Age Pension
CAPL	Child Abuse Prevention Law
CPA	Child Protection Agency
CPF	Central Provident Fund
CRC	Convention on the Rights of the Child
DPP	Democratic Progressive Party
EITC	Earned Income Tax Credit
FDI	Foreign direct investment
GDP	Gross domestic product
HDB	Housing Development Board
HKD	Hong Kong dollar
HKHA	Hong Kong Housing Authority
HOS	Home Ownership Scheme
HPLS	Home Purchase Loan Scheme
KMT	Kuomintang
LDP	Liberal Democratic Party
Legco	Legislative Council (Hong Kong legislative body)
LPH	Light public housing
MHLW	Ministry of Health, Labor and Welfare
MMD/SNTV	Multimember-district, single-nontransferable voting

MSF	Ministry of Social and Family Development
NPS	National Pension Service
NTD	New Taiwanese dollar
PBD	Purpose built dormitory
PLMPs	Passive labor market policies
PWM	Progressive Wage Model
ROC	Republic of China
SD	Singapore dollar
SFSTS	Sale of Flats to Sitting Tenants Scheme
SMEs	Small- and medium-sized enterprises
SOEs	State-owned enterprise
TFP	Total factor productivity
TPS	Tenants Purchase Scheme
URRPS	Urban and Rural Residents Pension Scheme
USD	United States dollar

MISERY BENEATH THE MIRACLE IN EAST ASIA

INTRODUCTION
Societies in Distress

East Asia's economic success is undeniable. The region experienced the most rapid growth of any other in the postwar era, and its stunning transformation inspired some scholars to speak of the East Asian miracle. Living up to its name, East Asia remains the world's fastest growing region and includes nations with some of the globe's highest standards of living. Perhaps the most remarkable story belongs to China, whose growth since 1980 has accounted for a large percentage of the increase in the world's gross domestic product (GDP) in that period. Moreover, many practitioners consider East Asian economies to be the exemplar in several policy areas, including the provision of infrastructure, trade promotion, and industrial development. They have also received high praise for making astute investments in human capital, by building the capacities of individuals through education, job training, and health care, and maintaining equitable distributions of income even as they grew quickly (except China). The region's policymakers and many scholars have trumpeted these accomplishments and noted their achievement even when government spending, especially on social policy, was kept to comparatively low levels.

Yet, a darker reality lurks beneath this picture of economic success and smart social investments. For some, the first hint that things were amiss may have been the critically acclaimed, Academy Award–winning film *Parasite*, which captured the sharp divisions in South Korean society and the hardships faced by ordinary citizens.[1] In reality, the headlines in major newspapers have revealed societies in distress for some time:

> "*No Country for Old Koreans: Moon Faces Senior Poverty Crisis*"
> "*Humans in Cages: Hong Kong's Shoebox Housing*"
> "*Record 219,000 Cases of Child Abuse Logged in Japan in Fiscal '22*"
> "*Long Working Hours and Low Pay Will Become the Norm in Taiwan*"
> "*Left-Behind Children a Poignant Reminder of the Cost of China's Development*"[2]

These articles are at odds with the well-established story of East Asia's many achievements, suggesting that a rewrite of the region's moniker to "misery beneath the miracle" is in order. South Korea, for instance, has been touted as a poster child for economic development, yet two-fifths of the individuals who made the miracle happen—currently elderly—live in poverty. Taiwan, whose strong economy initially produced sustained salary increases and rising household wealth, is now experiencing wage stagnation, even among the well-educated. Hong Kong has generated immense wealth and luxurious standards of living for elites, yet many citizens are resigned to living in scandalously deficient "cage" or "coffin" housing. Japan has prided itself on cherishing its offspring, but incidents of child maltreatment are growing in number and severity.

These paradoxical outcomes are alarming because neighboring China, which has followed a similar trajectory of rapid growth propelled by the main elements of the East Asian model, is experiencing many of the same serious social ills as it reaches the status of an upper-middle-income country. Old age poverty is endemic, income growth is slowing after years of rapidly rising wages, inequality has widened, cities are struggling to supply sufficient affordable housing, and the massive migration of workers from rural to urban areas that fueled rapid industrialization has left millions of children and seniors behind in precarious conditions.

East Asia's social welfare crises are having dire, far-reaching consequences for individual well-being, human capital development, the social fabric of communities, economic performance, and governance. Japan's child maltreatment crisis has cast a shadow over its long-run economic health, since victims are more prone to mental illness and end up being less productive in adulthood. South Korea's elderly poverty crisis has triggered a recent spike in suicides, crimes, and even incidents of prostitution among seniors. Taiwan's low-wage crisis has provoked a mass exodus of talented students and skilled workers to mainland China and the United States, depleting its human capital. Hong Kong's affordable housing crisis has contributed to acute income inequality that continues to threaten its political stability even after Beijing started to exert greater control over its affairs. In China, over sixty-seven million so-called left-behind children must fend for themselves while their parents work as migrant laborers in urban centers, rendering them prone to maltreatment and poverty. The incidence and high costs of these social welfare emergencies prompt one to ask: Why are these miracle economies experiencing such alarming problems today?[3]

This book analyzes this perplexing question in an innovative way by introducing a new methodological approach: dynamic integrated social welfare analysis. We contend that the extant social policy literature tends to be siloed, both in terms of focus and disciplinary approach, and thereby is susceptible to glossing over important interactions among different policy areas; static, by ignoring the impact of transformative processes such as urbanization and skill-biased technical change; and one-dimensional, by neglecting to look at problems and policies from the perspective of individuals and households, as well as policymakers. We posit that many valuable insights can be gained by studying multiple social policy issue areas simultaneously from the perspective of several disciplines in an integrated fashion, considering dynamic elements such as the welfare system's response to major trends, and adopting a dual micro/macro lens that captures the view from both the ground and above. This method requires treating the social welfare policy space as a complex system and examining the myriad of interactions among its elements when evaluating policies and outcomes.

The dynamic integrated approach led us to design four case studies that blend interdisciplinary research with powerful narratives of how government action (or inaction) shapes people's lives. Two of our studies involve the primary spheres of social welfare policy, which scholars typically identify as social insurance, social assistance, and labor market policies.[4] The chapter on South Korea focuses on old-age security, especially its main policy instrument, public pensions, which is the largest component of social insurance spending in most developed countries. The Taiwanese case probes labor market policies and income support initiatives for workers, which is a primary form of social assistance. The other two cases expand the scope of welfare analysis by exploring policy spheres that are frequently overlooked but have a major impact on individual well-being, social cohesion, and economic growth. Our study of Japan investigates the grave ramifications that rising maltreatment of children has for social well-being and economic performance, as well as the government's belated policy response. The chapter on Hong Kong analyzes public housing and the role it plays in shaping a variety of major economic, political, and social welfare outcomes.

Each of the social ills that we examine has been perceived as more acute in recent years, in some instances prompting the first ever consequential governmental response. Child maltreatment, old age poverty, and housing are long-standing social concerns in the region that have gained salience or intensified lately, whereas stagnant wages and declining standards of living for average families are relatively new phenomena. In the case of the former, the social problems in question may have posed significant difficulties previously, but, since they were occurring during a period of rapid growth, they were seen as standard for that stage of development and therefore something that could or even should be addressed in the future. The current level of income or development reached in these countries makes it hard to justify the view that these struggles are still normal or something that can comfortably be shelved for later. In the case of the latter, East Asian nations are beginning to confront some of the same labor market dilemmas that advanced industrial nations in the West have grappled with for decades.

To explore these crises, we have paired each substantive issue area with the nation where it has posed the greatest policy challenge. In three of the four cases—South Korea, Taiwan, and Hong Kong—the issue analyzed in each chapter has been the most severe social malaise faced by that society in recent times, although not necessarily by a large margin. In Japan, other social ills, such as old age and working poverty, have rivaled child maltreatment as the most pressing, but government policy toward mistreatment reveals hitherto understudied features of that country's social welfare system. In each chapter, we also review the experience of the other three nations as well as neighboring Singapore in addressing that particular social problem and find that they have also confronted numerous challenges.[5] China is the subject of a chapter of its own, in which we investigate how it has tackled the same four issues.

What we find strikes a raw nerve. The roots of the social crises plaguing these nations partly lie in the unique mix of progrowth policies that they implemented with apparent success during their period of rapid growth. Scholars have named their approach productivism to describe the general strategy of prioritizing economic outcomes at the expense of social welfare concerns.[6] Under productivism, governments kept safety nets purposefully threadbare but rewarded select groups, such as workers deemed to be critical for industrial development, with targeted social protection schemes. Since the state chose not to provide universal social assistance, it depended on corporations and families to serve as the principal means of managing socioeconomic risks for many citizens. Delegating this role to private actors allowed government officials to focus their attention on the development policies they believed were needed to sustain the economic miracle, most notably, social investment in education and health care.

China presents the more complicated case of "productivism with Chinese characteristics." Unlike the other nations discussed here, it had a planned economy and welfare system based on socialist principles until 1978, when a series of massive reforms pushed it toward a more capitalist structure accompanied by a market-based welfare model. Like their counterparts in other East Asian countries, policymakers concentrated on achieving rapid growth and consistently dedicated few resources to addressing social issues. Indeed, economic performance took on added significance in China because political leaders viewed it as the key to their legitimacy; in effect, they pledged to provide rapidly increasing standards of living in exchange for political and social quiescence. In the social welfare sphere, policymakers also favored certain groups in conferring benefits, such as urban workers. They relied on communities and families to provide needed support to vulnerable groups—notably, migrants, the elderly, and left-behind children—in the process creating tremendous disparities in welfare services.

Some scholars have cast the productivist approach in a positive light.[7] In their view, East Asian economies modernized quickly while enjoying a relatively equitable distribution of income—without the need for substantial government social spending. Rapid growth lowered the number of those living in absolute poverty and contributed to impressive improvements in human development indicators. Levels of human capital rose dramatically, permitting these countries to upgrade their economies in the face of the mounting international competition brought on by globalization. Private welfare solutions adequately protected the handful of citizens that needed assistance.

We contend that this is an overly rosy view of productivism that ignores several important deficiencies. We paint a more complete picture by analyzing the interplay between its different elements, examining how its impact has varied across social groups, and adopting a dynamic rather than static perspective in order to understand how it has evolved. We identify four characteristics of productivist systems that render them particularly ill-equipped to deal with the serious social problems now raging, especially those that disproportionately affect lower-income groups.

First, the basic structure of productivist welfare systems exposes sizable portions of society to significant social and economic risks. A stark dualism lies at the very heart of the productivist approach. East Asian nations dedicate considerable resources to managing the socioeconomic risks facing favored groups of citizens but eschew the policies needed to create a safety net for the working poor, unemployed, and other disadvantaged groups. For the latter, productivism is an empty promise that leaves them largely unprotected against serious hardship. In this, they differ from their Western peers in choosing a welfare strategy that excludes large segments of their populations from enjoying the economic success to which they have contributed. Productivist systems count on private actors, especially communities and families, to cushion the impact of adverse developments on these citizens. Yet, no guarantee exists that private mechanisms will materialize or suffice, especially as societies undergo major transformations that disrupt traditional support systems.

Second, every social welfare system must adapt to macro-level economic, political, and social trends in order to serve citizens effectively. Productivism struggles to adjust to the challenges they present because its policies are limited in scope and depth, making it difficult to ramp up spending or coverage in response to heightened demand, and because it relies excessively on private actors to furnish socioeconomic protection. Four ongoing, large-scale forces, namely, globalization and skill-biased technical change, extensive and rapid urbanization, powerful demographic trends, and changing family structures, are undermining the viability of the East Asian model. The socioeconomic insecurity felt by lower income groups in particular has been amplified by these developments. For instance, declining fertility and changing family structures have hindered the familial provision of welfare services at precisely the same time that skill-biased technical change has increased the need for it by heightening employment precariousness and earnings uncertainty among low-skill workers. Furthermore, some of these potent forces, notably, urbanization, are themselves the byproducts of the region's rapid growth. Exploring this feedback loop and its effect on the viability of key components of productivism yields a more dynamic conceptualization of East Asian social policy.

Third, the productivist model has engendered a political environment that facilitates its reproduction over time but hinders its ability to adapt to changing circumstances. Several scholars have argued that some East Asian governments are taking decisive action by expanding their welfare states and different strands of social policy are emerging across the region as a result.[8] On the contrary, we show that they mostly are holding fast, by implementing policies that appear to supply more protection to the needy but, in reality, are intended only to abate the most severe aspects of a problem and silence political criticism. The coalition that helped create and sustain productivism, consisting primarily of business and favored labor groups, remains intact and typically opposes the expansion of social assistance or income support. Governments may be spending more on social welfare, but they continue to withhold the resources needed to ameliorate the harm that crises are inflicting upon vulnerable groups. We label this politically expedient strategy of favoring appearance over action a *policy façade*.

Finally, the implementation of policy façades has taken a heavy human toll already. But the costs do not stop there. The systemic failure to address social crises adequately is having a significant but little discussed negative impact on the performance of East Asian economies. Moreover, the tendency of productivism to self-inflict serious economic harm is likely to damage the region's long-term growth prospects, thereby undercutting its principal perceived benefit. In Japan, the child maltreatment crisis has imposed costs of approximately USD16 billion each year and, as previously noted, victims are likely to experience decreased productivity and employability in adulthood. In South Korea, severe elderly poverty has turned a potential "silver economy" boom into a bust by suppressing the consumption of debt-ridden senior citizens. In Taiwan, persistent low wages have resulted in human capital flight and an increased risk of a downward spiral in the size of the labor force by discouraging many couples from marriage and childbearing. In Hong Kong, acute inequality heightened by the affordable housing crisis has hurt economic performance by undermining social mobility and limiting educational opportunities and skill development, especially for low-income children. In China, the failure to furnish adequate social services has forced households to guard against insecurity by saving at very high rates, making it difficult for the country to shift its economic model away from export-led growth toward the more sustainable domestic-driven consumption approach sought by the government.

By identifying both the welfare and economic costs of productivism, our study highlights the risks of maintaining an extreme imbalance between growth and social protection strategies. In this way, it contributes to the broader literature on the complex relationship between economic development and the provision of social welfare. Specifically, it lends support to the view, advanced by both historians and theoreticians, that certain types of social expenditures may be complementary to long-term growth by reducing socioeconomic risks for workers, allowing them to save less and spend more, promoting gender equality, and improving the investment climate for firms by creating a more stable, productive workforce.[9] The amount and type of social expenditures needed to maximize economic returns surely vary across countries, but it almost certainly requires higher and more diverse disbursements than indicated by those who believe social spending detracts from growth.

Understanding the strengths and weaknesses of productivism can also enrich theorizing about social welfare systems more generally. In chapter 1, we situate East Asia in comparative perspective by contrasting its systems to those in OECD (mostly Western) countries. There are startling differences in levels of overall social spending and expenditures in specific categories (notably, social assistance and unemployment compensation), as well as in the primary beneficiaries of public outlays. Chapter 7 delves deeper and shows that these differences have not diminished significantly for most nations despite the region's economic modernization and, in some cases, democratic reforms. We note, however, that Japan and (increasingly) South Korea have come to resemble liberal welfare states, a category frequently used in the comparative welfare literature on Western states.

In summary, this book helps readers to better understand the benefits and pitfalls of East Asia's approach to economic growth and social investment. Existing scholarship generally has overlooked the severity, persistence, and harmful consequences of social welfare crises in the region; this volume fills this gap and places a major asterisk on its economic achievements. It identifies the forces that are undermining the viability of the East Asian growth model and elucidates how policy façades leave those who need social protection the most without adequate support. These findings strongly confirm the emerging view among scholars that social welfare paradoxically may deteriorate for some households as economies develop and modernize, bringing the region into the ongoing debates about economic insecurity that have troubled the United States and other advanced industrialized countries. Certainly, East Asia deserves a more prominent place in the literature on social welfare due to its sizable population, growing significance on the world stage, and frequent mention as a model for other countries. Other emerging market countries will also begin to face the same challenges (if they have not already), probably without the advantage of the region's superior economic performance. They would do well to consider the East Asian experience as they design future public policies.

Using Narratives for Research and Teaching

One element of our integrated approach is the use of short composite narratives that provide intimate views on how ordinary citizens are coping with rising socioeconomic insecurity and the deficiency of government policy responses. Largely constructed through field research observations and interviews, journalistic accounts, and scholarly sources, they capture the lived experiences of representative individuals, which often involve pain, uncertainty, vulnerability, disbelief, and frustration, that are frequently difficult to evoke in conventional academic writing. Details on each of the narratives—what informed and inspired them—are noted in the individual chapters.

Why do we incorporate narratives in presenting our research? Cognitive scientists have shown that our brains are wired to learn through people-oriented stories because they lead to higher levels of engagement and remembering.[10] Storytelling has been deployed frequently in medical education, in areas such as illness narratives, and is increasingly used in social science research as a communication or teaching tool to convey urgency and deconstruct complex issues, especially when dealing with wicked problems like poverty.[11] Narratives also provide better contextualization for tragic outcomes like child abuse deaths, which are difficult to fathom through data analysis alone. In the realm of social welfare,

Andrea Campbell, Matthew Desmond, and Jacob Hacker are among those who have fused human stories with scholarly texts to provide a more complete picture of today's socioeconomic malaise and the ongoing public policy challenges in the United States.[12]

Storytelling can also be an important step in generating new research agendas and theories. The "epistemic value of storytelling" in social science is especially high for stories that are "anomalous" (i.e., when they show that existing models fall short of explaining real-world phenomena) or "immutable" (i.e., when they provide well-established details that reveal the shortcomings of a new model).[13] Stories also help us grasp data analysis and new statistical methods by providing real world examples of abstract reasoning and making our findings more accessible to those outside academia.[14]

In regard to teaching, our narratives are intended to promote active learning among students as they engage with the latest body of academic research. We have used unabridged versions of them at all levels of teaching—undergraduate, graduate, and executive education—for people from all walks of life and nations. One of the key pedagogical benefits of storytelling is the phenomenon of "learning by feeling" that enables readers to explore challenging, complex phenomena by experiencing the associated emotional dynamics.[15] Emotional engagement and personal relevance have been demonstrated to maximize knowledge transfer and its retention.[16] Narratives also promote a culturally responsive learning experience by helping students to better understand different societies and connect with people living in distant places.[17]

The narratives in the Japan and South Korea chapters adopt the innovative case writing style of the late Patricia Gercik, the former managing director of the Massachusetts Institute of Technology's Japan Program. Gercik's narratives featured engaging dialogues and nuanced contextual details on complicated issues such as North Korean abductions of Japanese citizens and the inner workings of Japanese corporate relations and practices.[18] They left an indelible mark on many generations of students in the popular Japanese politics course (dubbed Rawfish 101) cotaught with Dick Samuels. We honor and hope to carry on her legacy of creative, empathetic instructional efforts through this book.

A Note about Data

Assembling the data for this book presented specific challenges. Statistics on social protection spending and outcomes in the six countries studied here and OECD countries used in comparisons are available from several sources, but, in most cases, each reference covers only a subset of these nations and/or limited time periods. The Asian Development Bank (ADB) has developed an innovative data set on social protection outlays in Asia, but it does not include Hong Kong or Taiwan, and the latest statistics using this methodology are from 2015. The OECD has the most comprehensive data on social protection with statistics provided up to at least 2019 for most indicators, but they usually cover member states exclusively, which in our book means only Japan and South Korea. The International Labour Organization (ILO) reports figures on many social issues, but its data are drawn from various sources, and, oftentimes, the years provided vary greatly across countries. National governments also supply statistics on social spending, but they sometimes employ categories that differ significantly or data are aggregated in ways that make identifying specific expenditures problematic. As a consequence, we often had to pull figures from more than one source or omit specific countries on particular issues when compiling comparative statistics, especially in time series. When combining data sources, we made every effort to use measures that were as consistent as possible. In the case of nationally sourced data, we employed the methodology used by either the ADB or OECD (as the situation demanded) wherever possible to prepare our statistics. We note specific difficulties and how we addressed them in the notes wherever caution is required on the part of the reader in interpreting results. The data in this book are the latest available as of October 2023.

1

THE PROMISE AND PERILS OF PRODUCTIVISM

East Asia is widely known for its spectacular economic achievements. In the period 1960 to 2000, the region's nations grew at a rate unprecedented in world history. Real gross domestic product (GDP) per capita increased by a factor of 11.3 in Taiwan, 9.1 in Hong Kong, 8.2 in South Korea, 7.3 in Singapore, 5.0 in Japan, and 4.8 in China.[1] All six countries were among the world's top ten fastest growing economies during these four decades.[2] Their performance led to rapid modernization and development, improved standards of living, and greater economic and political importance on the global stage. Furthermore, some East Asian nations achieved these feats while maintaining a relatively egalitarian distribution of income, which contrasts with the experience of most other countries that have grown quickly.

Although these economies have cooled in the post-2000 period, notably, Japan, they continue to perform very well. Their GDP per capita place them among the world's richest nations, and their human development indicators rank among the highest. Nevertheless, East Asian societies are concurrently confronting a number of serious human crises. Old age poverty has increased to high and persistent levels, rising housing prices threaten affordability for many households, wages have stagnated, income inequality is climbing, and reported incidents of child maltreatment have soared. Thus far, the government response to these problems has been inconsistent, inadequate, and ineffective. Policymakers seem reluctant to allocate sufficient funds or devise lasting solutions to address these social issues.

We contend that these crises are partly a by-product of the particular development strategy that Hong Kong, Japan, South Korea, Singapore, and Taiwan followed during their period of fast economic growth—productivism. This approach led to excellent performance but also unleashed powerful forces that engendered serious social problems. The political coalitions that have coalesced around productivism have made it difficult for policymakers to implement a vigorous set of reforms or create a larger safety net to remedy deteriorating conditions if they were inclined to do so. Instead, they have adopted a largely reactive approach—what we term a *policy façade*—that favors appearance over action and entails high costs for vulnerable populations and national economies.

China also has pursued a high growth strategy, and its social policy has exhibited the main characteristics of productivism. It introduced major reforms starting in 1978 aimed at moving away from a command-and-control toward a more capitalist economy. This transformation was accompanied by a shift from direct state provision of welfare services to more market-based distribution. Nonetheless, the core of the government's approach remained wedded to the idea that social spending should be minimized in order to channel resources toward the greater goal of economic modernization. In recent years, officials have also shared the emphasis on human capital development typical of productivism in an attempt to upgrade the economy toward knowledge-intensive sectors. We find that China has not escaped the social ills confronting its peers; on the contrary, it faces even more severe difficulties because several of its institutional features amplify the effects of transformative forces like urbanization.

Scholars of comparative politics and political economy often have underestimated the undesirable consequences of East Asia's productivist model, perhaps blinded by the light of its outstanding economic performance. In particular, they have relied on the conventional wisdom that rapid growth was egalitarian to ignore any negative outgrowths of productivism, confident that the region's widely lauded investments in human capital would be sufficient to create opportunities for all households in the long run. As a result, they have overlooked emerging difficulties and missed the opportunity to develop a nuanced view of the region's economic strategy, one that comprehends its strengths and weaknesses as it confronts contemporary trends, like skill-biased technical change, that are disrupting welfare policy in all nations. To be clear, East Asia's social challenges must be viewed within an overall context of success. The region continues to be the object of envy on the part of citizens in other countries, particularly those that have struggled to sustain growth. Nevertheless, we point out that East Asian policymakers have chosen to allow these problems to persist and even worsen despite having ample means to address them head on.

We emphasize at the outset that we do not claim that productivism is the only cause of East Asia's misery today. The nations that we examine share several characteristics beyond the productivist approach, such as a tradition of Confucianism, political systems with often limited competition, and weak labor movements. A case can be made that one (or all) of these variables contributed to the crises facing the region, either directly or by acting to limit public spending to address them. This complicates the task of determining the specific role played by productivism in shaping social welfare outcomes. In terms of comparative method, it would be ideal if our analysis included nations that have not pursued a productivist model to better assess its importance as an explanatory variable, but no such country exists in the region. The nature of productivism does vary somewhat across countries, and we do consider if those differences contributed to distinct patterns in the features and impacts of social welfare policy, thereby shedding some light on this issue.

We also recognize that these shared factors likely played a role in leading East Asian public officials to adopt a productivist strategy. Nonetheless, we believe that productivism has had an independent effect on outcomes by virtue of integrating these elements into a fairly coherent worldview of social welfare that is distinct from others; that is, we consider it to be more than an intervening variable. No single factor could have given rise to a comprehensive strategy featuring all of productivism's specific characteristics of dualistic targeting of social protection, private provision of welfare, and heavy emphasis on human capital development. The whole of productivism is greater than the sum of its parts.

A remaining option for assessing the impact of productivism is to compare its outcomes to those of countries from outside the region that have adopted other social welfare models. The limitation of this approach is that it does not exclude the possibility that other differences between the regions, such as political institutions or culture, are responsible for any variation we see. For this exercise, we have opted to contrast social policies in East Asia to those in the West. The comparison to other developed nations is apt as they also have some form of advanced capitalist system and similar levels of GDP per capita. We find startling differences in their levels of social expenditures both overall and on specific types of programs, as well as in qualitative elements like the beneficiaries of these outlays. In general, developed nations in the West have experienced less severe social problems than in East Asia, at least in the issue areas covered in this book. We employ an analytical method that demonstrates how the various elements of productivism interacted as part of a complex system to shape outcomes in this way, lending credence to the hypothesis that this welfare strategy has played a major role in fostering crises in the region. We call this method dynamic integrated social welfare analysis.

This chapter begins by outlining our method and indicating why we believe it remedies blind spots encountered in many conventional studies of social policy. It then turns to an analysis of East Asia's economic model and performance, highlighting the factors that scholars have identified as responsible for its success. An examination of the region's welfare policy in comparative perspective follows, where we note its significant differences with the models commonly found in other developed countries. Next, we show that existing perspectives on productivism limit our understanding of its advantages and disadvantages, particularly with respect to its ability to cope with social problems. We offer a reconceptualization of productivism that identifies its structural weaknesses, such as its dualistic character, an inability to adapt to large-scale trends, like declining fertility, a strong bias to sustain the status quo, and the potential for self-infliction of serious economic costs. We find that the productivist approach leaves the poor and other disadvantaged groups exposed to serious economic risk and hardship.

Dynamic Integrated Social Welfare Analysis

This book advances a dynamic integrated approach to social welfare analysis that addresses gaps in existing research and expands our understanding of policy choices and outcomes. Much of the extant literature is siloed, both with respect to disciplinary approach and analytical focus, and overlooks critical interactions among policy areas; static, by ignoring the effects of critical trends, such as skill-biased technical change or declining fertility; and one-dimensional, by failing to consider social problems and government policies from the perspective of individuals and households as well as policymakers. Valuable insights can be obtained by examining multiple social welfare issue areas simultaneously from the perspective of different disciplines in an integrated fashion, considering dynamic elements such as the welfare system's ability to respond to large-scale forces like urbanization, exploring the interaction among its elements, and using a dual micro/macro lens to capture the views of ordinary citizens, as well as government officials. In other words, we treat the social welfare policy space as a complex system and include what scholars call system effects in our evaluation of policy outcomes.[3]

Viewing each social policy as part of a broader welfare system clarifies the ways in which a country's overarching strategy influences its design and implementation. In productivist systems, every policy area reflects the overall dualistic approach of targeting government benefits to select elements of society, such as workers who are deemed essential for industrial development, and not disadvantaged groups. The Taiwanese government, for instance, funneled resources into expanding already extensive tertiary education as opposed to training low-skill workers living near the poverty line. Similarly, the generous pensions for urban workers in China contrast sharply with the extremely low payments paid out to migrants and rural laborers.

A more complicated task is understanding the interactions among various policy spheres and how their evolution is reshaping the system itself. The most significant drawback of a siloed (and often single disciplinary) analysis of a social policy domain is its inability to identify interactive effects across multiple policy arenas and explore their consequences. In productivist welfare states, the interconnectivity of seemingly disparate policy spaces is extensive and has far-reaching, sometimes unintended consequences. For example, the heavy emphasis on improving human capital through privately funded education (social investment) has led many seniors in South Korea to dedicate most of their life savings to cover the high educational expenditures of their children; as a result, many elderly enter retirement with no nest egg and, due to inadequate pensions, fall into poverty (old age security). Another type of interconnectedness is revealed in the ways in which macro-level trends may undermine policies in key issue areas and, hence, compromise the viability of the overall social welfare strategy. For instance, urbanization and changes in family structure have diminished the ability of children to supply assistance to their aged parents (old age security) and of younger parents to care for their offspring properly (child welfare). The growing inability to rely on private welfare solutions is, in turn, generating pressure on governments to amend their strategy by augmenting levels of assistance, something that they have largely resisted doing so far.

Addressing these shortcomings, we develop an interdisciplinary, integrated approach to the study of social welfare that better captures the interactions among the elements of the system. Thus, we examine not just social insurance, social assistance, and labor market policies but also broaden the scope of the book to include often omitted topics such as housing and child welfare. Moreover, in aggregate, our country studies explore the welfare issues related to childhood, young adulthood, adulthood, and the senior years, thereby enabling us to explore interpolicy dynamics over an individual's life course. The analysis draws from not just economics, political science, and sociology, the mainstay of a great deal of work on social welfare systems, but also social work, anthropology, demography, psychology, and urban policy studies.

Another limitation of existing scholarship is that most research on national social welfare systems tends to be static in nature, restricting itself to taking a snapshot of a particular moment in time and, perhaps, weighing similarities to and differences with other countries. These studies frequently end up describing a steady-state structure and, thereby, overstate the system's stability as well as fail to assess how it may evolve over time. We adopt a more dynamic approach by exploring productivism's capacity to adapt to large-scale exogenous and endogenous developments, such as skill-biased technical change and urbanization. We also incorporate a temporal dimension by investigating the delayed effects of polices, as well as feedback loops affecting the system as a whole. Several elements of productivism, such as its reliance on private not public protection of vulnerable dependents, have undermined its potential to contribute to sustained economic growth. For instance, the insufficient response to child maltreatment in Japan has generated high direct and indirect economic costs in the contemporary period and is hindering the accumulation of human capital required to maintain growth in the face of a declining population.

Finally, with a few exceptions, studies of social welfare issues usually choose a macro lens that delineates their broad context but ignores the experiences of individuals and households within this setting. A top-down perspective is a necessary component of any social welfare analysis. National or subnational data reveal the scope, depth, and extent of a social problem and examining the policymaking framework identifies the key actors, institutional settings, and processes by which decisions are made and which instruments are available to government officials. Yet, individuals and households have important stories to tell as well. Seeing social ills from the perspective of ordinary citizens, that is, applying a micro lens that captures the views from the ground, helps us to identify the problems they face, how current government policy affects them, and how they are attempting to adjust to changing circumstances, yielding a more comprehensive analysis.

We introduce a micro lens through narratives that clarify what is at stake in human terms. These narratives are composites of personal stories constructed through field research observations, journalistic accounts, and interviews. Each chapter covering a social crisis begins with this view from the ground. It provides an intimate look into how ordinary citizens are coping with the crisis and the deficiency of government efforts to address the rising socioeconomic insecurity that derives from it. We link these individual experiences (the micro level) to the forces that are causing social ills, the features of the policymaking environment, and the government's policy response (the macro level).

East Asia's Pursuit of Growth

East Asia's economic performance since 1960 is unparalleled. The most remarkable growth occurred between 1980 and 2000, when the region as a whole grew by 6.1 percent annually in real terms.[4] Its achievements contrast markedly with the experience of other regions dominated by emerging economies. In the period 1980 to 2000, Latin America (0.1 percent), Sub-Saharan Africa (−0.6 percent), and the Middle East and North Africa (0.2 percent) all failed to generate sustained economic growth, even though many countries in these regions were better positioned initially than East Asian nations; South Asia performed well (3 percent) but still lagged East Asia considerably. The lack of growth left populations in some nations no better off (or even worse) in real terms than they were decades earlier.

The collective story of East Asian countries was praised in the widely read World Bank publication *The East Asian Miracle*.[5] The report attributed their success to their export orientation, rapid accumulation of physical and human capital, generally sound macroeconomic policies, and superior governance structures. As late industrializers, East Asian nations were able to copy available technology from abroad and leverage their lower production costs to move into sectors once dominated by Western economies. The outward orientation forced national firms to raise their productivity and efficiency to meet the test of international competition and enabled them to tap into economies of scale. Accumulation of human capital through public and private investment made workers more adaptable and capable of completing complex and nonroutine tasks, which is a prerequisite for countries hoping to compete in knowledge-intensive sectors. Governance structures provided a degree of autonomy for technocratic policymakers who were selected on the basis of merit and enabled them to design economic policy in the public interest, not just for narrow constituencies.[6] The Chinese case is more complicated because it underwent a transition from a closed, command-and-control economy to an export-oriented, more market-based one during this period.

Some researchers have additionally claimed that state intervention in the economy in the form of comprehensive industrial policies and protectionism was a key element, as it enabled East Asian nations to move up the value chain far more quickly, bypassing less sophisticated economic activities.[7] The so-called developmental state perspective suggests that without state guidance these countries might not have been able to compete in leading edge economic sectors already occupied by advanced industrial nations.[8] Others have argued that government efforts to steer industrial development actually harmed economic growth in some respects by channeling scarce resources to final users that could not deploy them most effectively, as seen in the low returns in several favored sectors (such as semiconductors).[9] Nonetheless, they acknowledge that East Asian nations managed their economies far more effectively overall, in part by implementing other government policies to offset the distortionary impact of misdirected state intervention.

Scholars have often claimed that East Asian countries grew quickly, while maintaining fairly equitable distributions of income (except China), in contrast to most emerging market nations where increases in inequality typically accompany modernization in the early stages. Table 1.1 only partially confirms this claim.[10] In 1965, South Korea and Taiwan, which were just initiating rapid growth, had after taxes and transfers (hereafter, *after*) Gini coefficients below 0.350 and they stayed low through 2015.[11] As points of comparison, the United States (0.397 in 1967), Germany (0.380 in 1964), and France (0.461 in 1965) evidenced substantially higher coefficients in the same period.[12] Hong Kong and Singapore, however, exhibited greater before taxes and transfers (hereafter,

TABLE 1.1 Before and after taxes and transfers Gini coefficients in East Asia, 1965–2015

		1965	1970	1980	1990	2000	2010	2015
China	Before	n/a	n/a	n/a	n/a	n/a	n/a	n/a
	After	n/a	n/a	0.310 (1981)	0.349	0.438	0.481	0.462
Hong Kong	Before	0.467 (1966)	0.409 (1971)	0.451 (1981)	0.476 (1991)	0.525 (2001)	0.537 (2011)	0.539 (2016)
	After	n/a	n/a	n/a	n/a	0.470 (2001)	0.475 (2011)	0.473 (2016)
Japan	Before	0.338	0.407	0.345 (1985)	0.403 (1995)	0.432	0.488	0.504
	After	n/a	n/a	0.304	0.312	0.337	0.336	0.339
South Korea	Before	n/a	n/a	0.324	0.292	0.324	0.341	0.341
	After	0.344	0.332	0.313	0.273	0.305	0.310	0.295
Singapore	Before	n/a	0.410 (1973)	0.442	0.410	0.444	0.480	0.463
	After	n/a	n/a	n/a	n/a	0.414	0.425	0.409
Taiwan	Before	n/a	n/a	0.278	0.312	0.326	0.342	0.336 (2016)
	After	0.321 (1964)	0.294	0.267 (1981)	0.271 (1991)	0.286	0.317	0.303 (2016)

Sources: For 1965–70: Solt, "Measuring Income Inequality." For 1980–2015: OECD, "Income Distribution"; Luxembourg Income Study, "Luxembourg Income Study Database," 2023; Zhuang and Shi, "Understanding Recent Trends in Income Inequality"; Hong Kong, "Hong Kong Annual Digest of Statistics 2012 Edition," November 2012; "Hong Kong Annual Digest of Statistics 2017 Edition," October 2017; Republic of Singapore, Ministry of Finance, "Income Growth, Inequality and Mobility Trends in Singapore," August 2015; Kang, "Globalization and Income Inequality in Korea: An Overview" (paper presentation, FDI, Human Capital and Education in Developing Countries FDI Technical Meeting, Paris, December 2001); Taiwan (ROC), National Development Council, "Taiwan Statistical Data Book 2019," National Development Council, May 2019

before) inequality than both their peers and many Western nations in this period, and continue to do so. They have also had high after coefficients from the time those data became available. Japan had low before inequality in 1965, but it rose rapidly thereafter to levels that by 2015 classified it as one of the most unequal advanced industrial countries (the OECD average was 0.471 in 2016). In contrast, its after inequality remained stable at levels slightly above most Western nations (the OECD average was 0.315 in 2016) throughout.[13]

Two factors help to explain the initial low degree of inequality in some East Asian economies. First, Japan, South Korea, and Taiwan implemented land reforms before industrializing, in effect redistributing wealth away from large landowners and helping to level the economic and political playing field.[14] These reforms improved agricultural productivity, enabling the sector to grow unimpeded; in contrast, many other countries taxed agriculture heavily to finance industrialization, which hindered its development, and incomes in rural areas dropped far below those in urban areas. Second, several writers have contended that political leaders implemented a policy of "shared growth," dividing increases in income far more equally between capitalists and workers than in other nations.[15] They did so by encouraging firms to grant steady wage increases to ensure that ordinary households experienced improving standards of living and, in a few cases, by providing subsidized housing. In some societies, policymakers adopted these measures as part of a sweeping bargain that offered material gains to citizens in exchange for political acquiescence. Nonetheless, most governments, notably, South Korea, also exercised firm control over workers in the belief that a disciplined, relatively low-cost labor force was essential for development.[16]

It is instructive to compare the trajectory of economic growth and inequality in the Scandinavian countries (Denmark, Finland, Norway, and Sweden) with the East Asian experience. Scandinavian economies grew at steady, albeit far slower, rates throughout this same time period and became well-known for their egalitarian distribution of income (see table 1.2). Their before Gini coefficients rose sharply, yet their after coefficients remained very low (well below those in East Asia)—under 0.28 in all countries, for all years. This is because Scandinavian governments aggressively redistributed income through social policy and taxes to achieve greater equality. East Asia's initial success in accomplishing both rapid growth and an equitable distribution without carrying out significant redistribution of income is a marked contrast. Similar levels of inequality in both regions might have reduced pressure on East Asia's conservative regimes to provide more social services as their economies flourished based on the conclusion that they were not needed to achieve desirable outcomes.

In short, East Asian governments seemingly were able to limit social expenditures and still attain some of the same outcomes prized by other advanced

TABLE 1.2 Economic growth rates and Gini coefficients for Scandinavian countries, 1985–2015

			1985	1995	2000	2010	2015
Denmark	Gini	Before	0.37	0.40	0.42	0.43	0.45
		After	0.22	0.23	0.23	0.25	0.26
	Growth rate		2.8	2.9	1.6	1.2	2.4
Finland	Gini	Before	n/a	0.40	0.48	0.49	0.51
		After	n/a	0.22	0.26	0.27	0.26
	Growth rate		2.9	4.8	3.2	0.6	1.8
Norway	Gini	Before	n/a	0.40	0.43	0.41	0.43
		After	n/a	0.24	0.26	0.25	0.27
	Growth rate		3.4	3.8	2.3	1.5	1.5
Sweden	Gini	Before	n/a	0.44	0.45	0.44	0.43
		After	n/a	0.21	0.24	0.27	0.28
	Growth rate		2.0	3.4	3.0	2.5	2.6

Source: OECD, "Income Distribution"; World Bank, "GDP Growth (Annual %)," World Development Indicators, 2023

industrial countries. Yet, a multitude of serious social problems now plague these societies and threaten to get worse. Can the region's nations persist in having minimal safety nets and still maintain high standards of living for all of their citizens? Can the productivist welfare model sustain rapid growth? In the following two sections, we begin to answer these questions by examining productivism's characteristics in detail and situating it within the universe of national welfare systems.

Situating East Asia in Comparative Welfare Studies

Productivism and Other Welfare Models

In most industrialized countries, economic development eventually led to the emergence of sizable welfare states, featuring a robust safety net and the provision of social insurance. Starting in the 1950s, a large body of research has explored how and why nations converged toward supplying more expansive social services as they encountered the disruptive changes associated with modernization, namely, transitioning from agriculture to industry, a closed to an open economy, and relationships based on personal kinship to impersonal exchanges.[17] By the late 1990s, scholars had identified divergent patterns of social welfare evolution among advanced industrial countries and formulated theories to explain them. Gøsta Esping-Andersen's pioneering research on the "three worlds of welfare states" captured much of the crucial variation among industrialized nations.[18] In *social democratic* welfare systems, found primarily in Scandinavian countries, governments spend an average of about 27 percent of GDP on social welfare and implement the most generous, universalistic, and redistributive programs. Many Western European countries, such as Germany, have *Bismarckian* systems built upon occupation-based social insurance schemes and expend an average of around 24 percent of their GDP on social welfare. Finally, Anglo-Saxon *liberal* welfare systems, exemplified by the United States, feature targeted, means-tested programs with limited benefits and modest levels of social insurance, and trail behind in social outlays at roughly 19 percent of GDP on average.

As scholars turned their eyes to East Asia, they discovered that countries were pursuing a mix of public policies that seemed largely unique to the region.[19] Ian Holliday was among the first to position them in the broader comparative literature, and he called their distinct social welfare strategy productivism.[20] Productivism described the general approach of subordinating social welfare to the dictates of a growth-oriented economic policy instead of allowing it to develop according to its own internal logic. This approach led governments to channel maximum resources toward the economy and resulted in a slim welfare state. The social expenditures they did make were concentrated in healthcare and education as these were viewed as necessary to increase human capital and equip workers to engage in a widening and more sophisticated set of economic activities.[21] Productivist regimes evidenced "limited commitment to the notion of welfare as a right of citizenship," in contrast to social democratic and Bismarckian welfare states that extended broad social rights.[22] Policymakers kept safety nets threadbare purposefully, opting to rely on corporations, families, and communities to manage socioeconomic risks for most citizens, but not all. Workers deemed to be critical for economic modernization, for instance, were rewarded with targeted protection schemes to gain their allegiance and boost their productivity.[23] In sum, in productivist systems, policies to assist the less fortunate, such as social assistance, appeared largely as afterthoughts, add-ons, or late additions to those focused on achieving rapid, sustained growth.

Holliday did not view productivism as a singular, homogenous model. He identified three broad strains of productivism in which states were differentiated primarily on the basis of their treatment of social insurance. In Hong Kong, which made up the "facilitative" subset, the government limited its involvement in the social welfare sphere in general but did intervene in certain markets, notably, housing, in order to supply the dwellings required to shelter the workers needed for industrialization. In Singapore, which comprised the "developmental-particularist" subset, policymakers established a mandatory individual savings vehicle, the Central Provident Fund, to help create affordable housing and advance old age security, mitigating the need for extensive social insurance. The government's housing policy was also a means of restructuring social relations in an ethnically divided society. Finally, the "developmental-universalist" subset, encompassing Japan, South Korea, and Taiwan, focused their efforts on the provision of social insurance, developing more comprehensive programs for health and old age.

In an equally important contribution, Ito Peng and Joseph Wong offered the complementary perspective that East Asia was not monolithic but rather exhibited two broad patterns of social policy evolution.[24] The first, seen in Japan, South Korea, and Taiwan, was an inclusive social insurance model that was beginning to develop redistributive programs based on universality and social solidarity. The second, found in China, Hong Kong, and Singapore, was characterized by an individualistic and market-based approach to social welfare. We agree that some differences in social policy do exist across these two country groupings, but, as we show throughout this book, they are more alike than not in certain key elements: low overall levels of social protection (with the exception of Japan), which is skewed heavily toward insurance; the identity of the groups that benefit the most from public outlays, namely, the nonpoor, as opposed to the poor; and minimal safety nets for vulnerable groups, as seen in very low levels of expenditures on social assistance. Moreover, the purported differences between the two groups frequently do not hold for individual issue areas. For instance, Japan has adopted a market-based housing policy, whereas in Singapore the government has built public units that house nearly 80 percent of the population, motivated in large part by the objective of promoting social solidarity.

We view productivism as a useful analytical construct that identifies a set of common policies and strategies across East Asia and helps to connect our cases. In other research, we show that some productivist welfare systems resemble the liberal welfare model found in Esping-Anderson's three worlds of welfare typology.[25] In both instances, social insurance vastly exceeds assistance, public benefits go disproportionately to the nonpoor, few programs aim to improve the prospects of low-skill workers and the unemployed, and nonstate actors supply many welfare services. A primary difference is that liberal welfare states have higher overall expenditures and more comprehensive and diverse social programs, reflecting the greater maturity of their systems. Japan stands out in as much as it straddles the productivist and liberal welfare models, sharing characteristics with both its East Asian and Western peers. Its total social spending is significantly higher than its neighbors and it has a more elaborate, mature set of programs, yet many of the qualitative features of its welfare system align with the productivist model; indeed, the only real difference is that Japan spends much more on insurance than other nations in the region. Adopting a broader view, recent empirical work, based on the concept of decommodification, has concluded that Japan is a liberal welfare state.[26] In the concluding chapter we suggest that viewing productivist and liberal welfare states as points on a continuum can sharpen our understanding of both systems. Specifically, both models engender political coalitions around welfare issues that make them vulnerable to the same types of social problems but less able to confront them effectively.

The next subsection situates East Asia in comparative perspective by examining the level of government social expenditures across industrialized countries. Spending is only one dimension of the extent and nature of the commitment to providing citizens with social protection. Thus, we also analyze other aspects of welfare policy, such as the identity of intended beneficiaries, the degree and scope of coverage, and the quality of social services (as well as greater details on spending) later in this chapter and throughout the book.

Relative Levels of Social Protection

Expenditures on social protection typically are divided into three broad categories—social insurance, social assistance, and active labor market programs (ALMPs). The classification of programs according to this typology was first developed to describe and analyze patterns of social spending in advanced industrial countries in the West.[27] Social insurance is comprised of pensions, health insurance, and other forms of insurance, including for unemployment and disability, and maternal benefits. Social assistance consists of welfare, child welfare, and elderly programs, as well as health and disability benefits to those who do not qualify for insurance. ALMPs involve measures to raise low wages through public employment training, job creation, and job placement services.

How do levels of social protection spending in East Asia and the OECD compare?[28] OECD countries are a useful point of comparison as their levels of economic development and national income are similar.[29] In 2015, overall social expenditures in East Asia, except Japan, were much lower, as table 1.3 shows.[30] The table includes three individual OECD countries that represent the welfare models discussed previously: Sweden (social democratic); Germany (Bismarckian); and the United States (liberal). We also have provided the averages for the pool of all thirty-seven OECD countries and the so-called OECD-18, a grouping of wealthier, original member states that is frequently the object of academic studies on social welfare.[31]

TABLE 1.3 Social protection in East Asia and OECD (as a % of GDP), 2015

	TOTAL PROTECTION	SOCIAL INSURANCE	SOCIAL ASSISTANCE	ALMP
China	7.7	6.9	0.6	0.1
Hong Kong*	5.4	3.6	1.8	0.1
Japan	21.9	19.9	1.8	0.2
South Korea	9.6	7.6	1.8	0.3
Singapore	5.3	4.1	0.9	0.3
Taiwan*	9.2	8.3	0.9	0.1
Germany	25.1	20.3	4.1	0.6
Sweden	26.1	19.0	5.8	1.2
United States	18.5	15.8	2.7	0.1
OECD average	20.1	16.7	2.9	0.5
OECD-18 average	23.8	19.6	3.5	0.7

* Hong Kong: ALMP, 2011; Taiwan: ALMP, 2010

Sources: Asian Development Bank, *Social Protection Indicator for Asia*; OECD, "Social Expenditure – Aggregated Data," OECD Social and Welfare Statistics, 2023; Hong Kong, "Hong Kong Annual Digest of Statistics 2019 Edition," October 2019; Chris K. C. Chan and Yujian Zhai, "Active Labour Market Policies in China: Towards Improved Labour Protection?," *Journal of Asian Public Policy* 6, no. 1 (2013): 10–25; Taiwan (ROC), Statistical Bureau, "Social Protection Expenditure," 2023

In all of East Asia, disbursements for both social insurance and assistance as a percentage of GDP were well below the OECD averages, with one exception (Japan, in the case of insurance). The gap in expenditures was especially pronounced for social assistance, where even the region's three highest spenders—Hong Kong, Japan, and South Korea (at 1.8 percent)—were well below the OECD and OECD-18 averages (2.9 percent and 3.5 percent, respectively), and for ALMPs, where only Singapore and South Korea (at 0.3 percent) were close to the OECD and OECD-18 averages (0.5 percent and 0.7 percent, respectively).[32] Nations in the region spent far more on insurance than assistance as their advanced industrial peers did, but the imbalance in their expenditures was generally much greater. Table 1.4 breaks down social insurance spending by type and reveals that there was no consistent pattern in East Asia of favoring outlays for pensions over health care, as OECD nations did.

Table 1.5 disaggregates social assistance spending, which serves as the foundation of safety nets for the poor, by category. No country in East Asia expended more than 0.9 percent of GDP on welfare assistance, which is the type of disbursement most specifically targeted toward low-income individuals. The International Labour Organization (ILO) supplies data for one major element of welfare assistance ("general social assistance for persons of active age"); for this component alone, the OECD and OECD-18 averages were 0.9 and 1.1 percent of GDP, respectively.[33]

TABLE 1.4 Social insurance expenditures in East Asia and OECD (as a % of GDP), 2015

	TOTAL INSURANCE	PENSIONS	HEALTHCARE	OTHER
China	6.9	3.3	1.8	1.8
Hong Kong	3.6	1.2	2.2	0.2
Japan	19.9	8.3	9.2	2.4
South Korea	7.6	2.6	3.8	1.2
Singapore	4.1	0.0	0.4	3.7
Taiwan	8.3	4.6	3.1	0.6
OECD average	16.7	7.4	5.7	3.6
OECD-18 average	19.6	8.7	6.3	4.6

Sources: Asian Development Bank, *Social Protection Indicator*; OECD, "Social Expenditure – Aggregated Data," OECD Social and Welfare Statistics, 2023; Hong Kong, "Annual Digest of Statistics 2019"; Chan and Zhai, "Active Labour Market Policies in China"; Taiwan (ROC), Statistical Bureau, "Social Protection Expenditure"

TABLE 1.5 Social assistance spending in East Asia by category (as a % of GDP), 2015

	TOTAL ASSISTANCE	WELFARE	ELDERLY	CHILD WELFARE	HEALTH	DISABILITY
China	0.6	0.4	–	0.1	–	0.1
Hong Kong	1.8	0.9	0.8	–	–	0.1
Japan	1.7	0.8	–	0.5	–	0.4
South Korea	1.8	0.3	0.6	0.4	0.4	–
Singapore	0.9	0.8	0.1	–	–	–
Taiwan	0.9	0.5	0.1	–	0.1	–

Sources: Asian Development Bank, *Social Protection Indicator*; Hong Kong, "Annual Digest of Statistics 2019"; Taiwan (ROC), Statistical Bureau, "Social Protection Expenditure"

At first glance, Japan's social welfare profile appears to be very similar to those of other OECD countries. A more careful look, however, reveals that the similarities have been confined to insurance spending, which was many multiples higher than assistance spending (11.4 times versus 4.0 for the OECD average). In the realm of social assistance, Japan more closely resembled its neighbors than nations in other regions. Remarkably, Japan expended the same amount on assistance as a percentage of GDP as Hong Kong or South Korea despite spending far more on social protection overall. This low level of assistance was not due to the fact that it was unneeded: Relative poverty in Japan has remained stubbornly high and totaled 15.7 percent in 2015.[34] In addition, its coverage rates for assistance programs were the lowest in the region in 2015 (see table 1.7). Studies have shown that Japan has designed eligibility criteria to be highly exclusionary in order to discourage applicants from receiving benefits.[35] Moreover, in the case of social insurance, expenditures on the nonpoor were more than double those on the poor, revealing that they were intended to benefit the middle class, not to protect the poor (see table 1.6).

Some scholars have argued that East Asian countries, notably, Japan and South Korea, had sizable functional equivalent programs that partially substituted for the lack of direct social protection spending discussed previously.[36] They included job protection, public works, agricultural subsidies, and policy interventions to boost specific economic sectors, such as trade protection for farmers or assistance for small- and medium-sized enterprises (SMEs). These programs were viewed as functional equivalents in that they created employment or provided income support, or helped to protect jobs by giving employers incentives to retain personnel in difficult economic times or imposing regulations that made layoffs costly.

We caution against the inclusion of functional equivalent programs in assessing the level of social protection for several reasons. First, this hypothesis has yet to undergo rigorous and comprehensive empirical testing to evaluate the effects of these programs on managing socio-economic risks and providing income maintenance over time. We do not know exactly who the beneficiaries are, how they receive their benefits, and what the value of their welfare substitution effect is. If functional equivalent programs were being used as a means of delivering benefits—and of doing so effectively—their primary impact would be on the market distribution of income, that is, prior to taxes and transfers. This does not appear to be the case in Japan, as it has experienced high and rising before taxes and transfers Gini coefficients (table 1.1). Second, functional equivalent programs often have offsetting negative impacts. Agricultural subsidies or protectionist barriers, for example, may boost the income of certain rural households or insure against income volatility, but simultaneously increase the price of food, leading to higher expenditures on a significant portion of a poor household's budget, particularly in urban areas.[37] The net effects of these programs as a means of providing social assistance or insurance, therefore, is an open question and their use raises a host of thorny distributional questions. Third, many functional equivalents are episodic in nature. Public works programs (for instance, new highway construction) create mostly temporary jobs that disappear once the project is completed. Finally, the primary purpose of most functional equivalent programs is not to advance social policy objectives. These interventions may have social welfare implications, but they are typically designed to meet other goals, such as delivering patronage to key constituencies. In Japan, the majority of regulatory or subsidy programs channel benefits to politically well-connected and already well-off businesses (including SMEs).[38] Their overall effect, therefore, may be to exacerbate rather than ameliorate inequality and reinforce the dualistic outcomes created by social protection programs. Similarly, employment protections in Japan and South Korea often deepen the existing insider–outsider cleavage in labor markets, leaving unprotected workers to fend for themselves at an even greater disadvantage. Thus, we view the majority of the previously mentioned programs not as functionally equivalent but as fundamentally economically or politically motivated programs that do little to enhance social protection schemes or offset their deficiencies in aggregate.

Reconceptualizing Productivism

Productivism has often been cast in a positive light because of East Asia's remarkable economic performance.[39] As the story goes, nations grew rapidly while maintaining a relatively equitable distribution of income. As a result, the number of absolute poor declined sharply and human development indicators showed constant improvement. Levels of human capital grew steadily, supplying the manpower needed to upgrade economies in the face of mounting international competition brought on by globalization. Governments smartly limited expenditures on social spending, thereby allowing resources to be mobilized in pursuit of superior economic performance and, in some cases, national security. Private welfare solutions adequately protected citizens in need.

We acknowledge these accomplishments but offer a more balanced assessment of productivism that highlights several major shortcomings as well. We use dynamic integrated social welfare analysis to dissect the interplay between its different elements and examine the impact it has had on a broad spectrum of social groups. We also move beyond a static picture of East Asian social policy to one that explores its ability to adapt to changing circumstances. Our analytical framework identifies four critical features of productivist systems that render them more likely to suffer serious welfare crises. First, their defining structural feature exposes sizable segments of society to significant social and economic risks. At the heart of productivism are dualistic social policies that cater to favored societal groups, while failing to fund safety nets for the needy. Second, they struggle to adapt to adverse developments because government programs are limited in scope and depth, making it difficult to ramp up spending or coverage in response to heightened need. Third, they create strong vested interests that are well situated to hinder reform. Finally, productivism tends to self-inflict serious economic harm that may damage growth prospects in the long run, undercutting its principle touted benefit.

A Dualistic Social Welfare System

THE ROBIN HOOD PARADOX OF SOCIAL PROTECTION

Social protection in East Asia presents a clear Robin Hood paradox: Those who need it the most get the least.[40] Table 1.6 disaggregates expenditures on social insurance and assistance by recipients classified as the nonpoor versus the poor.[41] Total social protection spending favored the nonpoor to a large degree. This pattern was most pronounced in the case of China, but in no country did the poor receive more than 30 percent of total disbursements. It is especially startling that in Singapore assistance outlays, which are those most critical to low-income households, benefitted the nonpoor over the poor. In China, Japan, and South Korea the poor received more social assistance than the nonpoor, but absolute expenditures were small. Governments channeled more spending to the nonpoor even though relative poverty rates in these countries remained stubbornly high. Poverty affected 34.2 percent of the population in China (2016), 15.7 in Japan (2015), and 17.6 in South Korea (2016), all well above the OECD average of 11.7 (2016).[42]

The tendency to neglect the poor is also seen in the number of eligible individuals who actually obtained social welfare benefits. Coverage rates for social insurance programs in East Asia were substantial, but those for assistance and ALMPs were very low, as indicated in table 1.7.[43] The rates for social insurance increased in all countries from 2009 to 2015, but those for social assistance actually dropped from already depressed levels in Japan and Singapore. Public assistance eligibility rules across the region are strict in order to discourage welfare dependency and reduce government expenditures. Studies have suggested that policymakers in some nations actively discourage eligible recipients from applying for means-tested benefits, contributing to the limited coverage rates.[44] In the concluding chapter, we examine how coverage rates in East Asia compare to those in OECD countries.

TABLE 1.6 Social protection per intended beneficiary in East Asia (as a % of GDP/capita), 2015

	POOR				NON-POOR			
	TOTAL	SOCIAL INSURANCE	SOCIAL ASSISTANCE	ALMP	TOTAL	SOCIAL INSURANCE	SOCIAL ASSISTANCE	ALMP
China	0.3	0.1	0.2	–	4.3	4.1	0.1	0.1
Japan	3.5	2.8	0.7	–	8.6	8.3	0.3	–
South Korea	1.2	0.3	0.9	–	4.1	3.8	0.3	–
Singapore	1.6	1.1	0.2	0.3	4.6	3.7	0.9	–

Source: Asian Development Bank, *Social Protection Indicator*

TABLE 1.7 Coverage of social protection in East Asia (% of intended beneficiaries), 2009 & 2015

	ALL CATEGORIES		INSURANCE		ASSISTANCE		ALMP	
	2009	2015	2009	2015	2009	2015	2009	2015
China	79.3	86.8	67.2	67.8	9.4	16.9	2.7	2.1
Japan	90.4	84.5	70.4	75.4	10.1	8.3	9.9	0.8
South Korea	73.1	102.4	58.8	85.3	9.5	13.0	4.8	4.1
Singapore	80.2	103.2	43.7	74.2	28.8	19.5	7.7	9.5

Source: Asian Development Bank, *Social Protection Indicator*

The subsequent chapters reveal stunning examples of the skewed pattern of social protection in East Asia. In Japan and South Korea, for instance, the government and private corporations have provided subsidized housing and substantial pensions to favored workforces, deepening an already considerable insider–outsider cleavage in labor markets. Individuals who were deemed peripheral, however, such as retired laborers and nonregular workers (i.e., part-time, casual, or irregular-hour employees), have been neglected and received the fewest benefits. In Hong Kong, the government has created a large stock of public housing but has not supplied adequate social protection for the most disadvantaged and vulnerable groups. Public officials have failed to exercise their control over land use to prioritize constructing affordable housing, opting instead to sell available lots to big developers in order to raise revenue. Consequently, thousands of citizens have been forced to live in substandard conditions, including the infamous coffin homes.

Tax policy in East Asian nations complements their approach to social welfare policy. Tax rates are generally low and governments rely more heavily on indirect duties, which are regressive, as opposed to forms of direct taxation, like income and wealth taxes, which may be progressive, than do other advanced industrial countries; consequently, tax policy in the region, on average, redistributes less income than in most of the developed world.[45] Table 1.8 displays before and after Gini coefficients and relative poverty rates for East Asian and OECD nations.[46] The difference between the before and after measures is a rough indicator of the degree to which government tax and transfer policies have influenced inequality. Taiwan and South Korea had lower before inequality than Western countries, the former markedly so. Taiwan's after coefficient was close to OECD averages, but South Korea's was somewhat higher, indicating a particularly low degree of income redistribution. All other East Asian nations had before coefficients that were roughly similar to or somewhat higher than the OECD averages. Of these, only Japan evidenced substantially lower after

TABLE 1.8 Degree of redistribution in East Asia and OECD, 2016 & 2018

	GINI COEFFICIENT (2016*)			RELATIVE POVERTY RATES** (2018)		
	BEFORE	AFTER	DIFFERENCE	BEFORE	AFTER	DIFFERENCE
China	0.548	0.514	0.034	n/a	n/a	n/a
Hong Kong	0.539	0.473	0.066	20.4	14.9	5.5
Japan	0.504	0.339	0.165	33.2	15.7	17.5
South Korea	0.396	0.352	0.044	19.9	16.7	3.2
Singapore	0.463	0.409	0.054	n/a	n/a	n/a
Taiwan	0.336	0.303	0.035	n/a	n/a	n/a
Germany	0.505	0.294	0.211	32.1	9.8	22.3
Sweden	0.435	0.282	0.153	24.6	8.8	15.9
United States	0.507	0.391	0.116	27.5	18.1	9.4
OECD average	0.471	0.315	0.156	28.2	11.7	16.5
OECD-18 average	0.484	0.303	0.181	29.3	10.3	19.0

* Exceptions for Gini coefficient: China, 2010; Japan, 2015; South Korea, 2015; Singapore, 2015

** Relative poverty is defined as income less than 50 percent of the national median

Sources: OECD, "Income Distribution"; Government of Hong Kong, "2016 Population By-Census, Thematic Report—Household Income Distribution in Hong Kong," 2017; "Hong Kong Poverty Situation Report 2018," December 2019; Republic of Singapore, Ministry of Finance, "Income Growth, Inequality and Mobility Trends"; Taiwan (ROC), National Development Council, "Statistical Data Book 2019"

inequality, though its level exceeded that in Western countries. After taxes and transfers, China, Hong Kong, and Singapore remained far more unequal than most OECD nations. In Hong Kong and South Korea, relative poverty rates dropped only slightly after taxes and transfers. They declined far more in Japan, roughly in line with other OECD nations, but still left relative poverty at a comparatively high level. Taken together, these data suggest that the standard view that the East Asian miracle yielded a monolithic region of egalitarian societies is inaccurate. What most of the region's countries actually had in common was that they redistributed very little income through tax policy and social spending (see column 3).

THE MAGNITUDE OF PRIVATE WELFARE: A MIXED PICTURE

The conventional wisdom is that East Asian policymakers were able to neglect social welfare concerns for decades because they could rely on families, corporations, and communities to care for the needy and keep a lid on social problems. Have private actors in fact compensated for the low levels of social protection provided by governments?

Many forms of private welfare spending are not easy to quantify, let alone observe, and not much comparative data are available. Table 1.9 displays the

TABLE 1.9 Ratio of private to public welfare expenditures in East Asia and OECD, 1990–2020

	1990	2000	2010	2015	2020
Japan	0.015	0.227*	0.164	0.140	0.132
South Korea	0.118	0.575*	0.260*	0.291*	0.268*
Germany	0.164*	0.119	0.126	0.139	0.145
Sweden	0.042	0.092	0.115	0.138	0.143
United States	0.598*	0.658*	0.595*	0.662*	0.678*
OECD average	0.144	0.169	0.163	0.183	0.154
OECD-18 average	0.157	0.204	0.215	0.226	0.189

* Denotes ratio above the OCED and OECD-18 averages for that year
Source: OECD, "Social Expenditure – Aggregated Data," OECD Social and Welfare Statistics, 2023

ratio of aggregate private to public welfare expenditures in Japan and South Korea, as well as several OECD countries.[47] We can draw only limited and tentative conclusions from these data, but they show that private spending generally has not compensated for low government spending in Japan and Korea. In 1990, the ratios in both countries were very small and well below their peer group. From 2000 onward, the ratios in South Korea rose and were higher than in the OECD; in Japan, they rose slightly, but, with the exception of 2000, were lower.[48] In all years, both nations had ratios well below those of the United States, which is often held out as an example of a country where elevated private spending counterbalances insufficient public outlays. One interpretation of these findings is that private actors in South Korea (but probably not Japan) took on more of the burden of protection after 1990, perhaps as social problems began to appear.

HUMAN CAPITAL INVESTMENT: DO THE CLAIMS MATCH THE REALITY?

Many analysts have viewed investments in human capital as evidence that East Asian governments were committed to improving social welfare in the long run. They assumed these investments would reduce the need for a broader safety net by opening the door to better job opportunities for those with precarious employment.[49] Government spending on education in the region, however, has been comparatively low. Table 1.10 shows public and private spending on education in East Asia and the OECD. East Asian governments seemingly have been very efficient in their spending, since educational (and health) outcomes in the region are generally excellent. No government spent more than the OECD averages in 2000 and 2015 and only Hong Kong did in 2019. But digging deeper, we

TABLE 1.10 Public and private education expenditures in East Asia and OECD (as a % of GDP), 2000, 2015, & 2019**

		2000	2015	2019
China	Public	1.9	4.0	4.1
	Private	n/a	2.5*	1.0*
Hong Kong	Public	4.0	3.3	4.4*
	Private	3.8*	1.5*	1.2*
Japan	Public	3.2	3.0	2.8
	Private	0.8	1.2*	1.1*
South Korea	Public	3.9	3.7	4.0
	Private	2.6*	1.6*	1.3*
Singapore	Public	4.6	2.8	2.7
	Private	n/a	n/a	1.3*
Taiwan	Public	4.3	3.7	3.6
	Private	1.5*	1.2*	1.1*
OECD average	Public	4.6	4.1	4.1
	Private	1.3	0.8	0.8
OECD-18 average	Public	5.0	4.3	4.2
	Private	0.5	0.6	0.7

* Denotes spending above the OECD and OECD-18 averages for that year

** China: Public, 1999, 2006; Private, 2009. Hong Kong: Private, 2014. Singapore, Private, 2017. Taiwan, Public & Private, 2001.

Sources: OECD, *Education at a Glance 2003* (Paris: OECD Publishing, 2003), and *Education at a Glance 2023* (Paris: OECD Publishing, 2023); Republic of China, National Bureau of Statistics, "China Statistical Yearbook," 2022; Hong Kong, "Annual Digest of Statistics 2022"; Government of Hong Kong, "2014/15 Household Expenditure Survey and the Rebasing of the Consumer Price Indices," April 2016, and "2019/20 Household Expenditure Survey and the Rebasing of the Consumer Price Indices," June 2021; Republic of Singapore, Ministry of Trade & Industry, "Report on the Household Expenditure Survey 2017/18," July 2019; World Bank, "Government Expenditure on Education, Total (% of GDP)," World Development Indicators, 2023; Taiwan (ROC), Statistical Bureau, "Net Government Expenditures of All Levels," 2023

see that spending by private households has been a critical element in achieving national educational goals. Private expenditures in all nations exceeded the OECD averages for every year (except for Japan in 2000, which did however outspend the OECD-18 average), often by a wide margin.

High educational expenditures have imposed a sizable financial burden on many households. The need to channel a large percentage of family savings toward scholastic expenses has undercut lifetime consumption smoothing for old-age security, as we demonstrate in chapter 2. It has also affected welfare outcomes in the short run by increasing income insecurity, which has been shown to be a major risk factor for child maltreatment. The claim that East Asia's emphasis on human capital investment has been unambiguously positive, therefore, must be reexamined with a fresh pair of eyes.

Factors Undermining the Viability of the Productivist Model

The literature on East Asian social welfare policy mostly has failed to consider whether productivism can adapt to macro-level trends, such as globalization and skill-biased technical change, extensive and rapid urbanization, demographic challenges, and changing family structures, that have the potential to undermine its ability to function efficaciously. We argue that these powerful forces have already had two deleterious effects on social welfare in the region. First, they have amplified the socioeconomic risks facing many households, which the productivist model is especially ill-equipped to manage. Second, they have exacerbated productivism's structural weaknesses, reinforcing its dualistic character and undermining the private welfare solutions on which it relies to compensate for low government spending. Urbanization and changing family structures, for instance, have impeded the familial provision of welfare services at precisely the same time that skill-biased technical change has increased the need for it by heightening earnings insecurity among low-skill workers. Similar trends have affected other developed countries, but their governments, unlike those in East Asia, have implemented reforms or stepped up spending to alleviate their pernicious effects on ordinary citizens.

Globalization and technological change are largely exogenous trends. East Asian nations avidly pursued an outward orientation that deepened their integration into the global economy, but globalization and technological change have been driven by broad structural forces that have affected nearly all countries. Shifts in demographics, urbanization, and changes in family structure, however, are to some degree endogenous. That is, these developments are partly by-products of East Asia's social strategy and rapid economic growth. Exploring this feedback loop and the ways in which it affects the viability of key components of the productivist system is essential for improving upon steady-state conceptualizations of social policy in the region.

GLOBALIZATION AND TECHNOLOGICAL CHANGE

Globalization and skill-biased technological change are economic forces that have had a large impact on wages and the distribution of income in East Asian countries as they have in other developed regions. Although they are separate factors, they tend to reinforce one another, thereby heightening their overall effect. In advanced industrial countries, they have resulted in stagnant wages, particularly for low-skill workers, augmenting the economic risks and insecurity that confront many households. In addition, they have exacerbated income inequality and added to a growing sense of deprivation among those being left behind.

Globalization has been a powerful force since at least 1980, contributing to shifts in the international division of labor and creating challenges and opportunities for all nations, firms, and households.[50] International trade and outsourcing may reduce the wages of low- and mid-skill workers in advanced industrial economies by forcing them to compete against similar individuals earning less in developing countries. At the same time, high-skill workers in developed nations typically experience increases in compensation as knowledge-based industries flourish when firms gain access to larger markets. The movement of people frequently reinforces these shifts in relative wages. Immigration, particularly to major cities, often brings in large numbers of low-skill workers who compete with residents and potentially limit real wage growth.[51] The combined effect of these trends is typically greater income inequality.

East Asian nations are highly integrated into the world economy in terms of both trade and investment and, hence, have felt the full force of globalization.[52] In particular, East and Southeast Asia have become tightly integrated through production networks and have forged complex supply chains with countries from outside the region. The impacts are particularly pronounced in the region's primary economic drivers, its major cities. Global cities have emerged as command-and-control centers for international business, a transformation that has profoundly altered the character of their economic activity.[53] They have become financial and logistical centers, and, in the process, traditional sectors, particularly, manufacturing, have declined. A sophisticated support network in the areas of accountancy, law, taxation, regulation, and telecommunications has developed to provide services to multinational companies and financial institutions creating new high-income jobs. At the same time, businesses that cater to high-income individuals, such as housekeeping, food, transportation, hospitality, and childcare, have grown in response to higher demand for personal services. As manufacturing declined, many low-skill and mid-skill workers lost access to positions paying good salaries and were pushed into these lower wage jobs. This transformation has been perhaps most pronounced in Hong Kong, but also has occurred in Beijing, Singapore, Seoul, Taipei, and Tokyo.

Outward foreign direct investment (FDI) from East Asian countries has exacerbated these trends. The volume of investments has increased dramatically in the last several decades as firms set up facilities in neighboring Southeast Asia, initially to take advantage of lower costs and subsequently to deepen modular production networks in the region.[54] In 2022, outward FDI from East Asia (excluding Japan) totaled USD268.9 billion and from Japan, USD323.6 billion.[55] Outward FDI has diminished some of the benefits of rapid economic development in the region for ordinary households, especially China, by enabling firms to avoid having to provide higher wages or benefits to retain workers.

Many economists believe that skill-biased technological change has been the critical factor in raising income inequality in advanced industrial countries. The majority of technical change in the past several decades has reduced demand for low- and mid-skill workers performing "routine" tasks and increased that for high- and low-skill workers performing "nonroutine" tasks.[56] The introduction of microprocessor technology is a well-known example of skill-biased technical change and its potential impacts. High-skill workers were able to use the new technologies to improve their productivity, as evidenced by the jump in the wage premium paid for individuals with more education (that is, college-educated versus high school graduates or less). In contrast, workers performing routine jobs saw little improvement (at least initially) and this led to meager or even no gains in their real compensation.[57]

Skill-biased technical change, along with globalization, has contributed to the increasing polarization of labor markets in advanced industrial economies, creating high- and low-wage jobs at the expense of middle-wage jobs.[58] The jobs most often lost are production jobs in the upper half of the noncollege labor force and middle management jobs in the lower half of the college workforce. In addition, employment in high-wage sectors, particularly, in finance, technology, and professional service industries (like law), has taken on a winner-take-all character, resulting in a small number of people in them to enjoy huge increases in income.[59] Thus, even though the education premium has persisted, within-group wage inequality has grown rapidly among college-educated workers even as it slowed among noncollege-educated workers.[60]

Technical change has had a significant impact in all of East Asia, but the most pronounced effects have occurred in China, where the skill premium exploded after being very low during the planned economy era; this development fueled an abrupt and sharp increase in inequality. Rising skill premiums also have contributed to higher inequality in Hong Kong, South Korea, and Singapore. The effects of skill-biased technical change are most pronounced in global cities, where big concentrations of skilled individuals in sectors with a winner-take-all character work alongside numerous workers in low-skill, routine sectors. Hong Kong and Singapore, with their sizeable financial and related service sectors, have been the most affected and it is no surprise that they have some of the highest levels of income inequality among developed countries.[61]

Globalization and technological change have heightened risk for East Asian households and made it harder to manage. Wages for many households have stagnated and they are the loss of a job or a serious illness away from poverty. In other developed countries, social safety nets that supply benefits, such as unemployment insurance and welfare assistance, protect households until they are able to recover. In East Asia, the lack of public assistance means they must turn to private parties, notably, the family unit, for relief, which may not be able to provide the needed support. Higher inequality, spurred by the explosion of incomes at the top, has pushed up prices for essential goods and services, increasing the sacrifice that families must make to procure quality housing, health care, and education for their children or even putting it out of reach. Additionally, rising income inequality fuels perceptions of relative poverty and these may harm physical and mental health. As the Japan case illustrates, an upturn in the number of people earning low wages and feeling left behind has resulted in more incidents of child maltreatment. All of these developments have undermined the promise of shared growth that generated support for the East Asian model.

The period of economic turbulence that began with the region's intense financial crisis amplified the already powerful effects of globalization and technical change. Governments that had enjoyed the luxury of making economic policy in a context of rising wages and low unemployment were suddenly faced with sharp downturns that pushed more people out of work and caused social distress. Hong Kong and Taiwan illustrate these points well.

In the 1980s and 1990s, Hong Kong began to restructure toward higher value-added activities as its comparative advantage shifted. Its transition toward a knowledge-based economy raised demand for professionals and managers with more education and skills and created new high-wage jobs. In contrast, less-educated, low-skill workers in manufacturing experienced reduced wages due to the migration of production facilities from Hong Kong to mainland China. In addition, immigrants from the mainland enlarged the pool of such workers at a time when demand for their labor was falling. These effects were exacerbated by a series of damaging events for the economy, including the Asian financial crisis (1997), the SARS epidemic (2003), and the Great Recession (2008). One consequence was that Hong Kong began experiencing working or in-work poverty, terms used to describe individuals who are employed but whose income falls below the poverty line. The relative poverty rate among economically active households was 15.4 percent in 2020, which was very high in comparative terms (the average of twenty Euro area countries was 7.4 percent).[62] Similar but lower rates of working poverty occurred in Japan (13 percent) and South Korea (12 percent) as well, indicating that the phenomenon was not limited to Hong Kong.[63]

After several decades of steady increases, wages in Taiwan stagnated starting around 2000. Low-skill workers have experienced a similar trend in wages as those in Hong Kong for essentially the same reasons and were also affected by a string of economic downturns, notably, the one caused by SARS. Taiwan's degree of working poverty seems to be lower, but it is difficult to say with certainty because the government does not disseminate these statistics. In contrast with Hong Kong, however, income inequality in Taiwan has decreased. This might be greeted as good news but for the fact that it stemmed from a decline in real compensation for well-educated workers, not an increase in income for low-skill workers. The wage gap between high- and low-skill workers has narrowed rather than widened, as in most advanced economies, because of a surprising drop in the wage premium for education. As the Taiwan chapter in this book details, this trend has been partly due to an oversupply of college-educated workers, a consequence of excessive investment in tertiary education that is a concrete manifestation of productivism's overemphasis on human capital development.

URBANIZATION

Economic growth generates market forces that lure people from rural to urban areas with the promise of better job prospects and superior education and health services.[64] Urbanization has accelerated across most parts of the globe over the last century; more than half of the world's population now live in urban areas.[65] Spearheading this trend, East Asia has experienced a tremendous wave of urban growth in the last few decades, ushering in major socioeconomic transformations. More than four hundred million people have migrated to urban centers in the period since 2000 alone (mostly in China) and the region boasted fifteen megacities (population over ten million) in 2023. The proportion of the population living in urban areas in Hong Kong (100 percent), Singapore (100 percent), Japan (92 percent), South Korea (82 percent), and Taiwan (78 percent) is very high by global standards, and urban population growth in China (59 percent) has averaged about 3 percent annually in the last decade.[66]

The intensification of urban development, while bringing benefits, has created living conditions that adversely affect the welfare of many citizens. One of the principal problems is housing availability, affordability, and quality.[67] The Hong Kong case illustrates the scope and depth of the potential difficulties. The city experienced a huge jump in population from 3.1 million in 1960 to 7.4 million in 2021, driven largely by several waves of immigration from rural areas in mainland China. This surge has been a primary factor in the steadily rising demand for flats that has resulted in housing price increases that have been especially acute since 2003. Flats have become mostly unaffordable for low and even middle-income families, threatening their ability to move up the homeownership ladder and accumulate a valuable asset. Many households spend an excessive share of their earnings on housing, and some have been pushed into deplorable subdivided apartments known as cage homes at the same time that luxury buildings proliferate for high income families. Housing inequality has exacerbated already elevated levels of income inequality and has fed resentment over the government's meager social spending and seeming unwillingness to increase it significantly. The absence of a safety net has been keenly felt as a large number of families headed by adults who earn low and stagnant wages have fallen through the cracks into poverty.

In addition to the affordability problems that drain household savings, urbanization has undermined the familial and community support systems that are vital mechanisms for income maintenance in the productivist model. Extensive research has uncovered the various means by which urbanization destroys the private safety net supplied by families and mutual aid.[68] Individuals lose kinship and family ties previously enjoyed in rural areas when they migrate into cities; urban anonymity and indifference hinder the development of supportive networks in their new surroundings. Without viable public and private safety nets, individuals face greater risk of becoming poor and experiencing deteriorating mental health. The case of South Korea's old age poverty illustrates this point well. Seoul was the sixth largest metropolitan area in the world in 2023 with 24.3 million people (around ten million within the city limits).[69] The finances of low-income elderly households have become strained because the city has a chronic shortage of affordable housing and the cost of basic necessities, such as groceries and clothing, is comparatively high.[70] At the same time, Korea's traditionally strong family bonds have waned considerably, especially in urban areas, and many seniors are essentially on their own. These circumstances call out for greater government intervention to protect one of society's most vulnerable groups. Nonetheless, the public safety net remains minimal, pushing the nation's elderly poverty and suicide rates to the highest levels among its peers.

The weakening of family ties and traditional social relationships in urban areas has also challenged the productivist model in the realm of child welfare, as demonstrated by the cases of Japan and China. Approximately 92 percent of Japan's population live in cities, making it one of the most urbanized countries in the world. Kinship and mutual support networks historically have played a vital role in protecting children from maltreatment. In urban centers, however, parents, especially those who have migrated from rural areas, often lack familial and community support, creating conditions that greatly increase the odds of abuse and neglect. The concerns are even greater for China because urbanization has played a role in the mistreatment of children nationwide. The mass migration of rural residents to cities in search of employment opportunities has separated family members and undermined community networks critical for mutual support back home.[71] The restrictive household registration system—*hukou*—makes it difficult legally and administratively for the nearly 269 million migrant workers in urban areas to bring their offspring with them. This signifies that the over sixty-seven million left-behind children in villages (nearly one-quarter of children below the age of seventeen nationwide) are often cared for by others who may not be ideal guardians while their parents are away.[72] Migrants' children living in urban centers—about seventy-one million—also face large risks because the *hukou* system restricts their access to quality childcare and education even if they were born there. Stressors such as overcrowding, precarious employment, poor living conditions, and weak supportive networks put an additional strain on child rearing, creating an environment ripe for abuse and neglect.

DEMOGRAPHIC CHALLENGES

Demographic trends in East Asia, displayed in table 1.11, are creating enormous challenges for policymakers. Low birth rates have already resulted in labor shortages that threaten the continuance of rapid economic growth. In addition, the graying of society is steadily raising the age dependency ratio as the elderly population grows and the quantity of workers supporting them stagnates.[73] Finally, low fertility is decreasing the average size of families, undermining their ability to provide financial support to compensate for relatively small government old age security programs.

Fertility rates have fallen sharply in the past few decades throughout the developed world but East Asia has been particularly affected. In the period 1950 to

TABLE 1.11 Key demographic data for East Asia, various years

	TOTAL FERTILITY RATE	% OF POPULATION 65+			MEDIAN AGE			AGE DEPENDENCY RATIO		
	2021	2000	2021	2050	2000	2021	2050	2000	2021	2050
China	1.7	6.8	13.1	30.1	30.0	37.9	48.0	10.0	19.0	51.5
Hong Kong	1.1	11.0	19.6	40.6	36.2	44.9	53.4	15.3	28.7	78.8
Japan	1.4	17.0	29.8	37.5	41.2	48.4	54.7	24.9	51.0	73.0
South Korea	1.1	7.2	16.7	39.4	31.9	43.7	56.5	10.0	23.3	75.2
Singapore	1.2	6.4	14.1	34.2	34.8	41.8	53.4	8.0	19.1	60.9
Taiwan	1.1	8.7	16.0	35.3	32.0	41.3	56.5	12.5	22.4	70.2
World	2.3	6.9	9.6	16.5	26.3	30.0	48.0	10.9	14.8	26.2

Sources: United Nations, Department of Economic and Social Affairs, "World Population Prospects," 2022, and "World Population Ageing," 2017; World Bank, "Population Estimates and Projections," Databank/World Development Indicators, 2023; Taiwan (ROC), National Development Council, "Demographic Indicators," 2023

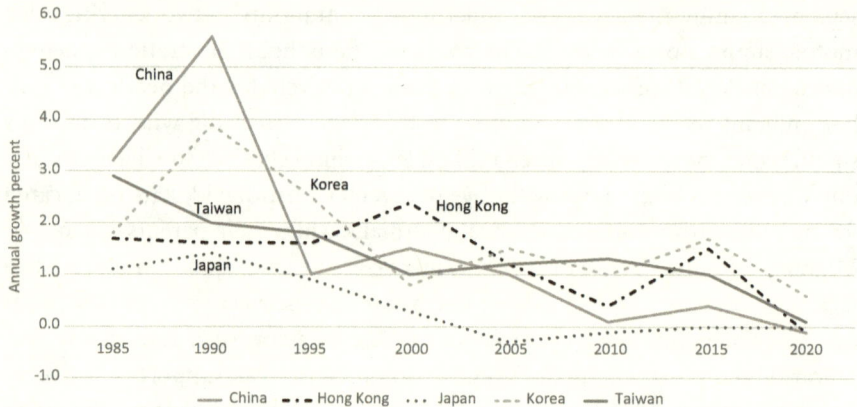

FIGURE 1.1 Labor force growth in East Asia (trailing five-year moving average), 1985–2020

Sources: Republic of China, National Bureau of Statistics, "Statistical Yearbook" (various years); Hong Kong, "Annual Digest of Statistics" (various years); Japan, Ministry of Internal Affairs and Communication, "Statistical Handbook of Japan," 2022; World Bank, "Labor Force, Total," World Development Indicators, 2023; Taiwan (ROC), Statistical Bureau, "Labor Force," 2023

1955, global average fertility (the number of children born per woman) was 4.97. This number dropped to 3.3 in 1990 and just 2.3 in 2021. In general, fertility rates today are the lowest in Europe and East Asia, clustering around 1.5. A decline in fertility, especially below the level needed to maintain the current size of the population (2.1), has significant and possibly alarming consequences for the long-run health of the economy and society and raises the socioeconomic risks facing households. To start with, an increase in population is required to raise the number of citizens available to engage in future economic activity. As figure 1.1 illustrates, growth of the labor force in East Asia has slowed significantly, most notably in Japan.[74] If expansion of the domestic labor pool is insufficient, governments may need to permit higher levels of immigration (as in Singapore) or intensify their use of labor-saving technology, such as robotics (as in Japan). Both alternatives pose difficulties. Immigration is a divisive political issue in many countries and creates numerous policy challenges, such as which immigrants to welcome and which government services to provide to foreigners. Automation typically displaces low-skill workers and others engaged in routine tasks and may depress their wages and worsen income inequality.

A decrease in fertility has also contributed to the graying of the population. East Asian societies are aging at a far more rapid rate than the world at large, as seen in table 1.11. The median age has risen sharply since 2000 and is well above the global average. The percentage of people aged sixty-five and over has roughly doubled since 2000 and is expected to rise much further by 2050. As the World Bank noted, Western nations took between fifty to one-hundred years to make the transition from young to old societies, but East Asia is completing that transformation in just twenty to twenty-five years.[75] A graying population places additional demands on government resources, driving up expenditures on entitlement programs with defined benefits, such as pensions and health care, and may restrain economic growth by reducing labor productivity.[76] In East Asia, the age dependency ratio has jumped dramatically and will continue to climb, casting doubt on the ability of governments to provide for the elderly over the long run. Similar trends have already pushed several European nations to reduce pensions and other social benefits out of concern that government revenue will fail to keep pace with expenditures.

Lower fertility in East Asia has another direct implication for the viability of the productivist model. Policymakers have relied upon the traditional family system to compensate for relatively small government entitlement programs. Declining birth rates, however, have decreased the size of the average family. Smaller families mean fewer potential caregivers and resources for supporting elderly dependents, who now live longer. This trend suggests that public officials inevitably will be forced to raise spending on seniors, expenditures that they once deemed wasteful. In some societies, notably Singapore, alarm over the need to raise public spending and mounting concern about the ability to sustain economic growth with a smaller population have prompted policymakers to implement various strategies to elevate the fertility rate, thus far with little or no success.[77]

The decrease in fertility is already producing great strains on households and their communities, as chapter 2 shows. In South Korea, the number of elderly people has ballooned at the same time fertility has dropped, leading to fast aging of the population and an increase in the age dependency ratio, both society wide and within the family unit. Despite the vital role that seniors played in the nation's economic miracle, the government has provided insufficient income support to them thus far. Shrinking family size has made it harder for children to fill the gap and a large percentage of seniors have fallen into poverty. As the next subsection details, the traditional family system is breaking down, making it less likely that the elderly (or other dependents) can rely on their immediate or extended families or local communities for assistance.

CHANGING FAMILY STRUCTURE

Maintaining a limited safety net might have sufficed at one point in time, but the traditional East Asian family structure has transformed in a manner that makes it less capable of supporting the elderly, children, siblings, and other dependents. The family unit has evolved in multiple ways as a consequence of rapidly changing demographics, economic opportunities and threats, and social norms. Family sizes are getting smaller; women, the traditional caregivers, are joining the labor force in larger numbers; adult children are moving away from home and even their communities for work; and the Confucian ideal that children have a strict set of duties to care for their aging parents has ebbed.

The most important development is probably declining birth rates leading to smaller families with a reduced number of potential caregivers. Lower fertility is one consequence of fewer and later marriages in East Asia. Economic and social changes have raised the opportunity costs of marriage for women, made it more difficult for men, especially those with less education, to fulfill the provider role, and heightened marriage market mismatches.[78] The result has been a steady decline in the number of children available to care for aged parents as smaller birth cohorts move into the main caring ages; in other words, the dependency ratio at the level of the family has increased. The impact of this trend is greatest on the poorest and most vulnerable social groups since they do not have as many resources to secure other forms of assistance.[79] Furthermore, higher life expectancy means that lots of seniors live to ages that require full-time, intensive care. In Japan, for instance, the ratio of elderly who suffer from senile dementia or are bedridden to potential caregivers is projected to rise appreciably, jeopardizing the provision of adequate support.[80]

A second significant trend is that a higher proportion of women, who remain the most likely caregivers, are being drawn into the paid workforce and are not available for full-time care. The rising cost of living has pushed many married women to accept employment in order to raise household income. In addition, a growing number of single women, especially in Japan, South Korea, and Taiwan, work to support themselves. The increasing opportunities afforded to women, who are now free to pursue careers that were previously difficult to enter, has made this possible. Furthermore, educated women are less willing—and are under less pressure—to sacrifice their careers for familial duties. In some countries, like Japan, boosting women's participation in the workforce has been an explicit objective of government policy.[81]

Finally, changing societal norms in East Asia have loosened the traditional bonds between children and their parents and made it acceptable for young adults to live outside the parental home.[82] This development is having a major impact on social welfare outcomes because seniors used to live with their children who served as caregivers or at least provided substantial assistance. Certain types of support, such as financial assistance, can be delivered from a distance, but providing help with day-to-day affairs is much harder, especially in dealing with the very old. In addition, the demands of their jobs or their own family life frequently hinder their ability to look after their parents. As a result, many elderly persons are more dependent on their own resources and outside help.

In Hong Kong, transforming family structures are augmenting the demand for public housing. One reason for the declining availability of affordable housing units is a decrease in the size of households. In recent years, larger numbers of children have moved out of their family's public rental units and into private apartments once they began to earn their own income.[83] This has created an additional source of demand for private units that has pushed up home prices. The government has been unable to supply sufficient public units to house those priced out of the private market; indeed, the average wait for public flats was 5.3 years in 2023.[84]

In Japan, changes in family structure have contributed to child maltreatment, a social problem that cannot be resolved by reliance on communities or extended families. It has experienced a surge in single motherhood, especially due to unexpected pregnancies. Single mothers tend to be poor and receive little or no government assistance. This combination of factors greatly augments the risks for child abuse and neglect. Victims of child maltreatment have higher divorce rates, which reinforces single parenthood and in turn perpetuates the cycle of abuse.[85]

Creating Policy Façades

Productivism in East Asia played an important part in its economic success, but it also sowed the seeds for future social crises. Foreseeing social problems might have been difficult for officials in the 1960s and 1970s, but subsequent policymakers failed to seize the opportunity to pivot their strategy when the pitfalls of the model began to emerge. Some authors have claimed that governments are taking decisive action by expanding their welfare systems to address social challenges.[86] We argue that even where policymakers have begun to shift gears, contemporary policies are inadequate to mitigate the crises. They have been reluctant to undertake the boost in spending required and continue to maintain that private actors are responsible for social welfare, not the state. As table 1.12 demonstrates, governments did not increase expenditures on social assistance to any meaningful degree over the last decade. They raised social insurance outlays significantly more, but in 2015 the bulk of these disbursements still targeted the nonpoor, not the poor (see table 1.6).[87] In addition, policymakers have resisted higher spending despite having enviable fiscal positions; the sole exception is Japan, which has run large deficits and faces a massive overhang of public debt. Hong Kong has enjoyed considerable budget surpluses during the past two decades and has accumulated fiscal reserves sufficient to cover more than one

TABLE 1.12 Social protection in East Asia (as a % of GDP), 2010, 2015, & 2019

	2010				2015				2019				CHANGE					
													2010–2015			2015–2019		
	TOTAL	SOCIAL INSURANCE	SOCIAL ASSISTANCE	ALMP	TOTAL	SOCIAL INSURANCE	SOCIAL ASSISTANCE	ALMP	TOTAL	SOCIAL INSURANCE	SOCIAL ASSISTANCE	ALMP	SOCIAL INSURANCE	SOCIAL ASSISTANCE	ALMP	SOCIAL INSURANCE	SOCIAL ASSISTANCE	ALMP
China	7.0	6.3	0.6	0.1	7.7	6.9	0.7	0.1	10.0	8.4	0.9	0.6	0.6	1.5	0.1	0.2	0.0	0.5
Hong Kong	4.5	3.4	1.1	n/a	5.4	3.6	1.8	n/a	6.0	4.1	1.9	n/a	0.2	0.5	0.7	0.1	–	–
Japan	21.0	19.3	1.5	0.3	21.9	19.9	1.8	0.2	22.8	20.5	2.1	0.2	0.6	0.6	0.3	0.3	-0.1	0.0
South Korea	7.9	6.4	1.2	0.3	9.6	7.6	1.8	0.3	12.3	8.5	2.5	0.4	1.2	0.9	0.3	0.7	0.0	0.1
Singapore	4.4	4.1	0.1	0.1	5.3	4.1	0.9	0.3	6.2	5.3	0.6	0.3	0.0	1.2	0.8	-0.3	0.2	0.1
Taiwan	8.4	7.4	1.0	n/a	9.2	8.3	0.9	n/a	9.7	8.7	1.0	n/a	0.9	0.4	-0.1	0.1	–	–

Sources: Asian Development Bank, *The Social Protection Index: Assessing Results for Asia and the Pacific* (Mandaluyong City, Philippines: Asian Development Bank, 2013), and *Social Protection Indicator*; Hong Kong, "Annual Digest of Statistics 2019"; Taiwan (ROC), Statistical Bureau, "Social Protection Expenditure"

year of government expenditures at prevailing levels.[88] Taiwan and South Korea have also run (smaller) budget surpluses in the same period and have significant reserves.

A comprehensive explanation for the reluctance of East Asian leaders to tackle social crises is beyond the scope of this book, but it is likely due to a combination of political opposition to altering the status quo, as well as their continued preference for productivist strategies. We return to this issue in the concluding chapter. We posit that the unwillingness to commit fully to resolving the crises has led to a common politically expedient approach to policymaking across the region: a largely reactive strategy that favors appearance over action that we call a policy façade. Policymakers create a policy façade when they eschew vigorous, fundamental reforms and implement only limited measures—sometimes in the form of temporary programs—aimed at abating the most severe aspects of a problem and silencing political criticism. In choosing this approach, they cater to business groups that generally oppose any significant changes in social policy, especially the expansion of assistance or income support for the needy.

By perpetuating the status quo, policy façades reinforce the historical dualism in social service provision. Façades are most common in areas of social welfare that supply benefits to disadvantaged groups, such as poor relief, since this is where public officials want to give the impression of addressing social ills without actually having to commit significant resources. In other policy areas, such as social insurance, policymakers may decide to meet challenges head on and expand benefits significantly because these can be funneled primarily to favored groups of individuals, such as the urban industrial workforce or retired public sector employees. In short, policy façades are the logical outgrowths of the productivist bias that East Asian countries have adopted. Our case studies in the following chapters illustrate the failure of governments to take decisive action to protect the most vulnerable citizens.

The social security façade in South Korea. South Korea's economic miracle has been tarnished by its exceptionally high and persistent old-age poverty. The government has done little to remedy the causes of elderly poverty, such as enforcing the recent ban on forced early retirement schemes, and has offered little in the way of income support. The national public assistance program does not include a minimum income guarantee for the elderly and supplementary, noncontributory old-age security measures provide only meager benefits. Instead of increasing levels of income support, national and local governments have turned to market mechanisms to alleviate the crisis by taking steps to facilitate the employment of seniors.

The labor market façade in Taiwan. Low earnings have exposed many Taiwanese households to economic risk and led to a variety of problems such as youth disenchantment and brain drain. Stagnant wages among low-skill workers are partly due to factors outside the control of government officials, namely, skill-biased technological change and globalization. Faced with the same challenge, other countries have designed income support policies, such as the Earned Income Tax Credit in the United States or United Kingdom's Working Tax Credit, to assist households headed by this class of workers, or implemented ALMPs to help them land better jobs.[89] Government policy in Taiwan, however, has been minimalist in this regard thus far. Policymakers have made only token efforts to improve worker training to prepare low-skill workers for other careers or boost their productivity. Instead, they focused their attention on expanding tertiary education initially in the belief that further human capital development would spur growth. This policy ended up flooding the labor market with college graduates possessing general skills, which drove down the wage premium associated with tertiary education and provoked a steady outflow of talented youth to other countries. Officials announced plans to raise the minimum wage aggressively (after many years of no change), but opposition from the business sector slowed the increases to a crawl. Consequently, the minimum wage's impact on the well-being of working-class households has turned out to be minor.

The child welfare façade in Japan. Despite an alarming, prolonged rise in child maltreatment incidents, the Japanese government has failed to address their root causes or consequences. Policymakers have focused on detecting and reporting cases of abuse, garnering headlines about the government's efforts to face up to the crisis. They have neglected, however, the rest of the necessary infrastructure, such as protection and rehabilitative systems, by leaving them chronically underfunded and understaffed. Specialized professionals, like mental health care providers, are in short supply, which greatly undermines counseling efforts for offenders and the recovery of traumatized children in government-regulated institutions. In addition, auxiliary measures, such as parental training, sex education, and mental health awareness programs, are also lacking. Consequently, the policy façade has led to a new record of detected cases each year, but not stronger protection for victims or rehabilitation of perpetrators.

The housing façade in Hong Kong. Hong Kong has been engulfed in an affordable housing crisis for several decades. The government has constructed a large stock of public flats but has not succeeded in providing adequate social protection for disadvantaged and vulnerable groups. Policymakers have opted not to wield their control over land use to prioritize building affordable housing, choosing instead to sell available parcels to big developers in order to fill the government's coffers (despite its large fiscal surpluses in recent decades). Low- and middle-income households that do not own their homes have put pressure on elected officials to moderate housing prices and provide more affordable public housing units. In response, policymakers have implemented a policy façade featuring a string of half-hearted measures that do just enough to quell public protests but not enough to aid the many city dwellers who reside in deplorable living conditions.

The Self-Inflicted Economic and Social Costs of Productivism

East Asian governments have missed multiple opportunities to take advantage of their growing wealth to develop more comprehensive social welfare programs. Proactive policies might have averted the worst effects of current crises or at least made their societies more resilient in the face of adverse developments like declining fertility. As the following chapters detail, the decision to deploy ineffectual policy façades in the face of large-scale, multidimensional social problems is gravely concerning on several fronts.

First and foremost, social problems have had devastating impacts on the lives of ordinary citizens and their communities. The elderly poverty crisis in South Korea has contributed to a shocking suicide rate and pushed some seniors into illegal activities to make ends meet. The low-wage crisis in Taiwan has brought a sizable portion of the working population to the brink of serious financial hardship, discouraging or delaying marriages and childbearing (adding to an already enormous decline in fertility). The child welfare crisis in Japan has resulted in gruesome deaths for some young victims and pernicious effects on the mental health of survivors, leaving them vulnerable to poverty, depression, and suicide in adulthood. The affordable housing crisis in Hong Kong has manifested itself in atrocious housing conditions that have been a major factor behind a surge in child abuse and physical and mental illnesses. In China, millions of left-behind rural children and elderly face mistreatment and poverty. These social problems have already inflicted a significant human toll on several generations of citizens; the use of a policy façade to address them will only prolong and possibly worsen this dire situation.

Second, the failure to address social ills has unleashed forces that are exerting a negative impact on economic performance. Ironically, a welfare strategy meant to promote rapid growth—one that largely succeeded—threatens future success. In Japan, the estimated losses associated with child abuse and neglect were at least USD16 billion in 2012.[90] Moreover, child maltreatment impedes the long-term accumulation of human capital because victims are more likely to have learning disorders that block personal development and heighten the chance of being unproductive or unemployed in adulthood. In South Korea, acute elderly poverty has turned a potential "silver economy" boom into a bust; many older adults are in debt and must rely on uncertain financial support from their children.[91]

Senior citizens in other advanced societies possess significant wealth and make up the largest and fastest growing group of consumers. Spending by individuals aged fifty and over amounted to over USD35 trillion in 2020, which represented half of all global consumer expenditure. In Taiwan, the low-wage crisis has provoked the mass exodus of talented students and skilled workers to neighboring countries, notably, China, as well as the United States. These individuals embody the type of human capital that was a critical factor in driving the nation's successful industrial upgrading, and its absence will surely undermine future economic growth. In Hong Kong, the affordable housing crisis has aggravated acute and still rising income inequality. A body of research has provided compelling evidence that excessive inequality hurts economic growth by undermining social mobility, limiting educational opportunities, and impeding skill development, especially for low-income children.[92] In China, the lack of a safety net has led citizens to save at very high rates to protect themselves against future economic risk. The paucity of household spending has hindered the government's efforts to switch from an export-led growth model to one based more on domestic consumption.

More generally, East Asian nations are at high risk of slowing economic growth due to decreasing birthrates, a phenomenon that limits the expansion of the domestic labor force.[93] The same is true for other advanced industrial nations, but few of these implemented policies that accelerated the slowdown as East Asia did. In the 1960s and early 1970s, policymakers feared that high fertility rates would lead families to spend less on health and educational services per child, weakening their development as skilled laborers. They implemented various measures to discourage childbirths, including some draconian measures like encouraging sterilization after the birth of a second child, that precipitated and then accelerated a decline in population growth.[94] Other by-products of productivism, such as unduly long working hours, have contributed to delayed marriages and a rise in singlehood, trends that are known to lower fertility rates.[95] As a consequence, expansion of the labor force has slowed markedly as population growth has ebbed (see figure 1.1), especially in Japan, where cumulative labor force growth was only 1 percent in the period 2000 to 2020.

Finally, the growing economic insecurity among citizens has heightened political disenchantment and fueled unrest. In Taiwan, the tough economic reality that awaits young college graduates has propelled some into the streets in protest. From student-led rallies calling for a hike in the minimum wage to outbursts of anger over revisions to the Labor Standards Act, discontent over the lack of a government response to economic insecurity has mounted.[96] Similarly, frustration over the lack of affordable housing and growing inequality were common themes in the virulent antigovernment protests that rocked Hong Kong in 2010s, fueling unrest that eventually prompted Beijing to crack down on dissent. At this point in time, implementing an effective response to social crises across the region would be challenging even if politicians should resolve to do so. East Asian nations do not have the governance structures or societal backing necessary to confront multiple social welfare crises forcefully, despite some signs that civic support is growing.

What Lies Ahead

East Asia's social crises have augmented the insecurity of numerous households and undermined the ability of nations to sustain long-term growth and perhaps even maintain political stability. The following four chapters dive into the social problems of old age poverty in South Korea, wage stagnation in Taiwan, child maltreatment in Japan, and housing affordability in Hong Kong. As discussed in the introduction, we have paired each substantive issue area with the country where it has posed the greatest policy challenge. In three of the four cases—South Korea, Taiwan, and Hong Kong—the problem that we examine has been the most acute social challenge faced by the country in recent times; in Japan, other social ills, such as old age and working poverty, have rivaled child maltreatment as the most pressing. Child maltreatment, old age poverty, and housing are long-standing social problems in the region that have intensified or gained salience lately, whereas stagnant wages and declining standards of living for the average household are new.

Each chapter opens with a composite narrative that illustrates real-life situations and captures the complex dynamics of a social crisis from the perspective of ordinary citizens. We then provide relevant historical background on the country and examine the magnitude, causes, and consequences of the welfare crisis under consideration. In doing so, we examine the features of productivism in each nation, how they contributed to the rise of the issue in question, and how macro level forces have begun to undermine the viability of this approach to social welfare. Each study also spotlights the deficiencies of the reactive policies that make up the policy façade that governments have implemented in response to the crisis. The last section of each chapter compares the experience in the country of focus with the situation in other East Asian nations and Singapore.

China is the subject of a chapter on its own. We analyze its welfare system, exploring how it evolved from direct state provision of benefits to a more market-based approach. We show that it too is vulnerable to the challenges facing other East Asian nations, namely, globalization and technical change, demographic trends, urbanization, and changes in family structure. We then examine its experience in the four areas of social policy scrutinized in the country studies. We conclude that several features unique to China—its unprecedented migration from rural to urban areas, reliance on local governments to implement social policy, stringent household registration system, and intrusive family planning measures—make it vulnerable to experiencing even more severe social problems than its neighbors.

The final chapter extends our analysis to explore the long-term trajectory of social policy within East Asia and better situate its experience in the comparative literature. It compares and contrasts social welfare policies and outcomes across the region's nations and concludes that although their overall strategy has not diverged significantly, disparities in total spending are emerging. We also analyze the features of social welfare systems in East Asia vis-à-vis those in the West and show they remain far apart in some respects, with two notable exceptions. Japan can now also be classified as a liberal welfare state, a model commonly found in the West, and South Korea is moving in that direction. Finally, the conclusion outlines a new research agenda that suggests how dynamic integrated social welfare analysis can contribute to future studies. Using the recent COVID-19 pandemic and climate changes as examples, we suggest that it has the potential to help scholars broaden the scope of social welfare studies and generate new insights.

2

MISERY IN THE GOLDEN YEARS
The Old Age Crisis in South Korea

Namsan Tower sits like an imposing trophy on a mountain top in central Seoul, overlooking a megapolis that is home to over twenty-five million people. The stunning panoramic views from the summit tell a powerful story. South Korea's transformation from a poor, rural, war-torn society to a leading industrial nation in less than two generations is one of the most noteworthy achievements in economic history. Today, it possesses an innovative, dynamic, and resilient economy and is celebrating three decades of democracy.

The view from the ground, however, tells a different story. The nation's elderly, who made personal sacrifices to help bring about the country's transformation, face exceptionally high poverty and suicide rates. Economic forces, notably skill-biased technical change, contributed to a deep schism in labor markets, pushing some workers into precarious employment with low earnings, few benefits, and scant opportunities to build a nest egg. Rapid modernization fueled intense urbanization that weakened community-based support networks for the aged and pushed up the cost of living in city centers to unaffordable levels. Declining fertility rates and longer life expectancy have increased the number of seniors per active worker, creating a larger financial burden for current and future generations. A strong emphasis on education to promote human capital investment backfired in one important respect; as their children's educational expenses ballooned, aging parents' savings for retirement dwindled. Yet changing family dynamics reduced the extent of care parents could expect to receive from their adult offspring. Above all, economic insecurity among senior citizens became pervasive because public officials chose to maintain a dualistic welfare system by erecting a policy façade instead of confronting old age poverty through comprehensive reforms.

South Korea offers a poignant lesson on how the relentless pursuit of economic growth can culminate in a rich country, poor elderly outcome. Seeing the old age crisis from the perspective of one family's struggles illuminates its multifaceted causes and detrimental consequences.

A View from the Ground

Lee Nam-Kyung idly watched the oversized clock hung high on the living room wall.[1] The time was 9:59 p.m. His wife's favorite K-drama, *The Night Watchman's Journal*, was about to start. The small dining room table was crowded with the essentials of her nighttime ritual: the handheld TV, bottles of nail polish, a basket holding rice crackers, and a cast iron teapot. Eun Mi had worked at a beauty salon specializing in eyebrows and lash extensions for nearly twenty years. But a routine summer day turned catastrophic when a neighbor found Eun Mi lying unconscious in the hallway. A massive stroke nearly took her life, and she was left severely impaired. Unable to communicate, walk, or eat on her own, she cried for hours and refused to eat the bland food the hospital served. Although most of her medical bills were paid by the national health insurance program, some expenses for her extended stay in the rehabilitation center and various therapy sessions were considered out of pocket. For decades, most of the Lee household income went to rent and their daughter's education. Living in Seoul was expensive, but they managed to rent a one-bedroom apartment in a central neighborhood so that their daughter, Sun-Ah, could attend one of the top public high schools in the country. Her graduation from college nine years ago marked the beginning of a new chapter in their lives since they were finally able to start saving for their retirement. Eun Mi had succeeded in saving nearly USD10,000, of which only a fraction now remained because of the mounting medical expenditures.

Nam-Kyung's savings were also dwindling. His nearly two-decade long career as an inventory manager at the Sam Won department store chain ended in the early 1990s. He had witnessed South Korea rise triumphantly from the double devastations of World War II and the Korean War. He took pride in what he and his fellow South Koreans had accomplished and firmly believed that diligence had been the key to their economic success. Nam-Kyung was a model worker—punctual, professional, and pleasant—who wore the company uniform with honor and joy and considered Sam Won to be his extended family. Nothing had prepared him for the day he was forced to retire. Contractually forced early retirement is the fate of many Korean workers, so he was simply handed USD5,000 in severance pay in the form of a retirement gift. He felt as if he were attending his own funeral as he witnessed the arrival of newly hired younger workers. Advances in personal computers, digitization, scanners, and customized software made it possible to collect and process detailed inventory, prices, and sales data for individual stores automatically. Sam Won management decided that it was not worthwhile retraining anyone over fifty in this era of new technology, and they systematically weeded out the workers who were now obsolete.

Despite the disappointing end to his inventory management career, Nam-Kyung still considered himself lucky. After being unemployed for nearly six months, he was given a second chance as a security guard at Sam Won's luxury designer boutique store in the Gangnam district, an affluent neighborhood in Seoul. The contract job offered low pay with no benefits, but he grabbed every overtime shift for the next fifteen years until life cruelly repeated itself. At the end of 2018, a new management team was brought in to cope with the rising competition from online vendors and discount stores. To cut overhead costs, the new managers replaced Nam-Kyung and a half dozen other guards with young Chinese immigrants of Korean descent. Ironically, the number of immigrants was growing because of ongoing government initiatives designed to address the aging, shrinking workforce. For the Sam Won management, it was a win-win situation. The new workers were young and willing to work long hours for half the regular pay. Many of them also spoke both Chinese and Korean fluently, which gave them an advantage in controlling the crowd of wealthy Chinese tourists that hunted for bargain-priced cashmere scarves and leather handbags.

Nam-Kyung sat alone in the dark, listening to the ticking of the clock. He had never envisioned that his many decades of hard work would produce *this* reality. As he lay in bed, he quietly waited for dawn to break.

The sweet aroma of freshly brewed coffee permeated throughout the restaurant as the early morning sunlight streamed through the front windows. Sun-Ah was visibly nervous to see her father at the Seoulful Café. His gaunt face and worried look did not help to calm her nerves.

"Dad, are you okay? You look like you lost a lot of weight."

Sun-Ah's concern for him came from a genuine place of kindness, which reminded Nam-Kyung that he had raised her right. She was the daughter everyone wanted. She had an impeccable academic record. Her stamina was remarkable too. She had spent close to seven hours each day studying at the after-school private crammer (*hagwon*), usually until midnight. She aced the nation's notoriously difficult college entrance exam, the Scholastic Aptitude Test (*Suneung*), and obtained a college degree—the first to do so in the Lee family—from the prestigious Seoul National University. She majored in economics and was recruited by the Jisun Financial Group six months before she graduated. With brisk, commanding strides, Sun-Ah had walked among the economic elites through the Myeong-Dong district, Seoul's financial and shopping center. She bought her first professional suit at the Sam Won designer boutique store where Nam-Kyung worked. She had her eyebrows and hair done regularly at a posh beauty salon. She had made it to the other side.

But today Sun-Ah looked a little scruffy and shaky. She bit her lip. "Dad, I meant to tell you sooner, but with mom's illness I knew you were overwhelmed. I quit Jisun three months ago. I couldn't take it anymore. The workplace stress was unreal. Managers bullied new recruits. One of them constantly harassed me. I was basically a personal assistant to my unit's managers for the first two years. Then the company gave me a fake promotion to become the office janitor, cleaning up the presentation materials used for board meetings, gathering data, and doing all the laborious tasks that the guys didn't want to do. They yelled and humiliated me in front of everyone for any little mistake I made. I hated it. Every workday meant overtime. I never prayed to God growing up, even before the college entrance exam. But earlier this year, I started stopping at the Myeong-Dong Cathedral after work. I prayed that one day I would regain my feelings and sense of purpose. I am a believer now. It was the divine wind that lifted me out of that misery and brought me here to the Seoulful Café."

Nam-Kyung did not know how to respond. He wondered if God were playing a cruel trick, testing him to see how he would respond. He gritted his teeth and responded, "This was a bad decision. You made a mistake. You should have stayed. Workplace conditions always get better. I encountered condescending customers all the time. Managers are stressed out because they are under enormous pressure to make money. Their meanness is not personal."

But Sun-Ah had already made up her mind. "Did you hear about Kim Joo-Hyun? He was my math tutor when I was in junior high school. He was so smart and very kind too. He got a job at an LCD factory and toiled away long hours. Well, he jumped from the roof of his dormitory and killed himself earlier this year. I don't want to write a letter saying 'I'm sorry' to you and mom. So, I quit. I can do better," she said in a defensive tone. "Besides I already have a job, here, at the café. The pay is not great, but I get to perform sometimes when the place turns into a jazz club at night. I'm still learning jazz piano, but I am quite good at it."

"You have a degree that most Koreans only dream of having and you are wasting it on a waitressing job?" Nam-Kyung asked harshly.

"No, Dad, I am not. I do all the inventory and accounting for the café. I also organize concerts and various community outreach programs. It feels good to be a part-time social entrepreneur. Don't worry about me, Dad. I am going to take care of myself. I can prove it." Her voice was calmer.

Nam-Kyung could not believe his ears. He distinctively remembered how he had forgone going to the dentist and his wife resisted buying a decent-sized TV because they could hardly afford Sun-Ah's classical piano lessons. His lump-sum retirement bonus had vanished to pay for her educational field trips and mounting private tutoring expenses. He fell silent. He did not have the stomach to tell Sun-Ah that he was struggling to find a job or about the acute financial distress plaguing the Lee household—perhaps because he did not want to admit that she was right about the lack of empathy businesses felt toward their workers.

That evening Nam-Kyung sat alone in the kitchen, listening to the ticking of the clock. He still could not believe that the family's enormous investment in his daughter's education would turn into a financial bust, or that Eun Mi, his backbone, would be fighting for her life. Staring into the empty living room, his mind began concocting a plan to turn his life around: dye his gray hair, attend a job fair, participate in the church's community activities, and maybe buy weekly Nanum Lotto tickets. As he waited for daylight, anxiety gripped his heart and mind once again. He prayed for a transfusion of resilience to help him fight the toughest battle of his life.

The Economic and Political Context

The widespread economic insecurity that plagues South Korea's elderly population is startling since the country is widely deemed to be one of the world's great success stories of economic and political transformation.[2] It endured oppressive colonial rule by Japan (1910–45), which exploited its natural resources and human capital to power its imperial expansion during World War II. After the war, the country imploded and split apart. The short but brutal Korean War (1950–53) took millions of lives, decimated families, flattened cities, and divided the nation into North and South. By 1953, South Korea was one of the poorest countries in the world with few prospects.

Rising from the ashes, the nation rebounded in a spectacular way. From 1960 onward, it experienced rapid economic growth propelled by an aggressive export-led strategy that featured labor-intensive manufacturing initially and then heavy industry. South Korea has often been showcased in the political economy literature as the quintessential developmental state. The government promoted industrialization by picking sectors (e.g., steel, shipbuilding and semiconductors) that were considered to be critical for long-term growth and imposed high trade barriers to protect them. Policymakers developed close ties with big business, particularly, the *chaebol*, and sought its collaboration with the implementation of strategic initiatives.[3] The financial sector, dominated by government-owned banks, was subordinate to industry and became a major tool in channeling low-cost funds to favored sectors. Finally, public officials strove to create a competitive edge in international markets by suppressing the labor movement to keep wages low.

South Korea has limited social welfare outlays in order to prioritize public expenditures for economic development purposes following quintessential productivist logic. The government expended less than 3 percent of gross domestic product (GDP) on social protection prior to the 1990s, but raised this amount to 9.6 percent in 2015, on par with other East Asian nations but well below the OECD average of 20.1.[4] Social insurance comprised the majority of this spending at 7.7 percent of GDP, whereas social assistance and active labor market policies (ALMPs) made up far less, at 1.8 and 0.3 percent, respectively. Social assistance expenditures were fairly equally divided among the welfare, elderly, child welfare, and health categories (table 1.5). The bulk of social protection spending went to the non-poor as opposed to the poor (table 1.6). The disbursements that did reach the needy were insufficient to make much of a dent in the elderly poverty problem. By 2015, coverage rates for insurance programs had improved significantly, but those for assistance remained very low (table 1.7). Social expenditures rose markedly in 2019, to a total of 12.3 percent of GDP, comprised of 9.4 percent on social insurance, 2.5 percent on social assistance, and 0.4 percent on ALMPs (table 1.12).

Korea has undergone major political change since the 1960s when the general Park Chung-Hee established an autocratic state. Long-brewing discontent among citizens over a lack of political freedoms erupted in social unrest in the 1980s, compelling the authoritarian regime to undertake democratic reforms that resulted in the first freely contested presidential elections in 1987.[5] Korea's democratic transition, however, soon faced a major challenge: a severe financial crisis in the period 1997 to 1998 that led to the collapse of the currency and a deep (but brief) recession. The crisis exposed extensive corruption involving top public officials and business leaders, a revelation that set in motion an intense process of reckoning that continues to this day.[6] Despite these adversities, South Korea has transformed into a stable democratic state and stood proud as the tenth largest economy in the world in 2021.

These great achievements, however, mask a gloomy contemporary reality. The generation that lifted the country from rural, poverty-stricken, post-war devastation to an affluent democracy is in dire straits: About 40 percent of all seniors live in relative poverty. What factors have contributed to this alarming rate of elderly poverty? What are the long-run ramifications? How have government officials responded to the growing distress among the aged? What role has Korea's productivist approach played in the old age crisis? Beyond Korea, how are other East Asian countries grappling with the issues presented by a rapidly aging population?

The Acute State of Elderly Poverty and Its Consequences
The Extent of Elderly Poverty

South Korea's senior poverty is the highest among advanced industrialized countries. Table 2.1 displays elderly (aged sixty-five and above) and total population relative poverty rates for select East Asian societies as well as the OECD average.[7] In 2020, Korea's elderly poverty rate of 40.4 percent exceeded those of Japan and Hong Kong by a wide margin and was nearly three times greater than the OECD average of 15.2 percent.[8] It has hovered between 40 and 50 percent since the early 2000s and was roughly three times higher than that of the total population—15.3 percent—in 2020. Seniors living alone fared the worst: 74 percent were poor.[9]

Figure 2.1 compares levels of poverty among different age groups in Korea and the OECD. It confirms the exceptionally high rates among Korean seniors vis-à-vis younger cohorts. In the OECD, by contrast, the younger population had a similar degree of poverty as the elderly. The Korean National Pension Research Institute reported that the income of older adults in 2014 was approximately 64 percent of average household income, well below that of the OECD, 88 percent.[10] A 2022 government survey found that a mere 8.7 percent of households felt "well prepared" for retirement. The high level of economic insecurity among the elderly has compelled many to "work until death," pushing the

TABLE 2.1 Old age and total relative poverty rates* in East Asia and OECD, latest years available

	OLD-AGE POVERTY	TOTAL POPULATION POVERTY
Hong Kong	32.0	15.8
Japan	20.0	15.7
South Korea	40.4	15.3
OECD average	15.2	12.0

* Relative poverty is defined as income less than 50 percent of the national median

Sources: OECD, "Income Distribution"; Government of Hong Kong, *Poverty Situation Report 2020*

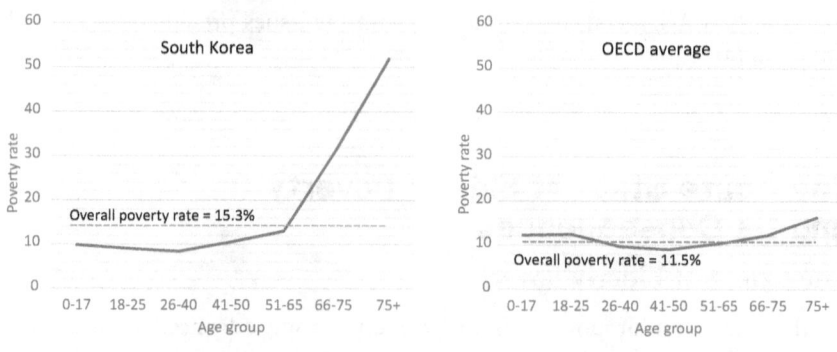

FIGURE 2.1 Demographic breakdown of poverty rates by age group: Korea versus OECD, 2020.

Source: OECD, "Income Distribution"

effective age of retirement to seventy-three, compared to the OECD average of sixty-five. An astonishing 69 percent of those sixty-five and older were employed in 2022, compared to the peer group average of 13.2 percent.[11]

Consequences

Many Korean elderly have responded to their economic insecurity by taking out loans, turning to crime, or committing suicide. The household debt-to-income ratio among seniors was around 161 percent in the 2010s, which was the highest among developed nations and far exceeded the younger generation's ratio of 128 percent.[12] Approximately 41 percent of elderly households were incapable of paying off the principal of their loans based on their current assets. The Seoul Central District Court announced that one in four bankruptcies during the first quarter of 2016 were filed by seniors, and this figure was expected to rise as more elderly persons faced greater financial risk.[13]

Anger and frustration over their deteriorating economic circumstances contributed to a nearly 75 percent surge in violent crimes (e.g., murder, aggravated assault, and rape) and thefts perpetrated by senior citizens from 2011 to 2017, a period in which the nation's overall crime rate declined.[14] From 2014 to 2016, financially motivated illegal prostitution by women in their fifties to eighties garnered media attention.[15] Known as the "Bacchus ladies," they sold Bacchus energy drinks in plazas and parks in Seoul and offered sex for less than USD30 at nearby motels. But perhaps the most distressing manifestation of acute elderly poverty has been the sharp rise in suicides among seniors. In recent years, Korea has experienced the highest incidence of suicide in both the overall and elderly population among peer countries. In 2020, the overall rate was 24.1 per 100,000 population compared to the OECD average of 10.[16] Suicide rates for the age groups 65 to 69, 70 to 74, 75 to 79, 80 to 84, and 85+ in South Korea were 37.1, 54.9, 72.5, 81.5, and 87.1, respectively, in 2015, versus the corresponding OECD averages of 15.2, 17.3, 19.7, 21, and 23.7.[17] The overall suicide rate for South Korea that year was 26.5, so all but one elderly age group had rates that were at least twice as high as the total population rate. A 2017 Ministry of Health and Welfare survey found that 21.1 percent of elderly respondents had depression.[18]

Korea's demographic trends are likely to compound old-age poverty and its associated problems. The country is projected to have the fastest aging society in the world, with the median age climbing precipitously from forty in 2015 to fifty-seven by 2050.[19] The elderly made up 11.5 percent of the population in 2020 but this will rise to 32.9 percent by 2040, a figure that will be considerably above the world average of 14.1 percent and second only to Japan in the region (35.2 percent); see table 1.9 for more details. The National Statistical Office estimated that 40.1 percent of the population will be elderly by 2050, making it the oldest society in the OECD.[20] The accelerated aging of Korean society is a consequence of plummeting fertility and rising life expectancy. In 1960, a woman gave birth to 6.0 children on average; that number dropped to just 0.7 in 2023. In the same period, average life expectancy jumped from fifty-three to eighty-two years.[21] The rapid pace of aging does not bode well for the financial situation of future seniors; if anything, their difficulties are likely to be exacerbated by the further strengthening of the political, economic, and societal causes of the old age poverty crisis, to which we now turn.

Understanding the Causes of Rising Elderly Poverty

The elderly are at great risk of falling into poverty due to multiple causes. They include poor health and high medical costs, inadequate pensions, the lack of good labor market opportunities during working age, low levels of education, family dissolution, unaffordable housing, serious debt, and financial scams and illiteracy.[22] All of these factors have the potential to contribute to low earnings or income losses that lead to impoverishment. Individuals have two primary forms of income maintenance to help guard against becoming destitute in their old age: personal resources (e.g., savings and familial support) and government assistance (e.g., pension and public assistance programs). Why have these two main defenses failed to prevent Korean seniors from slipping into poverty?

Depleting Personal Resources

Korea had a household savings rate of 8.5 percent in 2022, which was just slightly below that of most European countries.[23] Yet, a 2012 survey revealed that roughly 40 percent of individuals born between 1955 and 1974 had failed to make any preparations for retirement.[24] Why have ordinary Koreans had difficulty allocating financial resources for their old age? The main reasons are: (1) high private spending on education; (2) intense urbanization, which has raised the cost of living and weakened family support networks; and (3) loss of income due to early contractual mandatory retirement.

HIGH EDUCATIONAL EXPENSES

Productivism places a heavy emphasis on educational achievement, and this has contributed to old age poverty in Korea. Many seniors have struggled to accumulate retirement savings because of the protracted burden of covering the scholastic expenses of their offspring.[25] The country's ultracompetitive education system and job market compel parents to make enormous financial investments on behalf of their children. Schooling for ages six to fifteen is free, and high schools impose only modest tuition fees, but payments for cram schools (*hagwon*), tutors, English-language classes, and extracurricular activities are a substantial drain on household income. Private expenditures on education amounted to 1.3 percent of GDP in 2019, well above the OECD average of 0.8 percent. Private spending accounted for 10 percent of primary to postsecondary (nontertiary) expenditures and for 62 percent of tertiary, compared to the OECD averages of 10 and 31 percent, respectively.[26] The impact on families was significant; in 2011, scholastic expenses added up to nearly one-quarter of household income on average. Indirect costs may also be high. The education arms race has pushed some parents to live in more expensive urban neighborhoods in order to enroll their children in the best schools and link up with private educational resource networks.[27] One study found that these financial pressures caused depression among fathers (but not mothers).[28]

URBANIZATION: THE AFFORDABILITY PROBLEM AND THE BREAKDOWN OF FAMILIAL NETWORKS

Korea's astonishing economic advance fueled explosive urban growth that has contributed to lower household savings and debilitated the familial support networks that are vital for combating elderly poverty. The proportion of urban residents jumped from a little over 50 percent in the late 1970s to 81.5 percent in 2022; Seoul, with a population of ten million, is one of the largest municipalities in the world.[29] According to the Worldwide Cost of Living Survey 2021, Seoul ranked as the twelfth most expensive city in the world. Its chronic shortage of affordable housing has created a tremendous financial burden for many families.[30] In addition, the price of basic necessities, such as groceries, clothing, and utilities, has risen sharply, which has affected low-income households the hardest since they spend a larger proportion of their income on such goods.

Urbanization has also played a part in the breakdown of the Confucian family support system. High spending on offspring yields dividends when an established quid pro quo scheme obliges children to care for their aging parents. A large body of research confirms that an intergenerational exchange of resources in the form of financial support from children and coresidency helps to reduce elderly poverty.[31] In Korea, the Confucian tradition conferred on the eldest son (and, if he married, the daughter-in-law) the responsibility to care for his parents and the pooling of financial resources among family members was the norm. The country's traditionally strong family bonds, however, have diminished considerably, especially in cities. In 2016 only 32 percent of South Koreans believed that children should take care of their aging parents, a huge drop from 90 percent in 1998.[32] Nearly 72 percent of seniors' total income came from child-to-parent monetary transfers in 1980. By 2003, this figure had dropped to 31 percent and has continued to decline; a more recent estimate put it below 25 percent.[33] The weakening of the family system is seen also in the rise of lonely deaths—elderly dying alone at home and being left undiscovered for a long period of time.[34] These incidents are likely to increase further as the proportion of single elderly households rises from 25 percent in 2010 to an estimated 40 percent in 2030.[35]

CONTRACTUAL EARLY MANDATORY RETIREMENT

Korea's labor market regulations and practices have had the effect of restricting personal savings for retirement. Traditional contractual mandatory retirement practices have forced many workers to exit their career jobs at around fifty years of age—when their earnings are peaking—through a practice known as "honorary retirement."[36] An individual's prime working years, therefore, are cut short, severely reducing lifetime earnings and the ability to save for old age. The law on contractual early retirement was amended in 2013, lifting the official retirement age to sixty by 2016 for large companies and by 2017 for small- and medium-sized enterprises (SMEs); it will be raised to sixty-five for those born in or after 1969. Whether these adjustments will improve old-age financial security is an open question. Employers, especially in the financial, manufacturing, and service sectors, persist in forcing their workers to retire earlier through informal mechanisms (e.g., "voluntary" honorable retirement or by demoting workers to demeaning jobs) despite several government incentives to keep older workers on the job.[37] They embrace the practice because it purges high-cost older workers (who receive wage increases based on seniority) and creates openings for low-cost young workers who are also believed to be more productive. Numerous studies, however, have found little to no evidence that firm productivity actually improved after forcing older workers to retire.[38]

As a general practice, early retirees receive severance pay (a so-called retirement allowance) amounting to five times their monthly salary. The gap between the typical age of forced early retirement and the age of eligibility for a pension, which varies between sixty-three and sixty-five years, is very long. This compels many retirees to begin second careers as low-paying, nonregular workers in service sector jobs such as security guards, street cleaners, laundromat attendants, and cashiers.[39] These positions are highly vulnerable to elimination or downward wage pressure due to skill-biased technological change. Some seniors are also recruited by so-called silver businesses, where they might make dumplings and tea at cafés or deliver business parcels and jewelry using senior-discount fares as silver couriers.[40] Others leverage their severance payment to take out loans to open small retail shops or restaurants since the barriers to entry are low. In 2015, 54.3 percent of business owners were previously salaried employees and 62.8 percent of total self-employed persons were aged fifty or above.[41] These businesses generally earn low profits and have a high occurrence of bankruptcy.[42]

Policy Responses

Old Age Income Security Policies

Pensions (also known as social security or old age security) insure individuals against income losses due to old age and are the principal line of defense against elderly poverty in most countries. They help to smooth consumption by transferring economic resources from the employment to retirement phase in one's life course. Their income replacement component ensures that retirement income mirrors the living standards achieved during the employment stage to some extent. Pension schemes vary in design, income replacement rate, coverage, and their extent of redistribution (that is, whether they provide low-income individuals with a higher percentage of previous earnings). Germany, Japan, the United States, and Korea have developed an earnings-based Bismarckian system that is funded primarily by employers and employee contributions.[43] This contribution-financed approach focuses on status maintenance and is less concerned with old-age poverty relief. The United Kingdom and Denmark, on the other hand, have adopted a Beveridgean pension system.[44] This type of system seeks a degree of redistribution through a universal flat-rate pension financed by taxes (or tax-like contributions).

Most countries—whether Bismarckian or Beveridgean—have sought to establish a minimum floor of social protection through noncontributory social assistance schemes financed by general taxes. That is, they add to pension income as needed to alleviate old age poverty.[45] For example, Canada and the United Kingdom integrate the safety net and social insurance systems by offering a basic, near universal national pension plan supplemented by an income-tested program for the elderly. In the case of Canada, the Old Age Security program caters to the general aged population and its income-tested Guaranteed Income Supplement program extends the safety net to seniors in need.

A Dualistic Social Welfare System and the Contemporary Policy Façade

Korea has developed a seemingly comprehensive multi-pillar pension system to reduce old age risk, but it fails to furnish sufficient income to the elderly in need. Seniors' total income was comprised of 50 percent earned income versus 30 percent from pension schemes; the remainder consisted of income-yielding assets and a small amount of public assistance.[46] In contrast, public pensions were the predominant source of income in most Western nations (the OECD average was 55 percent).

The Korean pension system consists of four pillars. Two "zero pillar" programs meant to furnish a minimal level of social protection comprise the base of the Korean old age safety net: the Basic Old Age Pension (renamed the New Basic Old Age Pension, or BOAP, in 2014) and the Basic Livelihood Security Program (BLSP). BOAP is a noncontributory maintenance scheme for the elderly that supplements the income of those enrolled in a contribution-based government plan; BLSP is a means-tested, entitlement-based social assistance program for the poor at large, many of whom are incapacitated. The "first pillar" consists of the contribution-based National Pension Service (NPS) and government-sponsored pension programs for civil servants and military officials (the primary of which is the Government Employees Pension Service). The "second pillar" is comprised of occupation-based pensions, like those for teachers, and company-administered programs. It also includes corporate schemes that give employees the option of converting their mandatory lump-sum severance payments (i.e., retirement allowance) into a defined benefit or contribution pension plan.[47] Finally, individual savings make up the "third pillar."

In aggregate, the Korean government spent the equivalent of 3.1 percent of GDP on programs for the elderly in 2020, which is a relatively low level; expenditures on seniors in China, Japan, and Taiwan amounted to 5, 12.4, and 1.2 percent, respectively, and over 10 percent in most European countries.[48] Outlays on the country's main social security system, the NPS, were only equivalent to 1.2 percent of GDP in 2020, providing further evidence of the inadequate nature of the old age security system. The government expended a slightly higher amount, equal to 1.3 percent of GDP, on the various government employee pension schemes. Finally, expenditures on noncontributory transfers through the BOAP amounted to 0.8 percent of GDP.[49] The following subsections examine Korea's various old age security measures in greater detail. We contend that although the government has expanded pension programs and increased benefits in the last decade, these efforts are merely a policy façade: They appear to address the issue of old age poverty but actually do little to prevent or lift individuals out of it.

THE NATIONAL PENSION SERVICE

South Korea's principal old age security program, the NPS, is considerably newer (1988) than those in other countries, for example, Japan (1941), the United States (1935), Sweden (1913), and Germany (1889).[50] Individuals must contribute for at least ten years to become eligible for partial benefits, twenty years for half benefits, and forty years for full benefits. The contribution rate of 9 percent is split equally between employers and employees; self-employed workers pay the entire premium themselves. The NPS has two distinct benefits components: a flat rate payment that depends entirely on the number of years that contributions have been made and another based on individual earnings.[51] Workers with lower earnings receive higher replacement rates because of the flat rate component of the pension scheme but net replacement rates in general are very low compared to OECD peers.

The relatively late launch of the NPS means that many current workers have made contributions for only a short period of time. The widespread practice of early forced retirement has also prevented many recent retirees from reaching the ten-year benefit eligibility mark.[52] Those who were forced to retire early took on irregular or temporary employment during which they were either exempt from or unable to pay their NPS contributions. Consequently, the NPS has not functioned as an effective old age risk management system as of yet. Only around 30 percent of senior citizens over sixty-five actually received the NPS in 2013 since most individuals were ineligible to receive benefits.[53] NPS administrators predicted that it would take until the year 2070 to raise the beneficiary rate to 70 percent.[54]

When the NPS was launched, the maximum replacement rate (a person's gross post-retirement income divided by their preretirement income) was slated to be 70 percent; in 2013, it was reduced to 40 percent effective as of 2028.[55] The net replacement rate (net pensions as a ratio of net earnings) for a full career worker earning average wages is 35 percent, well below the OECD average of 62 percent.[56] The average net replacement rate is considerably lower because of early retirement or career breaks due to unemployment or childcare, both of which are commonplace in South Korea. The negative impact of a career break of ten years on pension payouts, for instance, is the greatest in the OECD and among the highest for a break of five years.[57]

A more basic reason why many seniors cannot rely on the NPS as their principle means of old age income maintenance is that it cannot overcome the inequities that stem from the fundamental labor market divide between insiders and outsiders. The schism in labor markets has deepened as skill-biased technical change has accentuated the relative wages paid to different classes of workers. The OECD stated bluntly that this cleavage was "one of the main obstacles towards enlarging social insurance coverage in Korea."[58] The NPS ends up exacerbating rather than ameliorating old age inequality because workers with stable, high wage jobs who are able to contribute to their retirement for a longer period of time get the most out of the system.[59] These individuals also tend to receive corporate benefits that augment their savings, such as retirement allowances, bonuses, and overtime pay.[60] In contrast, the pension system is highly disadvantageous for those with precarious employment (i.e., nonregular workers, such as those with contractual or part-time jobs), the self-employed, or employees in small businesses. Korea had one of the highest ratios of nonregular laborers among salaried workers—roughly one-third in 2016, twice the OECD average; moreover, 38.5 percent of these employees work only part time. A particularly high share of nonregular workers in Korea were employed in small and micro businesses (72.1 percent in firms with thirty employees or less).[61] Job tenure at such firms was extremely short; about half of all individuals stayed with their firm for less than one year. On average, non-regular workers received 34.6 percent less per hour than regular ones despite having broadly similar skills. In addition, the number of nonregular and regular employees in SMEs who had pension coverage was significantly lower (49.7 percent and 67.3 percent, respectively).[62] They also tended to possess smaller personal savings because they were less likely to receive retirement allowances, overtime pay, and bonuses.

THE NONCONTRIBUTORY SOCIAL INSURANCE PROGRAM

The NPS has had limited coverage and redistributive effects, which prodded the government to introduce a noncontributory social insurance program, the BOAP, in 2008. This tax-financed income support program supplements the income of older adults who had not enrolled in or contributed sufficiently to the NPS. It was designed to have wide coverage, as the means-test criteria did not focus on the neediest, but meager in benefits, rendering it ineffective at fighting elderly poverty.[63] The government expanded the BOAP in 2014. The revamped program dispensed funds that ranged from USD98 to USD196 per recipient monthly and targeted individuals in the bottom seventieth percentile of the earned income distribution. Former President Moon Jae-In's administration hiked the monthly allowance to around USD250 in 2019, but this increase was offset by a reduction in a recipient's public assistance benefits since the higher allowance was treated as additional income. The Yoon Suk Yeol administration has stated that it plans to expand the BOAP, but the new proposed benefit level remains insufficient for combatting old age poverty. To do so effectively would require both lowering the income threshold and concomitantly increasing benefit levels.

THE LAST RESORT SAFETY NET

The government implemented a means-tested public assistance system, the BLSP, in 2002 in response to the socioeconomic hardship caused by the financial crisis.[64] This scheme is available to older adults below the de facto poverty line. The take-up rate was just 3.2 percent, however, and expenditures amounted to 0.2 percent of GDP in 2016.[65] Even though two-fifths of elderly were poor, only about 10 percent of seniors received assistance because eligibility rules were extremely strict in order to discourage welfare dependency and reduce public expenditures. The government restricted access to the program by testing income and assets, the capacity to work, and the availability of familial support from siblings, children, and in-laws. Moreover, prospective applicants could be deemed ineligible for the basic living allowance if they received benefits from the BOAP.[66] Finally, a sense of shame has deterred many seniors from participating in public welfare schemes such as this one. Governments in northern Europe have sought to dispel the stigma attached to public welfare, but Korean officials have yet to make any effort to do so.

The Korean government also instituted an Earned Income Tax Credit (EITC) in 2008 and has slowly modified its eligibility requirements to include 1.4 million households by 2016 (or about 7 percent of all households). Workers enrolled in the BLPS are not eligible for the EITC. Two-thirds of all EITC households are headed by someone fifty years or older, and 47 percent of these are single-person.[67] Benefit levels are very low: The average payment in 2016 was only 2.2 percent of the average wage. The OECD concluded that the "EITC has a positive impact on labour supply and poverty for certain groups. Yet, EITC alone is insufficient to reduce the high level of in-work poverty among older workers in Korea and thus can only be one element in a broader strategy."[68]

The Political Economy of Social Insurance without Protection

The root causes of the deficit in social protection for the needy lie in Korea's initial pro-economic growth agenda under authoritarian rule. The focus on rapid development gave rise to a coalition of private actors that supported the government's strategy. The *chaebol*, Korea's large industrial conglomerates, were the key actors. They established direct, intimate links with public officials and aided in formulating and implementing industrial policies; in the process, they accumulated massive economic power and gained political influence. Parallel to the growing political and economic clout of large businesses was the emergence of a class of privileged workers—a sort of labor aristocracy—within large companies.[69] They enjoyed longer employment tenure, higher wages, corporate welfare benefits, and generous retirement allowances. These circumstances weakened their incentive to press for greater public social welfare spending and their interests aligned with those of their employers, not other workers.[70] Consequently, working class mobilization remained mostly fragmented, leaving non-regular laborers, the self-employed, and employees in small businesses to fend for themselves. Unlike the organized labor unions that played an important role in constructing welfare states in Europe, their Korean counterparts did little to advance a solidaristic social policy.

The strength of business vis-à-vis labor helps explain the delay in the development of the social security system during the authoritarian era and the durability of early forced retirement practices. The government proposed a national pension scheme in 1973, but the primary goal of mobilizing funds from its citizens was capital investment, not providing financial security for old age. The business community, however, resisted and postponed its enactment until the late 1980s. Similarly, the government acquiesced to early forced retirement practices in the corporate world. Occasional efforts to introduce retirement age legislation stalled because of the strong political influence of the Korea Employers Federation. It opposed raising the mandatory retirement age on the grounds that it would allow unproductive workers to stay on the job and compromise the labor market flexibility needed to succeed in a global, competitive environment.[71]

The introduction of the NPS and the roll out of universal health care in 1989 is surely related to the impact of democratic reforms that began with the massive protests of June 1987 and the first free presidential elections held later that year. These events forced politicians to view issues of social protection from an explicitly political perspective and consider how their stances on old age security, health care, social assistance, and labor market policies would play with voters. The influence of the *chaebol* remained strong after Korea's transition, however. The country's de facto majoritarian-based electoral system gives political representatives an incentive to cater to narrow, district needs at the expense of broad, national concerns such as social welfare.[72] Business has a tremendous advantage in defending its policy preferences under these circumstances as it is well-organized, has ample resources, and can rely on an existing network of leaders and lobbyists with links to important politicians. In addition, a party focused on the interests of labor has yet to develop into a potent political force in Korean politics, leaving it without a strong voice in policymaking. The result has been the slow and uneven increase of social protection described above that has maintained a dualistic nature despite clear signs—like widespread elderly poverty—that certain segments of the population are in dire straits.

One consequence of the slow progress in enlarging the national government's role in social protection is that cities have also stepped into the mix. In response to the old age poverty crisis, their approach has been to promote market-based solutions. The Seoul Metropolitan Government, for example, has advocated a type of do-it-yourself welfare that encourages the reemployment of seniors. Firms who are willing to employ workers aged fifty-seven or above are eligible to receive government subsidies.[73] The city has run one of the largest annual senior citizen jobs fairs in Asia that attracts nearly one million retirees.[74] It has also offered short training programs on topics such as cyber and mobile literacy, small enterprise courses, and postretirement life design workshops. Finally, it has created a talent bank of seniors to help place older adults in local firms that can profit from their skills.

Policymakers at all levels of government have also attempted to mobilize non-state actors in order to limit the need for greater public social welfare spending.[75] Thousands of volunteers and caregivers throughout the country, for example, are trained by the government each year to detect the early warning signs of elderly suicide and conduct telephone checks. Churches, especially in urban centers, often provide various social services for the elderly poor, including mobile soup kitchens and psychological counseling. Moreover, public officials continue to rely heavily on familial support even as evidence mounts that urbanization and changing social norms are dismantling the once dominant Confucian tradition.[76]

The scandals of recent years have begun to check the abuse of political power and corruption that has marred Korean politics and open the door to elected officials who are less beholden to vested interests. The massive Candlelight Revolution in 2016 led to Park Geun-Hye becoming the first democratically elected president to be impeached; she was subsequently arrested for corruption and sentenced to twenty-four years in prison. Only time will tell if the change in political climate is sufficient to bring about a definitive shift away from the pattern of skewed social policy responses that have characterized Korea's productivist political economy. As already noted, social spending has risen substantially, but the majority of funds still flow to favored social groups, not the needy. Initiatives to address elderly economic insecurity like the BOAP remain circumscribed and mainly function as band-aid solutions to deeper, structural problems. The old age security crisis is likely to endure in this land of economic miracles.

The Old Age Crisis in East Asia

East Asia accounts for about 31 percent of the world's elderly population and is the fastest aging region in the world.[77] Seniors will constitute over 30 percent of the total population in each country by 2060: China (33.2 percent), Hong Kong (38.7 percent), Japan (38.8 percent), South Korea (40.2 percent), Singapore (32.2 percent), and Taiwan (39.3 percent).[78] The graying process has accelerated because life expectancy in the region climbed from sixty-five in 1960 to eighty-five in 2020, the longest in the world. In addition, the number of births continues to plummet. In 1950, the region's fertility rate was 5.4; in 2020 it was only 1.2. These demographic trends point to the likelihood of an ever-growing number of elderly who find themselves living in or near poverty in the future.

Japan

The OECD estimated that 20 percent of Japanese elderly lived in poverty in 2020, significantly above the rate for the total population (15.7 percent).[79] The hardships that many seniors face have been well documented. As in South Korea, thousands of elderly across Japan die alone (*kodokushi*) each year and often remain undiscovered for an extended period of time.[80] People sixty years or older committed close to 38 percent of the nation's suicides in 2022 (nearly 21,000 incidents per year, one of the highest rates in the world).[81] Furthermore, seniors accounted for over 20 percent of all crimes (double the rate of two decades ago). A growing number of elderly perpetrators view prisons as akin to nursing homes where they can receive better shelter and free meals and escape isolation.[82]

These social trends—and the elderly poverty issue—will persist because the government does not guarantee a minimum income for senior citizens. Japan's principal mandatory social security system—the National Pension (Kokumin Nenkin)—covers self-employed persons, salaried private-sector workers, government employees, and the dependent spouses of the latter two groups. One must contribute for forty years or more to obtain full benefits, and income replacement rates are considerably lower than the OECD average across all earnings levels. In 2020, the replacement rate for average income earners was 38.7 percent versus the OECD average of 62.4 percent.[83]

As in Korea, Japan's main social assistance program for the poor, the Livelihood Protection (Seikatsu Hogo), has exceptionally strict eligibility rules that require recipients to be virtually penniless, homeless, and family-less to qualify for assistance. Policymakers have pursued an approach that strives to secure employment for needy seniors in lieu of providing cash transfers. In the last decade, the government has raised the retirement age from sixty to sixty-five, and it is being increased to seventy in incremental steps over a period of several years (starting April 2021). But in reality, firms retain discretion over retirement policies and corporate practices vary greatly, especially between large firms and SMEs.[84] In 2016, over 80 percent of companies, both large and small, had a mandatory retirement age of sixty—which is five years ahead of the pension eligibility age—leaving many retirees with insufficient income during the gap period.[85] The government has offered subsidies to employers to retain or hire older workers and amended labor regulations to oblige firms that have an early retirement age to rehire affected workers on a contract basis through the age of sixty-five. Four-fifths of employers have continued to mandate early retirement at age sixty or shifted full-time core workers to irregular employment arrangements at generally less than half their previous salary.[86] The COVID-19 pandemic hit this growing group of elderly irregular workers particularly hard, with many losing their jobs and even going hungry.[87] Government efforts to reskill older workers have been generally lackluster.

Singapore

The Singaporean government has not adopted an official poverty line and, therefore, does not disseminate old age or total population poverty statistics. Several scholars have attempted to calculate poverty rates based on the methodology used by the OECD but note that their analyses were limited by incomplete data on household income. Irene Ng, for instance, found that the total population poverty rate was 24 percent in 2017.[88] Anecdotal reports have confirmed the relative magnitude of this estimate and documented the growing number of elderly working poor and the heightened degree of social isolation among low-income seniors.[89]

The country's old age security scheme relies on a compulsory non-redistributive savings plan called the Central Provident Fund (CPF) Retirement Account. Workers with higher-paying, stable jobs are able to make larger contributions to their retirement accounts and, hence, enjoy greater income security in old age. Since CPF accounts only yield 2.5 percent interest, well below the rate paid by private pension funds, the government has adopted a lease buyback scheme on Housing Development Board (HDB) flats to improve the cash flow of senior citizens.[90] Older adults who live in a four-room or smaller HDB flat are eligible to sell a portion of their lease to receive a monthly cash payout. This policy—akin to a reverse mortgage in other parts of the world—may have a pernicious effect on the cycle of intergenerational poverty because it reduces the inheritance of offspring.

The government's other line of defense against elderly poverty is Com-Care Long Term Assistance.[91] Under ComCare, a two-person senior household receives 1,080 Singapore dollars (SD)—about USD790—in cash assistance per month to meet basic needs. Eligibility is restricted to individuals who are physically incapacitated due to illness, disability, or old age and lack assets or familial support. As a supplement to public assistance, the government also introduced the Silver Support Scheme in 2016. It covers living expenses (providing from SD180 to SD900 every three months) for older adults who meet a means test that considers earnings, properties, and accumulated CPF contributions.[92] The strong stigma surrounding public assistance, however, has led many seniors, even those in dire need, to reject state largess and choose to work in low-paying jobs instead.

Hong Kong

The issue of elderly poverty in Hong Kong has gained prominence with frequent media reports depicting seniors living in cage or coffin homes, taking refuge in McDonald's restaurants (becoming McRefugees), scavenging for food in dumpsters, or collecting scrap cardboard to earn money for basic necessities.[93] In 2019, 32 percent of older adults lived in relative poverty, double the rate for the total population (15.8 percent).[94]

High levels of aged poverty are a direct result of limited government spending on social security programs. Expenditures on pensions amounted to just 1.4 percent of GDP in 2019. Hong Kong has a three-pillar approach to old-age security, consisting of: (1) the Mandatory Provident Fund; (2) noncontributory programs (including the Comprehensive Social Security Assistance Scheme [CSSA], Old Age Allowance [commonly referred to as fruit money], Old Age Living Allowance [OALA], and Disability Allowance); and (3) private savings.[95] By 2012, it had become obvious that the three-pronged approach, at least at existing benefit levels, was inadequate for addressing persistent elderly poverty. In response, the chief executive announced a new means-tested old age living allowance to enhance financial support for low-income seniors. The proposal proved controversial, with some critics arguing that elderly income was so low generally that all seniors should be eligible for the new payment. Citing demographic trends, policymakers responded that making the allowance a non–means-tested benefit was not fiscally sustainable. In 2017, the government relented by easing eligibility requirements (thereby expanding access to 74 percent of all elderly) and increasing the amount of payments. The government also eliminated the so-called bad son letter that adult children previously had to write asserting that they were unable or unwilling to support their aged parents in order for them to be eligible for the CSSA, the primary income support scheme. In 2022, it merged the two OALA programs and began providing an additional 995 Hong Kong dollars—about USD127—to approximately 50,000 poor elderly persons.[96] Nevertheless, public officials have continued to resist the creation of a universal pension scheme, which is favored by 90 percent of citizens, on the grounds that it would prove too costly and due to strong business opposition.[97]

Taiwan

The official poverty line in Taiwan is set at 60 percent of median disposable income (unlike the 50 percent measure used by the OECD and most researchers). The total poverty rate was 1.3 percent in 2019, but some observers have asserted that this is an artificially low figure.[98] The government does not supply statistics on old age poverty, but several studies have concluded that it is around 30 percent.[99] Consistent with this observation, the Directorate-General of Budget, Accounting and Statistics reported that 56 percent of all seniors fell into the lowest income quintile and their households were among the poorest in Taiwan. The average annual disposable income of these households (generally consisting of two persons) was less than 300,000 Taiwanese dollars (NTD)—or about USD10,000.

Elderly poverty is unchecked because the country's old age security system supplies very limited benefits (the replacement rate is roughly 7 percent of average wages) and emphasizes maintenance of income status over redistribution.[100] The two main social insurance programs are the earnings-related Labor Insurance or Labor Pension programs and the flat-rate National Pension introduced in 2008 to cover individuals not insured by other public pension programs. Some scholars have lauded the latter program as offering greater social protection to vulnerable sectors and representing a turn toward more redistributive policies, but its results have been disappointing. Most of the private sector workforce is enrolled in the old Labor Insurance or new Labor Pension schemes, which are mandatory for workers between the ages of fifteen and sixty who work in firms with more than five employees; contributions are made by the employer, government, and employee.[101] Benefits are calculated based on the worker's seniority and average monthly salary. The National Pension provides a monthly supplementary allowance payment of NTD3,628 (USD120) for low-income pensioners under its Old Age Basic Guaranteed Pension Scheme.[102]

Taiwan's occupation-based social security arrangements supply a degree of old age social protection for individuals with high pay and longer tenure but not less privileged workers. The latter include the self-employed, workers in small enterprises (less than five employees), the working poor (around 20 percent of the labor force), and the unemployed. The arrangements also exacerbate gender inequality because a large number of women do not participate in the formal economy but work instead in family businesses like small retail shops and restaurants.[103] Thus, some critics have claimed that the current social security system does not act as a safety net but instead reinforces social stratification.

East Asia's journey from rags to riches has led to a surprising twist of fate: an old age poverty crisis. The region boasts the fastest aging societies in the world and its current large elderly population faces numerous and considerable economic hardships. The dreadful circumstances facing seniors have resulted in silver-age working poverty, homelessness, social isolation, suicides, petty crimes, and even prostitution. There are few indications that future retirees will fare much better.

The dire situation in South Korea illustrates the underlying causes of elderly poverty in the region and beyond and offers powerful lessons on the pitfalls of the productivist approach to social welfare. Economic advances accelerated urbanization, which became a transformative process that destroyed community-based networks and weakened family-centered safety nets for seniors. High private expenditures on education sapped savings for retirement but have not always set up young adults for success. Declining fertility rates and longer life expectancy increased the age dependency ratio, creating a larger and growing financial burden on the young. Above all, economic insecurity among senior citizens became pervasive because of skewed and insufficient government responses. The government has provided insurance to workers with stable, high-wage jobs but offered low-wage workers the least amount of protection against various socioeconomic risks. For impoverished seniors, Korea's old age income maintenance scheme is a policy façade that appears to address their plight but in reality does not commit anywhere close to enough resources to make a real difference. The old age crisis is likely to persist given the chronic social welfare policy shortfall that has its origins in a productivist political economy that protects the interests of business and a labor aristocracy but neglects disadvantaged societal groups.

3

BROKEN PROMISES
The Low Wage Crisis in High Performing Taiwan

The iconic super skyscraper Taipei 101 proudly soars over Taiwan's capital city, a tangible manifestation of its impressive economic success. The nation's economy has enjoyed one of the world's fastest and most consistent growth rates since 1960. Taiwanese multinational firms, such as the electronics giants Acer and Foxconn, have established a firm foothold in global supply chains, become large investors in mainland China and Southeast Asia, and emerged as major players in international trade. This bright economic picture, however, is not reflected in the lackluster reality confronting many workers. After years of steadily rising earnings, working poverty plagues the low-skill labor force and highly educated workers struggle to find jobs that justify the time and cost of obtaining a university degree.

Wages in East Asia rose quickly until the mid-1990s driven by rapid economic modernization and large investments in human capital. A period of turbulence that began with the region's financial crisis brought an end to this golden era. Governments that had enjoyed the luxury of making economic policy in a context of increasing standards of living and low unemployment were suddenly faced with sharp downturns that pushed people out of work or into working poverty and led to the expansion of the nontraditional workforce. Some scholars saw this upheaval as an opportunity for governments to reorient the welfare–work nexus away from private toward public solutions to adverse labor market developments.[1] Policymakers did introduce a handful of new labor policies aimed at cushioning the blow on households and facilitating job retraining and placement, but the magnitude of these efforts fell far short of what some other advanced industrial countries have done when faced with similar circumstances.

Low-skill workers in many developed countries have experienced mostly stagnant earnings since the early 1980s as a consequence of skill-biased technical change and globalization. An unusual feature of the Taiwanese case is that both low- and high-skill workers have had difficulty finding work that pays well. The college-educated have seen the return on their education decline, manifested in a reduction in the wage premium that they enjoy over less-educated workers, even as skill-biased technological change raised the demand for their labor. This puzzling outcome is due to several factors. First, the government undertook an aggressive expansion of tertiary education that greatly increased the supply of well-educated workers. Second, this jump in supply occurred at a time when globalization was pushing Taiwanese companies to offshore a great deal of their production to mainland China and Southeast Asia, which reduced the number of high-quality jobs available in Taiwan. Third, college-educated workers often did not have the skill sets that firms needed, especially in high-tech sectors, so recent graduates in particular found it difficult to land good job placements.

More broadly, the Taiwan case reveals the potential limitations of a key element of the productivist strategy, namely, heavy investments aimed at accumulating more sophisticated human capital, without also providing adequate government support for struggling low-skill workers. The failure to create a more balanced and comprehensive labor strategy may jeopardize the goal of achieving rising standards of living for the majority of households, even in a society with one of the most astonishing records of sustained high growth in world economic history. It also shows that macro-level demographic trends and changes in family structure may make private provision of protection against economic insecurity as an alternative solution less likely to succeed. The stories of three talented young adults related below demonstrate the high stakes for a new generation of Taiwanese.[2]

The View from the Ground

Huang Tsai took a big breath and sighed deeply. Taking a break from cleaning out his locker and desk, he slouched in his chair as if it were his final resting place. Huang had just wrapped up nearly forty years of teaching at one of Taipei's municipal schools. Teaching junior high school math in Taiwan was heavy-duty work. Teachers were under enormous pressure to cover a packed curriculum that included advanced algebra, geometry, and statistics. These subjects were main components of the Basic Competency Test and, later, the University Entrance

Examination. Moreover, building quantitative skills was seen as the key to securing a high-paying job in fields such as engineering, computer science, and finance.

Over a decade ago, a group of talented and highly motivated students had given him a handmade globe shaped like a hot air balloon. It was the final object sitting atop his emptied desk. The math whiz, Pu-Ching Tan, had inserted the latitude and longitude lines and weaved together the basket. Peter Zheng had put his engineering skills to work and installed tiny light bulbs that illuminated the globe beautifully at night. The computer nerd, Lin "Bill" Chen, had created a display that showed the time and temperature and attached it to the basket. Huang had taken great comfort from the endearing gift on the numerous occasions his job had gotten tough, uplifted by the conviction that Peter, Pu-Ching, Lin, and the countless other students whose lives he had touched were chasing their dreams and winning in life.

Peter Zheng's parents were always fishing for compliments about their gifted only child. They owned a small beef noodle shop that featured a large brass antique cash register near the door. When customers inquired about the shop's curiosity piece, his parents quickly responded: "Amazing, right?! Our son refurbished it when he was only eight years old. It still works!" Peter's delicate hands were soft and smooth but they could transform into sophisticated tools capable of fixing practically anything. As a child he had spent countless hours creating elaborate battlefields and electrified amusement parks using the knock-off Lego bricks that his mother purchased at the local night market.

The family's delectable ginger anise–flavored beef broth recipe earned them a living, but Peter's college diploma—the first in the Zheng clan—gave them hope of upward mobility. At the National Taiwan University of Science and Technology, one of the top engineering schools in Taipei, he had gained the technical skills and experience of working in teams that were highly valued by employers. The Golden Gate Enterprise, a company manufacturing heavy-duty cast iron security gates located near the university, had recruited Peter upon graduation. That summer, he had proposed to his girlfriend, Wenting, and a baby girl was born the following year. His ever-so-proud parents gushed about their granddaughter whenever customers smiled at the adorable baby photos that were now plastered all over the cash registrar.

Custom-made gates for luxury apartments and mansions were in high demand as lavish buildings popped up everywhere in and around Taipei. Peter's crew was in charge of installing, repairing, and maintaining the electrical and mechanical components of the massive cast iron gates. They worked long hours without receiving overtime pay—even on weekends and late at night—but no member of his crew ever complained and tackled each task with a great sense of responsibility and pride. Despite the signs of rising wealth everywhere, Peter's annual salary, around 820,000 Taiwanese dollars (NTD), about USD25,000, as an electrical engineer, barely budged over time. His wife had begun to work a few hours at the noodle shop to supplement their household income, but the job was becoming more and more unbearable as the Zheng matriarch increasingly pontificated about child rearing. Wenting had nudged Peter to relocate to Kaohsiung, the largest city in southern Taiwan. Kaohsiung was thriving as an international port with robust refinery, machinery, shipbuilding and petrochemicals sectors, offering Peter a variety of job opportunities. Peter flirted with the idea of relocation but he quickly backtracked. Joining his wife's family in Kaohsiung would deeply hurt his parents. He was stuck between a rock and a hard place.

Pu-Ching loved all things math and Hello Kitty. She had thick glasses and a quirky personality that attracted loads of friends. But there was another reason she was popular. In high school, everyone had sought her out when they needed help with math homework. Like many of her classmates, Pu-Ching had pushed herself hard to get into a top university. She had majored in economics and statistics and begun her career as an analyst for a major national bank in Taiwan. Her attention to details, superb data analysis, and report writing skills had helped her to advance to the associate level within a year; at nearly NTD690,000 (USD21,500), her salary was considerably higher than her peers. A few years later, however, her career had stalled. Advances in statistical and database software made it easier for students to become adept at research and quantitative reporting. Year after year a growing horde of recent college graduates put downward pressure on her earnings. Furthermore, managerial positions proved difficult to secure for women like Pu-Ching, who were deemed "star assistants," not leaders.

Her love life was also seemingly going nowhere. Her boyfriend had left for Japan to receive managerial training at the Mitsukoshi department store, but distance had not made her heart grow fonder. The relationship remained official so that she could dodge her parents' get-married-faster lecture. The last thing on her mind was getting married and having children, given her hectic work schedule and meagre salary. Her mother frequently admonished her for not having nabbed Justin Tien, her middle school sweetheart and the son of a wealthy businessman. He had crossed the Pacific to attend an American university after failing to get into one of the good Taiwanese universities. Upon returning, he had invented wildly popular rum-soaked pineapple gummy bears and had become a shining star of Taipei nightlife. His social media accounts were filled with pictures of a Ferrari, a silver Persian cat, and Michelin-star dining. Pu-Ching was impressed but also dismayed that Justin had achieved financial success by playing hard at night after faring poorly academically. Is winning in life about taking big risks? Having good luck? Ingenuity? Family wealth? Destiny? Her mind was mired in doubts over her self-worth, past choices, and future.

Lin's tall frame and broad shoulders were perfect for playing basketball, so he did and fell in love with the sport. He had revered NBA superstar Tim Duncan of the San Antonio Spurs so much so that he changed his English name from Daniel to Tim when he was eleven years old. A year later, a severely broken ankle had forced him to quit basketball. Being immobile, he had spent long hours on the couch playing video games. This setback had changed his life. Something about the creative visuals and interface of video games had captivated his mind. Sensing his newfound fascination, his parents had arranged for him to be enrolled in after school computer classes and bought various books and educational videos. By the time he had started junior high school, he changed his name yet again, this time to Bill, after the Microsoft founder, and he aspired to become a software programmer.

These career aspirations were auspicious because they fit with the Taiwanese government's ambitious national strategy to strengthen its software development industry. The government subsidized Nankang Software Park in Taipei served as the Asian headquarters for many IT giants, including Hewlett-Packard, Microsoft Innovation Center, IBM, and Intel. The Taiwanese version of Silicon Valley also housed many smaller local IT firms, like iNavi, which had developed a video game–like car navigation system with interactive maps, superior digital images, and dynamic audio. Bill had been working there for five years as a senior software programmer.

The company and nearly two dozen other smaller firms were crammed into the seventh floor of Nankang Park's main tower. Far from the glamorous image of technology companies, Bill's workplace was dingy, austere, and musty, despite the central air conditioning. His hunched shoulders and forward-bending spine said it all. He was envious of his friends who had moved to Silicon Valley and were making six figures and enjoying company benefits, such as free buffet meals, yoga classes at work, and a month-long paid sabbatical. His annual salary of NTD900,000 (USD28,000) was almost the same as when he joined the firm despite its robust growth. Intense competition compelled firms like iNavi to reinvest most of their profits in order to expand research and development. Moreover, IT firms commonly hired non-Taiwanese engineers, especially from mainland China, India, and Southeast Asia, which further dampened salaries. It looked like it might be game over for Bill at iNavi but a new beginning loomed on the horizon. A former coworker, who had been recently hired by a video game giant in Tokyo, contacted Bill about an opening in his unit. This was his chance to become unstuck.

The Political and Economic Context

Taiwan has been widely lauded because of its metamorphosis into an advanced industrial economy in a very short period of time. Thus, it may be puzzling to learn that after its initial success in raising standards of living across the board, wages have stagnated for most workers—even those who are highly educated. A brief tour of Taiwan's history and stunning political and economic transformations provides some context for explaining this dramatic halt in progress for many of the nation's citizens.

Japan colonized Taiwan in 1895 and began to develop the island economically, albeit almost entirely for its own benefit, but it remained isolated internationally. The situation changed in 1949 with the exodus of the Republic of China (ROC), led by Chiang Kai-shek, from the Chinese mainland after its defeat in the Chinese Civil War. Approximately two million mainlanders joined members of the Kuomintang (KMT) who had been brought to the island by the United States to administer the territory after the formal surrender of Japan. The already-high tensions between Taiwanese-born people and the KMT escalated further, creating a divided society composed of two very different cultures and linguistic groups.

The ROC used martial law in 1949 to suppress political opposition by anti-KMT and procommunist groups in a period known as the White Terror; martial law was finally repealed only in 1987. Throughout this period, the ROC maintained an authoritarian, one-party government that legitimized its rule by invoking national security concerns and, subsequently, promising material benefits to its citizens. Chiang Kai-shek's son and successor as president, Chiang Ching-kuo, initiated a process of political liberalization in the mid-1980s. The Democratic Progressive Party (DPP) was created in 1986 and became the country's first true opposition party. Over succeeding years, the influence of non-KMT political groups slowly rose and, in 2000, Chen Shui-bian of the DPP was elected president.

Taiwan's democracy has thrived in spite of a historically high degree of corruption among its political leaders. The president, who is chosen by popular vote, is the head of state and can serve a maximum of two four-year terms. The president appoints the members of the cabinet, including its head, the premier, which is responsible for policymaking and administration. Nonetheless, the Office of the President, rather than the premier, retains most critical executive powers. The unicameral Legislative Yuan is the primary legislative body and has 113 members who are chosen through a mixed electoral system.[3] The legislature is able to pass laws without the support of the president or premiere. In recent decades, the issue that has divided politicians and their parties the most has been the question of whether Taiwan should be unified with mainland China. Economic issues have been less divisive, in large part because performance has been so strong.

As in other East Asian nations, the central goal of public policy has been to sustain fast economic growth. Taiwan initially adopted import substitution industrialization but shifted to an export-led growth strategy by the late 1950s when it became apparent that its inward orientation faced limitations. The nation began to confront stiff competition in the 1980s, first from Southeast Asia and then China, and this contributed to deindustrialization as it lost its footing in manufacturing. In response, government officials devised an industrial policy that sought to create comparative advantage in increasingly sophisticated economic activities. In addition, they dedicated ample resources to creating physical infrastructure and accumulating human capital in order to improve competitiveness. The rapid upgrading of the labor force has been cited as one of the primary reasons for Taiwan's success.[4] It created a pool of skilled and flexible workers capable of engaging in more advanced economic activities, enabling firms to enter new sectors and modernize production methods continuously. Yet, as this chapter shows, aggressively expanding tertiary education in an attempt to accelerate human capital development did not guarantee superior welfare outcomes; instead, it ended up creating serious challenges for a wide swath of workers.

Public officials eschewed the creation of a safety net for workers, even as the country's wealth rose, delegating the responsibility for helping struggling individuals to family and community instead. Taiwan spent somewhat more than its East Asian peers on total social protection in 2015—9.2 percent of gross domestic product (GDP)—but this amount fell far short of the average for OECD countries, 20.1. The bulk of the expenditures went for social insurance—8.3 percent—not social assistance—a mere 0.9 percent; this latter figure was actually a decrease from 1 percent in 2009.[5] In the early 2010s, a scant 1.8 percent of the population was eligible for welfare assistance.[6] Total spending climbed to 9.7 percent of GDP in 2019, almost entirely due to an increase in social insurance (to 8.7 percent); social assistance, in contrast, rose only slightly to 1 percent.

The Low Wage Crisis and Its Consequences

Wage Trends

Earnings in Taiwan followed the upward trend typical of fast-growing emerging market countries until 2000. Table 3.1 shows five-year moving averages for annual real wage growth in East Asia. In Taiwan, salaries went up at an annual rate of 4.8 percent from 1980 to 2000, resulting in a threefold rise in compensation.

TABLE 3.1 Annual real wage growth in East Asia (five-year moving average), 1980–2019

	1980–84	1985–89	1990–94	1995–99	2000–4	2005–9	2010–14	2015–19
China*	n/a	n/a	6.9	7.7	12.8	12.4	8.4	7.8
Hong Kong	n/a	3.0	1.4	0.6	1.8	–0.2	0.7	0.3
Japan	4.4	3.0	2.5	0.5	–1.0	–0.6	–0.7	0.7
South Korea	n/a	n/a	n/a	3.5	2.8	1.4	0.8	3.0
Singapore*	n/a	n/a	n/a	n/a	1.6	1.6	1.8	3.9
Taiwan*	5.8	8.2	5.6	2.0	0.8	–1.6	1.2	1.6

* China: 2015–17; Singapore: 2015–18; Taiwan: 1981–84

Sources: Republic of China, National Bureau of Statistics, "Statistical Yearbook (2017, 2018, 2022)"; Hong Kong, "Annual Digest of Statistics (2009, 2012, 2017, 2019, 2022)"; OECD, "Average Wages"; Republic of Singapore, Ministry of Manpower, "Gross Monthly Income," 2023; Taiwan (ROC), Statistical Bureau, "Average Monthly Earnings"

This increase was in line with the rapid expansion of the economy (7.3 percent) and labor productivity (4.6 percent) during this period.[7] Real wages stagnated after 2000, however; earnings in 2015 were only slightly above those fifteen years earlier. GDP growth, on the other hand, remained robust (7.5 percent) and labor productivity continued to rise though somewhat more slowly (3.7 percent).[8] These trends indicate that capital not labor reaped the rewards of the increase in the nation's output. One study determined that the distributional consequences were substantial: Labor's share of national income fell from 55 percent in 1995 to 47 percent in 2012.[9]

Stagnation of median household income is observed frequently in advanced industrial countries. In the United States, for example, average real wages have barely budged in the last forty years.[10] It is also commonplace in other East Asian nations. Earnings growth in Hong Kong and Japan has slowed over the last two decades to rates similar to or lower than Taiwan's. In contrast, South Korea and Singapore, which have had a similar growth trajectory as Taiwan (and have a higher GDP per capita), continued to experience solid increases in compensation after 2000. China, starting from a far lower level of economic development, has witnessed staggeringly rapid real wage growth that actually accelerated after 2000.

Taiwan's average salary is low for a developed country. In 2022, average monthly salaries in East Asia—Singapore (USD4,340), South Korea (USD3,635), Japan (USD3,459), and Hong Kong (USD2,133)—were significantly higher than in Taiwan (USD1,977); they were only lower in China (USD1,380). As a point of comparison, the average in OECD countries was USD4,522.[11] On the positive side, unemployment in Taiwan, as in most of the region, has remained low, hovering around 4 percent. One reason for depressed average monthly salaries in Taiwan has been a low minimum wage. The nominal minimum wage rose steadily until 1996 but then remained unchanged for ten years. Policymakers have increased it since 2006, albeit at a slow rate. The monthly minimum wage was NTD26,400 in September 2023 (about USD4.70 per hour), which is on the low side for a developed nation.[12]

What truly stands out about the trajectory of Taiwan's wages, however, is that real compensation for highly educated workers, particularly their starting salaries, has taken the biggest hit relatively.[13] The education premium (compensation for college versus high school graduates) in Taiwan shrank dramatically in the 1990s, falling from 67 to 25 percent; it continued to decline until at least 2012.[14] As a point of comparison, the education premium in Hong Kong rose from 75 to 105 percent in roughly the same time period.[15] Prolonged declines in the education premium are not common in developed countries but have occurred in developing and emerging market countries, notably in Latin America.[16]

One noteworthy consequence of these wage trends is that inequality in Taiwan, unlike other East Asian countries (and, more generally, other developed countries), has not risen substantially in the past few decades. Before and after tax and transfers Gini coefficients rose from 0.278 and 0.267, respectively, in 1970, to a high of 0.342 and 0.317 in 2010, before declining slightly to 0.338 and 0.303 in 2015. Taiwan's most recent levels are well below both the before and after tax and transfers coefficients for other East Asian countries, with the exception of South Korea.[17]

The Consequences of Declining or Stagnant Wages

IN-WORK POVERTY

Poverty in Taiwan has been very low historically, though this may be partly an artifact of the way the government defines poverty.[18] The official rate in 2019 was 1.3 percent. Unlike many countries, the Taiwanese government does not report figures for working poverty. One academic study, using standard OECD methodology, calculated the rate of working poverty to be 15.8 percent in 2006, up from 14 percent in 2003.[19] Journalistic accounts have also discussed in-work poverty frequently, defining it as workers whose income is clustered around or below the prevailing monthly minimum wage.[20] A sizable pool of workers fall into this category, living paycheck to paycheck and one family emergency or loss of a job away from serious hardship. Workers who do not have a fixed term of employment— that is, part-time, dispatch, and temporary workers—make up a large percentage of this pool. This group was comprised of 374,000 workers (4.2 percent of the total workforce) in May 2019 and their average salary was NTD19,931 (USD644) per month, which was below the minimum wage.[21] Employees earning this level of income would find it difficult to make ends meet, especially in metropolitan areas like Taipei, according to most observers.

Government assistance to the poor in Taiwan is strictly means tested, and benefits are provided on an all-or-nothing basis. Payments are generally small as they are designed to push households just over the poverty line.[22] Reflecting the conviction that family members should take care of their own, officials consider the income and assets of an applicant's parents, even if they live separately, as well as those of grandparents who do reside with them; in the past, the income of an applicant's siblings and former spouses were also considered. Policymakers have increased the threshold for benefits fairly often in order to calibrate the number of people that are eligible. The threshold is critically important—workers earning just above the official poverty line, such as those making the minimum wage, are not eligible for any government aid. These individuals often end up turning to nongovernmental organizations (NGOs), like the Taiwan Fund for Children and Families, that distribute funds as well as assistance in the form of staples such as rice and oil.

In January 2018, government officials announced that they would seek to establish a minimum monthly salary of NTD30,000 (approximately USD975) for all workers. They did not explain why this specific level of income was chosen, how they planned to reach it, or by when, but by stating this objective they set a new implicit standard by which to define in-work poverty.[23] Approximately 2.7 million workers, or roughly one-third of the labor force, earned less than this amount in 2018, including most individuals who worked for small- and medium-sized enterprises (SMEs). As of this writing, the goal has not been met; in 2023, the minimum monthly salary had climbed to only NTD26,400 (about USD820).

YOUTH DISENCHANTMENT

Many young Taiwanese, even those graduating from college, are well aware that they will start their careers with a low salary and, more importantly, confront the prospect of stagnant wages for many years to come. The Ministry of Labor reported that the average university graduate received a starting monthly salary of NTD30,000 (about USD940) in 2022, a gain of less than NTD2,000 over the year 2000.[24] Consequently, students have become increasingly politicized and started to protest against low earnings and the lack of job prospects.[25] Disenchantment also played a role in the Sunflower Movement that erupted in March 2014. The demonstrations centered on a new service sector trade pact with mainland China that many students believed would make Taiwan economically (and politically) dependent on China. As in the case of Hong Kong's Umbrella Movement, disillusionment with the economic opportunities available to young people also contributed to this wave of unrest.

BRAIN DRAIN

Low salaries in Taiwan have led to a massive brain drain as workers, particularly recent college graduates and high-skill individuals, exit the country in search of better employment opportunities. Initially, Taiwanese professionals primarily emigrated to Japan and the United States. Many of these emigrants were students who studied abroad and did not return home after completing their degrees. Starting in 2000, China and Southeast Asia also became common destinations. By one estimate, 700,000 Taiwanese-born residents lived in the Shanghai area alone in 2010, although what proportion of these were permanent residents was unclear.[26] By 2021, over two million Taiwanese were abroad, with the majority residing in North America (1.3 million) and Asia (0.6 million).[27]

The Chinese government is well aware of the emigration of high-skill individuals and has attempted to poach top talent, especially in science, technology, engineering, and mathematics fields, drawing the ire of Taiwanese officials.[28] Recruitment efforts begin well before graduation. In 2010, Chinese officials announced that Taiwanese high school students who scored in the top 12 percent on the country's General Scholastic Ability Test—approximately 15,000 students—could skip the Chinese college entrance examination and apply for admission directly. The Taiwanese government did not recognize diplomas from Chinese universities, so those who availed themselves of this opportunity and studied on the mainland were unlikely to return to the country.

The mass exodus of talented students and high-skill workers is bound to hurt long-run economic growth by depriving Taiwan of some of its best human capital. A study by Oxford Economics concluded that the combination of the brain drain and difficulty in attracting high-skill individuals would make Taiwan the most talent deficient of the 46 nations in its survey. It indicated that low earnings were largely responsible for these trends and urged the government to find ways of improving the country's salary structure.[29]

DECLINE IN THE FERTILITY RATE

Low or uncertain income is a powerful deterrent to having children, especially among the highly educated in developed countries.[30] This deterrent is especially large if essential goods and services such as education and housing are not affordable. Under these circumstances, individuals may decide to delay marriage or forgo it entirely, which will lower the fertility rate. Taiwan exemplifies the link between economic insecurity and fertility among the well-educated workforce.[31]

It had the lowest total fertility rate in the world in 2022 at 0.87 children per women, well below the critical level (2.1) required to sustain a nation's population over the long run.[32] Multiple government policies to reverse the trend, such as offering cash or tax benefits to families with children and organizing dating events to facilitate marriage among young singles, have met with little success.[33] These measures are insufficient to overcome the challenges of stagnant wages, the uncertain financial future facing young college graduates, and the high cost of living that are contributing to fewer and later marriages. A recent survey conducted by Yes123, an online job search company, reported that respondents cited inadequate income to support a family, unaffordable housing, and the lack of time to care for a child as the three main reasons for avoiding parenthood (in that order).[34]

The Causes of the Low Wage Crisis

Earnings for low-skill workers have grown slowly if at all in many developed countries in the last few decades, but high-skill workers have generally fared better. This disparity, due to the wage premium enjoyed by more educated workers, has contributed to increasing income inequality in several countries, like the United States and China. Taiwan is unusual in that this premium has shrunk dramatically, lessening the pay gap between workers. What accounts for this startling fact?

Factors Behind Low Wages in Developed Countries

Two forces have played major roles in the stagnation of wages for low- and mid-skill workers, as well as a sharp jump in inequality in developed countries: globalization and skill-biased technological change. These two factors typically reinforce one another, intensifying their overall effect on earnings and income inequality.

The creation of global value chains and expanded international trade are two facets of globalization that have had a significant impact on earnings and income distribution. Trade and outsourcing through supply chains have put low- and mid-skill workers in advanced industrial countries in competition against similar individuals receiving lower pay in developing and emerging market countries. In some nations, such as the United Kingdom, the immigration of low-skill workers has deepened this effect by increasing the supply of this type of manpower at home. At the same time, well-educated workers in developed countries have experienced higher demand for their labor, as firms engaged in skill- and knowledge-based activities flourish with greater access to world markets. The combination of these two trends has held down the salaries of low- and mid-skilled workers and raised those of high-skill workers, thereby worsening the distribution of income in advanced economies.

Skill-biased technological change has had an even bigger impact on relative wages and the distribution of income. In advanced industrial countries, technical change has reduced demand for low-skill laborers and mid-skill individuals among the college-educated while increasing it for the high-skill individuals who are able to leverage new technology to improve their productivity.[35] The net effect is a widening gap in the earnings of the two categories of workers that translates into a rise in income inequality.

The Causes of Low Wages in Taiwan

Skill-biased technical change and globalization have also contributed to stagnant earnings in Taiwan. The nation ran into tougher economic times starting around 2000, as did most economies in the region. It escaped most of the pain of the Asian financial crisis, but it was the nation hardest hit by the SARS crisis (2003) and the Great Recession (2008). Unemployment rose sharply for the first time and other major disruptive changes took place in labor markets, such as a large jump in nonstandard employment. Yet, Taiwan has experienced a distinctive outcome—wages for high-skill, along with low-skill, individuals have declined in real terms. Two developments were largely responsible. First, it undertook an unprecedented expansion of tertiary education that produced an excess supply of well-educated workers who did not necessarily have the skill profile that employers wanted. Second, it underwent a massive wave of offshoring that fundamentally altered patterns of production and employment precisely when more turbulent economic times took hold.

OFFSHORING

Taiwan has experienced a tremendous relocation of production and employment abroad, especially in manufacturing. Taiwanese manufacturers did just 7.4 percent of their production overseas in 2001, but that figure jumped to 38.1 percent by 2011.[36] The surge in offshoring occurred after the DPP won elections in 2000 and began to permit companies to move their operations overseas. A former presidential advisor summed it up thusly: "This relaxation of Taiwan's cross-strait policies led to an exodus of manufacturers on a scale that no other country has ever seen."[37] Offshoring is exceptionally high because of the nation's heavy reliance on contract manufacturing combined with close economic ties to China.[38]

Offshoring has had a tremendous impact on Taiwanese labor markets, with lower wages in China acting as a restraint on compensation at home, particularly in the manufacturing sector.[39] But the effects have gone much further. China's recent efforts to transform from being an assembler of final products to an innovator in the knowledge economy have also attracted high tech Taiwanese firms. This trend has limited salaries among more skilled Taiwanese workers who now must compete with comparable workers in mainland China for jobs. Offshoring to China may have reached its peak, however. Increasing production costs, notably, rising salaries, and a rash of labor disputes on the mainland have pushed several major companies, such as Foxconn, to relocate portions of their production back to Taiwan.[40] Taiwanese companies seeking a platform abroad are now more likely to move operations to Southeast Asia where costs remain low and workers are increasingly more skilled.

LABOR MARKET DEVELOPMENTS

Several long-term labor market trends in Taiwan also have affected wages. First, immigration of low-skill foreign workers, largely from Southeast Asia, has heightened competition in segments of the labor market, particularly in manufacturing and social services (e.g., elderly care).[41] Although Taiwan has high levels of emigration, its net migration—immigrants minus emigrants—was positive from 1997 to 2019, before turning negative in 2020. A study commissioned by the Ministry of Labor found that net migration had contributed to wage stagnation for domestic low-skill workers.[42] Second, as in many developed countries, Taiwanese firms are making much greater use of part-time, dispatch, and temporary workers. In industries where firm-specific work experience is not critical, the use of nonstandard workers allows firms to reduce costs by paying lower salaries and offering fewer benefits. These workers compete with full time employees, who may become hesitant to demand higher wages out of fear of being replaced. Finally, Taiwan's labor markets are partially segregated along gender lines. Women often end up working in small family-owned businesses, generally in the informal sector, where compensation is very low and the prospects for increases in earnings are limited.[43]

TRANSITION TO A SERVICE ECONOMY

Most developed economies evolve away from manufacturing toward services as they mature. This has also been the case for Taiwan. The service sector accounts for 70 percent of national output and employs 60 percent of the labor force. Most firms in the service field are SMEs in the nontraded sector.[44] Improvements in labor productivity in services and among SMEs tend to be lower than in manufacturing and large corporations. Limited productivity gains mean that the marginal product of labor rises slowly and this restrains the growth of employee compensation.⁴⁵ Moreover, Taiwan's service industry has experienced an oversupply of labor in recent years because a larger number of college graduates have chosen not to work in manufacturing.⁴⁶

MASSIFICATION OF TERTIARY EDUCATION

A noteworthy feature of Taiwan (and Korea) is the very high percentage of young adults who attend and graduate from institutions of higher education. In 2015, 43 percent of all Taiwanese held a college or university degree, well above the average for OECD countries (33 percent); moreover, 68 percent of those aged 20 to 24 were currently attending a tertiary institution. In 2012, a record 1.3 million students were enrolled in higher education, up from only 6,665 in 1950 and 345,736 in 1986. That year, one out of every 3.7 undergraduates ended up attending graduate school, which led to over 60,000 students completing master's programs and 4,000 finishing doctoral programs.⁴⁷

These high enrollments were due to the so-called massification of tertiary education that began in the 2000s.⁴⁸ Policymakers hoped this expansion would create a large, highly skilled workforce capable of powering a quick transition toward a knowledge economy. Prior to 1994, the government had controlled the size of tertiary institutions, appointed presidents, set admission quotas and curriculum standards, supervised faculty and student affairs on campus, and limited the creation of new facilities, both public and private.⁴⁹ Reforms began in 2002 when the government abolished the Joint Entrance Exam for selecting applicants and adopted the new Multiple Examination Program. High school graduates now had two ways to gain admission to universities: (1) application or recommendation screening, or (2) examination and placement. This greatly increased the accessibility of tertiary education, transforming it from an elite to universal system.

In 2003, the government launched the ambitious Plan to Develop First-Class Universities and Top-Level Research Centers. It distributed NTD50 billion (USD1.45 billion) to twelve universities over five years to achieve this goal; the plan was renewed in 2011. In 2005, policymakers undertook several additional reforms to encourage the growth of four-year colleges. First, they revised the University Law to give institutions more flexibility in designing their organizational structures, making staff appointments, and establishing working conditions. Second, they prodded two-year vocational schools to become four-year universities and shift their focus from high-level technical training to more general education.⁵⁰ These reforms led to a jump in the number of tertiary institutions from seven in 1950, to 121 in 1990, and 163 in 2010; the proliferation was greatest among private institutions.⁵¹ The rapid expansion of four-year schools led to immediate concerns about a decline in the quality of tertiary education, as well as its effects on equality of opportunity.[52]

One consequence of the shifts in tertiary education policy was an oversupply of college-educated workers with general as opposed to concrete technical skills. Taiwan's robust vocational training system played a key role in fostering its early economic development, especially of its export industries.[53] The government reforms to expand vocational training by creating additional institutions at the secondary and tertiary levels had unintended consequences. At the secondary level, critics argued that an overemphasis on academic versus real-world learning by doing left students unprepared for more advanced vocational studies.[54] At the tertiary level, the government's efforts to convert two-year vocational schools into four-year technological colleges ended up diluting technical training. Thus, at a time when employers were looking for workers with specific technical skills, Taiwan was starting to produce an army of generalists.[55] This mismatch led to a deficit in the type of labor Taiwanese firms need to raise productivity and remain competitive in international markets.[56]

The costs to individuals have also been significant. The massification of tertiary education has been a primary factor behind the precipitous decline in the wage premium enjoyed by college-educated workers by increasing their supply above demand for their labor.[57] University graduates have been dealt a double blow—paying more for a college degree but obtaining lower returns on their investment. A close historical parallel to the impact of increased university enrollments in Taiwan happened in the first half of the twentieth century in the United States.[58] Technological advances raised the need for skilled labor but the surge in the supply of college-educated individuals outpaced demand; this reduced the wage premium they enjoyed over high school graduates. The education premium only began rising again in the 1970s when skill-biased technical change continued to lift the demand for highly educated workers, but the supply of such workers waned because of declining educational achievement.

The shrinking of the education premium and collapsing birth rates eventually led to a drop in demand for higher education in Taiwan. In 2015, the Ministry of Education announced plans to reduce the number of universities significantly based on projections that enrollments in tertiary institutions would fall by one-third by 2023.[59] The objective was to close (or merge) eight to twelve of the fifty-one public and twenty to forty of the 101 private universities by that year. This goal was not met—only three universities actually ceased operations by 2023. The government also launched several initiatives to meet the demand for specific technical skills and enhance the future productivity of college graduates.[60] The rollout of a new twelve-year plan, the Curriculum for Basic Education by 2018, was one of the primary steps toward achieving these goals.[61]

Policy Responses
Income Support and Measures to Lift Wages

Governments around the world have implemented various types of income support policies for the working poor (and their households) as well as measures to raise salaries or make individuals more employable; the latter are called active labor market policies (ALMPs).[62] The objectives of these programs are related but distinct. ALMPs are designed to help workers upgrade or acquire new skills in order to secure employment, find better jobs, and augment earnings, whereas income support policies, a form of social assistance, seek to supplement the salaries of those making low wages. It is tempting and mostly correct to view ALMPs as addressing the root causes of in-work poverty and income support measures as lessening its consequences. Low household income, however, may stem from several causes, such as one partner's nonparticipation in the workforce, so raising the wages of the working partner may still leave the family in a precarious position.

Income support policies may come in a variety of forms.[63] They include minimum wage legislation; earned income tax, dependent, or child tax credits; cash payments to workers or their families; and childcare, wage, transportation, or health care subsidies. ALMPs involve employment training or retraining programs, job creation, or job placement initiatives.[64] The effectiveness of these policies has varied greatly across countries and over time, but studies suggest that well-designed measures tailored to specific settings can have a positive impact.[65]

Passive labor market policies (PLMPs) are usually important components of the policy mix as well. They are forms of social protection, like unemployment insurance, that are intended to provide temporary assistance to workers if they lose their livelihood.[66] This sort of protection is most critical in periods when rapid economic change disrupts labor markets by eliminating some types of jobs or altering the structure of work. Globalization and skill-biased technical change count amongst the most powerful forces causing major upheavals in employment.

Taiwan's Policy Façade: Human Capital Investment without Protection

Taiwan has implemented only a limited set of income support policies. The government began providing assistance to certain low-income individuals (e.g., those with disabilities) in 1951, but payments were generally very small.[67] In contrast, public officials created generous social insurance schemes for select groups of workers, including military servicemen, civil servants, farmers, and school teachers, in an attempt to maintain their political loyalty.[68] Joseph Wong has contended that Taiwan's process of democratization, which moved forward in fits and starts beginning in the late 1980s, prompted the expansion of health care, but had little effect on labor market policies.[69]

The government began to expand aid to low-income households starting in 2010 with the revision of the Social Assistance Act, but amounts remained very small. Policymakers have adjusted eligibility criteria several times, but the government's all-or-nothing approach to supplying assistance has left many vulnerable families without crucial support. In 2019, expenditures on social assistance totaled just 1 percent of GDP. As noted previously, Taiwan has a minimum wage and it has become an important policy instrument in the last two decades. Policymakers have raised the wage more quickly, and it reached USD832 per month in September 2023, which was well below the level promised by previous administrations. Finally, the government has waived income taxes for workers earning below the minimum wage since 2017 as a means of bolstering household incomes.

Policymakers implemented several ALMPs in the 2000s as concerns mounted over an unemployment rate that surpassed 5 percent in 2002 (up from 2 percent). The measures concentrated on addressing temporary displacement as opposed to long-term structural unemployment and their primary targets were single parents, youth, and the disabled. They included wage subsidies, employment training, the creation of temporary jobs in the public sector, and public employment placement services. In 2010, expenditures on these programs amounted to a mere 0.1% of GDP.[70] The government has not expanded the scope of or increased funding for ALMPs significantly over the last decade.

The first notable PLMP emerged in response to higher unemployment caused by the Asian financial crisis.[71] The two most significant initiatives were the Labour Insurance (1999) and the Employment Insurance (2002) Acts. The Employment Insurance Act implemented a workfare requirement that obliged unemployed individuals to search for new jobs, take vocational training courses, or undergo employment consultation arranged by public service employment agencies.[72] Unemployment insurance in Taiwan is underfunded and offers inadequate benefits (for most workers, 60 percent of average wages over the preceding half year for a duration of six months). Government spending on unemployment programs amounted to only 0.1 percent of GDP in 2019, down from 0.2 percent in 2010. One study found that if the unemployment rate were to rise above 5.5 percent (as it did in 2009) insurance funds would be in deficit.[73] In 2020, only 11.1 percent of unemployed received benefits because of strict eligibility criteria; this rate was the lowest in the region (except Hong Kong) and far below the averages of 53.1 and 68.9 percent, respectively, for OECD and OECD-18 countries.[74]

The duration of benefits was also considerably shorter and replacement rates were well below those of other East Asian nations.[75]

The clear evidence that Taiwan's workers, especially those with low skills, are struggling to earn sufficient income has not prompted the government to redefine its obligations toward their social welfare. Public officials have usually backtracked when business groups have opposed proposals that would raise wages or benefits. They have implemented a handful of initiatives to support low-income workers, but they watered down even some of these cautious measures, like minimum wage hikes, in order to appease businesses. In effect, the government has created a policy façade. Policymakers appear to be responding to growing concerns about low incomes, but they remain unwilling to adopt a more comprehensive strategy involving substantial expenditures or reforms that would ensure that all households are able to maintain a decent standard of living.

Government officials have been mostly able to ignore the interests of labor in their policy deliberations. Workers in Taiwan are poorly organized and lack the ability to pressure the government to enact legislation that would improve their situation. With the exception of a few industries, the degree of unionization is low. Moreover, trade unions historically have operated within a state corporatist structure in which they are expected to function as the extended arms of the government within civil society. Labor advocates had hoped unions would be more proactive about representing worker's interests after democratization, but they largely have failed to do so.[76]

In contrast to its reluctance to protect low-income workers, the Taiwanese government has been proactive in one area of labor policy. In line with the productivist approach, it has promoted investment in human capital aggressively in the hope that it would provide the push needed for the nation to succeed in the knowledge economy. The heavy investment in education played a major role in the country's initial success and improving the standards of living for workers. Extension of these efforts to the massification of tertiary education, however, had deleterious effects on the compensation of well-educated individuals and shifted skill formation away from what employers actually needed in their workforce, thereby creating an imbalance in the labor market. Taiwan's high level of openness and unique relationship to mainland China aggravated the consequences of these developments by intensifying the brain drain of high talent workers. Government leaders acknowledged these problems and instituted reforms to "rationalize" higher education and reorient skill formation, but for those who passed through the university system in this period these efforts were too little too late.

In Taiwan, as in other productivist nations, the strategies that contributed to excellent economic performance have eventually created negative side effects. Policymakers pursuing a strategy of social investment without protection lacked the vision to adjust their approach as problems such as stagnant wages began to emerge; indeed, they exacerbated the difficulties by redoubling their efforts to accumulate human capital by expanding the university system. Moreover, the vested interests created during the high growth era remain firmly entrenched and make adopting a more evenhanded approach toward labor and capital difficult in the contemporary era.

Wage Trends and Policy Responses in Other East Asian Countries

Skill-biased technical change and globalization have disrupted labor markets throughout East Asia. The economic turbulence of the 1990s and 2000s amplified the impact of these forces, and policymakers that had long basked in an environment of steadily rising wages and low unemployment were suddenly faced with discomfiting choices. The policy responses to this turn of events have varied somewhat. Most countries expanded PLMPs to a degree, and some made use of ALMPs for the first time, but, with the possible exception of Singapore, these efforts did not alter fundamentally their approach to the welfare–work nexus.

Hong Kong

As in Taiwan, real wages in Hong Kong have stagnated, hitting low-skill workers particularly hard. Real wage growth from 2000 to 2021 was only 0.3 percent per annum despite the fact that labor productivity rose by 3.3 percent.[77] The average annual wage was USD25,596 in 2022. Starting in the 1980s, Hong Kong aggressively restructured its economy toward higher value-added activities. Its efforts to transform into a knowledge-based economy raised the demand for educated professionals. The need for less educated laborers fell drastically, however, as manufacturing facilities migrated to mainland China. To make matters worse, Chinese immigrants enlarged the worker pool in the city at the same time that the need for their labor was falling. The changes in relative demand for different types of labor increased the compensation of well-educated, high-skill individuals considerably, while depressing the earnings of less educated ones by the 2000s. The wage premium associated with a university degree soared to 105 percent in 2002, which marked a 40 percent jump over the previous decade.[78]

The widening gap between high- and low-skill workers has resulted in elevated levels of income inequality and coincided with a surge in the number of poor families.[79] Hong Kong has experienced the worst working poverty in the region at 15.4 percent in 2020, up from 14.1 percent in 2009.[80] As in Taiwan, the lack of a robust safety net has left many low-income households in precarious financial circumstances. The government's response was to impose workfare requirements on the beneficiaries of assistance in order to reinforce the message of self-reliance. The Comprehensive Social Security Assistance program made it compulsory for able-bodied adult recipients to participate in the Support for Self-Reliance (SFS) scheme or have their benefits terminated.[81] The government only began enforcing minimum wage legislation starting in 2011 largely due to the vigorous opposition of business groups that claimed it would raise operating costs and force job cuts. It was only five US dollars in 2023, an hourly rate slightly above Taiwan's. Policymakers stepped up the use of ALMPs after multiple economic shocks in the 1990s roiled labor markets, but expenditures have been modest at about 0.1 percent of GDP.[82]

Hong Kong's high level of human capital helped spark its rapid growth, but recent bottlenecks in the tertiary education system have resulted in an inadequate supply of college graduates that has held back economic performance.[83] Many more students routinely qualify for enrollment in universities than there are seats available, leading to rationing and inequality of educational attainment based on income.[84] Moreover, employers have complained repeatedly that university curricula fail to provide the skills needed in their new economic activities. The problem is made worse by Hong Kong's relative lack of success in attracting talented foreign professionals in science and technology, the arts, business and finance, and health care to supplement its local workforce.

Singapore

Singapore's response to the problem of turbulent labor markets offers an instructive contrast to Taiwan and Hong Kong. Low-skill workers in Singapore have experienced comparable difficulties, but policymakers have managed to improve the standard of living of some of them by implementing an innovative ALMP. This policy indicates that the government has adopted a different approach than its regional peers in at least one respect and may be beginning to redefine its role in the welfare–labor nexus.

Real wage growth in Singapore has exceeded that of all other East Asian economies except China (see table 3.1 for details). Real wages rose by 2.5 percent annually from 2000 to 2022, which was almost directly in line with improvements in labor productivity (2.4 percent).[85] The increases accelerated after 2015, with low-income workers seeing the largest gains, a trend not seen elsewhere in the region.[86] Singapore's average annual wage in 2022 (USD52,080) was similar to that of the average OECD country (USD53,416), and well above that of other East Asian nations.[87] Labor's share of national income, 42.5 percent, was below that of most industrialized countries in 2015; this share had risen, however, off a low of 41 percent in 2005.[88]

The government's main instrument for assisting low-income workers is the Workfare Income Supplement. Individuals must be at least thirty years of age, earn a monthly gross income of 2,500 Singaporean dollars (SD) or less, and not own significant property, to be eligible.[89] The government has not established a minimum wage (with a few exceptions noted later in this section) due to business opposition. In collaboration with unions and employers, however, it implemented an innovative ALMP in 2012, called the Progressive Wage Model (PWM). This program aimed to increase salaries in the cleaning, security, landscape, lift and escalator, retail, food services, and waste management sectors, by raising worker productivity through training programs designed to upgrade skills.[90] Wages in these sectors were stagnant due to an abundant supply of labor, contracts that locked in salaries for long periods of time, and the inability of unions to bargain for pay raises in an effective manner.[91] A key feature of the PWM is guidance provided by the National Wages Council on appropriate wage levels for these categories of workers; the council's guidelines became mandatory in 2023 (most companies were already abiding by them on a voluntary basis). Employers have embraced PWM as a means of addressing high employee turnover and low productivity that have often resulted in the poor quality of services they offer clients. Salary increases mandated by the council are one reason why earnings for low-income laborers have grown more quickly than for other income groups and inequality declined from 2010 to 2022, as measured by both before (from 0.480 to 0.437) and after tax and transfers (from 0.425 to 0.378) Gini coefficients.[92]

We speculate that Singapore's leaders implemented the PWM because of increasing political competition in the country's tightly controlled political arena. Electoral support for the People's Action Party (PAP), long the unchallenged force in the nation's politics, has declined over the course of the last decade, resulting in the loss of seats to the opposition Worker's Party.[93] Officials might have decided to adopt policies that benefit low-skill workers in order to reduce the appeal of the Worker's Party. Buoyed by the PWM's success and the apparent greater receptivity of the PAP, labor unions, such as the National Trades Union Congress, have called for the expansion of the PWM to other sectors, as well as the introduction of minimum wage and insurance schemes for workers who are in the process of changing jobs.[94]

Japan

The average annual salary in Japan has changed very little in recent years and was USD41,509 in 2022. Real monthly wages declined by 1 percent annually from 2000 to 2019 but rose by 0.4 percent from 2019 to 2022.[95] The decrease in the former period occurred despite essentially flat labor productivity in both the manufacturing and services sectors.[96] Labor's share of national income in Japan is considerably higher than in other East Asian economies at around 60 percent, but this is a substantial drop from 70 percent in 1980.[97]

Japan's labor markets are highly dualistic. Regular workers enjoy strong legal protections, high salaries, generous benefits, and reliable pensions; nonregular workers, in contrast, frequently work only part-time, receive low pay and fewer benefits, and have little job security. Nonregular workers comprised about 35 percent of the workforce in 2019 (up markedly since 1990) and were particularly pervasive in the service sector.[98] The uptake of nonregular workers accelerated in the past decade as more elderly, pushed by poverty, and women, encouraged by Abenomics, joined the workforce. Their earnings have risen moderately (by 2 percent in 2016) due to high demand, mainly because they are less expensive to hire, whereas those for regular workers have barely budged.[99]

Several factors account for sluggish wages.[100] First, business activity has been lethargic as the general malaise that has affected Japan since the bursting of its financial bubble in 1989 endures. Faced with a shrinking population and restrained domestic spending, firms have been reluctant to raise employee compensation. Second, productivity in the service sector, which employs about 70 percent of the workforce, has been flat in the past two decades, making it difficult to justify salary increases on the basis of economic criteria.[101] Finally, labor unions, which solely represent regular workers, have failed to push for substantial wage hikes because they value job security over pay hikes. In addition, most unions are formed at the company rather than industry or interindustry level, so employees usually identify more with their firm than other workers.

Historically, Japan had a firm-centric approach to labor market issues that relied on employers to take care of their workforce through corporate welfare policies.[102] The weakening of the lifelong employment model and rise of nonregular laborers has finally prompted the government to react to low wages. In 2015, then Prime Minister Abe Shinzō proposed raising the minimum wage, which was 800 yen (or USD6.61) per hour, by 3 percent annually until 2020; by October 2023, it stood at 1,002 yen, but, because of a depreciating currency, it had risen in USD terms to only 6.76.[103] In 2018, Abe also pressured companies to begin granting employees 3 percent raises, a request that was seconded by the main business lobby, Keidanren. The government, however, has yet to make use of ALMPs to create more economic opportunities for low-wage workers. It spent a mere 0.15 percent of GDP on these programs in 2019, down from 0.3 in 2010.[104]

South Korea

The average annual salary in South Korea was USD43,620 in 2022. Real wages rose by a respectable 1.8 percent annually from 2000 to 2019, but this was far less than improvements in labor productivity, which averaged 3.9 percent per year.[105] Labor's share of national income fell precipitously as a consequence, from 70 to 50 percent in the period 1970 to 2015.[106]

Korea's labor markets are highly dualistic, like Japan's. In 2016, nonregular laborers were paid 34.6 percent less per hour than regular salaried workers, even though their skills were broadly the same.[107] In 2020, 21.3 percent of workers earned less than 50 percent of the median income, and the mean poverty gap ratio was 30.2; 4.4 percent of the labor force received the minimum wage or less.[108] Women had especially depressed salaries, reflected in a gender wage gap that was the highest in the OECD at 34.1 percent in 2018.[109] Moon Jae-In, who was elected president in 2017, ran a populist campaign promising to boost salaries for low-income workers and shorten working hours, which were the longest in the OECD. In 2018, his administration lifted the minimum wage, the government's primary tool to help low-income workers, by 16.4 percent, the largest jump in twenty years, and pledged to raise it by an additional 30 percent to 10,000 won by 2020. This increase was projected to benefit 4.6 million citizens.[110] SMEs, however, contended that the sharp rise in the wage would destroy their profitability. Their opposition resonated with a surprisingly large portion of the public and the government relented. After 2019, increases in the minimum wage slowed considerably, and, in 2024, it will stand at only 9,860 won—short of the 2020 target.[111]

The government has gradually raised the percentage of unemployed who received benefits. It climbed from 27.5 percent in 2005 to 43.4 percent in 2020, a figure that remained below the OECD average of 53 percent.[112] Policymakers have made little use of ALMPs to create more economic opportunities for low wage workers historically. Programming has expanded in the last decade, however, and spending as a percent of GDP rose to 0.32 percent in 2017.[113] Since 2009, Korea has been one of the few countries where expenditures on ALMPs exceed those on unemployment benefits.[114] The need for ALMPs has never been greater. The employment gap for disadvantaged groups, 31.8 percent, is well above the OECD average of 24.7 percent.[115] A key initiative to improve the employment prospects of these groups is the Employment Success Package Programme, which began in 2017.[116] As in Taiwan, creating opportunities for the young has been particularly challenging, since many college graduates (70 percent of youth had degrees in 2020, the highest ratio in the OECD) are inactive or unemployed. Korea's youth employment rate in 2021 was 44.2 percent, almost 9 percent less than the OECD average, and many young adults are nonregular workers.[117] Two causes of the reduced rate are the low level of vocational training and mismatch between university curricula and the skills demanded by employers. Policymakers have implemented numerous measures to address youth employment, such as subsidies and tax benefits for employers, but it is widely recognized that they have been ineffective.[118] The employment situation of older workers is also concerning. As discussed in the previous chapter, many seniors must work to supplement their income, often after forced early retirement, and are frequently relegated to nonregular, low paying positions. Thus far, the government has done little to train older workers in new technologies, a failure that leaves them in unproductive jobs and could endanger the country's ability to sustain long-term economic growth as the population ages.[119]

Skill-biased technical change and globalization have shifted the relative demand for factors of production worldwide, mostly favoring the owners of capital and high-skill workers. Demographic trends have slowed the growth of the labor force, altered the mix of workers available to participate in the economy, and increased the burden aged dependents place on active workers. These forces have augmented the challenges confronting policymakers grappling with labor market and human capital policies. Signs of stress have appeared in East Asian societies, notably, in the form of stagnating earnings for low-skill workers and a declining labor share of national income. Unlike their peers in the majority of developed countries, policymakers in the region are in the advantageous position that these macro level trends have materialized in an economic context of above average growth.

Wages for low-skill workers in East Asia rose quickly during the high growth period, when nations focused on labor-intensive manufacturing, but began to stagnate as they moved into more high-valued added activities. East Asian countries have productivist welfare systems that have socialized very little economic risk, so these laborers are highly exposed to the damaging impacts of rapid economic changes. Thus far, only Singapore has gone beyond the usual step of raising the minimum wage by providing them with further training and encouraging firms to increase compensation in line with improvements in labor productivity. Labor's declining share of national income is a product of the fundamental shift in East Asian economies away from labor-intensive to capital-, skill-, and knowledge-intensive industries. Nonetheless, it also reflects the continuing inability of workers in the region to organize and bargain collectively for better salaries and working conditions. Without effective representation, they are unable to push back against the downward pressure that the forces of globalization and technical change have put on their earnings.

In all but one East Asian nation, the wage premium has risen as demand for educated workers has ratcheted up. Taiwan is unique in that earnings for high-skill labor have also stagnated. This is due to the unusual but not unheard-of circumstance in which the supply of well-educated workers grows faster than the demand for them. The sharp increase in supply in Taiwan was the direct result of the government's vigorous efforts to massify tertiary education rapidly, an outgrowth of the paramount importance that the productivist approach places on human capital investment. Policymakers hoped that creating a universal system of higher education would provide the push Taiwan needed to succeed in the knowledge economy, but instead it depressed the compensation of well-educated workers and shifted skill formation away from what employers actually needed in their workforce. Ironically, it has fed a brain drain that is depriving the country of some of its most talented individuals. The Taiwanese experience serves as a cautionary tale of the perils of social investment without protection.

4

ABUSED AND NEGLECTED
The Other Children's Welfare Crisis in Japan

Japan is known internationally as a society that does everything possible to promote the well-being of children. Parents and community members work tirelessly to ensure their children's safety year-round. Conspicuous signs are placed outside of residential homes and in taxis designating them as safe havens in case a child has an emergency. Groups of vigilant volunteer mothers monitor networks of sidewalks designed as a walk-to-school system. The education of children is a national priority. The enormous investment in learning is reflected in the demanding curriculum, long school hours that include sophisticated extracurricular programs, and the large sums of money spent each year on tutoring and cram schools.

The children who receive this abundance of care contrast sharply with Japan's "other" children—those who are abused, neglected, poor, and live in despair. They are voiceless, forgotten, and remain largely invisible, sometimes until their lifeless bodies are discovered. This outcome is best encapsulated by what social scientists describe as the Robin Hood paradox: The vulnerable children who need social protection the most receive the least. Alarmingly, child abuse cases in Japan are rising sharply, setting a new record each year. The number of incidents reported to the child consultation centers scattered throughout the country has increased more than two hundred–fold since 1990, from 1,101 to 219,170 in 2022 (figure 4.1). The contemporary rise in maltreatment conflicts with Japan's well-honed image as a child-centric society. It is, however, consistent with the workings of a productivist system with a dualistic

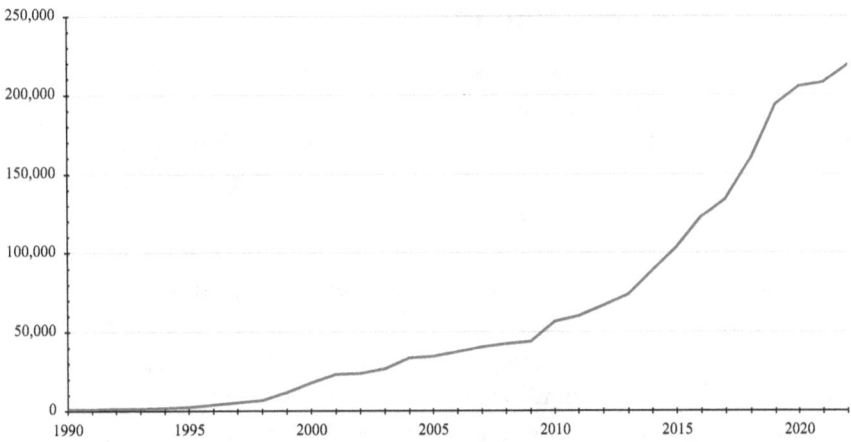

FIGURE 4.1 The rise of reported child abuse cases in Japan, 1990–2022.

Source: Japan, Children and Family Agency, "Reiwa 4 nendo"

pattern of welfare provision that leaves numerous vulnerable children to fend for themselves.

The comparative social policy literature provides valuable theoretical and empirical tools to help identify the origins and broad features of different national welfare systems. Nevertheless, it omits insights from comparative social work that can advance our understanding of both the general pattern of welfare outcomes and those in specific areas like child welfare. This chapter breaks down the barriers between these two siloed literatures in order to develop a multifaceted explanation of child maltreatment in the context of a broader cultural, economic, political, and social milieu. In doing so, it describes the dualistic orientation of Japan's child welfare system and reveals how it has failed to adjust to the powerful forces that are altering the ecology of family life and contours of the policy landscape. Skill-biased technical change and globalization have increased economic insecurity that has heightened the risk of maltreatment in many households. Urbanization has weakened community networks that traditionally have protected against abuse and aided in rehabilitation. Demographic trends, notably, the rise of unwanted pregnancies and single-parent households, have expanded the pool of vulnerable children and guardians prone to engaging in maltreatment. Finally, structural changes have weakened the family's resilience and ability to protect children. The tragic lives of two siblings in the narrative below illustrate how this complex web of forces may lead to the neglect, abuse, and even death of our most vulnerable citizens.

CHAPTER 4

A View from the Ground

Three-year-old Megumi lay still as the oppressive heat parched her throat.[1] Navigating the piles of trash on the living room floor, she crawled through a tight space to check on her little brother, Takeshi. Megumi's nudging yielded no response. She tried to pinch his sunken cheeks, but her fingers could barely grab a hold. Overwhelmed by a sense of responsibility to protect her brother, Megumi began banging on the door, walls, floor, and anything else that created a sound. The white, newly painted walls were plastered with collages of little handprints, depicting the desperate struggle of their creator. "Mama, where are you? Open the door, please. I am sorry," Megumi said softly. Being locked up in the living room, she knew, meant punishment, but for what she did not know. She felt tears well up behind her eyes as fond memories of her mother flooded her mind. Curled up in a fetal position, she began counting how long it would take for her mother to open the door. *One, two, three . . .*

A loud chorus of cicadas woke Kanda Masato, the manager of the apartment complex. The air conditioners were struggling to keep up with the glaring ferocity of the morning sun. Summer was in full swing. Masato's daily work routine for the last thirty years began with checking for maintenance requests. Complaints of a foul odor had inundated his mailbox in recent days, but they came from different floors, which made pinpointing the source quite a challenge. He had already checked the main air ducts for dead rodents. As he took a break from sorting the work orders, he was greeted by one of his favorite tenants.

Nishida Sakura bowed gingerly. "Good morning, Kanda-san."

Masato gently patted Sakura's hunched back. "Wow, you are up so early *oba-chan*. Is everything okay? Is there anything I can do to help? Any problems with your light bulbs? Or do you need someone to finish your beer?"

"No, nothing this week," Sakura answered, laughing. She paused for a moment. "Actually, I wanted to talk to you about the smell. I might know where it's coming from. It's strongest when I walk in front of apartment #702. I don't know who lives there, but I think they have two small children. I haven't seen them in recent months. Is it unoccupied now? Maybe they forgot to take out the trash before moving away." Her brows furrowed in concern.

"I will check on that immediately. What would I do without you?" Masato held her hand with gratitude.

Sada Yoshiko, a hostess at a nearby nightclub, occupied apartment #702. One of the most popular joints in town, JIN paid their dancers high wages in an effort to retain them for at least a few years to build up loyalty-club members. Yoshiko's one-year lease was cosigned by JIN, so Masato was not worried about her breaking the contract. His main concern was that she was a young single mother with toddlers, which, from his many years of experience, meant crayon-marked walls and indented refrigerator rims. He grabbed the master key and ventured up to the seventh floor.

Upon arriving in front of #702, he noticed two sticky notes posted on the door. They were from child welfare services requesting Yoshiko to call back. He was not surprised to see the notes, since he had seen her children playing during the day in the hallway by themselves. Given the nocturnal nature of her job, Masato, or her neighbors for that matter, rarely saw her. Knocking at the door, Masato called politely: "Sada-san, it's me, Kanda, the apartment manager." He paused for a moment and continued: "Are you there?" Failing to get any response, he leaned towards the door to detect any sound, but instead got a whiff of a putrid scent.

He cleared his throat and tried again. "Sada-san, are you there? If not, I will open the door, if you don't mind. I just want to make sure that everything is okay." Masato counted up to three to turn the key. *One, two, three* . . . Opening the door released an unbearably strong wave of stench, but he saw nothing unusual at first glance. The walls were in good shape and the refrigerator was nick-free. When he looked toward the living room door, just a few feet away from where he stood, he noticed that it had been sealed with layers of tape. He felt a cold shiver go down his spine. Quickly backing out of the apartment, he slammed the entrance door and called the police. Masato slouched against the wall and covered his ears with both hands. Unable to silence the deafening sound of cicadas in his mind, he knew that he had just witnessed a horrific scene that would haunt him for the rest of his life.

Masato had been glued to the TV for nearly two days. The national news services had picked up the story and showed pictures of the two deceased toddlers, Megumi and Takeshi, during happier times. Their infectious smiles translated into pain and confusion for many. Yoshiko was apprehended at her boyfriend's flat, just a few miles away from the apartment. The police confirmed that she had starved them to death based on her confession. She had sealed off the living room with several layers of tape and locked the door from the outside to prevent Megumi from opening it. Authorities found their naked bodies in the middle of the room, surrounded by excrement and a mountain of trash that Yoshiko had not bothered to dispose of for months. She had stopped changing Takeshi's diapers, denied the toddlers baths or regular meals, and routinely left them alone at night. She catered to male clients at JIN until midnight, and then switched roles and frequented a so-called host club where female customers pay for male company until early morning. When Yoshiko started dating her new boyfriend, she told him that her children were with their grandparents. She related to the investigators how Megumi used to jump and give her high fives at dinner time, grinning from ear to ear. But when she began feeding them only once a day—a small rice ball and piece of biscuit—Megumi's once sparkling smile disappeared into a grimacing, sunken face, and she kept her tiny hands to herself in protest. The police speculated that she had imprisoned her children and starved them to death in their own home so that, ironically, she could feel free, alive, and loved.

Interviews with the apartment tenants were featured prominently in the news. One popular daytime TV host blamed them and the management for turning a blind eye to the children's calls for help. "The neighbors heard them cry incessantly for weeks and did nothing about it. Typical city people, cold and ungenerous," he scoffed. "This is an urban issue. In rural areas where community ties are strong, everyone helps out. It's all about *tasukeai* [mutual aid] in traditional Japanese towns or villages. You never hear about cases like this."

A guest commentator from a child welfare advocacy organization lamented that the tragedy had unfolded because of a perfect storm of an unbalanced education system, a threadbare safety net, and the rising number of single mothers. "Times have changed. Unwanted pregnancies and single motherhood are up, and many mothers face dire financial circumstances with little prospect of escaping poverty. It's rather ironic that we invest so much in education and yet we fail to provide our children with sex education in schools or parental education programs that could promote their future well-being."

A social welfare policy expert jumped into the discussion. "The Japanese government was largely dormant on the problem of child abuse and neglect until the mid-1990s precisely because it was understood to be a private family issue. In the last decade, it has enacted several measures to prevent abuse, but one of the major obstacles is funding. The number of reported cases has been rising but, due to the tight budget, child welfare services are understaffed and unable to review and address each case thoroughly. Tragedies like this will continue to happen as long as the government remains reluctant to intervene actively to protect the most at-risk children."

Masato turned off the TV and tried to come to grips with the feeling that the only finger he could point was at himself. He knew that the children were neglected when he first laid eyes on them. "Why didn't I offer to help Yoshiko as I have done for other tenants?" he asked unforgivingly. "I should have checked on them sooner. I could have saved them." He stood up and walked outside to the balcony. Gazing at the magnificent blue sky temporarily relieved his pain. There was a faint golden tinge to the clouds. Masato closed his eyes and prayed that Megumi and Takeshi were playing somewhere high above.

The Political and Economic Context

Observers often marvel at how Japan's government programs—from transportation to public safety—seem to work seamlessly. Therefore, learning of gruesome child abuse incidents or a broken safety net that does little to protect the needy is confounding. A brief overview of the country's history and institutions helps to provide a frame of reference for exploring the *other* Japan, where the suffering of the most vulnerable segments of the population falls by the wayside.

At the turn of the twentieth century, Japan became the first non-Western country to industrialize and introduce democratic institutions. The country's great economic and political transformation came at a high cost: It gave rise to powerful economic elites who created a skewed democratic system that provided only minimum social protection for disadvantaged groups.[2] The government's economic policies concentrated scarce capital in the hands of a few privileged firms with strong links to government officials, creating the large, family-controlled financial industrial conglomerates called *zaibatsu*; these firms went on to become one of the hallmarks of the modern Japanese economy.[3] The *zaibatsu* demonstrated skillful political entrepreneurship and quickly gained influence and power. As the boundaries between state and market blurred, political leaders engineered Japan's democratic institutions to augment the power of organized economic interests.[4] They extended voting rights (to men only) in several steps: first to large agrarian landholders in 1890, to urban industrialists in 1900, to small businesses and other landholders in 1919, and, finally, to the laboring class in 1925.

One product of this political engineering was the introduction of a multimember-district single-nontransferable voting electoral system (MMD/SNTV) in 1925. The MMD/SNTV had two major consequences. First, it engendered nomination strategies and malapportionment that contributed to the half-century long dominance of the conservative, probusiness Liberal Democratic Party (LDP).[5] Second, it compelled politicians to deliver material benefits to narrow constituencies in order to build political support. Together, these features created a political economy that hindered the development of a universalistic social policy and gave rise to a productivist welfare system.[6] Although Japan's electoral system later changed to a mix of plurality and proportionality, the LDP has remained the clearly dominant party.[7]

Unlike its East Asian peers, Japan began developing a social welfare system a century ago (at roughly the same time as Western nations) and currently expends a similar amount on social protection—21.9 percent of gross domestic product (GDP) in 2015—as liberal welfare states (table 1.3). The vast majority of these expenditures—91 percent—were dedicated to social insurance. In the area of social assistance, Japan spent a mere 1.8 percent of GDP and more closely resembled its neighbors than advanced industrial nations in other regions. The ADB determined that expenditures on nonpoor recipients were more than double those on the poor, revealing that social spending was intended to benefit the middle class, not to protect the needy (table 1.6). Welfare spending amounted to a mere 0.8 percent of GDP in 2015, and coverage rates for social assistance programs were extremely low (tables 1.5 and 1.7). In addition, research has shown that Japan has established eligibility criteria in ways that are meant to discourage applicants from receiving benefits.[8] Social expenditures increased only slightly by 2019 to 22.8 percent of GDP, with social insurance and assistance registering at 20.5 and 2.1 percent, respectively (table 1.12).

Japan's productivist orientation has spawned child welfare practices that have contributed to today's maltreatment crisis. Parents, teachers, civil society groups, corporations, and the government invest heavily in the development of children in order to produce self-reliant adults who will join the productive workforce, build families, and reinvest in their offspring's future. In contrast, the other children, whose circumstances call for a greater need for aid and protection, whether due to a parental divorce, health emergency, or low wages, have received little assistance.

The Child Welfare Crisis and Its Consequences

A Growing Wave of Abuse and Neglect

Child maltreatment has become a more prominent issue in the Japanese national media over the last two decades.[9] Four high-profile cases in particular have grabbed the nation's attention. In Tokyo, Funato Yua's parents regularly beat her, kept her on a near-starvation diet, and confined her to a room without electricity, where she wrote letters begging for their forgiveness and love. She succumbed to pneumonia in June 2018, leaving behind her emaciated, bruised body with traces of frostbite.[10] Kurihara Mia from Chiba Prefecture cried out for assistance in a confidential school questionnaire on bullying, stating that her father deprived her of sleep and physically abused her. Despite her courageous call for help, she was found beaten to death in a bathtub in February 2019.[11] In the summer of 2020, a twenty-four-year-old single mother in Tokyo abandoned three-year old Kakehashi Noa for eight days in order to visit her boyfriend in Kagoshima Prefecture. After months of neglecting her daughter, she imprisoned her in the living room by blocking the door with a sofa. She died of severe dehydration and starvation.[12] In the summer of 2023, an investigative panel found that the late boy band producer, Johnny Kitagawa of the talent agency Johnny & Associates, sexually assaulted and abused hundreds of boys over half a century.[13] For many, these cases illustrated the pressing need for more active government intervention to protect vulnerable children.

Article 2 of the Law for Prevention of Child Abuse enacted in 2000 (with minor revisions in 2004, 2007, and 2019) defines child abuse as consisting of violent, sexually inappropriate, negligent, or emotionally scarring acts committed by a custodian (i.e., individuals with parental authority or a legal guardian).[14] The law recognizes four broad categories of abuse and neglect. In 2022, psychological abuse was the most common form of maltreatment, accounting for 59 percent of all cases, followed by physical abuse (24 percent), neglect (16 percent), and sexual abuse (1 percent).[15] One study found that Japanese parents involved in maltreatment cases were "characterized by poverty, personality problems, parental conflict and complicated family relations, followed by societal isolation, their own childhood family problems and unintended pregnancy."[16]

Cross-national studies of child abuse and neglect are limited due to widespread underreporting of incidents, inconsistent definitions, and the large number and variety of public and private actors involved in providing child welfare services across countries.[17] Nevertheless, most experts and government officials believe that the extent of child maltreatment in Japan is alarming.[18] As noted earlier, the quantity of child abuse cases reported to the approximately 220 child consultation centers (*jidō sōdanjo*) throughout the country rose from 1,101 cases in 1990, when the Ministry of Health, Labor and Welfare (MHLW) first began compiling child abuse statistics, to 219,170 in 2022 (figure 4.1). The National Police Agency referred 112,965 incidents (nearly half of the total) to the child consultation centers in 2022, which represented a 19 percent jump from the previous year.

National statistics, however, offer only a partial glimpse of the pervasiveness of child maltreatment; the number of cases is undoubtedly much higher than official counts since underreporting is commonplace. Underreporting occurs because maltreatment often happens behind closed doors and to infants below the age of two—the group with the highest incidence of abuse—who are voiceless and helpless.[19] When witnesses exist, they may forgo notifying authorities out of fear of retaliation. One study concluded that nine out of ten child abuse cases in high income countries go uncounted.[20] Vastly different estimates of child maltreatment deaths in Japan also suggest that official figures understate the extent of the problem. The MHLW asserted that eighty child abuse and neglect fatalities occurred from 2015 to 2016, whereas a nongovernmental research report put the number at about two hundred.[21] The Japan Pediatric Society estimated that 350 such deaths occur on average per year.[22] The higher estimates are probably more accurate since prolonged medical neglect that results in death is difficult to prove, inconclusive autopsy reports in suspected cases are common, and the lack of coordination among the police, welfare officials, and medical personnel hinders case reporting. The surge in the official numbers of maltreatment against the backdrop of vast underreporting is concerning since the factors driving abuse continue unabated.

The Consequences of Child Maltreatment

The effects of child abuse and neglect are profound and devastating. More than four decades of research by clinicians and academics have documented that victims are more likely to endure psychological, behavioral, physiological, cognitive, and emotional difficulties, as well as problems of low self-esteem, than nonabused children.[23] Individuals who have experienced child abuse have a higher risk for depression, anxiety, substance abuse, suicidal tendencies, and obesity. Victims also were more likely to have learning disorders, memory impairment, and aggressive behaviors.[24] A recent government survey showed that nearly 70 percent of child abuse victims in Japan lagged behind academically, and 20 percent had impaired or delayed physiological development.[25] Other studies have determined that injuries or insufficient nutritional intake in children under the age of two may hamper physical and cognitive development, leading to stunted growth, hearing impairment, and physical disability. In the case of disabled children, researchers found that their condition worsened over time when negligent parents denied them treatment and physical therapy.[26] Negative health outcomes increase the likelihood of poverty, unemployment, and low productivity in adulthood, which in turn can further undermine mental health and psychological well-being.[27] A Japanese government survey established that one out of every six victims had engaged in an illegal or criminal activity.[28] In a related finding, researchers at Chiba University reported that nearly 50 percent of inmates in their large-scale study had experienced childhood abuse.[29]

Child maltreatment also results in significant, nationwide economic losses that silently wreak havoc year after year.[30] The direct costs include expenditures for operating child social welfare service facilities, foster homes, and child consultation centers. The indirect losses stem from medical issues, divorce, unemployment, crime, and a decline in worker productivity. One study estimated that in 2012 the economic costs of child abuse in Japan were around USD16 billion each year and emphasized that these would continue to accumulate annually.[31]

The Causes of the Child Welfare Crisis
Historical Developments in Comparative Perspective

Putting the issue of child maltreatment into historical and comparative perspectives provides needed context for Japan's crisis. At various points in human history, many forms of cruelty to children—such as disciplinary beating and confinement, ritualistic murder, trafficking, prostitution, and slavery—were acceptable practices and received very little public attention and legal response.[32]

Children were not treated as individuals with basic human rights and parents had "established power" over their offspring.[33] This general narrative also applies to Japan where a substantial body of research has confirmed that child abuse and neglect have been pervasive from ancient to modern times.[34] Examples have included the killing of children to reduce the economic burden on families (*mabiki*), forced child labor in factories during the Industrial Revolution, the military use of children during World War II, and the abandonment of infants during the postwar baby boom. As Japan moved from rags to riches, its affluence diminished the need to exploit children for economic gains. Takenaka Tetsuo asserted that the end to various forms of "societal child abuse" marked the beginning of "household child abuse," in which the nexus of maltreatment shifted to parents at home.[35]

The medical profession's discovery of child abuse in the United States and Europe in the 1960s put the spotlight firmly on the household.[36] A group of radiologists, pediatricians, and psychiatric specialists published a seminal article, "The Battered-Child Syndrome," in 1962. It offered clinical evidence that child abuse was not a mere byproduct of poverty or mental illness but a ubiquitous problem that warranted urgent societal intervention.[37] Adding to the momentum for change, studies on childhood trauma identified the pernicious effects that violence against children has on the individuals involved and society at large.[38] With journalistic accounts raising public awareness and mounting pressure from child advocacy groups, legislators responded by mandating the reporting of abuse cases and criminalizing child maltreatment. In the United States, for example, all fifty states passed legislation to protect children from abusive caretakers by the late 1970s. Internationally, the General Assembly of the United Nations adopted the Convention on the Rights of the Child (CRC) in 1989. The CRC declared that children had the right to be protected "from all forms of physical or mental violence."[39] Influenced by the growing international movement, the Japanese medical community and a handful of social scientists began conducting their own studies and surveys of maltreatment in the early 1970s.[40] The Ministry of Welfare carried out its first survey in 1975 and the term child abuse victim syndrome (*hi gyakutai ji shōkōgun*) surfaced in the academic discourse in this period.[41]

Efforts to protect Japanese children from violence strengthened significantly in the early 1990s for several reasons. First, the country signed the CRC in 1990 and ratified it four years later. Second, the Ministry of Welfare officially defined "child abuse" (*jidō gyakutai*) and started publishing statistics on reported cases annually. Third, the 1990s witnessed the emergence of a more robust civil society in urban centers. For example, Osaka's Child Abuse Prevention Association (Jidō Gyakutai Bōshi Kyōkai), one of the first nongovernmental organizations (NGOs) dedicated to combating child abuse, was established in 1990. The following year, lawyers, pediatricians, psychologists, school officials, teachers, and hygienists formed the Center for Child Abuse Prevention in Tokyo. These associations and other voluntary groups played a key role in creating some of the nation's first child maltreatment counseling centers and reporting hotlines.[42]

In response to growing calls to protect children from violence and neglect, the national government adopted the Child Abuse Prevention Law (CAPL) in 2000. It focused on early detection of child maltreatment by requiring a wide array of community members and professionals (e.g., educators, dentists, doctors, nurses, and lawyers) to report any concerns related to abuse. The law gave child consultation centers the key role in evaluating each report and formulating an appropriate response in coordination with the police, foster facilities, family courts, and other professionals.[43] The CAPL was amended in 2004 and 2007 to expand the definition of child abuse to include witnessing domestic violence and strengthen the obligation of local authorities to take all necessary measures to ensure a child's safety. The amendments also defined child abuse as a human rights infringement and reinforced the responsibility of the medical community to cooperate with relevant stakeholders in order to prevent child abuse.[44] The CAPL underwent additional revision in 2019 to ban all forms of corporal punishment.

Japan's child welfare crisis remains acute despite legislative initiatives and shifts in societal values towards protecting children from maltreatment. The reform of child welfare policies, especially those pertaining to reporting, certainly increased the sheer volume of maltreatment reports.[45] But the surge in number was not merely a function of better reporting. The causes included a complex set of factors that constitute the so-called ecology of high-risk environments.[46] Urban areas, for example, contain more stressors (e.g., congestion) that make caretakers more prone to abuse and neglect children. The ecology of family life also has an impact; parents without adequate family and community support systems are more likely to maltreat children.[47] The legal and cultural ecologies matter as well, especially the characteristics that hinder or discourage perpetrators and victims from seeking and receiving help. Finally, the public policy landscape shapes the availability of solutions and preventative measures to curtail maltreatment over time. The following subsections explore the ecology of child maltreatment in order to gain a holistic, integrated understanding of the crisis plaguing Japan.[48] Although child abuse can occur in hospitals, schools, and orphanages, our focus here is on understanding its causes within a household.

Contemporary Factors Driving the Crisis

URBANIZATION

The degree of urbanization is positively associated with a rise in child abuse and neglect. A primary reason is that city dwellers have a higher level of stress and susceptibility to mental disorders. Overcrowding, congestion, noise, air pollution, voluminous information, and the fast pace of cities can overstimulate the senses and damage mental health.[49] These urban stressors increase the chances of child maltreatment when the frustration of caregivers turns into aggressive behaviors or poor stress management leads to deficient care for oneself and others.[50]

Urban areas are also high-risk environments for child maltreatment because parents have greater difficulty in obtaining assistance, and others find it harder to help them. In particular, the challenges of moving into a new community raise the likelihood of child maltreatment because the caregivers' previous support network dematerializes; it takes time and effort to rebuild one in a new environment.[51] Anonymity, isolation, confusion, mistrust, and loneliness characterize the lives of many urban residents, and they lack the support system provided by families, friends, neighbors, and communities in rural areas. Approximately 92 percent of Japan's population lives in cities, making it one of the most urbanized countries in the world.[52] The high degree of urbanization has weakened traditional social relationships significantly. According to the World Values Survey, Japan had the highest degree of social isolation globally. Approximately 16 percent of the population responded that they rarely, if ever, spent time with friends, colleagues, or other social groups.[53] Thus, it is no surprise that nearly 30 percent of all reported cases typically come from three major metropolitan areas: Tokyo, Yokohama or Kanagawa, and Osaka.[54]

Beyond the general weakness of the social support system in urban areas, the compartmentalized design of housing units and high turnover of residents in rental and so-called weekly apartment buildings exacerbate the degree of impersonality and prevent mutual aid networks from forming. The auto-lock security systems so ubiquitous in cities inadvertently hinder child welfare officers' ability to enter buildings and investigate reports of maltreatment. Additionally, a Japanese government survey revealed that over 80 percent of child welfare officers found work in urban areas more difficult than in rural ones because information was not readily available due to privacy concerns and coordination among neighbors was limited.[55]

POVERTY AND INEQUALITY OF OPPORTUNITY

Incidents of child maltreatment in advanced industrialized countries increase when income inequality and poverty rise.[56] The macro-level forces of skill-biased technical change and globalization, analyzed in previous chapters, have wrought major economic changes that have disrupted labor markets, raised poverty rates and income inequality, and heightened the economic risks facing households, particularly those of low-income families. A lack of economic resources means greater stress for caregivers, whether it be worries about rent or food for their children or coping with numerous life course risks (e.g., sickness, unemployment, and divorce) that lead to income losses. From a long-run perspective, strong evidence has pointed to the existence of a vicious cycle of poverty and abuse. Poor children are more likely to be victims of abuse, and this heightens their risk of falling into poverty and unemployment in adulthood, which in turn increases the likelihood that they will maltreat their own offspring.[57]

Studies have established a strong empirical link between child maltreatment and poverty in Japan.[58] One-third of all child abuse-related deaths in the last few decades have been mother–child suicides brought on by economic hardship.[59] A 2003 survey conducted across child consultation centers in Hokkaido Prefecture involving 119 cases of maltreatment found that 72.3 percent of the offenders had experienced economic difficulties; only 10 percent owned a home as opposed to the 56 percent rate for Hokkaido residents overall.[60] A nationwide study discovered that 21 percent of male and 25 percent of female public assistance recipients had experienced abuse.[61] Finally, a Tokyo Metropolitan Government survey conducted in 2004 revealed that 32 percent of the city's 1,477 child abuse cases occurred in single-parent households, and 31 percent of these households faced acute economic insecurity.[62]

Many Japanese households are very vulnerable to economic shocks due to the country's threadbare safety net.[63] Macroeconomic trends, therefore, merit close attention as a factor influencing levels of maltreatment. Several studies have documented that economic recessions increase abuse. One retrospective study of children admitted to hospitals determined that "rates of admissions for physical abuse and high-risk traumatic brain injury were significantly related to increases in local mortgage foreclosure and delinquency rates in the associated metropolitan areas."[64] The start of the Japanese child welfare crisis coincided with the country's lost decades, a period that featured a financial crisis, stagnant economy, and growing poverty. In addition, a wave of labor market deregulation put more workers in precarious situations including depressed wages and long-term unemployment. The rate of working poverty rose to approximately 25 percent and the proportion of children living in a household below the poverty line steadily increased from 10.9 percent in 1985 to a record-high 16.3 percent in 2012.[65] Child abuse incidents also climbed sharply after the Lehman shock of 2008 and the global recession that followed, as more workers were compelled to relocate in search of jobs and lost their social support networks for childrearing.[66]

DEMOGRAPHIC SHIFT: THE RISE OF SINGLE MOTHERS AND UNWANTED PREGNANCIES

Studies have found that the greater the proportion of single mothers in a community, the greater the rate of child abuse. The strong association between single motherhood and maltreatment is mainly due to this group bearing an elevated risk of falling into poverty and lacking a supportive network.[67] Japanese single mothers have one of the highest employment rates in the advanced industrialized world at around 86 percent.[68] Many of them, however, occupy the lowest stratum of the labor market, one that offers the least pay and employment protection. Nearly 50 percent of Japanese lone parents are poor, the highest rate among OECD countries.[69] The employment rate of Japanese single mothers is concerning from a childcare standpoint because research shows that neglect rates are positively associated with the proportion of employed mothers.[70]

Japan has witnessed a substantial increase in the number of single mothers since the 1990s. In 2021, over 1.3 million households were headed by single parents (1.2 million by single mothers and 0.1 million by single fathers), 50 percent more than two decades ago.[71] A key dynamic behind this trend was unintended pregnancies. A study of 206 pregnant women in Sukagawa City, Fukushima Prefecture, determined that unintended pregnancy was strongly correlated with higher incidents of adverse child-rearing outcomes; these included decreased mother-to-child attachment and greater negative feelings towards child rearing. Moreover, fathers were less likely to participate in caring for their offspring.[72] The same researchers found that 97 percent of single women's first pregnancies were unintended compared to 10 percent for married women.[73] Young couples that "marry because of unintended pregnancy" (*dekichatta kekkon*) are also on the rise. The 2019 census showed that 80 percent of mothers aged fifteen to nineteen and 55 percent of those aged twenty to twenty-four married due to pregnancy.[74]

One notable intervening factor for child maltreatment is psychological disorders among young parents. Psychologists are alarmed by elevated narcissism combined with delayed adulthood among younger generations and their potential effects on escalating violence and negligence towards children.[75] Many warn that the number of severely violent, torturous incidents is likely to rise further.[76] A child welfare historian observed that when mothers of past generations faced economic hardship, some resorted to mother–child suicide (*boshi shinjū*) to spare the child from suffering; that is, the decision to kill themselves was often grounded in concern for their child's well-being. Mother–child suicides have decreased, replaced by situations in which abusive and negligent parents hurt their children to gain freedom or self-satisfaction.[77] "Adult children" prefer to read youth comic books and play virtual games and often shirk household responsibilities such as doing the dishes.[78] Even the seemingly innocuous Peter Pan Syndrome—millennials who shy away from adult responsibilities and refuse to become productive members of society—can have devastating consequences.[79]

CULTURAL AND LEGAL IMPEDIMENTS

Cultural and legal contexts may hinder the adoption of preventative measures or provision of aid for child abuse victims in several ways. Firstly, authorities or community members may hesitate to intervene, fearing that they are outsiders (*soto*) intruding on internal (*uchi*) family affairs.[80] Prior to 1947, as part of the Japanese "family system" (*ie seido*), children were considered to be private assets, and their welfare and protection were legally treated as family issues.[81] This system was abolished in 1947, and child abuse reporting laws subsequently were strengthened to protect children's rights. Nonetheless, many individuals continue to regard maltreatment reporting as interference in familial matters. In a similar vein, anecdotal evidence has revealed that many child welfare professionals, including social workers, teachers, and the police, remain uneasy about challenging parental authority.[82]

Secondly, Japan's legal framework for child welfare and protection remains weak. Japan was a laggard in ratifying the United Nations Convention on the Rights of the Child (in 1994 as the 158th country) and did so with very little discussion of what children's rights really meant. According to Masuzawa Takashi and Ishikura Yōko, the Japanese tend to conflate "rights" and "power." They often deny children's rights fearing that acknowledging them would augment children's power vis-à-vis their parents and society.[83] The Child Welfare Law (Article 33–6) specifies that abusive parents will be forced to forfeit their parental rights (*shinken*), but the courts rarely revoke them even when their children are under the temporary custody of a child guidance center.[84]

Although the Japanese government banned corporal punishment starting in 2020 (through amendments to the CAPL and Child Welfare Act), the country's failure to protect children legally still manifests itself in several ways. First, the punishment for child abuse is exceptionally lenient. Most abuse and neglect cases in Japan are settled without any criminal charges for the offenders. When charges are filed, punishments are light. In contrast to the sentencing guidelines for child maltreatment deaths in other advanced industrialized countries, which range from fifteen to twenty-five years, Japan's are typically less than seven years.[85] Second, although witnesses of child abuse are legally responsible to report incidents, they do not face any professional or criminal sanctions if they fail to do so.[86] These legal shortfalls not only weaken deterrence against maltreatment but also hinder its early detection and prevention. Third, limited adherence to children's rights and entrenched gender inequality have resulted in family laws that disproportionately place the burden of care and financial responsibility on divorced mothers, which puts them at a higher risk of poverty and stress.[87] Japan's divorce rate has risen in the last three decades with an estimated one-third of marriages ending in divorce. Nearly 80 percent of single-mother households are the products of divorce and, in over 70 percent of cases, mothers are designated as the sole custodians. One study determined that rising divorce rates and the associated growth in single-mother families had a detrimental impact on the time parents spent with children, a factor that influences child maltreatment.[88] Approximately 47 percent of single-mother households have some form of child support arrangements, but only 28 percent actually receive payments.[89] In contrast, over 60 percent of custodial parents in the United States and Germany receive legally settled and enforced child support from noncustodial parents.[90] Beyond single mothers, we need to make space for exploring families at the margins and their welfare in the Japanese context.[91]

Lastly, the enforcement of individual privacy rights has had the unintended consequence of hampering child welfare protection. Concerned citizens in Japanese cities have attempted to recreate the mutual aid networks (*chiiki no tsunagari*) commonly found in rural areas in order to protect children. Privacy laws, however, have blocked community members from determining where and how many children live in their residential area or even their own building. Landlords and property management firms are not permitted to disclose information about their tenants, so they have difficulty even obtaining the telephone numbers of their neighbors. These privacy and confidentiality clauses are designed to secure the safety of the victims of domestic violence and their children, sexual assault victims, and other vulnerable groups, but they have also inadvertently hampered community-based monitoring of and voluntary protective assistance for children.[92]

Policy Responses
The Child Protection Policy Framework

Government policies are vital for tackling child abuse and neglect. Most advanced industrialized countries, including Japan, have adopted the four-stage child protection policy framework illustrated in figure 4.2. Its main elements are (1) detection and reporting, (2) investigation, (3) protection, and (4) rehabilitation.

In the detection and reporting stage, the government introduces measures, such as child abuse hotlines, that encourage and facilitate reporting of suspected cases. In addition, it requires professionals and citizens to report child maltreatment and, concomitantly, takes steps to raise public awareness.

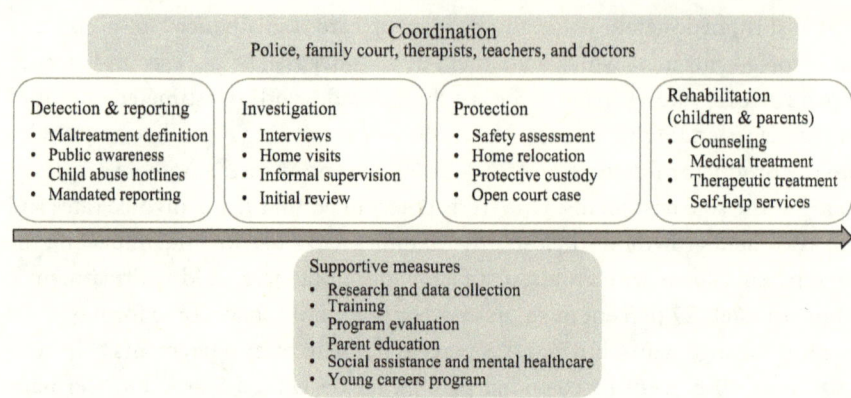

FIGURE 4.2 Child protection policy framework in Japan

Government-sponsored child protection services investigate suspected cases through home visits and interviews of the purported victims and perpetrators and then produce their initial findings. From this stage forward, coordination with law enforcement officials, family court prosecutors, therapists, teachers, and doctors is required. Once credible evidence of child maltreatment is found, responses may entail providing protective custody, finding safe living arrangements, or opening a court case. The final stage consists of rehabilitative services for both the mistreated child and parents, such as medical treatment, counseling, and self-help services. Other supportive measures include research, data collection, training, program evaluation, and parental education. The broader social safety net and the mental health care system also play important roles in preventing child maltreatment, especially in the case of poor single mothers. One study found that even a small amount of government assistance to single parents has the potential to decrease the incidence of child abuse significantly.[93]

The Child Welfare Policy Façade

The Japanese government has erected a policy façade to deal with the ongoing child abuse crisis. Policymakers have emphasized the detection of maltreatment cases without offering victims protection against abuse or treatment (or rehabilitation of perpetrators) and mobilized only limited government resources to combat the growing crisis. This strategy stems from a productivist approach to social welfare that features social investment without the creation of a safety net for the vulnerable and high reliance on private resources to achieve human capital goals.

Detection without protection. Policymakers have concentrated on detecting and reporting child maltreatment cases and neglected the rest of the necessary infrastructure, such as protection and rehabilitative systems, by leaving them chronically underfunded and understaffed. In recent years, professionals and many citizens have sounded alarm bells about the frightening rise of maltreatment nationwide. Yet, government officials have failed to build a child protection system that responds to each and every report in a timely and adequate manner. They maintain that providing abuse hotline services and encouraging whistleblowing will lead to the early prevention of child abuse, but this only holds true if a timely investigation takes place and sufficient aftercare and preventative measures are provided.[94]

Limited government resources. Japan's underfunded system is chronically understaffed and its workers are undertrained. Around 220 child consultation centers exist throughout the country employing nearly 5,800 staff.[95] They have long been stretched beyond their capacity and do not have the personnel to attend to all of the abused and neglected children in their caseloads. On average, each caseworker manages over 100 cases per year, which is five times the average in other advanced industrialized countries.[96] Many cases are left unresolved and have severe, even fatal, consequences.

The starvation death case of five-year-old Saitō Riku in Atsugi City, Kanagawa Prefecture, is a case in point. In the early 2000s, Riku's mother abandoned the toddler to escape domestic violence at the hands of his father, Saitō Yukihiro. Thereafter, signs that Yukihiro was abusing and neglecting Riku were evident. According to a court document:

> Riku was taken into protective custody for a short time after he had run out of the house barefoot and wearing nothing but a diaper. While at the child welfare center, Riku was examined and found to have marks on his body signifying possible abuse. A short while later, after the identity of Riku's father was established, staff members at the child welfare center met with Yukihiro and decided that an officer from the center would visit the home to establish whether or not the environment was fit for a young child. However, over the following four years, not one visit took place. A spokesperson for the child welfare center said at the time: "Whether or not the individual in charge of the case forgot or was too busy, we do not know, and it doesn't matter. The fact remains that no home visits were conducted."[97]

Yukihiro left his son without any food, water, or electricity and eloped with his girlfriend in 2007. Authorities discovered Riku's skeletal remains surrounded by four tons of trash on the living room floor in 2014. The father had continued to pay the rent in order to conceal the body and receive the child allowance. Authorities should have found the body much sooner since Riku never showed up at the elementary school he was registered to attend. A staff member of the child consultation center admitted that Riku's case constituted professional negligence resulting from the center's lack of resources to handle all reported cases.[98] The 2019 child abuse death case involving a call for help made by ten-year-old Kurihara, the victim herself, has also been attributed to the lack of public funding and staffing to protect the vulnerable.[99]

To address the chronic staff shortages at child consultation centers, the government began allowing the use of artificial intelligence (AI) to determine whether temporary protection should be provided to children at risk in 2020. The child abuse death of a four-year-old girl in the city of Tsu in Mie Prefecture, however, has sounded a cautionary note. The girl died after officials decided not to take her into custody based on the AI assessment of her case, which calculated the level of the need for protection to be 39 percent. A visit from an officer of the child consultation center to visually confirm her safety did not take place for nearly a year after she stopped going to daycare, strongly suggesting that staffing to respond to cases remains short.[100]

Beyond the general understaffing issue, child consultation centers also suffer from a severe shortage of experts and trained professionals.[101] Responding to child maltreatment cases requires an experienced team with the capacity to decide about placements and counseling as well as coordinate with other authorities effectively. The majority of staff in child consultation centers, however, are not licensed as social workers; around 35 percent are part-time employees with little or no training in child maltreatment, which the government does not furnish.[102] The turnover rate of staff is very high. A typical staff person only works for three years on average and then quits for a better paying, less stressful job. Specialized professionals, such as mental healthcare providers, are also in short supply, which greatly undermines counseling efforts for offenders and the rehabilitation of traumatized children in government-regulated institutions. Auxiliary measures, such as parental training, sex education, and mental health awareness programs, are also insufficient.[103]

Social investment without a safety net. The failure of the government's policy façade approach to child welfare is also attributable to a threadbare safety net that elevates the risks of maltreatment. The Dependent Children's Allowance (Jidō Fuyō Teate) offers cash assistance to employable poor single mothers; monthly benefits range from just 10,000 to 40,000 yen (around USD80–320) depending on the beneficiary's income. The duration of benefits is generally less than two years and nearly half of the recipients receive only partial payments.[104] Single mothers who are unemployable due to circumstances such as disability and illness receive a modest monthly allowance called Supplementary Welfare Benefits for Mothers and Children (Boshi Kasan) that is meant to cover a portion of expenses for food, clothing, and education. The program is circumscribed in scope because it is administered through the country's main public assistance system, Livelihood Protection (Seikatsu Hogo), which operates under very strict eligibility guidelines.[105] A consequence of the meager social assistance afforded to poor single mothers is that juvenile detention centers and prisons have become the de facto safety net of last resort for abused children where they can receive protection, daily meals, and health care.[106]

As noted at the outset, Japan has a structurally biased welfare system that delivers the least benefits to the neediest. The vast majority of expenditures are for health care and social security programs, and a mere 0.7 percent of GDP per capita went to social assistance for the poor in 2015 (table 1.6). Other social welfare programs that could potentially aid low-income groups vulnerable to child maltreatment (e.g., affordable housing assistance, employment training and placements, and unemployment benefits) are also insubstantial. In 2023, the Children and Families Agency was launched as an extraministerial bureau of the Cabinet Office to design a more comprehensive strategy. It serves as the command center for the diverse range of child welfare related programs that were previously overseen by multiple ministries and agencies. Though the new agency is responsible for issues such as child poverty, child-rearing, and child abuse, its efforts to reverse Japan's declining birthrate may end up receiving the greatest attention given the insistence of some public officials to add "Families" to its name.

High Reliance on Private Resources. In line with productivism, the Japanese government has promoted investments in human capital in an attempt to spur economic growth. Children in families with fewer financial resources are at a disadvantage because private spending has underpinned the nation's efforts to build human capital to a great extent.[107] Japan's public expenditures on education as a percentage of GDP in 2019 were the lowest among OECD countries at 2.8 percent of GDP (the average was 4.1 percent, as indicated in table 1.10). Private spending at 1.1 percent, however, was higher than the OECD average of 0.8 percent. The heavy reliance on private resources has strained the finances of all households, especially those of low-income families, increasing the risk of child maltreatment.

The State of Child Maltreatment and Policy Responses in East Asia

The issue of child maltreatment is gaining more attention than ever before across East Asia as cases multiply, filling newspapers with gruesome headlines of abuse and neglect. Risk factors, such as urbanization, economic insecurity, and single parenthood have all risen in the past decade, suggesting that the problem is unlikely to improve without more vigorous government intervention. Overall, the region's productivist emphasis on investing in children as a key part of building human capital has not extended to providing welfare protection to the most vulnerable members of society. East Asian governments spent an average of 0.9 percent of GDP on social protection of children in the period 2009 to 2015, only half the OECD average of 1.8 percent.[108] The policy responses to child maltreatment vary across the region, but authorities in all nations share a general reluctance to intercede more forcefully or commit more resources.

South Korea

According to the Korean National Child Protection Agency (CPA), confirmed child abuse and neglect cases rose almost fourteenfold from 3,891 in 2004 to 53,932 in 2021.[109] The growing number of child maltreatment incidents has been attributed to urbanization, prolonged economic downturns, exceptionally high alcohol consumption fueled by a so-called drinking culture, and the rise in divorce rates and single parenthood.[110] In addition, several studies have confirmed that child maltreatment has been a perennial problem in South Korea because of the persistence of Confucian values that uphold the parent–child hierarchy and discipline (*sarangeei mae* or whip of love).[111]

The South Korean government has created a legislative framework to address child abuse that resembles the situation in Japan. The 1981 Korean Child Welfare Act has been revised multiple times in the last two decades to require professionals (e.g., teachers and doctors) to report suspected cases and facilitate intervention by family courts.[112] In addition, the revised law designated the CPA as accountable for investigative, counseling, and child placement services. The government operates a twenty-four-hour hotline to the CPA and has increased the number of child protection centers throughout the country from seventeen in 2000 to around ninety-five in 2022. The country lacks facilities to house children who need to be removed from their homes, however. Child protection centers are severely understaffed, with only seven or eight workers per facility.[113] Thus, despite ongoing efforts to improve public awareness, reporting, and legal interventions, insufficient public funding leaves vulnerable children at great risk of abuse and neglect.

Taiwan

Child maltreatment has been a persistent problem in Taiwan, with indications that it has worsened considerably since the year 2000.[114] Scholars have attributed the precipitous rise in child abuse to rapid urbanization, growing inequality, weakening of family ties, a higher divorce rate, and the increasing number of single parent families. Physical abuse was the most common form of maltreatment (35 percent), followed by neglect (32 percent), and sexual abuse (14 percent). It is not uncommon for child-rearing practices in Taiwan to include corporal punishment to inculcate discipline and obedience and for parents to assert their authority.[115] One recent case involved a naked, emaciated, and bruised three-year-old boy found tied to a balcony with zip ties by his father. He was bound for hours and attempted to eat his own feces out of hunger.[116] The father admitted to hitting the child with his fist and slapping him with slippers for wetting the bed. Another grisly case involved a Taiwanese couple charged with abusing and beating their three children to death and then burying their bodies in a hidden location.[117]

Taiwan's legislative responses have paralleled Japan's. The 1973 Child Welfare Act, modeled after Japan's child welfare law, was the first statute promoting child welfare. It was amended in 1993 to require professionals to report suspected cases. The Ministry of the Interior's Children's Bureau established the first national database to track child abuse cases in 1999. Various legislative measures on child welfare were combined into the Protection of Children and Youth Welfare and Rights Act in 2012. They operationalized the concept of child abuse and increased public awareness of the problem, but the government did little to alter the policy detection approach that limits investigative, protective, and rehabilitative efforts. The shortage of funds allocated to child welfare has led to just 7 percent of suspected child abuse and neglect reports being investigated.[118]

Singapore

Child abuse and neglect cases have risen noticeably in Singapore. The Ministry of Social and Family Development (MSF) has received more than 3,000 reports of child abuse annually since it introduced more systematic and streamlined screening tools to improve the detection and reporting of incidents. It announced that the number of investigated cases has risen almost sevenfold from 279 in 2009 to 2,141 in 2021.[119] The majority of cases investigated by the agency involved neglect, followed by physical and sexual abuse.

The MSF has trained more than 2,500 professionals, including social workers, health care providers, and educators to handle maltreatment cases. The Child Protective Service is designated to safeguard children's welfare and has the legal authority to remove victims from their families. The MSF has yet to assess the factors behind the rise in child maltreatment officially, but academics have attributed it to changing family dynamics and growing economic insecurity among ordinary citizens. The decrease in the number of nuclear families has diminished the support network that parents can rely on for childrearing purposes. A much lower fertility rate and the increasing number of two–working-parent families may also be increasing the stressors that trigger child abuse.

With the rise of child abuse and neglect incidents, the Singaporean government has turned to civil society to meet the growing demand to protect children. One major player is Big Love, a child protection center created in 2013 under the management of Montfort Care, a charity organization comprised of professionals and volunteers.[120] Funded by the MSF, it serves as a one-stop shop for a wide range of child protection services: caseload management, risk assessment and counseling services for parents and children, professional training, child welfare advocacy, public education, and community outreach events. Big Love handles cases with moderate levels of protection concerns, such as families confronting high financial stress, whereas the MSF manages those that involve more serious issues like intentional physical harm and negligent medical care.[121]

Hong Kong

Child abuse in Hong Kong has received enormous media attention in recent years, feeding widespread public concerns that the government has failed to protect children.[122] In one notorious 2018 case, a five-year-old girl, Chan Sui-lam, was killed after she was thrown at the ceiling and stabbed in the chest with scissors. Her father and stepmother had forced her to sleep in the cold, given her very little food, and physically assaulted her for several years. The Social Welfare Department reported 1,439 cases of child abuse and neglect in 2022, a figure considerably higher than the annual average (900 cases) over the previous decade.[123] A University of Hong Kong study, however, revealed that official figures have underreported the actual number by a wide margin. It estimated that around 70,000 children experience "severe violence" by means of corporal punishment at the hands of their parents each year.[124] It also disclosed that 45 percent of children surveyed responded that they had experienced abuse. Systemic underreporting is a consequence of Hong Kong's failure to adopt a mandatory reporting law for suspected incidents; in addition, professionals like teachers and doctors are undertrained to identify the signs of child maltreatment. The recent spike in child abuse finally prompted the government to propose a bill in 2023 to institute mandatory reporting for professionals that interact with children.[125]

Beyond Hong Kong's weak policy infrastructure to combat child abuse, socioeconomic, legal, and demographic factors have contributed to child abuse and neglect. First, areas with higher poverty rates have more incidents, pointing to Hong Kong's threadbare social assistance program for low-income households as an underlying cause of abuse.[126] Second, a government study revealed that child abuse is positively correlated with the proportion of public rental units in a geographic area. The findings confirmed previous research that detected a negative correlation between the quality of housing and child abuse.[127] Third, the former Chair of the Legislative Council Subcommittee on Children's Rights, Fernando Cheung Chiu-hung, noted that households headed by teenage mothers and new immigrants were at particularly high risk of child maltreatment outcomes because they had limited familial and supportive networks.[128] Lastly, Hong Kong's legal framework has done little to protect children's rights since punitive measures against offenders remain weak.

East Asian societies place great emphasis on child development. Investing in children is seen as a means of creating a sound foundation for a strong family, community, economy, and nation. Recent reports of a spike in child abuse and neglect in Japan and the rest of East Asia, therefore, are a disquieting trend, one that is even more puzzling given the dwindling number of children across the region. Our study of Japan reveals that many of the risk factors for child maltreatment, such as urbanization, economic insecurity, and single parenthood, have all risen during the last two decades. Moreover, the public policy response to this increasingly acute crisis has been grossly inadequate. Government officials have erected a policy façade, primarily focusing on detecting and reporting child maltreatment cases, while leaving the rest of the necessary infrastructure, such as protection and rehabilitative systems, chronically underfunded and understaffed. Implementing weak institutional mechanisms to protect the most vulnerable segments of Japan's child population is consistent with a productivist approach that prioritizes policies to promote economic growth, such as investments in education to build human capital, over the social welfare concerns of the needy. Similar policy shortfalls in neighboring countries, some considerably more severe than Japan's, raise grave concerns for the future of the region given the significant humanitarian, health, behavioral, economic, and social costs associated with child maltreatment.

5
IN THE SHADOW OF VICTORIA PEAK
The Affordable Housing Crisis in Hong Kong

Hong Kong is one of the world's leading cities by any conceivable measure. Its dramatic harbor, sleek modern buildings, luxury shopping, and world-class restaurants make it a glamorous setting for wealthy residents and expatriates. The magnificent mansions on Victoria Peak, costing upwards of USD100 million, perch above the metropolis, offering unforgettable views by day and an unparalleled display of city lights at night, punctuated by a stunning laser show at 8:00 p.m. every evening. The signs of conspicuous consumption are everywhere: children shuttled to school by chauffeur-driven luxury automobiles, jam-packed jewelry stores, and high-end restaurants and nightclubs bustling every night of the week. Beneath this dazzling surface, however, lurks a different reality for many other residents. The income gap between elites and ordinary citizens has widened, elevated levels of poverty persist, and the cost of living keeps rising. Yet, the problem that stands out the most starkly is sharply escalating housing costs that have put decent homes out of the reach of large segments of the population and exposed them to grave socioeconomic risks.

The dearth of affordable housing is caused by several powerful forces, including the macro-level trends that have been discussed throughout this volume. Rapid population growth fueled by waves of immigration from mainland China has intensified urbanization in an already crowded city, raising the demand for flats and pushing prices up to stratospheric levels. Other demographic trends, notably, dropping fertility and profound changes in family structure have decreased the size of households, while multiplying their number, further adding to the demand for apartments. Globalization and skill-biased technical change have contributed to low and stagnant wages for many workers and high inequality, leaving many families unable to afford private homes and utterly dependent on scarce public flats. And, of course, there is Hong Kong's complicated topography that restricts the amount of land available for construction, making it expensive and logistically difficult to increase housing supply.

Successive Hong Kong governments have crafted numerous plans for addressing the affordability crisis over the past several decades, but they have been met with little public enthusiasm and fallen far short of expectations. The current strategy has emerged from a long and tortuous evolution of policies that have fluctuated between prioritizing rental units or home ownership, and private-market or public-housing solutions. In addition, policymakers have had to navigate a fraught political environment that has pitted big real estate developers against lower socioeconomic groups and their advocates. Thus far, the government's productivist orientation has led officials to favor developers, since land sales for the construction of luxury housing provide a painless source of government revenue that keeps taxes low and helps to maintain a friendly business environment. Limiting the supply of public housing also sustains the value of the primary asset of most middle-class families, their home. These groups benefit at the expense of the less fortunate, who must scramble to find inexpensive rentals.

Shining a spotlight on how the other half lives adds a different and often overlooked perspective to our understanding of the causes and consequences of Hong Kong's affordable housing crisis. Here are a handful of stories that capture facets of life in the shadow of Victoria Peak.[1]

The View from the Ground

In the western part of Kowloon on a dingy side street in Mong Kok, twenty men live in a 480–square-foot apartment carved out from an old industrial loft, each occupying fifteen–square-foot bunks. They share a single small bathroom and two burners in a closet space that serves as a rudimentary kitchen. One of the tenants is Feng Xiaohu, a migrant worker in the fast-food industry. Xiaohu moved to Hong Kong from Gansu province six years ago after his wife passed away and has toiled in service jobs ever since, making about 7,500 Hong Kong dollars (HKD) monthly (USD938). He feels fortunate to have steady work at a salary above minimum wage considering his low level of education and lack of job skills.

In spite of the cramped and unsanitary conditions, Xiaohu pays HKD3,850 (USD481) in rent. Ineligible for public housing because of his nonresident status, he is resigned to his current living arrangements but usually is able to put a positive spin on his personal circumstances. His "cage" apartment is, after all, better than the "coffin" homes some of his workmates must endure. Nevertheless, he has quarreled with two of his flatmates recently over their lack of hygiene after he developed a persistent rash.

Just a couple of kilometers to the north, in Sham Shui Po, Zhou Chulan lives with her two children, eight and twelve, in a forty-five–square-foot room, one of eight created by subdividing an apartment in a building from the 1930s. A bunk bed and cabinet take up most of the space, leaving little room to stand up, let alone to move about. The family shares the communal kitchen and two toilets with the other residents. All the tenants are orderly and clean, but the decrepit state of the building has contributed to frequent asthma attacks in her daughter, Nancy. Her poor health has impeded her performance at school, and she is exhibiting signs of stress.

Chulan was forced to move here after her husband abandoned the family unexpectedly one night two years ago. She works as a cleaner in the nearby Golden Shopping Centre mall, making the apartment's location very convenient. She dreams of moving to a more spacious and modern public flat in order to improve the living conditions of her children. Her name is on the waitlist for public housing, and she hopes they will be offered a flat soon, since families with children and the elderly are given priority. Chulan fears, however, that they will be asked to relocate to the New Territories and she will be forced to quit her job and find a new one. Her current position does not pay especially well, but her supervisor treats her kindly, and she is close friends with several of her coworkers.

In Kennedy Town on Hong Kong Island, Wang Lei, sixty-seven, a retired widower with two adult children, lives off meager savings and the government's old age living allowance, which is just enough to keep him above the poverty line. He lives in a flat in Sai Wan Estate, one of Hong Kong's oldest existing public housing projects (constructed in 1958). His tiny apartment is worn out and lacks light, but it is located on a relatively quiet street near most necessities.

Like many of his friends, Lei heads for the local McDonald's when he gets tired of his surroundings. He sits for hours venting about his kids to a group of elderly homeless (dubbed McRefugees) who regularly spend much of the day at the restaurant. His children moved into their own apartments after they got married and did not offer to take him in after his wife died, citing a lack of room in their small units. He does not accept that claim and complains that their refusal reflects a lamentable shift in society's values, in particular, the changing views on children's obligations to their parents. He was deeply embarrassed when they had to write "bad son" letters to the welfare agency stating that they could or would not provide him with financial support in order to qualify for the old age living allowance. They usually visit once a week bringing food, but the rest of the time he must fend for himself. His biggest concern is medical care. Lei is prone to respiratory difficulties, exacerbated by the thick air pollution in his neighborhood, and must make frequent visits to the doctor on weekdays when his children are at work. Traveling to the clinic on his own is exhausting and makes him very anxious.

In Tsuen Wan in the New Territories, the Wu family lives in an apartment built in the 1980s. Shum Wu is a driver for a charter bus company located near North Point and Yan Wu works in a retail shop in Wan Chai. The family moved here recently because their old flat in Ho Man Tin in Kowloon was much too small and the rent was rising very quickly. Their new home has an area of 496 square feet for the family of four—compared to their old unit of 324 square feet—and is cheaper and more cheerful than apartments in more desirable areas on Hong Kong Island or in Kowloon.

The main disadvantage of their new home is that Shum and Yan now must commute over an hour to work each way. In addition, the Wu's believe that the children's new school is unsatisfactory. Wilson, fifteen, and Angel, seventeen, will soon be taking the Hong Kong Diploma of Secondary Education exam to qualify for admission into one of the city's universities, and their parents fear they are underprepared. Although the family's combined income places them solidly in the lower middle class, they have little savings to spare, and paying for tutoring would be a severe strain on the family's resources.

The Political and Economic Context

Hong Kong has always been somewhat of an enigma. It grew rapidly with laissez-faire policies in a region where interventionist development states reigned. The city prospered under British colonial rule but has done almost equally well after its handover to China. It has produced great wealth but it is shared very unequally. A brief review of Hong Kong's history and unique political and economic institutions provides some context for understanding the underlying factors that have created the deep schism between luxury housing on Victoria Peak and the hardship down below.

China regained sovereignty over Hong Kong on July 1, 1997, after 156 years of British colonial rule and it is now a Special Administrative Region (SAR). As a condition of the handover, Chinese officials pledged to maintain its distinct way of life for the next fifty years. The "one country, two systems" approach enshrined in the Basic Law, Hong Kong's de facto constitution, guaranteed the territory a substantial degree of autonomy, except in the areas of foreign policy and defense. In recent years, however, Beijing has asserted its political control over the city in ways that have alarmed many citizens who, despite feeling allegiance to the mainland, cherish their autonomy. A series of mass protests over electoral reforms and civil rights, notably, those surrounding the Umbrella Revolution in 2014, eventually were met with a sharp response from the Hong Kong government. Prodded by Beijing, it passed a new national security law in 2020 that severely restricted political freedoms and imposed harsh penalties for dissent, including among elected legislative officials. By 2022, no prodemocracy politicians held political office.

The executive branch dominates the Hong Kong political system. It has the authority to formulate strategy, promulgate legislation, and execute public policies. The chief executive is the highest-ranking government official and wields a wide range of powers, including signing bills and budgets, approving government policies, and issuing executive orders. The Election Commission, a 1,500-member body comprised mainly of representatives from various so-called functional constituencies (essentially, professional interest groups, like real estate and construction or financial services) and officials handpicked by the Chinese Communist Party, selects the chief executive, not citizens through universal suffrage. A promise to move toward the direct election of the chief executive was scrapped when popular protests broke out in 2014 over the party's insistence that it reserved the right to screen candidates and reject those that it deemed unsuitable. Beijing and a large portion of Hong Kong's business elite have fostered a strong alliance based on shared political and economic interests. Specifically, neither wishes to see the emergence of a candidate who might adopt redistributive policies that could threaten the status quo.[2]

Strategically located adjacent to mainland China and at the heart of East Asia, Hong Kong is one of the most densely populated places in the world. It has an area of only 426 square miles, roughly six times the size of Washington, DC, featuring a severe topography that makes urban development complicated, time consuming, and very costly. The sea that surrounds the city combined with mountainous terrain confine the population of over seven million people to increasingly more congested spaces near the waterfront. It is comprised of three main territories—Hong Kong Island, Kowloon Peninsula, and the New Territories—and an outlying area, Lantau Island, which mostly consists of natural parkland, the airport, and tourist attractions such as the Giant Buddha and Disneyland theme park.

Hong Kong has had one of the world's best performing economies in the last six decades. From 1960 to 2000, its gross domestic product (GDP) per capita grew at an annual rate of 5.7 percent, making it the third fastest growing economy in the world.[3] Growth has slowed more recently, but during the decade leading up to 2022 real GDP per capita still rose 1.2 percent annually, despite sharp downturns related to COVID-19 and political unrest.[4] Hong Kong has embraced its status as a fully open economy and adapted nimbly as its original comparative advantage shifted to other nations with the deepening of globalization. Once a manufacturing powerhouse, it has thrived subsequently as one of the globe's leading financial, logistics, and trade centers, taking full advantage of its proximity to other strong economies in the region. The adjustments involved in shifting economic activities, however, have heightened the financial insecurity experienced by many individuals, particularly, low-skill workers and their families.

To foster competitiveness, policymakers have attempted to create a favorable business environment, featuring low tax rates and levels of government spending. Expenditures on social protection in Hong Kong have been particularly low, amounting to just 5.4 percent of GDP in 2015, far below the OECD average of 20.1.[5] Following typical productivist logic, public officials have eschewed creating a social safety net and left the burden of supporting the needy to families. Social assistance was equivalent to 1.8 percent of GDP in 2015, considerably less than the OECD average of 2.9 percent. Total social spending increased to 6 percent of GDP in 2019, broken down into 4.1 percent on insurance and 1.9 percent on assistance.

Despite its great economic success, Hong Kong has failed to furnish a large number of its citizens with the quality of life typically expected of a developed economy. Income inequality is extremely high, relative poverty is pervasive, especially among the elderly, and many citizens reside in dangerous, deplorable, and yet very expensive housing with little prospect of significantly improving their living conditions. The government has intervened extensively in housing markets during the past seventy years, but its policies have generated more controversy than success, particularly when compared to a frequent point of reference, Singapore. Why has Hong Kong consistently fallen short in one of the policy areas that matters the most to its citizens?

The Affordable Housing Crisis and Its Consequences

Not Enough Flats

Housing affordability has become a major policy issue in many urban areas around the world. Rising prices have made it increasingly difficult for low- and middle-income families to rent a decent flat, let alone buy a residence, jeopardizing their ability to move up the home ownership ladder and accumulate a valuable asset. In the United States, for instance, households in the lowest and second lowest income quintiles spend roughly 50 and 30 percent of their incomes, respectively, on housing, placing them in the Department of Housing and Urban Development's "severely cost-burdened" and "cost-burdened" categories.[6] In less affluent neighborhoods, gentrification is pushing out existing tenants as rents climb and developers build more luxury housing to appeal to working professionals. Consequently, numerous families are forced to move farther from work and schools or accept substandard housing in more central areas. In older cities, the lack of space makes building new affordable housing difficult and expensive.

Property prices in Hong Kong began to rise rapidly in the early 1980s, fueled by cheap credit, home financing schemes, and a flood of Chinese immigrants into Hong Kong. They collapsed in 1997 due to the harsh economic and financial conditions ushered in by the Asian financial crisis but renewed their vertiginous climb in 2003 as the SARS epidemic subsided; property values rose 370 percent by 2017.[7] All categories of privately owned homes (small, medium, and large) experienced price increases that outpaced income growth significantly, while rents followed a similar but less pronounced trajectory.[8]

Hong Kong's real estate was the second most expensive in the world (after Monaco) on a square meter basis in 2023.[9] In addition, the 2023 Demographia survey concluded that Hong Kong's housing was the least affordable out of 325 metropolitan areas worldwide. Its housing affordability index score was 18.8, signifying that a four-person family had to spend almost nineteen times its annual income to purchase a 400–square-foot flat in a central neighborhood.[10] This was the highest score for any locality since the survey commenced and well above that of other global cities: London (8.7), New York (7.1), and Singapore (5.3). Consequently, most residents have been forced to buy or, more likely, rent a modest flat outside the central districts where they work or tolerate suboptimal living conditions near their jobs. Among active workers, just 21.4 percent had employment in their home districts, one of the lowest percentages globally. Furthermore, the average commute time in Hong Kong was forty-six minutes, even though the city has one of the most efficient public transit systems in the world, second among global metropolitan areas (Tokyo is first).[11]

The Consequences of Unaffordability

HEAVY RELIANCE ON PUBLIC HOUSING

Many residents must turn to public housing since the private marketplace is so expensive. Hong Kong boasts one of the largest public housing stocks in the world and it continues to grow. In 2022, it consisted of 850,700 rental units and 441,700 flats that had been sold at subsidized prices. The government added an average of 13,400 public rental flats annually in the period 2016 to 2022.[12] In 2021, over 3.3 million people, or 46 percent of the total population, lived in public housing (see table 5.1). The majority of tenants were located in the New

TABLE 5.1 Population by housing types in Hong Kong (%), 2005–21

	2005	2010	2015	2021
Public permanent housing	48.7	47.0	45.6	45.7
Rental housing	30.4	29.3	29.2	30.0
Subsidized sale flats	18.3	17.7	16.4	15.7
Private permanent housing	50.6	52.4	53.9	53.7
Temporary housing	0.7	0.7	0.5	0.6

Source: Hong Kong, Census and Statistics Department, "Hong Kong Annual Digest of Statistics 2009 Edition," November 2009, and "Hong Kong Annual Digest of Statistics 2017 Edition," October 2017; Government of Hong Kong, "Housing in Figures 2022"

Territories (56.6 percent), followed by Kowloon (34.6 percent), and Hong Kong Island (8.8 percent).[13]

The steady increase in public housing stock has not been sufficient to meet incessantly rising demand. At the end of June 2023, the Hong Kong Housing Authority (HKHA) reported that the average waiting time for public rental units was 5.3 years, up from 4.7 in 2017. Single senior citizens, one of the most vulnerable social groups, faced an average wait of 3.9 years, up from 2.7 in 2017.[14] Several nongovernmental organizations have contended that the housing situation is considerably worse than the government's figures indicate because the waitlist does not include single adults and new immigrants.[15]

THE DECLINING QUALITY OF HOUSING AND WELL-BEING

A defining feature of housing units in Hong Kong is their comparatively small size, even by East Asian standards. The average floor space per person is only 161 square feet, the lowest by far of any developed nation.[16] In public flats it is lower still, a mere 146 square feet. Only 16.4 percent of public housing rental units, even those intended for families of four or more, are larger than 430 square feet.[17] By law, public flats must have at least 70 square feet per person, but Hong Kong has not established a minimum living space for private units. The lack of such a standard has enabled the explosive growth of subdivided apartments, resulting in an abundance of tiny living spaces. In addition, many flats in Hong Kong are of poor quality. Almost two-thirds of all public units were built more than twenty years ago and are in various states of disrepair; private apartments, except in the luxury market, are typically of even worse quality.[18]

The most severe manifestations of small size and bad living conditions are so-called cubicle, cage, coffin, and rooftop slum homes.[19] The number of residents living in these types of dwellings has soared as high property prices closed the door on regular housing for low-income earners. The Census and Statistics

Department reported that in 2015 approximately 199,000 people lived in miniature units in 88,800 subdivided flats that once housed a single family, a dramatic increase over its estimate of 64,900 people in 2012.[20] The government issues licenses for cubicle homes if they meet certain guidelines, but conditions are often atrocious even in legal dwellings; many residences, for instance, do not have basic amenities such as kitchen facilities, an independent toilet, or water supply. Rent on a subdivided apartment is one-third more expensive than a regular flat on a per–square-foot basis and absorbs about 40 percent of the tenant's income on average.[21]

Substandard housing is associated with low self-esteem and a greater propensity for residents to suffer physical and mental illnesses.[22] Evidence is also mounting that cramped and poor living conditions have played a role in the rise in the number of child abuse cases in Hong Kong.[23] A government study found that abuse is positively correlated with the proportion of public rental units in a district, even after controlling for other variables such as income.[24] The results led the researchers to recommend allocating more preventive and remedial child welfare services to districts with a high percentage of public rental housing.

GROWING UNEQUAL: CREATING A MORE VULNERABLE POPULATION

Unaffordable home prices affect the material well-being of families at all income levels but have a particularly large and pernicious impact on low- and middle-class households since they spend a greater share of their budget on accommodations. In Hong Kong, rising housing inequality has gone hand in hand with widening income inequality. Hong Kong is the most unequal advanced industrialized society. Its Gini coefficients for before taxes and transfers income for the years 1981, 2001, and 2016 were 0.451, 0.525, and 0.539, respectively, revealing a steady trajectory toward increased income disparity; post-transfer coefficients for 2001 (0.470) and 2016 (0.473) show a less pronounced upward trend.[25] As a point of comparison, the average coefficients for OECD nations were 0.478 for pre and 0.314 for posttax and transfers income.

The number of people living below the poverty line in Hong Kong before taxes and transfers was persistently high in the 2010s, averaging around 20 percent, and reached a record of 23.6 percent in 2020.[26] The largest group of impoverished is the elderly, especially women; approximately 32 percent of seniors were poor in 2020.[27] Seniors are generally on a fixed income, so they struggle to cover housing costs if rents rise and may be forced to cut back on other expenditures, such as for food or medicine. The level of in-work poverty was also elevated in 2020 at 15.4 percent.[28] Migrant workers, who make up a disproportionately large share of the working poor, are also deeply affected by higher home prices; in contrast with the elderly, they lack even the most minimal safety net because they are not eligible for public housing or most other government benefits.

Anger over the increasing disparity in incomes has mounted as more households find it difficult to rent or purchase an apartment in the private marketplace. Adding fuel to the fire, it is well known that numerous families with incomes above the eligibility threshold currently live in public flats, occupying units that would otherwise go to those in need.[29] Housing and inequality were common themes in the frequent antigovernment protests of the 2010s. Frustration over affordability, for instance, was a prominent theme in the momentous 2014 Umbrella Revolution. Rising property prices have also stoked deep resentment toward wealthy real estate developers. Many residents believe that government officials routinely put the interests of large developers, including several from mainland China, ahead of those of ordinary citizens.

The Causes of the Affordable Housing Crisis

Demand and supply factors, such as real GDP per capita, population growth and related demographic trends, the level of real domestic credit, construction costs, land availability, and the real interest rate, are the primary determinants of property prices. On the demand side, all other things being equal, a growing population or declining household size leads to a greater need for housing units and hence an increase in prices. Rising GDP per capita provides individuals with additional income to spend on housing, which usually augments demand; moreover, some economists believe that housing is a luxury good, so demand may rise disproportionately with respect to income.[30] Greater levels of real domestic credit signify that more financing is available for home purchases, which also tends to elevate demand. On the other hand, higher real interest rates raise financing costs, which will suppress demand and thereby reduce prices. On the supply side, less availability of land and an increase in construction costs will reduce housing stock and thereby push up prices.

These fundamental factors have also been significant in the case of Hong Kong. One study determined that real GDP per capita had the greatest long-run impact on home prices, followed by the availability of land, which had an effect with a significant lag.[31] Real GDP per capita has grown very rapidly in Hong Kong, averaging about 2.4 percent annually since 1960, which has increased demand for housing. Greater wealth in East Asia has created a pool of foreign buyers for Hong Kong real estate. Investors from mainland China in particular have flooded into the market spurring the construction of luxury units.[32] Easy credit terms due to ultra-low interest rates contributed to this surge and also propelled purchases by residents.[33]

Demographic trends and changes in family structure have also heightened the need for flats, demonstrating again the importance of macro-level forces in shaping the social policy context. A surge in cross-border marriages and the inflow of migrant workers following the handover of Hong Kong to China have overwhelmed the market for low-income homes, pushing up rents and giving landlords an incentive to subdivide existing apartments.[34] A reduction in the size of households living in public housing, due to climbing divorce rates, lower fertility, and changing family norms, has also had a noticeable impact.[35] Although the number of households in public flats has increased steadily, the number of individuals living in them decreased by 600,000 from 1990 to 2016 despite the addition of 150,000 units.[36] Children moving out of their family's public rental into private apartments of their own or ones purchased by the family as an investment (or additional residence) is a major cause of this trend.[37] The number of households living in private rentals jumped from 351,000 in 2006 to 529,000 in 2016 partly as a consequence.[38] These individuals have two motivations. One is the desire for more comfortable or independent living arrangements, a decision that marks a clear change in social norms. Another is that the children's departure reduces the income of the remaining household and makes their parents eligible for lower rents.

In general, housing supply in Hong Kong has failed to keep up with the rising need for residential real estate. Its small geographic size and mountainous topography limit the land suitable for development to a thin strip along the coast (with the exception of Southern Kowloon). Only 24 percent of Hong Kong's geographic area is built up, and a mere 7 percent is dedicated to residential use; the remaining 76 percent is comprised of wood, shrub, grass, and wetlands.[39] The pace of land creation has slowed to a few hundred hectares per year, down sharply from the 2000s, as the options for expanding habitable areas become more difficult and costly and public concerns over adverse environmental impacts grow.[40] Supply constraints are also the result of burdensome regulatory and construction costs. Regulation taxes—the time and money a developer expends to clear government and political hurdles for authorization of a project—are onerous in Hong Kong.[41] Most new residential developments are located in areas outside regular zoning and require a long and complicated political and bureaucratic process to secure approvals. Property developers also face strict building codes, rigid rules on land use conversions, and long delays in obtaining permits. In addition, Hong Kong's formidable topography results in comparatively high construction costs that directly affect property prices. In 2015, average residential building costs were USD3,090 per square meter, second only to London.[42] The pace of construction is also the slowest in the world because of the variety of technical difficulties involved and a frequent shortage of labor due to dangerous working conditions.

The demolition of existing housing stock to make room for new development is infrequent in Hong Kong. Publicly subsidized flats, for example, are jointly owned by the government and households, greatly complicating the transfer of property to developers for new construction. Therefore, builders must usually acquire scarce unused land or undertake a costly land use conversion (typically, from industrial or agricultural uses) to create a new housing project instead of simply tearing down and replacing old estates. As a later section discusses, government officials, who control land use, have brought new lots to market only in small quantities, intending to maximize the revenue they obtain from sales. In contrast, Tokyo has met the surge in demand for flats caused by steady population growth by demolishing existing stock and replacing it with large-capacity high rise buildings; it had an astonishing 142,417 housing starts in 2014 alone.[43] Consequently, supply largely has kept pace with demand and property prices have been fairly stable over the last three decades.

Policy Responses
Affordable Housing

Governments intervene in housing markets based on various rationales, such as correcting market failures or advancing urban planning objectives. Policies vary greatly in terms of their points of focus or time frames. Public officials may attempt to influence the demand for housing or its supply, seek to promote home ownership or provide rental units, or concentrate on the short or the long run. Housing strategies also differ on their redistributive effects, as seen in the priority they place on affordability. Even in the realm of affordable housing, policymakers may target disadvantaged groups, such as the elderly or poor, or opt to focus on particular income groups, like the lower middle class. Finally, the actors designated to carry out housing schemes vary. In some nations, private agents are regarded as the main agents, in others, government bureaus take the lead or act through public-private partnerships. Macro-level trends, such as deepening urbanization, aging of the population, and evolving family structure, may change not only the priorities of housing policy or the identity of groups needing special assistance, but also the constraints policymakers face in pursuing objectives.

Public officials have a wide range of measures at their disposal to pursue policy objectives. They may produce housing units directly or offer financial incentives, such as subsidies or tax breaks to developers or buyers, to influence housing construction or purchase decisions. Zoning laws and land use permits enable them to control what is built and where. They can implement regulations on every aspect of planning and construction, including building and fire safety codes, permit and inspection requirements, and procedural steps, in order to affect supply. To influence property prices, they may impose transaction or real estate taxes or establish the requirements for issuing mortgages (e.g., the minimum down payment for purchases).

The Housing Policy Façade

The Hong Kong government has a long history of intervening in housing markets using several of the instruments mentioned in this chapter. Its policies, however, have been inconsistent and generally ineffective in addressing the myriad challenges posed by the city's difficult circumstances, especially with respect to providing adequate housing security for the disadvantaged and vulnerable. Policymakers have erected a policy façade that has resulted in the construction of a large but insufficient number of public flats. Various measures could increase the supply of affordable homes to meet demand, but they have chosen not to implement them consistently or at all. They include modifying regulations to create more flexible housing markets; enforcing existing laws to evict tenants of public units who no longer meet eligibility requirements; experimenting with new modalities of housing development, including demolishing low-capacity buildings to make way for new high-capacity ones; and exercising control over land use to dedicate more lots to affordable housing. Taken as a whole, the prevailing set of policies has favored big real estate developers and current homeowners over the numerous citizens who must fend for themselves in overpriced private markets or hope to secure public units when they become available.

The government did not create its policy façade overnight. Housing policy initially achieved a reasonable balance between the competing needs of affordability and private development, but it slowly evolved into a façade that has left a large segment of the population at risk. This transformation began in the 1990s and accelerated as land became scarcer and, hence more valuable, raising the opportunity costs of constructing more public flats instead of selling available lots to the developers of luxury homes. The current policy reflects the government's overall productivist orientation, as officials have chosen to prioritize maintaining a business-friendly, progrowth environment over increasing expenditures on housing and other social welfare programs that would improve the lives of Hong Kong's neediest.

HISTORICAL EVOLUTION

Housing policy in Hong Kong has passed through five stages.[44] During the first housing boom stage (1954–71), the government began to operate a large-scale public rentals program with the objective of ensuring a stable supply of workers for the growing manufacturing industry. The first units came in the form of emergency homes to resettle those displaced by the massive Shek Kip Mei fire in 1953; thereafter, the HKHA started to build big, low-cost estates. The construction of public housing was also a means to secure badly needed land that was being occupied by squatters for urban development.[45] By 1973, 1.8 million people lived in public units.

The second stage (1972–86) primarily concentrated on quality improvement initiatives. The main policy objectives were creating better public housing and addressing the growing calls for home ownership. The government redeveloped many old resettlement estates and built more permanent rental flats. In general, the new rental apartments were superior to comparable private ones, which were not only more expensive but also substandard, sometimes dangerously so. To satisfy the emerging demand for home ownership, the HKHA introduced several initiatives to help finance purchases, including the Home Ownership Scheme (HOS) and Public Sector Participation Scheme. The HOS constructed flats and offered them for sale to means-tested households at discounts of between 25 and 50 percent to market prices. The HOS proved to be successful in targeting low-income families and purchasers had relatively low levels of default. Approximately 240,000 HOS units were sold between 1979 and 1997.[46]

The third stage (1987–96) witnessed a neoliberalism-inspired wave of privatization that began with the Long-Term Housing Strategy introduced in 1987. The strategy shifted policy from the direct construction of public rental flats toward encouraging citizens to buy homes. Specifically, it attempted to tap into the ability of developers to mobilize private resources by introducing the Home Purchase Loan Scheme (HPLS). The HPLS granted interest-free loans to public rental tenants and other eligible citizens to finance the purchase of private properties. In 1991, public officials also proposed the Sale of Flats to Sitting Tenants Scheme (SFSTS), in which the government offered to sell 3,000 to 4,000 apartments in newer public estates to tenants on favorable terms. They expected these initiatives to reduce government expenditures on housing in the interest of sustaining a fiscal approach of low spending and taxation.

The share of public rental units in total housing stock declined from 45 percent in 1976 to 35 percent in 1997, but the government's hope of reducing the need for public rentals eventually hit a serious roadblock.[47] The loan amounts offered under the HPLS and SFSTS failed to keep up with the jump in housing prices during this period. In addition, another government agency adopted a measure that counteracted the home ownership drive. In 1991, the Monetary Authority raised the required down payment for home purchases from 5 to 10 to 30 percent in an effort to protect the solvency of the banking system. It claimed that this step was necessary to reduce bank exposure to the real estate sector, but the large payment required upfront prevented many families from purchasing a flat. In effect, the increase in down payments shut the door on latecomers to the private housing market. Consequently, the demand for public rentals remained strong and, by 1997, the waiting time for flats reached 6.6 years.[48]

The government's renewed home ownership effort characterized the fourth stage (1997–2001). The then chief executive Tung Chee-hwa announced an increase in housing production to 85,000 units annually with the goal of shortening the waiting time for flats to three years and pledged to raise the home ownership rate to 70 percent of the population. To encourage higher income households to acquire their own apartments, the HKHA unveiled the Tenants Purchase Scheme (TPS) in 1998. TPS was intended to provide 250,000 families living in public rentals with the opportunity to purchase their flats at reduced cost. It tried to correct the failures of the unsuccessful SFSTS by setting home prices below those of the HOS. The Asian financial crisis (1997–98) foiled the government's ambitious plans, however, and it soon abandoned its housing policy objectives, with the exception of achieving shorter waiting times for public apartments.

Real estate developers augmented their influence over housing policy after the handover of Hong Kong to China. Beijing and much of the business community shared an interest in preventing groups that advocated for shifting government strategy toward greater redistribution from gaining a more potent political voice. Chinese leadership could count on developers to help select their preferred candidates for the chief executive and legislature in exchange for their support for sustaining business-friendly policies. Developers made no secret of wanting to secure land in order to construct luxury buildings that were more profitable than public housing projects. Government officials were only too happy to oblige by designing a policy façade that would advance their own interests as well by creating a reliable source of government revenue, as described in the next section.

Accordingly, policymakers initiated the fifth stage (2002–17) distinguished by a retreat to rentals.[49] In a sharp reversal, officials announced that henceforth the government would concentrate its efforts on public rental assistance and land supply issues. Resources allocated for subsidized home ownership schemes like the HOS and TPS would be shifted to constructing public rental units and these would be reserved exclusively for low-income families who could not afford private flats. Government intervention also extended to multiple attempts to affect property values directly and indirectly in this period, as the next section details.

CONTEMPORARY POLICIES AND INITIATIVES

The administrations headed by the chief executives Donald Tsang (2005–12), Leung Chun-ying (2012–17), and Carrie Lam (2017–22) declared repeatedly that affordable housing was a top government priority, often as a response to signs of growing unrest that sometimes materialized into antigovernment demonstrations. Yet in the end they implemented measures that mostly served to reinforce the policy façade that ignored the needs of disadvantaged groups.

Tsang took office after a prolonged period of depressed property values. Prices had dropped after the 1997 Asian financial crisis and only recovered in 2003 after the SARS epidemic subsided. By 2000, public officials had shifted priorities away from promoting affordability to halting the decline in prices that was cutting into developers' profits and the value of current owners' flats. In 2001, the government announced that the sale of HOS flats would be halted for ten months in order to check the expansion of housing supply. In 2002, Tsang, then chief secretary of administration, declared that HOS sales would resume, but be capped to avoid competition with the private real estate sector.[50] This policy was effective: Annual growth in housing supply, including private, subsidized, and public rental units, dipped from 59,800 homes in 2006 to 25,700 in 2016, and property prices resumed their upward trajectory with a vengeance.[51] This policy shift epitomized Hong Kong's housing policy façade. When the goal of affordability conflicted with that of keeping home prices high to benefit developers and current homeowners, public officials did not hesitate to abandon it. It did not matter that the wait time for public flats, which had fallen to two years in 2003, began to climb again at a time when many households were being priced out of private housing markets.

In an about-face, by 2009 soaring prices renewed concerns of a housing bubble. Moderating price increases through administrative means, but not measures to augment the supply of flats, became a primary focus of government policy. Two prudential measures stand out. First, the Hong Kong Monetary Authority raised the required down payment—the loan-to-value ratio—from 30 to between 40 and 50 percent by 2010. Second, the Inland Revenue Department implemented several anti-speculation regulations, notably, a special stamp duty tax of 15 percent on real estate transactions.[52] R. Sean Craig and Changchun Hua found that both policies had statistically significant effects on housing prices, but they were temporary and only slowed but did not alter the rising trend in property prices.[53]

Tsang's successor, Leung, pledged to increase the supply of affordable housing by constructing 75,000 new public units from 2013 to 2018 and an additional 100,000 from 2018 to 2023. He also promised that 17,000 new HOS homes would become available from 2016 to 2020 and encouraged the Hong Kong Housing Society, a nongovernmental organization, to construct more subsidized flats.

Finally, the chief executive outlined steps to expand the supply of land for building residential real estate, including reducing red tape for approvals, opening undeveloped land for housing starts, and exploring the conversion of underground spaces.[54] Leung cautioned that the government's initiatives would not bring quick relief, noting that it frequently took ten to twenty years to approve and build large housing developments due to the need for public consultation, often complex engineering, and completion of associated infrastructure projects like new subway stations.

Critics of the government protested that the new measures were grossly inadequate. Many focused on the fact that even with the increase in public flats, available housing stock would fall far short of demand. Sze Lai-Shan, from the Society for Community Organization, stated: "The housing authority plans to build 15,000 units on average in the next five years. That will hardly solve the problem. . . . Including the new units and around 5,000 units more that are returned every year, the annual number of available units is around 20,000, but there are more than 160,000 families waiting for them."[55] Sze urged the government to build many more apartments, claiming that the current budget surplus and positive fiscal outlook made extra construction not only possible but a moral imperative.

Public housing advocates advanced two ideas as potential means of improving access to affordable units. First, they suggested that the government should create more economic opportunities in outlying areas where construction was less problematic and costly in order to persuade low-income residents to move; providing incentives such as offering larger, better-quality flats and more generous transportation subsidies might also encourage relocation. Second, and more controversially, some activists argued that no public space, even parkland or private golf courses, should be considered off limits for housing development given the dire living circumstances faced by many residents.[56] They pointed out that less than 25 percent of Hong Kong's land was developed, but country parks and nature reserves occupied nearly 40 percent. This proposal met with staunch opposition by environmentalists, citizens who relied on parks for recreation, and city health officials who feared that a reduction in green space might worsen already bad air quality and lower the level of physical activity among citizens.

Other observers claimed that the housing shortage also might be alleviated by managing the existing stock more efficiently through three measures. First, the HKHA should enforce rules governing the means test for residency more strictly.[57] Many tenants whose income had risen above eligibility thresholds continued to live in public estates. In some cases, well-off tenants had even purchased private properties as investments or additional residences.[58] The government had been slow to address this issue, meaning that families in need were unable to obtain public housing.[59] Second, the HKHA ought to modify the terms governing the sale of government-subsidized homes on the secondary market, permitting those who were willing to downsize to smaller living quarters or switch to a private rental to sell in order to make way for new tenants.[60] The restrictions on subdividing public flats similarly could be lifted to help meet the demand for small, inexpensive units. Finally, many privately owned apartments remained unoccupied. Developers often did not release newly constructed units because they anticipated higher sale prices in the near future or those who purchased them for speculative purposes kept them empty to avoid the bother of leasing them. A punitive tax on vacant investment properties would provide an incentive to sell or rent them, thereby increasing the supply of private housing.

Lam proposed several new policies in 2018 that represented a shift away from the prevailing focus on supplying only public rentals and were carefully designed to address the criticisms leveled against past governments. She pledged to make homes more affordable for first-time buyers: "The goal of our policy is property ownership. We aim to build a property ladder for families with different incomes and reignite their hope for buying property."[61] To do so, the government planned to increase the level of subsidies available to purchasers in order to lower the cost of an apartment from roughly 70 percent of market value to 52 percent. Lam also vowed to impose punitive vacancy fees on properties that were not sold or occupied in one year's time. Finally, she announced the government would rescind the rights it had recently granted to private firms to develop nine sites and instead use the land to build an additional 10,600 affordable public rental units.

Critics denounced the chief executive's proposals as "mere window dressing" and contended that they did little to address the fundamental factors restraining the supply of public housing, most notably, insufficient land set aside for the construction of affordable homes.[62] They pointed out that the government's expenditures on housing had dropped significantly, from 14 percent of overall public spending in 2001 (equivalent to 2.6 percent of GDP) to just 5.2 percent in 2021 (1.3 percent of GDP).[63] They argued that this was a clear indication that public officials could do more if they really wished. In response, the chief executive conceded that the administration's policies would not resolve all problems but claimed that the measures "demonstrate the political determination and innovation of this government."[64]

The most recent chief executive, John Lee Ka-chiu (2022–), introduced several housing initiatives in his first policy address and declared that they were a priority for his administration.[65] The government established two new bodies to formulate a fresh overall housing strategy and accelerate the development process: the Steering Committee on Land and Housing Supply and Task Force on Public Housing Projects. Second, it announced the creation of a new form of dwelling, Light Public Housing (LPH). LPH was conceived as a type of transitory living quarters to accommodate families and individuals while they waited for permanent public housing. The government pledged it would construct 30,000 such units as part of 158,000 new flats by 2027 with the aim of shortening the wait time for a public apartment from six to 4.5 years. Third, officials indicated that they would give private developers more incentives to construct affordable apartments by implementing inclusionary zoning.[66] Finally, they encouraged builders to adopt a new modality of housing delivery, modular integrated construction, that permits standardized units to be built offsite and assembled onsite whenever possible. This approach has been employed successfully in several major cities like New York.

CHOOSING DEVELOPERS OVER AFFORDABILITY

The trajectory of Hong Kong's housing policies reveals that policymakers have struggled, as they have in many societies, with the question of how much affordable housing to supply and whether to provide flats directly or support private markets. They have a diverse set of tools in their arsenal, but their most powerful weapon is their absolute control over land use. The government owns all the land in the territory and chooses how to allot available parcels to competing users. Decisions on how much land to release for residential development and by what means are deeply controversial since they directly affect real estate prices and determine the identity of winners and losers in housing markets.

The government's land use policies generally have favored big developers and current property holders over low-income households. The convergence of interests between developers and public officials has been greatly facilitated by Hong Kong's political structure. Many elected officials are accountable to organized interest groups, not the general public. The economic importance of sectors like real estate and finance and their political influence through their role as functional constituencies that help select the chief executive make it difficult for leaders to ignore their requests. In contrast, ordinary citizens, especially those from lower socioeconomic groups, have little voice in the political system, allowing officials to largely neglect their interests. Political parties that advocated for working-class families once played a role in Hong Kong's legislature, the seventy-member Legislative Council (Legco), but this body has always been at best a weak check on the executive branch.[67] All such parties have been effectively silenced since Chinese authorities tightened their grip on Hong Kong. No opposition politician held political office as of 2023; most were either imprisoned or in exile. Furthermore, the frequent robust prodemocracy protests demanding a greater say for ordinary citizens and redistribution (including more abundant and better public housing) that once shook public officials and prodded them to introduce at least some reforms have come to a screeching halt.

Policymakers have not favored developers simply because they wished to curry favor with important constituents. The goal of keeping direct taxation as low as possible has pushed them to exploit land leases for revenue; in 2018, land sales comprised roughly 30 percent of government receipts.[68] Extracting so much revenue from leases continues even though Hong Kong has run very large fiscal surpluses in recent years. The surplus in 2022 was 1 percent of GDP, down from a peak of 5.6 percent in 2017.[69] The government's reserves in 2022 were sufficient to cover 1.3 years of expenditures (based on spending in 2022); in some years (e.g., 1998), reserves were sufficient to finance more than two years of outlays.[70] Nations that have adopted a productivist approach generally favor keeping taxes and government spending low as a means of improving their international competitiveness, but only Singapore has taken this directive to the same extreme that Hong Kong has.

In order to maximize proceeds, the government has sold land mainly in the form of big parcels by auction to the highest bidder. This approach has made it difficult for anyone but the largest private developers to purchase desirable tracts and resulted in a concentrated real estate sector.[71] Since land is scarce and expensive, those who win bids almost always opt to construct high-end residential buildings to maximize their profits as opposed to more modest structures with smaller margins. In addition, developers often hold off on building on the land they have purchased in the hopes that property prices will increase further; in December 2017, for example, investors owned 2,471 acres of undeveloped tracts still classified as farmland.[72]

Policymakers occasionally have altered the rules governing auctions to serve specific housing policy objectives. They instituted an application list system in 1999 in which bidders submitted offers for sites on an inventory of available land; a bid that reached 80 percent of the government's undisclosed reserve price would trigger a public auction. This process enabled developers to influence the supply of land by either placing or withholding bids for available lots as it best suited them.[73] The list system reinforced government efforts to push up property prices from the depressed levels reached after the Asian financial crisis. The government scrapped the system definitively in 2013 to reclaim full control over land supply and has relied on regular auctions ever since.

In the final analysis, the government's land use policies have displayed a reluctance to expand affordable housing more rapidly. As critics have noted, policymakers have the option of introducing other criteria, such as community impact, into the decision-making process on how to allocate available land, as many European cities do; such a modification would undoubtedly lead to a greater supply of affordable flats over time.[74] When the goal of promoting affordability has conflicted with the objectives of raising government revenue or securing the support of big developers and middle-class homeowners, they have chosen the latter. Perhaps the best example of this happened after the Asian financial crisis when officials canceled plans to construct 85,000 units annually, the main recommendation of the Long-Term Housing Strategy Steering Committee, in a rush to prop up falling housing prices. The former chief executive Leung alleged that the decision to abandon low-income households was a grave error, stating pointedly that if the initiative had proceeded "today's housing problems would not exist."[75] This choice was certainly not based on a shortage of funds, as the government fiscal situation was excellent as noted previously. The fact that outlays on housing declined drastically from 14 percent of total expenditures in 2001 to just 5.2 percent in 2022 reveals where the government's true priorities have lain.

The State of Affordable Housing and Policy Responses in East Asia

Other East Asian nations face housing issues similar to those of Hong Kong, namely, unequal access to quality dwellings, the lack of affordable flats in cities, and concerns over how to supply homes to the most vulnerable, like the elderly or single-parent families. These challenges are often due to the same factors as in Hong Kong: deepening urbanization, skill-biased technical changes, evolving family structures, and adverse demographic trends. Yet, housing policy in East Asia varies considerably across nations. The quantity and characteristics of public housing, the scope and depth of government intervention in private housing markets, and the degree to which public officials use housing policy to effect redistribution differ markedly.

Singapore

Singapore confronts housing challenges that resemble Hong Kong's: scarce land, high population density, shrinking household size, and rapid economic development. Nonetheless, it has accomplished far more by managing to achieve near-universal affordable housing. Indeed, Singapore is often showcased as a major success story in the literature alongside Western nations such as the Netherlands and Finland.[76] The Housing Development Board (HDB) has built around one million units of public housing since 1960. Today, over 80 percent of Singaporeans live in public estates, 90 percent of whom own the ninety-nine–year leases on their homes; the government also assists citizens in the lowest income decile to rent homes. The legal system permits officials to acquire land cheaply and quickly and this, along with subsidies, has kept the cost of building public units and their purchase price well below market rates.

The government has adopted measures in other policy spheres to support housing goals. The most important is the Central Provident Fund (CPF), a compulsory tax-exempt savings scheme for all citizens.[77] Deposited funds are used to purchase government bonds that in turn finance loans and subsidies to the HDB; this funding source enables the HDB to reduce construction costs by circumventing more expensive borrowing from commercial lending institutions. The CPF was also designed to incentivize and assist citizens to purchase housing. The government has encouraged public housing tenants to own flats rather than rent since the 1960s. Under the Home Ownership Scheme, eligible individuals are permitted to use their CPF savings to make the required 20 percent down payment and monthly CPF contributions to cover payments on HDB mortgages. Thus, the purchasers of public dwellings are able to finance their homes without experiencing a decrease in monthly disposable income. In Hong Kong, some political parties have proposed introducing a pension plan similar to the CPF and permitting citizens to use it for home purchases, but strong opposition from the business sector has blocked their efforts.

Private housing prices in Singapore roughly doubled from 2009 to 2022.[78] This increase is attributable in part to the government's aggressive promotion of foreign investment in the aftermath of the Asian financial crisis and SARS outbreak, which brought a lot of foreigners into the private property market.[79] High property values have affected single Singaporeans and nontraditional couples the most because they are largely excluded from owning or renting public flats. These groups are penalized twofold—once for not being in a traditional marriage and twice because recent policies have allowed the prices of homes they can access to soar. Officials have implemented several measures to curb property prices, including stamp duties and stricter mortgage terms, but these have met with limited success.

Singapore's exclusive focus on its citizens in designing housing policy has also left foreign workers—especially those holding low-wage jobs—likely to confront substandard living conditions. This issue is concerning because migrant workers, mainly from China, Bangladesh, India, Malaysia, and other Southeast Asian countries, account for nearly one-fifth of Singapore's population.[80] Employers must provide accommodations for their foreign workers under the Ministry of Manpower's guidelines and the Employment Act. Housing options for non-Malaysian foreign workers are limited because they are subject to a government quota on residency, set at 8 percent of flats in a neighborhood and 11 percent in a block.[81] Therefore, most of these workers live in commercially run purpose-built dormitories (PBDs), factory-converted dorms, or temporary quarters on construction sites. In the case of PBDs, employers pay landlords a monthly rent that averaged about USD350 per worker in 2023.[82]

Human rights groups have criticized these accommodations—especially those at industrial or construction sites—for lacking proper sanitation, space, and safety. Some activists have claimed the PBDs constitute an apartheid system that segregates migrants from the rest of society.[83] Most PBDs are located far from the city center and are self-contained to restrict workers' spatial movements. Surveillance is also very common, with dozens of cameras continuously monitoring residents' activities.[84] Workers' discontent over their perceived social exclusion took a violent turn in 2013. Hundreds of South Asian migrant workers rioted in the city's Little India district, leaving thirty-nine police officers injured, twenty-five vehicles damaged, and dozens arrested.

In the wake of the country's worst riots in over forty years, prime minister Lee Hsien Loong vowed to improve the living conditions, legal protection, and safety of foreign workers.[85] The government increased financial and criminal penalties for employer violations, revamped its enforcement and inspection efforts, and provided more information to migrant workers about their rights and responsibilities. Officials also urged employers to utilize well-managed PBDs instead of quarters at construction sites or factory-converted dorms.[86]

Japan

Japan's housing policy has been oriented toward private development and primarily designed to benefit middle-class households.[87] The central goal has been to assist families in moving up the housing ladder and acquiring a valuable asset that provides financial stability and protection against some forms of economic risk, thereby lessening the need for public social spending. Policymakers have also viewed this process as a means of expanding the middle class. The government has supported the private housing market by providing subsidies to builders and low-cost loans to middle-income households. In addition, it has adopted lax land use and zoning regulations that have kept regulatory and construction costs for real estate developers low, helping to contain price increases. In contrast to Hong Kong, residential properties in Japan are generally affordable, with the exception of the Tokyo–Yokohama and Osaka–Kobe–Kyoto metropolitan areas—and even in those locales, homes are less expensive than in most other megacities worldwide.

The government started building public flats after World War II to address a desperate housing shortage that affected a sizable portion of the population.[88] Municipalities built and managed public housing estates that were largely financed by central government subsidies, a practice that continues to this day.

Government efforts were supplemented by large firms that constructed estates for their employees as one element of Japan's extensive corporate welfare system. Policymakers initially supplied public units to "core" members of society, such as military personnel or coal miners; they only targeted the poorest segments of society later on when the pressing need for low-cost housing became apparent. Japan's extensive working poor population continues to experience difficulty finding affordable flats, but the government has not made housing security for low-income families a top priority. In 2019, public rental units made up only 3.5 percent of total dwellings, half the OECD average of seven.[89]

South Korea

South Korea's housing strategy has resembled that of Japan in many important respects, particularly in preferring private market over public solutions and favoring middle-class households. In the broadest terms, policymakers viewed housing as one ingredient in its recipe for achieving rapid economic growth. Government policy concentrated on encouraging the private sector to build an adequate number of homes for workers, especially those in priority sectors, devoting little attention to the issue of affordability. Officials emphasized home ownership over rentals; as in Japan, government subsidies for the purchase of private housing primarily benefitted middle-class families and investors, not the poor.[90] The government started to construct estates for low-income families in the 1960s in response to social unrest. The Roh Tae-Woo administration (1988–93) formulated the first comprehensive plan to cope with the scarcity of flats in the greater Seoul area. Nonetheless, officials only began to build a significant number of public rental units in 2002. A major expansion took place in the 2010s and by 2020 public rentals made up 9 percent of all dwellings, somewhat above the OECD average of 7 percent.[91]

These efforts did not suffice to meet the growing demand for affordable homes. The cost of flats in urban areas, notably, Seoul, has increased dramatically in the last decade and many residents have opted to rent rather than own, typically through Korea's unique *jeonse* system.[92] Most quality rental housing is too expensive for lower income groups and they are forced to live in poor conditions or relocate farther away from work and good schools in search of lower rents. As seen in the film *Parasite*, many families resign themselves to living in semi-basement apartments called *banjiha*; there were 330,000 *banjiha* nationwide in 2020, with 200,000 in Seoul alone.[93] The outcry over the conditions depicted in the film led the Seoul city government to announce that it would provide up to USD2,600 to *banjiha* families that earned less than 60 percent of median income—about 1,500 households—to find better living quarters.[94] After four people died in flooding in 2022, it stipulated it would no longer permit new *banjiha* apartments and compel owners to convert existing units into nonresidential space within ten to twenty years.[95]

The Moon Jae-In administration (2017–22), which rode into office on a populist platform, vowed to address the burgeoning housing crisis head on. It initially focused on curbing real estate speculation, but the failure of this approach led to several measures aimed at improving supply, including the direct provision of flats.[96] Growing anger over the scarcity of affordable homes, especially among young adults, finally erupted and property prices became a central issue in the 2022 presidential elections.[97] The winner of those elections, Yoon Suk-Yeol, of the opposition Democratic Party, had campaigned on the promise of adopting policies that would enable private market forces to increase the supply of new homes. In August 2022, the government pledged to add 2.7 million residence units nationwide by 2027, including 500,000 low-cost flats specifically for young adults, by easing restrictions on urban redevelopment and reconstruction.[98]

Taiwan

Taiwan has followed the most private-market–oriented housing policy in East Asia. Unlike Japan and Korea, the government has proffered only limited amounts of credit or subsidies to builders or homebuyers. Programs to help buyers secure low interest mortgages have been the primary vehicle to spur construction since 1990. As in Korea, policymakers initially thought of housing mainly in terms of its impacts on economic development and national security, such as ensuring there is an adequate number of dwellings for civil servants and military personnel. They have emphasized that family and community, not the government, should take care of the majority of other housing needs.

The government first began to build small quantities of public units in 1976, primarily as a safety net for the very neediest; by 2002, a mere 5.3 percent of Taiwan's housing stock was public and a miniscule 0.1 percent was in the form of rental apartments.[99] The provision of even this limited amount of public housing occurred mainly because of the increase in political competition facing the Kuomintang ruling party.[100] Housing has become a salient political issue recently because of the tripling of property values since 2005. Taipei now rivals Hong Kong in having some of the least affordable housing in the world, according to the Demographia Survey; in 2015 it had a score of 15.7 versus 17.0 for Hong Kong.[101] Rising prices have been caused by a surge in demand by Chinese buyers and reinvestment of repatriated earnings by Taiwanese citizens, as well as an upturn in vacancies created by investors who purchase properties but do not inhabit them.¹⁰² They have forced many families out of Taipei into surrounding towns and added impetus to the brain drain of young professionals. The government has pledged to address the growing concern by building more public housing units and regulating the rental housing market more closely. Among the announced measures are incentives for developers to transform hotels and other structures into so-called social housing, small rent subsidies for low-income individuals, and regulations to limit real estate speculation.¹⁰³

The lack of affordable housing in Hong Kong has been a perennial problem that has impinged upon many aspects of citizen's lives. Other East Asian nations, with the exception of Singapore, have experienced a lack of affordable homes as well, and the situation is likely to worsen in the future. The Hong Kong government has had some notable successes in housing policy, such as constructing dwellings for large numbers of workers in the 1950s and 1960s. Nonetheless, during long periods of time, Hong Kong's policies have been inconsistent and ineffective in addressing the city's housing challenges. Indecision about whether to rely on government or private market solutions or emphasize rentals or subsidized homes has led to policy reversals that have distorted markets and resulted in ineffectual management of housing stock.

Hong Kong officials are caught between a rock and a hard place. On the one hand, they face criticism that the government has not done enough to assist low-income households and first-time homebuyers or control runaway property values. This accusation is especially potent since expenditures on housing have declined even as the government has enjoyed fiscal surpluses, sometimes very large ones, over the past two decades. On the other, their efforts to increase the availability of affordable housing and dampen price increases antagonize influential developers and current homeowners who oppose any measure that might decrease the value of their most important asset. In the same vein, public officials prefer to limit social spending and maintain the lucrative land sales that provide a steady source of revenue and keep taxes low, policies consistent with an overall productivist strategy. Consequently, they end up adopting, repeatedly, incomplete housing measures that they know in advance will be insufficient to stem the crisis and provide adequate protection to the city's most vulnerable populations. This policy façade is unlikely to fall unless an unforeseen event alters Hong Kong's political institutions in a way that makes leaders more accountable to the general electorate, the government opts to reduce its reliance on land sales as a source of revenue, or Beijing determines that its political interests are better served by ending the privileged status of big developers.

6

LEFT BEHIND
Misery beneath the Miracle in China

A defining feature of the East Asian model that has achieved such great economic success over the past six decades is the productivist approach to social welfare. As the preceding chapters have shown, productivism might have promoted rapid growth for a time, but it also contributed directly to the social problems now appearing across the region with a vengeance. China is often grouped together with its neighbors, yet it differs in significant ways. It underwent a transformation from a command-and-control to market economy and took longer to reach middle-income status; even today, its per capita income is well below that of others in the region. In addition, it is a geographically large country with a huge population and has evolved toward a complex federalist system in which local governments play a critical role in policy design and implementation. Nevertheless, China also resembles its peers in many important respects and has pursued some of the same basic strategies. Its leaders have emphasized fast economic growth and kept social spending low, betting that rising material prosperity would assure labor peace and political acquiescence. The Confucian tradition, with its emphasis on hard work and the protective role of family and community, has influenced public policy, especially in the social realm. Social spending has mostly benefited core members of the workforce, not society's most vulnerable groups.

The striking contrasts and similarities between China and other East Asian nations suggest that examining its social policy can refine our understanding of social welfare trends in the region. In which ways has China's experience with productivism been comparable with its peers? Has it led to similar outcomes? What does the pattern of social misery beneath the economic miracle encountered elsewhere in East Asia mean for China as it follows in their footsteps? Is it too late for Chinese policymakers to learn any lessons from the broader regional experience?

This chapter begins by outlining China's transition from a planned to market economy. By any conceivable measure, its economic performance has been unprecedented and its success in virtually eliminating absolute poverty in such a short time is extraordinary. We then explore the country's social policy model, reviewing how it too transformed toward a more market-based approach. Its social welfare system exhibits a dualistic structure that seems intrinsic to productivist systems, leaving it vulnerable to the negative impacts of macro-level trends affecting other nations in the region, namely, globalization and technological change, demographic trends, urbanization, and evolving family structures. In China's case, social policies have favored urban workers at the epicenter of economic activities and largely neglected rural residents and migrant workers. Finally, the chapter analyzes China's experience in the four social policy areas analyzed in the other East Asian nations, namely, old age security, labor markets, child welfare, and affordable housing. We conclude that several features unique to China—its unprecedented migration from rural to urban areas, reliance on local governments to implement social policy, stringent *hukou* household registration system, and intrusive family planning measures—make addressing these social problems even more daunting.

China's Economic Transformation

The contemporary Chinese economy resembles those of its East Asian peers in many respects. It underwent a period of incredibly fast growth, had an aggressive outward orientation, featured extensive government intervention, and took advantage of compliant, low-cost labor. Its experience differs in that China was once a command-and-control economy based on state-owned enterprises (SOEs) and collective agricultural production. Its transformation toward a more market-based capitalist system was surprisingly quick and had tremendous repercussions for many areas of public policy, including social welfare.

The Chinese government once exercised almost complete control over the economy and kept it isolated from the outside world. It based its planning and development model on the Soviet Union's, and that country supplied technology and technical advisors for a number of years.[1] As in most developing nations, leaders viewed agricultural surpluses as a source of funds for fostering rapid heavy industrialization.[2] The government taxed agriculture more moderately than many other countries, however, because rural areas were a traditional stronghold for the Communist Party. Agricultural production continued to grow, albeit slowly, throughout the period of Mao Zedong's rule and beyond. In the period 1953 to 1978, Chinese gross domestic product (GDP) per capita rose at an average real annual rate of 3.6 percent, largely because of high industrial growth during the First Five Year Plan (1953–57).[3] Economic performance deteriorated sharply during the Great Leap Forward (1958–62) and somewhat less so during the Cultural Revolution (1966–76) because policymakers implemented policies that removed material incentives for key producers and weakened other market forces.[4]

Emerging from years of poor economic performance during the Cultural Revolution with a large, underemployed population and low standards of living, political leaders viewed fast growth as essential to promoting national security, material well-being, and social and political stability. A new strategy started to take shape at the Third Plenary Session in December 1978, which put in motion the first set of substantial market-oriented reforms. Policymakers liberalized agricultural markets by allowing prices to rise, scaling down production teams, permitting farmers to sell their goods to market directly, and introducing the Household Responsibility System; these measures had the immediate effect of raising productivity in the sector.[5] They also allowed the creation of small rural firms and a limited amount of foreign direct investment (FDI), which contributed to an increase in total factor productivity (TFP). Starting in 1985, the government transformed the nonagricultural goods sectors by taking steps to unwind the planned economy, develop the private sector, and marketize and then privatize SOEs.[6] Finally, it began to integrate China into the international economy through various actions that together have been labeled the Open Door policy. The key measures were decentralizing foreign trade institutions, promoting exports, and encouraging FDI and other modes of technology transfer.[7] Collectively, these reforms represented the development of what political leaders called "socialism with Chinese characteristics."

China's restructuring ushered in a period of phenomenal performance that, given its large size, constituted what the World Bank dubbed the greatest growth surprise in economic history. China's GDP grew at an average of 9.5 in real terms annually from 1979 to 2018.[8] The structure of the economy changed dramatically. Agriculture accounted for 30 percent of output and occupied 75 percent of labor in 1977, but only 5 percent of output and 30 percent of labor in 2012. The massive shift of resources and manpower from agriculture to industry and services increased TFP. In addition, China took advantage of its status as a late (late) industrializer to adopt existing technologies and leverage its low production costs to insert itself deeply into global supply chains and expand its exports quickly, enabling it to tap into economies of scale. Scholars identify the increase in nonagriculture TFP and very high levels of domestic investment, made possible by an elevated rate of savings and access to cheap capital, as the two key factors that spurred growth.[9]

China now confronts the challenge of transforming its economy from being a follower to innovator in order to avoid getting stuck in the middle-income trap. It has lost its advantage in low-tech, labor-intensive manufacturing due to a sharp rise in production costs, and these activities have moved to lower-cost countries in Southeast Asia and elsewhere. It has limited the losses from this shift in comparative advantage by permitting Chinese firms to invest abroad and launching the ambitious Belt and Road Initiative. But the government's real hopes for the future lie in high-tech, knowledge-intensive industries, and officials have introduced a host of policies, including strengthening tertiary education, higher expenditures on research and development, and various sector-specific policies that are part of the Made in China 2025 initiative (supplemented by China Standards 2035), to develop these sectors. In addition, policymakers have come to realize that they cannot depend on continuous increases in domestic investment and exports to sustain China's economic performance and need to rely more on bolstering domestic consumption by an expanding middle class.

The political economy of Chinese economic policy is similar to that of other East Asian nations in important ways. Leadership has been committed to rapid growth and faced little opposition to dedicating the bulk of available resources to achieving it. The government has numerous tools at its disposal for implementing ambitious industrial policies and protectionist schemes. It differs in the almost absolute control that the Communist Party has enjoyed over all areas of public policy, as compared to the more dispersed political power in other nations, even in periods in which some (namely, South Korea, Singapore, and Taiwan) had authoritarian regimes. It has been able to stifle societal dissent, exercise considerable control over the distribution of the factors of production, regulate and restrict internal migration, subdue labor, and effect huge public expenditures when required to offset the business cycle. This massive, largely unchecked power, however, has not been exercised to provide greater social protection to the needy.

Social Welfare Policy in China: From the "Iron Rice Bowl" to Productivism

Social policy in China has undergone profound changes that mirror the economy's transformation toward a more market-based capitalist system. The transition has involved moving from the direct provision of social welfare by SOEs to a more complex approach that has severed most of the links between employment and social protection, shifted the delivery of services to local governments, and introduced market-based elements.[10] The government has raised social spending in the last decade, especially on health care, but continued to prioritize growth and seems even more reluctant than its peers to expand safety nets significantly.[11] A dualistic system has emerged, in which high-skill workers receive adequate social protection, but low-income individuals must rely on their families and communities, especially in rural areas. This dualism has been reinforced by a restrictive household registration system—*hukou*—that makes social and economic mobility difficult. In a nutshell, the country now exhibits productivism with Chinese characteristics.

In the prereform period, the socialist model stressed the central roles of the state and Communist Party and deemphasized the importance of families in all areas of social welfare (although in reality they carried a heavy burden). The scope of benefits was very small, however, and mainly confined to a select few, despite the promise of "cradle-to-grave" welfare. This privileged group consisted of "productive" urban workers employed by industrial SOEs; employees in the service, commercial, and financial sectors, however, were usually classified as "unproductive."[12] SOEs set aside funds to provide an "iron rice bowl" of benefits to career productive workers that included housing, education, health care, pensions, and basic income.[13] Urban residents who were not part of the state production system and the rural population received few or no services. Thus, a welfare state created by a regime that had a stated goal of eradicating income inequality ended up widening the income gap, as Nara Dillon has shown.[14] Policymakers restricted means-tested social assistance to orphans, the disabled, and the aged because they believed that more generous relief might disincentivize work and drain state resources.[15]

After the economic transition, policymakers slowly forged a society-wide welfare system to replace the firm-based one. This change was driven by necessity. As SOEs began to compete against private firms and in international markets, providing employee benefits became burdensome; the cost of benefits measured as a proportion of the total wage bill jumped from 13.7 percent in 1978 to approximately 30 percent in the early 1990s.[16] In some instances, they had to obtain additional subsidies from the state to fulfill their obligations to workers. As the losses of SOEs mounted, policymakers came to see their restructuring as a critical step in the emergence of a more productive economy. They quickly realized that devising alternative forms of delivering and funding social welfare was a prerequisite for this reform. Workers were reluctant to leave SOEs for the private sector and relinquish their welfare benefits, and they resisted the layoffs that were central to the restructuring process. Moreover, the growing number of workers in the private sector had little or no social protection. By the mid-1990s, 70 percent of workers were employed in private firms and were not covered by work-unit based welfare or government programs.

Improving social welfare services became a priority once leaders decided that an inadequate safety net threatened their political authority. In the words of Elizabeth Croll, "social welfare . . . emerged as one of the most important issues underlying a new and explicit social contract between persons and the party-state: support for its legitimacy or mandate to rule in return for social security, welfare and services."[17] In 1994, the government drew up the guidelines for a social security system that decoupled benefits from employers and, later in the decade, introduced limited forms of insurance, such as a basic pension and health care services. The changes extended to other social policy areas as well. In the housing sphere, for example, before 1978, work units normally supplied homes to their workers; after 1978, local governments, per central government directives, contracted with private developers to construct public flats and new policies discouraged SOEs from provisioning apartments to employees.

A related change, driven by a desire to reduce government spending, was diversifying delivery systems. The responsibility for social welfare benefits and activities was transferred from the central to local governments and private and nongovernmental organizations. Many welfare providers, such as health clinics, schools, and nursing homes, started offering services based on a fee structure in order to raise money to cover their costs. Market-delivered social services enabled the government to reduce its expenditures and concentrate its funding on education, health, and supplying social benefits to those truly unable to afford them. In addition, policymakers encouraged local communities and families to step up efforts to meet welfare needs, especially in rural and disadvantaged urban areas.[18]

The government had few resources during the early years of its economic transformation, but its rapid growth since that time has generated huge sums of revenue that could be dedicated to social protection.[19] Overall public spending in absolute terms surged from USD26 billion in 1980 (26.8 percent of GDP) to USD817 billion (21.5 percent of GDP) in 2021.[20] Social welfare expenditures were very low in the early 2010s but have climbed subsequently. In 2015, China expended a total of 7.7 percent of GDP on social protection, broken down into 6.9 on social insurance, 0.6 on social assistance, and 0.1 on active labor market policies (ALMPs).[21] Almost all social spending went to the nonpoor, as opposed to the poor (4.3 percent versus 0.3 percent of GDP/capita), and coverage rates for welfare programs were only 17 percent. Moreover, the government did not expand outlays appreciably as rapid modernization caused disruptive changes that increased the need for social protection. From 2009 to 2015, it raised spending on insurance, which went almost exclusively to the middle class, from 4.3 to

6.9 percent of GDP, but actually reduced assistance from 0.7 to 0.6 percent of GDP and cut ALMP expenditures by half. In 2019, total social outlays rose to 10 percent of GDP, which was comprised of 8.4 percent on insurance, 0.9 percent on assistance, and 0.6 percent on ALMPs, according to the OECD.[22] Increases in spending on insurance dwarfed those on assistance by a margin of nearly eight to one.

The family has played the primary role in offering protection against economic risk, especially for seniors. The familial support system is based on multigenerational coresidence guided by the Confucian concept of reciprocal filial piety.[23] The elderly obtain financial assistance, health care, and companionship from their adult children or extended family as gratitude for their upbringing. Public officials sought to codify the obligation of intergenerational support and care by incorporating it into the constitution and passing other measures prescribing family-based assistance, like elderly support clauses, in marriage contracts. More recently, the government has promoted Family Support Agreements (*jiating shanyang xieyi*)—voluntary but enforceable contracts that stipulate a level of support by children for elderly parents—out of concern that such assistance was declining.[24]

China initially placed less emphasis on developing human capital than other East Asian nations. It focused instead on investing in physical infrastructure and taking advantage of its low cost of manpower to fuel an export-led growth strategy. Over time, policymakers began to prioritize human capital as the country attempted to move up the ladder of comparative advantage. They have redoubled their efforts in the contemporary era as China attempts to transform from a low-cost producer and assembler of goods to competitor in knowledge-intensive sectors. Consequently, they have shifted their attention to improving the quality of primary and secondary education nationwide and increasing the enrollments and capacities of universities. One indication of this new point of emphasis is that public spending on education doubled from 1.9 percent of GDP in 1999 to 4 percent in 2021.[25]

Productivism with Chinese Characteristics

China's social welfare strategy is broadly consistent with the productivist model. The government has prioritized economic growth, especially since 1978; increased expenditures on social insurance while keeping welfare assistance to a minimum; implemented dualistic policies that favor certain classes of workers over others; and relied on extended families for social protection. More recently, policymakers have also dedicated ample resources to building human capital in ways that mirror their neighbors during their period of rapid growth. Nonetheless, two features distinctive to China—its *hukou* registration system and complex intergovernmental structure—set it apart from its peers.

THE *HUKOU* HOUSEHOLD REGISTRATION SYSTEM

A feature unique to Chinese social policy is that the government delivers social services to individuals based on their residential status or household registration, called *hukou*. The government introduced the *hukou* system in the 1950s to enable the state to control the internal flow of people. Individuals seeking to move had to obtain permission to reside (temporarily) in a new locale or attempt to live outside the system altogether.[26] The system played a vital role in economic policy. Public officials viewed rural residents as being a critical piece for supporting industrialization since they produced the foodstuffs required for the subsistence of urban workers. *Hukou* enabled them to block rural to urban migration as necessary in order to prevent a decline in agricultural production as well as overcrowding of urban areas.

An individual's *hukou* status moves with them, so if a woman migrates from a rural to an urban area, she continues to receive benefits intended for rural not urban residents. Thus, migrants are not eligible for the welfare services reserved for permanent residents in their new locality, such as health care, pensions, housing, and children's schooling. This policy was meant to make workers more productive by encouraging them to leave their children behind when they relocated and, hence, not waste time and energy on child-rearing.[27] Some scholars have contended that this feature of *hukou* created an underclass of low-cost workers that could be called upon as needed for industrialization efforts without having to permit them to live permanently in urban areas. In other countries, migration to urban areas creates economic opportunities for poor rural residents and gives family members access to better education and health services, encouraging upward mobility across generations.[28] The *hukou* system has mostly blocked this critical means of social mobility, at least until very recently.

Urban residents always have received far more generous benefits than the rural population.[29] Under Mao, political leaders proclaimed that the government would take direct responsibility for the social welfare of urban dwellers, but rural communities were expected to be self-reliant. The commitment to urban workers stemmed from their central role in the process of modernization, particularly industrialization. In addition, officials feared that urban residents were more likely to cause unrest because they could organize more easily and had better access to ideas that challenged the status quo. The benefits provided to urban inhabitants included ration cards, housing, health care, education for their children, unemployment insurance, retirement benefits, and even arranged employment.[30] With the exception of educational facilities and care for the aged funded by local enterprises, government-subsidized services in rural areas were limited to a minimal safety net for those unable to work, such as the disabled and veterans; others were obliged to rely on family or neighbors for support. Since rural inhabitants were also excluded from most services when they migrated to urban areas, they often ended up recreating a similar type of self-provisioning welfare system in their new locale.[31]

Criticism of the sharp disparity in social welfare benefits has prodded the central government to step up its efforts to improve rural services, as well as reduce the differences in treatment between permanent and temporary urban residents. In 2014, the central government announced the National New-Type Urbanization Plan and State Council Opinions on Further Promoting the Household Registration System Reform. These directives gave local governments greater freedom to set rules covering *hukou* registrations and stipulated that migrants and locals should have equal rights and benefits henceforth.[32] It instructed smaller cities to abolish their registration system completely and larger municipalities to relax restrictions. In response, major cities like Shanghai established a point system for gaining household registration that was designed to attract young high-skill individuals, but becoming permanent residents remained out of reach for many regular workers. The government met its goal of one hundred million new urban *hukou* registrations by 2020, but the migrant population grew much faster than expected, resulting in an even larger percentage of the urban population without a local registration than previously. The so-called urban social benefits deficit—the percentage of the population without access to services provided to permanent residents—grew from 18.5 to 26.6 percent, instead of falling to the target of 15 percent.[33] A barrier to increasing the number of urban *hukou* registrations moving forward is resistance by municipalities that do not possess the financial resources to supply social services for a larger population. The lack of funding is partly a product of China's decentralized governmental structure, to which we now turn.

CHINA'S INTERGOVERNMENTAL STRUCTURE

China is a unitary state with five tiers of government: central, provincial, prefectural, county, and township. The intergovernmental structure has profoundly influenced the design, implementation, and results of social policy. The central government sets social policy goals for the nation but subnational governments, which have enjoyed a high degree of autonomy historically, execute its directives.[34] They raise the majority of funds expended on social protection, design and implement welfare programs, and allocate available resources within their communities. The financial and administrative capacity of local governments is thus a critical factor in the national government's ability to achieve policy goals. The unevenness of social welfare outcomes across provinces and cities nationwide is partly due to the variation in the competency of local and state officials.

Intergovernmental relations have been an obstacle to the successful implementation of several major initiatives, notably, the expansion of public housing. The problem resides in the distinct preferences and motivations of officials at different levels of government. In particular, the financial incentives of local officers are frequently not aligned with the goals of national policy. Subnational governments account for 85 percent of all public expenditures in China (the highest percentage worldwide), yet they only raise 60 percent of all tax revenue.[35] The central government establishes the rates for all major taxes, so local officials are unable to hike them in order to secure more funds. Consequently, they rely heavily on transfers from the national government to finance programming. Transfers fluctuate depending on economic conditions and are seldom sufficient to cover all spending; in point of fact, subnational governments have run large deficits consistently since 1994, when the current fiscal system was created. This reality has pushed them to seek other means of raising money and these often undermine national policy objectives. The propensity to reclassify and sell prime land to private developers to maximize revenue as opposed to using it to expand quality public housing or achieve other social objectives is a good example of this. In addition, local officials generally are more concerned with maintaining growth instead of providing better social services because their career prospects often are determined by how well they fare in the intense competition with other cities for the best economic performance.[36]

Challenges Facing the Chinese Productivist Model

China's social welfare system confronts challenges similar to those its East Asian peers face, namely, globalization and technological change, exacting demographic trends, intense urbanization, and fundamental shifts in family structure. Moreover, it must tackle these threats while having to create a safety net essentially from scratch. In contrast, neighboring nations confront the easier task of modifying or, more likely, expanding their existing welfare programs. China's burden is also greater because unprecedented migration from rural to urban areas in combination with a stringent household registration system and intrusive family planning measures have amplified the potency of these four macro level forces.

Globalization and Technological Change

China plunged into international markets with the launch of its Open Door policy. In a relatively short time, it became the world's largest trading nation in terms of absolute volume. Policymakers also encouraged FDI, which brought in new technology and designed policies to connect domestic firms to international supply chains. Chinese firms adopted new technologies at a rapid pace as they rushed to modernize and become competitive.[37] The country's opening precipitated a massive wave of changes throughout the economy, notably, the shift of huge amounts of resources, especially workers, from rural to urban areas. Skill-biased technical change altered modes of production and shifted the relative demand for different types of labor. Displaced workers were exposed to new types of economic insecurity as they transitioned into new sectors or became unemployed.

Globalization and technical change had a profound impact on social conditions. Wages for urban workers soared, and their households experienced a rapid and sustained improvement in standards of living; the level of absolute poverty in rural areas also declined sharply. Nonetheless, disparities in income climbed, and the mounting demand for more skilled and educated workers drove up the wage premium for college graduates. The premium was very low in the command-and-control economy, but, by 2013, the rate of return on attending college had risen to 54 to 76 percent, and obtaining a postsecondary degree raised it to 59 to 90 percent.[38] China's Gini coefficient leapt from 0.310 in 1980 to 0.481 in 2010; inequality within both rural and urban communities increased, as did the gap between urban and rural areas.[39] High-skill workers in urban centers have attained an excellent quality of life, but low-skill laborers have experienced much smaller gains. Moreover, as the basis for much of China's traditional economic activity—low wages and other production costs—erodes further and the country intensifies its push into artificial intelligence (AI) and robotics, the disparity between different types of workers is likely to grow further, and those with fewer skills will be exposed to even more economic risk.

As discussed throughout this book, high inequality presents numerous challenges for policymakers. Investments in human capital have the potential to alleviate income disparities if they create more options for low-income and high-income individuals alike. As it attempts to upgrade its economy toward knowledge-intensive industries, China has focused on human capital development, particularly through improvements in education, and this may end up generating more opportunities for all, but that outcome is far from guaranteed.

Demographic Trends: Low Fertility and the Graying of Society

Like other East Asian societies, China has experienced dropping fertility rates and rapid aging of the population. Its total fertility was as high as 6.16 in 1965, but fell below the replacement rate in 1993 and collapsed to a new low of 1.16 in 2021.[40] The government implemented stringent family planning measures in the past, including the infamous one-child policy (1979) that imposed fines on couples that had more than a single child.[41] The evidence suggests, however, that this policy played only a minor role in bringing down the birth rate.[42] Most of the decline was due to the same factors that have led to decreases in other nations, namely, larger incomes, increased levels of education, higher costs of raising children, later marriages, and the changing roles of women. Officials replaced the one-child with a two-child policy in October 2015 in an effort to boost fertility.[43] The announcement led to an initial jump in births in 2016 but, as demographers predicted, the policy shift was not sufficient to reverse the trend in fertility. Undaunted, policymakers introduced a three-child policy in 2021.

China will soon have the largest elderly population in the world in absolute terms. The number of citizens aged sixty or above reached 257 million in 2021, which represented 18.1 percent of the population. It is expected to reach 487 million, or 38.8 percent of the population, in 2050.[44] This enormous pool of seniors will require more government services, such as old age assistance and health care. Yet, the country's capacity to provide this support is in doubt as the age dependency ratio will triple to 51.5 elderly per one hundred people of working age, up from nineteen in 2021.[45] The ability of China's pension system to meet future challenges is discussed in a later section.

Urbanization

China has experienced the most intense urbanization in world history. In 2022, 65.2 percent of the population lived in urban areas, up from 19.4 and 50 percent in 1980 and 2010, respectively.[46] Urbanization deepened after 2000, largely driven by massive rural to urban migration. According to the 2020 census, China's "floating population" was 375.8 million people, up by almost 70 percent from 2010.[47] The number of rural migrants working in urban areas, particularly along the east coast, rose to 295.6 million, which represented roughly one-third of the national workforce.[48] The government has also encouraged urbanization as a policy goal in recent years. In 2014, Xi Jinping's government announced a plan to move an additional 250 million people to cities by 2026 by relocating rural residents and constructing entirely new cities.[49]

Urbanization on such a large scale has created numerous social policy challenges. The surge in urban population has overwhelmed delivery systems in many municipalities, leading to deterioration in the quality and reach of social services. Even if migrants are not eligible for specific services, they still may contribute to higher demand. For instance, overcrowding may have played a role in the large price increases that have pushed many households out of the quality housing market or made private schooling prohibitively expensive in some localities. As we discuss later, these developments have contributed to child maltreatment in Chinese cities for reasons that were discussed at length in chapter 4.

Migrant workers and their families in urban areas are particularly exposed to economic insecurity and have a greater need for social protection. These individuals often hold low-paying, insecure jobs with irregular hours and lack even the most basic of formal safety nets in the event of a loss in income. Moreover, intense urbanization and ambitious city restructuring have led to the dismantling of informal employment-based welfare networks that once channeled community assistance in times of need.[50] The problems associated with urbanization, however, are not limited to the cities to which migrants move. As we discuss later, the children of rural migrants who stay behind are frequently victims of neglect, physical and sexual abuse, mental health issues, and physical illness.[51] Left-behind older adults also face difficulties such as depression, loneliness, and poverty.

Changes in Family Structure

The traditional family-based welfare system that has long served as a private safety net in China is weakening as the structure of the family undergoes changes, threatening a critical pillar in its approach to social protection. Multigenerational families are giving way to increasingly smaller nuclear units. Adult children are fewer in number and are frequently less able or willing to contribute much to their parent's welfare. Less than half (41 percent) of Chinese over age sixty lived with their adult children in the period 2011 to 2012.[52] Changes in family structure are due to several factors: weakening Confucian values, particularly filial piety; a decline in fertility; higher divorce rates; urbanization; and mass migration that has dispersed family members, creating left-behind children and seniors.

Similar to other East Asian societies, the norm of children's obligation to help their elderly parents is waning, and they now provide less assistance in adulthood.[53] As noted earlier, recognition of this trend has led to a government effort to require adult children to provide care to their aged parents through marriage contracts and Family Support Agreements. Young Chinese are more focused on their careers and individual interests, marry later, divorce more frequently, and are more willing to live far from home. Financial aid for elderly dependents can be provided at a distance, but other crucial forms of support, such as help with day-to-day activities, cannot. A growing pool of well-educated working women have chosen to exit the marriage market altogether, decreasing the supply of daughters-in-law to care for seniors. Even in cases where children wish to support their elders, it is frequently more difficult to do so. The total fertility rate in China dropped to 1.16 since 2021, well below the replacement rate. Many households, especially in urban areas, have only one child, putting a large and often unbearable burden on them to assist elderly parents. A growing number of couples have no children at all; the number of childless seniors is forecast to rise from 3.5 million in 2005 to ten million by 2035.[54]

Social Welfare Crises in China

The effectiveness of China's social policy model is being undermined by globalization and technological change, demographic trends, urbanization, and changes in family structure. Previous chapters found that these same forces have vitiated the capacity of other East Asian societies to address crises in old age living conditions, household wages, child welfare, and housing markets. China confronts similar—if not greater—challenges in these same policy areas. The country's unprecedented internal migration and intense urbanization, dependence on local governments to implement policy, stringent *hukou* registration system, and intrusive family planning measures pose additional difficulties in managing these social ills. We examine each one of these social crises in the Chinese context in turn.

Old Age Poverty

China has experienced a high level of old age poverty. In the past decade, the government has succeeded in reducing the level of absolute elderly poverty considerably, but the relative level remains high. The number of poor older adults in China is gravely concerning from a humanitarian perspective because it has the largest senior population in the world. In 2021, 24 percent of the world's population over the age of sixty lived in China.

The Chinese government has measured poverty using an absolute standard in contrast to most developed countries that use a relative measure, such as incomes at or below 50 or 60 percent of the national median. Additionally, it has adopted a poverty line of just USD2.25 per day for rural areas (no official line exists for urban settings), not the rate that the World Bank typically applies to upper middle-income countries like China: USD6.85.[55] Jinquan Gong and colleagues used the official rate to measure rural poverty and adjusted it to compute urban poverty by applying a multiplier of 1.412. They determined that the overall elderly poverty rate was 35.2 percent in 2011 but fell to 13.1 percent in 2020. The difference between elderly poverty in urban and rural areas was stark: 4.3 percent in urban versus 16.8 percent in rural areas.[56] Björn Gustafsson and Ding Sai calculated rates in urban China using various concepts of relative poverty. They found that the elderly poverty rate in 2013 was 12 and 18.1 percent using the 50 percent and 60 percent of median income measures, respectively, and it had risen steadily since 1998.[57] Whatever the exact rate, the low-income levels of many older adults continue to lead to serious mental and physical ills. A third of seniors are in poor physical health, 40 percent show signs of depression, and the elderly suicide rate is high and climbing.[58]

One reason for high elderly poverty is that many individuals enter retirement without sufficient savings. Core household expenditures have risen in recent years, making it more difficult for individuals to smooth consumption over their lifetimes by saving during their working years. Expenditures on education and health, for instance, have surged, straining the budgets of low-income households in particular.[59] In addition, China's early retirement policy restricts the period of time individuals have to accumulate savings. China has a very low average retirement age of around fifty-four years, compared to the OECD average of sixty-four years.[60] The country's archaic retirement law enacted in the late 1970s has yet to be updated to reflect the dramatic improvement in life expectancy, from fifty-nine in 1970 to seventy-eight years in 2020.[61] Forcing individuals to quit work at a young age has augmented the economic insecurity of older women in particular. Women white-collar professionals (e.g., medical personnel, teachers, and administrators) are mandated to stop working at fifty-five and women blue-collar laborers at fifty in an effort to compel them to serve as caregivers for their aging parents.[62] Women were paid about 72 percent of what men earned on average (in 2015) and had a longer life expectancy (eighty-one versus seventy-five for men in 2020), so their shortened, lower-paying careers in conjunction with extended lifespans heightened their risk of falling into old age poverty.[63]

The family has been the first line of defense against elderly poverty historically, especially in rural areas where the majority of the aged have resided. Seniors are increasingly unable to rely on the resources of household members, however, because of the changes in family structure. Consequently, the government-sponsored social security system is fast becoming the primary contingency plan for many elderly persons. The Chinese government has managed to create a national pension system that provides nearly universal coverage for the adult population (a little over one billion people) in a short period, which is a remarkable achievement. As in the case of other social protection schemes, however, a startling gap in the benefits afforded salaried urban versus rural or migrant workers is evident. The government has erected a policy façade that follows a familiar productivist logic: It confers adequate old age protection to skilled and educated workers that are vital to economic growth but neglects others. Although it has begun to extend coverage to previously excluded groups, the benefits provided are so meager that they must continue to rely on other sources of income almost exclusively. The dualism is of sufficient magnitude to exacerbate national income inequality.[64]

China introduced a two-tier pension system for urban workers in 1998 that is administered by provincial governments; it was revised significantly in 2006. The first tier consists of the Basic Old Age Insurance (BOAI), which is funded by employers. It requires employees to have a minimum of fifteen years of contributions and "pays 1 percent of the average of the indexed individual wage and the province-wide average earnings for each year of coverage."[65] The second tier, which is not available in all provinces, consists of a defined contributions scheme in which the employee contributes 8 percent of their salary and employers approximately 20 percent (later reduced to 16 percent). Select groups of workers also have access to two supplementary plans that have appended a third tier to the pension system. One is the Employer-Sponsored Annuity program that is administered by large SOEs and had approximately 27 million participants (about 3.5 percent of all workers) in 2020. In 2022, the government also allowed urban workers to open private individual retirement accounts.[66] In sum, urban workers have multiple layers of old-age protection and benefits are substantial: the average income replacement rate is equivalent to about 50 percent of the average wage of the entire pool of urban employees.[67] These schemes covered 503 million people at the end of 2022, which represented 71 percent of urban workers.[68]

Workers in rural areas and the unemployed or flexible workers in urban settings have not fared as well. They were excluded from the national pension system until 2009 and still receive very little government support. Policymakers introduced two voluntary programs, funded by individual contributions with partial government subsidies as needed: the Urban Resident Pension scheme (2009), which covered urban unemployed residents, and the New Rural Pension program (2011), which protected rural workers. The two programs were merged in 2014 under the Urban and Rural Residents Pension Scheme (URRPS).[69] Although 549 million people were insured by the URRPS at the end of 2022, their benefit rate is far too low to act as a safeguard against poverty. The average monthly payment in the URRPS was only 179 yuan (about USD25), as compared with 3,326 yuan (about USD460) in the BOAI.[70] The disparity in overall spending on the two programs is even more pronounced. Expenditures on the BOAI were equivalent to 5 percent of GDP in 2019, whereas those on the URRPS amounted to just 0.3 percent.[71]

The old age security system has two additional gaps in coverage. First, new migrant workers are seldom enrolled in the BOAI because obtaining urban *hukou* registration takes considerable time, if it can be done at all. In 2017, only approximately 22 percent of migrant workers received a basic pension (or medical insurance).[72] Second, most women engaged in informal employment are not included in national pension programs. These gaps are detrimental because if these individuals fall into poverty as seniors, which is likely, they are forced to rely on the country's meager safety net: the Minimum Living Standard Assurance program (commonly known as Dibao). The Dibao program has limited funding, estimated to be between 0.25 and 0.33 percent of GDP, and falls far short of addressing elderly poverty effectively.[73] It has tight eligibility rules, delivers inadequate benefits in general, has targeting errors, and provides less social protection to the rural population where the need is greatest. Jennifer Pan has suggested that policymakers have reshaped Dibao from a vehicle to alleviate poverty to a tool of surveillance and repression.[74] She warned that this transformation has the potential to diminish the legitimacy of the government and feed resentment among those denied benefits.

The lack of old age insurance has had the most severe consequences for the largest groups of seniors in China—migrants and those residing in rural areas. They typically have fewer savings than workers in urban areas because of lower lifetime earnings and must rely on increasingly uncertain financial support from their children. Some elderly orphans who no longer live with their spouses or children are taking the extreme step of putting themselves up for adoption.[75] At the macro level, the lack of adequate pensions may become a drag on economic growth by forcing individuals to save too much during their working years, hindering the government's efforts to develop an economy that is based on domestic consumption instead of exports.

The pension system itself is coming under strain. Studies have concluded that the system's finances are not sustainable given the rapidly increasing number of retired persons and old-age dependency ratio. Moreover, the average age of migrant workers is rising much more quickly than that of urban workers, and they will soon swell the ranks of the elderly.[76] Any effort to bring their very low benefit levels more in line with those of urban workers will have a ruinous impact on the viability of the pension system. Both the BOAI and URRPS are already projected to show a deficit in 2028 and run out of funds sometime around 2035.[77] Raising the retirement age and adjusting contributions are critical steps to improving sustainability but will not solve the problems of insufficient financing and inequity completely. Some scholars have suggested that the only viable solution is to create a single centrally coordinated national pension system that covers all citizens irrespective of their geographic or registration status, but as of 2023 this does not seem probable. Thus far the government has shown its enduring bias in favor of urban workers by dedicating funds to shoring up the BOAI as opposed to raising benefit levels in the URRPS.[78] This suggests that old age poverty is likely to persist in rural areas and among the many millions of migrants who have toiled tirelessly to fuel China's economic success story.

Labor Markets and Trends in Wages

In the command-and-control economy era, planners in the Bureau of Labour and Personnel determined the allocation of labor and wage levels. They kept salaries low to minimize production costs, confident that state-subsidized food and the welfare benefits provided by enterprises would be sufficient to maintain labor peace. They established eight pay grades for factory workers and technicians and twenty-four for administrative and managerial personnel. Differences in pay among the grades were small and raises were based on seniority rather than performance.[79] These rules gave workers little incentive to excel at their jobs and, hence, firms were plagued by low productivity and poor allocation of available manpower.

Wages rose with the transition toward a market economy as firms, especially in the private sector, were permitted to pay higher salaries and compensate more productive employees with better pay. Workers also had greater freedom to switch employers in search of better compensation, albeit within the confines of the *hukou* system. The competition from the private sector for quality workers sped up reform in SOEs and pushed up salaries in all categories of firms in a very short period. Compensation also surged because rapid economic growth (averaging close to 10 percent annually) steadily raised the demand for workers and nonagricultural productivity climbed, increasing the marginal product of labor. Finally, labor force growth slowed starting in 2000 because of declining fertility, contributing to labor shortages in some regions that added to wage pressure.[80]

The increase in earnings for Chinese workers of all skill levels nationwide has been substantial, but the largest gains have accrued to high-skill workers in urban areas along the East Coast. Data limitations make it difficult to measure longitudinal trends precisely, but average salaries have risen by many multiples since the start of China's transition to a market economy.[81] Real annual wage growth was slow until the mid-1990s but accelerated to an average of 7.6 percent from 2012 to 2021.[82] One reason for the rapid decline in the level of absolute poverty was that even the earnings of workers in the lowest income decile rose by 61 percent in the period 1980 to 2015.[83] Average wages did not keep up with improvements in labor productivity, however, leading to a widening gap between workers' compensation and average labor output.[84] As in other East Asian economies, one consequence of this trend was a decline in labor's share of national income by 12.5 percent from 1978 to 2007, to about 45 percent; in other words, the owners of capital captured a disproportionate share of the fruits of the productivity increase.[85] Some authors have claimed that low-skill workers will face more difficult conditions moving forward as Chinese manufacturing firms contract or move operations offshore.[86]

The education premium in China was very low in the command-and-control economy since wage scales were compressed by design. During the Cultural Revolution, more educated individuals, who were often the target of Mao's reeducation efforts, sometimes earned even less than manual laborers. The premium grew quickly after 1978 as decentralized market forces generated greater demand for workers with higher levels of education. This trend intensified in the 1990s as the Chinese economy modernized and shifted toward complex economic activities requiring a highly skilled workforce. The rate of return on schooling rose dramatically, from 4 percent in 1988 to 10.2 percent in 2001.[87] This leap occurred despite a large increase in the supply of more educated individuals. Average years of schooling went up and the percentage of workers with a college degree jumped from 13 percent in 1988 to 28 percent in 2001. The initial surge in demand for skilled labor outpaced the growth in supply and, therefore, wages for this group of workers continued to ascend. Educational achievement was (and remains) the primary means by which rural residents were able to migrate into better paying jobs in urban settings.

Estimates of the education premium in China vary considerably due to different data sets and methodologies but it is, by all accounts, very large in comparative terms and has not stopped climbing.[88] Le Wang reported that the premium enjoyed by college-educated workers was 37.8 and 87.9 percent in 1995 and 2002, respectively.[89] Xinyang Chang found that the premium for workers with a junior college education or above was 45.4 percent in 2007.[90] Xiaohua Feng concluded that the education premium in high-skill and low-skill manufacturing sectors was 160 and 173 percent, respectively, in 2008, and that it had risen substantially since 2001.[91] Qiao Wen calculated that the rate of return to attending college was between 54 and 76 percent and obtaining a postsecondary degree between 59 and 90 percent in 2013.[92] The greatest returns on education have probably been in the high-tech sector. Worker compensation has gone up the most in Beijing and Shenzhen, where many technology companies are located.[93] These firms have heavily recruited college graduates in STEM fields, often attempting to lure workers away from rival firms, both domestic and foreign. Many of the foreign workers are Taiwanese so, in one sense, that nation has exported wage increases for its best workers to the Chinese mainland instead of benefiting from them itself. In the last decade, the supply of college graduates in China has expanded and many are encountering difficulties in landing suitable jobs, so future trends in the education wage premium are uncertain.

The jump in the education premium since 1978 has contributed to the surge in inequality that China has experienced since its transition. Its posttax and transfers Gini coefficient leapt from 0.310 in 1980 to a high of 0.491 in 2008. The coefficient leveled off and even declined slightly afterwards (it was 0.466 in 2021). This decrease has been due to a fall in the share of the top income quintile—a consequence of the introduction of a more progressive income tax—and gains for the middle of the income distribution, not an increase in the share of the bottom 30 percent.[94] Labor market trends suggest that additional government efforts will be needed to reduce inequality further, both in incomes and across provinces. High inequality has already fed resentment among low-income individuals and contributed to social protests, putting pressure on Communist Party leadership to act more forcefully.[95]

The government has largely ignored the plight of low-skill workers, as in the case of Taiwan, opting to construct a policy façade instead of pursuing a more progressive labor market policy. Spending on ALMPs, which once averaged 0.1 percent of GDP, jumped up to 0.6 percent in 2019.[96] Nevertheless, the primary policy, called Employment First, is geared toward creating jobs for college-educated adults (the target in 2019 was eleven million positions), not helping low-skill workers through public employment training (as in Singapore).[97] Youth unemployment has become a highly salient issue in the last decade as more recent college graduates have refused to accept low skill jobs, pushing the rate to 20 percent in April 2023.[98] Passive labor market policies (PLMPs) have also provided meager support. Unemployment insurance covered less than half of urban workers and in 2020 only 5.2 million people out of the twenty-six million unemployed actually received benefits.[99] Some regional governments have occasionally cut firm contribution levels in an effort to boost output by reducing business costs and enforcement of rules is weak.

Finally, policymakers have yet to make use of income support programs for low-income workers (and their households) apart from the minimum wage. They introduced a comprehensive minimum wage policy in 2004 (after a half-hearted attempt in the early 1990s). Minimum wages are set at the provincial level and vary greatly across provinces and even within them by design.[100] They are fixed through negotiations involving local government officials, labor unions, business associations, and the chamber of commerce, and adjusted every two years. Regional variation is mostly due to differences in levels of output and income, but one study determined that subnational governments also use the minimum wage for political ends.[101] Economic performance plays a large role in promotion decisions so local officials have an incentive to increase the minimum wage to attract the attention of political superiors by signaling that their province is a top performer.

Child Maltreatment

Official data do not exist, but a sizable literature has determined that child maltreatment is pervasive in China. Over fifty provincial- or city-level studies were conducted in the last two decades and they found a high prevalence of child maltreatment. A meta-analysis of ten surveys conducted across the country estimated that the child maltreatment rate was 54 percent and indicated that the predominant forms were physical and emotional abuse and neglect.[102] A review of thirty-two studies that polled college students calculated that 64.7 percent had experienced childhood maltreatment.[103] Though gender-differentiated data are scarce, some researchers have ascertained that Chinese boys are more likely to experience severe parental abuse than girls. This is because parents expect boys "to take over the family lineage and business," whereas they treat daughters as "outsiders" who leave the family when they marry.[104] Unlike neighboring societies, where high profile incidents generally involve abuse or neglect in the home, the Chinese media most frequently publishes articles on physical and sexual abuse in schools and at health care providers.[105]

The government's response thus far has been more limited than the policy façade of detection without protection observed in Japan and South Korea. China ratified the United Nations Convention on the Rights of the Child in 1992 but only defined child abuse and neglect officially in the 2015 Family Violence Law. Policymakers have not created the basic public infrastructure for reporting incidents or established social service networks and child welfare agencies to protect and rehabilitate victims. Cultural and legal institutions have hindered the development of a national child protection system even as some risk factors for abuse, such as urbanization and migration, grow unabated. The country's idiosyncratic family planning policies and *hukou* registry system have amplified the impact of these factors, putting millions of children at risk of maltreatment in both urban and rural areas.

The economic cost of child abuse was estimated to be more than 1.5 percent of GDP in 2010: 0.84 percent (USD50 billion) from physical abuse, 0.47 (USD28 billion) from emotional abuse, and 0.39 percent (USD23 billion) from sexual abuse.[106] This was a conservative number since these calculations did not include the toll of child maltreatment related deaths. In addition, these figures did not take account into incidents of neglect, which can be as emotionally and economically costly as physical and verbal abuse.

The causes of child maltreatment in China are similar to those identified in the comparative literature, but also involve a few unique factors. Consistent with earlier findings, one study observed a positive association between neglect and the number of disabled children and unemployed persons in a family, younger mothers, parents with less education, and weak family support networks.[107] The stressors typical of urban areas—overcrowding, precarious employment, poor living conditions, and weak supportive networks—put additional strain on child-rearing, creating a high-risk environment for abuse and neglect. As elsewhere in the region, cultural and legal frameworks have supported uncontested parental authority, even treating measures such as restraining and beatings as legitimate disciplinary actions until the enactment of 2015 Family Violence Law. Some scholars have argued that reluctance on the part of Chinese policymakers and society at large to be more protective of children's rights is due to the perception that child abuse is an imported Western concept.[108] The media has continued to report that many cases of child maltreatment are not prosecuted vigorously, especially if they involve public officials, despite the new law.[109]

Social protection for unmarried parents and their offspring—a group deemed at high risk for maltreatment—is weak in China, as it is in other East Asian nations. Many households headed by unmarried parents are not entitled to health insurance or employer-supplied maternity leave, making it difficult for mothers to give their children proper care. The government has created an additional burden by making out-of-wedlock children illegal under population and family planning law and permitting provincial governments to impose an administrative fine called the social support expenditure on unmarried parents.[110] This practice has resulted in underreporting of out-of-wedlock children, complicating efforts to obtain accurate figures on the purported rise in single parenthood and the number of children affected.

What truly sets China apart from other countries, however, are how its unprecedented rural to urban migration, rigid household registration system, and intense urbanization have contributed to child maltreatment. The mass migration of rural residents to cities has broken up families and damaged community networks critical for mutual support in rural areas and the networks that spring up in urban areas are inadequate to serve this function. The national government issued a new set of guidelines in 2016 encouraging migrant parents to bring along their children, but they have faced challenges in doing so because they continue to lack access to social services, notably, housing and schooling, and their low pay renders private options unaffordable.[111] In 2020, seventy-one million migrant children resided with their parents in their new location, whereas sixty-seven million remained in their hometown.[112] Of those left behind in rural villages, thirty million boys and girls were housed in state boarding schools and had very little contact with their immediate and extended families.[113] The children of migrant workers in cities have not fared much better since their parents confront multiple challenges in providing them with adequate care.

> The vast majority of migrant workers . . . simply do not have the time, ability or resources to provide their children with the support they need. They are either physically separated for long periods of time, work long and anti-social hours, or lack the education needed to help their children with their schoolwork. Most migrant workers spend far less time reading to their children and helping with their homework than their middle-class urban counterparts and cannot afford to pay for the books and extra-curricular activities urban children take for granted.[114]

Child abuse and neglect in China are widespread in both urban and rural areas, unlike most developed countries where they are more prevalent in cities. A 2019 white paper on the mental status of left-behind children revealed that in the largely rural Jiangxi, Anhui, and Yunnan provinces, 65.1 percent of children suffered physical abuse, 91.3 percent mental abuse, 30.6 percent sexual abuse, and 40.6 percent suffered from neglect; 14 percent had experienced all four categories of mistreatment.[115] A 2013 study conducted in Anhui province determined that over 50 percent were abused by their temporary caregivers.[116] The lack of guardianship also made left-behind girls vulnerable to sexual assault and harassment. The Women's Federation of Guangdong Province, for example, found that left-behind girls accounted for 94 percent of sex crime victims in Huazhou.[117] As a result, these children were reported to have a higher incidence of a range of behavioral and mental health issues and perform more poorly in school than their peers.[118]

The extent of child abuse in urban settings is equally staggering. Studies conducted in the major cities of Guangzhou and Changsha found that 27 and 62 percent of surveyed children experienced abuse in the former and latter, respectively.[119] Migrant girls in urban centers are at especially high risk; one study determined that they made up 88 percent of sexual assault victims in some districts of Shenzhen.[120]

China's one-child policy (1979–2015) also compounded the risk for children nationwide. The "onlies" (commonly referred to as the little emperors or little suns) are perceived as more egocentric and harder to discipline (due to over-indulgence and overprotection), and parents may resort to extreme measures including violence to instill parental authority.[121] Furthermore, under the one child policy, a forbidden second child (*heihaizi* or illegal child) was barred from being registered in the *hukou* system.[122] They are thus largely invisible to the relevant authorities and more vulnerable to maltreatment. The national government recently ordered local governments to provide health care and education to *heihaizi*, but many of them still have restricted access to social services.

National and subnational governments are ill-equipped to undertake the task of addressing child abuse.[123] The central government spent a scant 0.2 percent of GDP on child welfare assistance in 2009 (the latest year for which there are data) and the agencies that oversee children's well-being have been reluctant to acknowledge that child mistreatment is a serious issue.[124] Children's calls for help are ignored routinely, as mandatory reporting requirements are still relatively new, coordination of professionals (e.g., police, doctors, teachers) to identify and protect victims is inadequate, and healthcare professionals lack the training and confidence to intervene in suspected cases.[125] The effective coverage of government protection programs was an astonishingly low 3 percent of children nationwide in 2020 (up only slightly from 2.2 percent in 2009).[126]

In conclusion, Chinese policymakers have only just started to react in the face of abundant evidence that a maltreatment crisis is taking place and likely to persist since trends like mass migration continue unabated. Their failure to act has put millions of the country's most vulnerable citizens at high risk of distress and may jeopardize social stability and economic performance in the future as the current generation matures into adults.

Affordable Housing

China's housing policy has undergone the greatest transformation of any nation in East Asia. Until 1978, most homes in China were publicly owned and allocated through work units (*danwei*) as part of the enterprise-based welfare system.[127] Housing built and managed by state-work units comprised between 60 to 75 percent of the total urban stock; municipal public housing, which mostly consisted of poor-quality, nationalized private flats built before 1949, made up the rest. The government owned all urban land and controlled the production, operation, financing, and pricing of residential properties.[128] Chronic underinvestment in housing stock led to serious shortages of units in major cities and poor living standards for residents. Homes in rural areas were self-built and privately owned.

Housing policy changed course as China transitioned from direct state provision of social welfare services to a more market-oriented approach. The government shifted from supplying apartments through SOEs to encouraging private developers to meet the ever-growing need for flats by building affordable units for sale or rent and constructing "commodity" housing for purchase on the open market.[129] In other words, the distribution of housing changed radically from in-kind and free to monetary and market-based. Access to the various types of affordable housing for sale—so-called economic comfortable housing, capped price housing, and shared ownership housing—was means-tested and intended solely for those who did not own a home. The category named cheap rental housing was also means-tested and supplied only to the poorest families who lacked the means of owning property. Developers of affordable units were entitled to earn a maximum profit of only between 3 to 5 percent over construction costs. The government also returned confiscated private property to their previous owners, transferred some of the burden of public housing costs to urban residents by gradually increasing their rent, and privatized much of the public stock of homes by selling existing rental units to tenants. By 2011, approximately 90 percent of urban residents owned their own residence and 10 percent were in rental units.[130]

Housing inequality was evident from the start of the transformation of government policy and worsened over time. Access to most public units was based strictly on the *hukou* system. Local residence was required to purchase a dwelling and certain vocations enjoyed preferential treatment. Migrant workers were excluded from all public flats except public rental housing.[131] This type of housing emerged in several Southern cities in 2008 and had no means-test or residency requirement (though a temporary living permit was obligatory), but it was priced just below private market rates making it very expensive.[132] Thus, migrants often had to settle for substandard living conditions, such as residing in upcycled shipping containers or being crowded into small, dilapidated units, or live far from their workplace. This disadvantage exacerbated already existing disparities in employment opportunities that greatly favored urban residents.[133]

Housing policy proceeded in an ad hoc fashion until the announcement of the Decision on Deepening the Urban Housing Reform in 1994. This reform definitively ended the in-kind distribution of flats, altered the system of home ownership from public to private, and instituted market rates for public rentals.[134] In 1998, local governments began providing cash subsidies to private developers to encourage construction. The subsidy policy was triggered by the economic downturn that followed the East Asian financial crisis and worries about the rapid growth of public expenditures on housing.[135] The authorities' goal was to divide the housing market into three segments: 70 to 80 percent affordable flats built by subsidized private developers, 10 to 15 percent high-quality private apartments for upper income families, and 10 to 15 percent subsidized units supplied by employers or municipalities.[136] The government also created the Housing Provident Fund (HPF) in 1999 to assist urban workers in the purchase of homes. The HPF was financed by contributions from both employers and employees.[137] By 2000, between 60 to 80 percent of the population, primarily lower- and middle-class households, lived in affordable units built by private developers receiving subsidies.

The supply of housing in cities, however, could not keep up with the incredible surge in demand fueled by rapid urbanization and this led to soaring prices after 2000, especially in the eastern provinces.[138] Elites were still able to purchase luxury flats in prime neighborhoods, but salaried workers frequently had to commute long distances in order to obtain affordable homes. To make matters worse, some wealthy individuals purchased dwellings, often two or three at a time, as investment vehicles instead of residences.[139] In 2022, the vacancy rates in first-tier, second-tier, and third-tier cities were 7, 12, and 16 percent, respectively, which are very high by global standards.[140]

By 2010, the widening gap in access to quality flats was exacerbating tensions over rising income inequality. Affordability became a major element of the broader social justice initiatives that emerged from Hu Jintao's vision of the "harmonious society" (2006) that sought to improve political and social stability.[141] In addition, policymakers viewed the expansion of inexpensive housing as a key component of a new initiative to deepen urbanization. Urban growth was seen as necessary for pooling skilled labor and capturing the agglomeration economies that are essential for becoming competitive in knowledge-intensive industries. Building this type of workforce would not be sustainable unless a sufficient number of affordable quality flats were available. Increasing the supply of low-priced units would also spur economic growth by freeing up funds that households could spend on other goods and services and thus help in efforts to reorient the economy away from exports toward domestic consumption.[142]

The government undertook a large expansion of public housing in 2011 with the objective of building thirty-six million units for low-income families by 2015.[143] Three-fifths of the units were intended for home ownership and two-fifths for rentals. The main policy instrument was again to offer supply-side subsidies to developers as opposed to demand-side financial assistance to tenants. Developers favored building commodity housing over affordable units since the former was not covered by rules limiting profits, the size of units, or means testing, so subsidies were necessary. Local officials had great discretion in carrying out the expansion of affordable housing. They designated and sold land for housing projects and allocated subsidies and bank loan guarantees to property developers. Many localities created Finance and Construction Enterprises (FCEs) as intermediaries, giving them responsibility for finding land, raising funds and organizing construction. Overall, the central government, local governments, and FCEs supplied 10, 20, and 70 percent of the total investment, respectively. Notwithstanding, local government guarantees were not always sufficiently large or reliable, so property developers sometimes had to secure bank loans by mortgaging their own assets.[144]

The central government's push to expand affordable public housing has encountered serious obstacles, the chief of which is China's intergovernmental structure.[145] Local officials frequently have failed to construct sufficient affordable units because their financial incentives are not aligned with the goals of national policy. As noted previously, subnational governments account for 85 percent of total government spending but only raise 60 percent of tax revenues. Consequently, they must search for ways to secure funds through nontax means, such as fees, levies, penalties, and the sale of land-use rights.[146] Similar to Hong Kong, municipalities often reserve the best land for private luxury developments instead of affordable homes because they generate the highest financial return for the city. In 2017, reclassifying and selling rural land for urban development comprised almost 40 percent of their total revenue.[147] The capacity to implement national housing policy also varies greatly leading to uneven outcomes across the country. Local governments with high levels of debt or fewer resources have had difficulty financing housing initiatives.[148] Many western cities in particular have lacked the funds (or expertise) to promote major construction projects. Finally, corruption surrounding housing developments has been widespread. A government auditor found that close to USD1.5 billion allocated toward them was misappropriated or stolen in 2014.[149]

An additional problem is that affordable public housing is generally of poor quality and not well connected to social services, such as schools and health care, public transportation, and job opportunities because it is typically built on the fringes of urban areas.[150] The decision to locate these projects in peripheral areas stems from the strategic calculus of city officials who reserve superior central locations for private developments.[151] The failure to construct housing that is connected to key services and networks has contributed to the housing poverty experienced by many low- to middle-income households in public units.[152] To overcome this problem, some cities have experimented with public–private partnerships in which officials permit developers to build commercial housing in prime spaces in exchange for setting aside a certain percentage of units as affordable, a policy that is often referred to as 80/20 after its use in New York City.

The situation for migrants, who have been excluded from most public housing historically, is markedly worse as already noted. Some cities (e.g., Beijing, Chengdu, Chongqing, and Shanghai) have started to allow rural migrants to apply for public rentals and even offered financial assistance or established a provident fund system for home purchases. Cities that have opened housing to migrants typically still require a minimum number of years of residential status along with a company guarantee or professional certification that identifies the applicant as skilled or semi-skilled. These requirements are an insurmountable barrier for most; in 2016, just 3 percent were able to purchase affordable housing or live in public rentals.[153] To make matters worse, major city governments have started to eliminate illegal dwellings occupied by migrants in the name of reducing overcrowding and abolishing "big city disease." In addition, Beijing and Shanghai have announced their intention to impose population caps of 23 million and 25 million people, respectively.[154] Some observers have claimed that these policies are intended to force out migrants and other low skill workers and steer them to so-called ghost cities, municipalities that have experienced massive construction of apartments that remain under-occupied because of a mismatch between supply and demand.[155]

In summary, housing policy in China has striking parallels to the policy façade in Hong Kong. Chinese leaders have professed concern about the needs of low-income individuals and made some efforts to increase the supply of affordable homes, but in reality they have shaped policy with an eye toward national economic performance.[156] Housing projects are viewed as a means of raising investment levels, ensuring that cities have sufficient manpower, boosting consumption, and accelerating the transition of the economy from an export to domestic orientation. Skepticism over the government's motives has been exacerbated by the government's changing points of emphasis and inability to provide a clear mission statement for its housing strategy.[157] The façade has also been evident in the tendency of housing policy to further the interests of local governments and developers. Local officials have struggled to find ways to raise sufficient revenue and land sales have been a primary means of doing so. In their drive to maximize revenue, they usually choose to allocate land to the luxury housing projects that developers favor over affordable housing that would benefit the most citizens, especially those in greater need.

Nevertheless, a few tentative signs suggest that government priorities may be evolving. Policymakers have announced plans to construct an additional 6.5 million public rental units that would accommodate twenty million people across forty major cities by 2025. Many of these flats would be allocated to rural migrants who have struggled to find affordable homes of any kind. By the start of 2026, public rentals could house up to an estimated 12 percent of the migrant population (about sixty million people).[158] Shenzhen has also introduced a pilot program offering "shared ownership" housing (in which the buyer acquires half of the unit and the government retains the other half) in January 2023.[159] As of early 2023, 3.3 million units that can hold ten million people have been completed.

China's growth after its transformation from a command-and-control to market-based economy has been astounding. Though inequality has increased sharply, the rise in real income has been sufficient to lift living standards for ordinary households and reduce absolute poverty dramatically, an admirable achievement that has improved the lives of millions. Yet the government lags in improving the overall social welfare of its citizens. Social protection is highly dualistic along urban–rural lines, and migrants have been largely excluded from receiving adequate government benefits because of the stringent *hukou* registration system. The level of social protection is generally low, most notably, concerning old age support, in the hope that family and community can step in when needed. And policymakers have yet to grapple seriously with other urgent social issues, such as child maltreatment and mental health.

China's approach to social welfare closely resembles the East Asian productivist model; if anything, its willingness to sacrifice social goals to a laser-like focus on prioritizing economic growth is even more pronounced. Certainly, it has much farther to go than its peers in creating an adequate safety net. National leaders seemingly have learned little from the social crises brewing right next door. The government is taking many of the right steps: increasing investment in human capital, but at a measured pace; attempting to alleviate glaring inequalities among regions; and shifting toward a more sustainable overall economic strategy. But its reluctance to enhance social protection for vulnerable groups is likely to result in widespread misery in the near future, as the population ages, technical change accelerates, the structure of families transforms, and urbanization deepens further.

The lack of a safety net may also threaten the sacred cow of economic growth if citizens continue to spend too little and save too much because they cannot rely on public social protection. The government has run large deficits repeatedly in order to implement fiscal stimulus packages to counteract economic slowdowns and quell potential political and social unrest. Some economists worry that China has fallen into a high savings trap, in which domestic demand is chronically insufficient and the government or SOEs must borrow and spend excessively to maintain economic expansion. One solution to this predicament is to limit public borrowing and lending to corporations and instead boost domestic consumption through social expenditures. Brad Setser noted that achieving this objective will "take far more aggressive reforms—and by reform, I mean reforms that expand access to social insurance and raise transfers to low-income workers financed through progressive taxes, not just reforms to state banks and state firms—than China's leaders have considered to date."[160] If policymakers fail to heed this advice, we fear that the country may become the ultimate example of misery beneath the miracle.

CONCLUSION
Lessons from East Asia and Advancing a New Research Agenda

East Asia presents a vivid paradox. The region has grown rapidly over the last five decades and achieved high-income status, yet its nations are currently beset by social crises that have put large swaths of their populations in dire straits. We contend that these crises are a direct outgrowth of the predominant social welfare strategy that governments in the region have adopted—productivism. The productivist approach has exposed many groups to high levels of economic insecurity exacerbated by macro-level trends, like skill-biased technical change and urbanization, and contributed to rising inequality in nations once known for their equitable distribution of income. Moreover, a welfare strategy that was originally designed to spur economic development is generating forces that may impede growth in the future. Instead of adapting to these new realities, authorities have dug in their heels, continuing to provide social protection to select groups, while erecting policy façades that only give the appearance of responding to the needs of those who require the most social protection.

Using dynamic integrated social welfare analysis, we have explored social policy in East Asia with fresh eyes and assessed its fundamental strengths and weaknesses. We have examined multiple social welfare issues in each country from the perspective of several disciplines, considered dynamic elements such as feedback loops and the ability of productivist systems to respond to major trends, and adopted a dual micro–macro lens in order to evaluate policies from the bottom-up, as well as the top-down. This has enabled us to distinguish the common and distinctive policy elements across countries in both their overall approach and individual issue areas. In this concluding chapter, we extend the analysis of these empirical patterns to synthesize our findings and identify new avenues for further comparative research.

In the first section we ask: How alike are East Asian nations with respect to social protection? We conclude that they remain more similar than dissimilar in the composition of their social expenditures but detect some divergence in the evolution of overall spending. We uncover some differences on individual issues, but any significant variation is typically limited to only one country per policy area. The most noteworthy divergence is observed in the pairing of South Korea and Taiwan. Some scholars expected both nations to augment spending significantly in response to rapid growth and democratization. South Korea has raised social expenditures substantially, but Taiwan has done so only slightly. We briefly consider whether the continuity that we observe in the region's welfare policies is due more to policymakers responding to the demands of key constituents who oppose reform or pursuing their own preferences or political incentives.

The analysis in this section also serves a broader purpose by shedding light on the relationship between economic growth, democracy, and social welfare. Are growth and democracy good for the poor, as has long been claimed, or do they mostly result in greater social services for the nonpoor? Increases in national income and political competition have had mixed effects on social protection in East Asia. South Korea has raised social spending far more than Taiwan, but both countries have resisted higher disbursements on welfare assistance and labor policies that help low-skill workers (Taiwan more so). A large body of research has probed how growth affects the features of social welfare systems. The East Asian experience indicates that the reverse causal relationship also deserves close attention. Under what conditions will social protection strategies impede rather than promote growth in the long run, as we find they do in East Asia?

As the preceding chapters show, social welfare systems in East Asia and other developed nations have differed markedly in the past, both in their level of government spending and qualitative features. Do they still? The second section explores this question. In doing so it addresses the argument that East Asian nations are bound to move toward social welfare models found in the West as greater wealth diminishes budgetary constraints and, in some cases, democratization increases demand for social protection. If productivism is not a unique approach but simply an earlier stage in the evolution of previously identified systems, then time should erase the apparent dissimilarities.

We discover only limited evidence of such convergence—primarily in social insurance spending in Japan and South Korea. The fundamental characteristics of a distinct productivist approach—low levels of protection, a strong focus on policies aimed at spurring growth, and heavy emphasis on building human capital—remain very much in place. Confronted by globalization and technical change, declining fertility and aging populations, intense urbanization, and shifts in family structure, policymakers have opted to implement policy façades instead of engaging in serious reform. This choice has exposed their vulnerable populations to additional economic hardship, not alleviated it.

This comparison is important in another respect. For too long, East Asian nations have been neglected in the comparative analysis of social welfare. Scholars have contended that their level of spending did not qualify them as true welfare states or they represented a distinct model that had little in common with those found in the West.[1] We believe both claims are misguided. East Asian nations are welfare states. They dedicate considerable (and growing) resources to social programs—but their priorities differ from those of many other developed nations, but not all. In this chapter, we argue that Japan also fits the profile of a liberal welfare state very well, a conclusion supported by several other studies. South Korea's rapid increase in insurance expenditures suggests that it is moving in that direction as well, but still has a long way to go. These observations are a strong argument for removing the scholarly barriers between East and West and opening up new avenues of research into the origins and evolution of national welfare systems.

The final section of this chapter considers how dynamic integrated social welfare analysis can contribute to comparative welfare studies more broadly. We use the recent COVID-19 pandemic and ongoing challenges associated with climate change to illustrate how a conceptual framework that is multidisciplinary not siloed, dynamic as opposed to static, and includes a wider range of social policy areas is able to generate additional insights, even in areas that have already been the object of extensive research. It does so by surfacing issues that interact with various spheres of social welfare, such as mental health and suicides, but are often neglected, or by leading scholars to consider the impact of ecological forces on the effectiveness of national welfare systems.

Commonalities Outnumber Differences in East Asia

Individual Issue Areas

The preceding chapters show that in general East Asian nations have similar policies and outcomes in the individual social policy areas that we examine. The variation that we observe is typically limited to just one country in a single issue area. Moreover, a different nation is the outlier in each case, except for Singapore (in housing and the use of active labor market policies [ALMPs]).

Rapidly aging East Asia has higher levels of relative elderly poverty than OECD countries and, with the exception of Japan, lackluster old age security systems. Seniors in the region are disproportionately poorer than the total population. In contrast, the poverty rates for the general and elderly populations in the majority of OECD countries are roughly the same. South Korea has the highest rate of any developed country, but the rate in China and Hong Kong—and possibly Singapore and Taiwan—is also very high.[2] Policymakers in China, Hong Kong, and South Korea have acknowledged that old age poverty is a problem and formulated policies to address it, but the funds allocated to these initiatives have been insufficient to improve the situation significantly.

Japan's elderly poverty rate is below those of other nations in the region but exceeds those in the West. Its social security system is more mature and it experienced rapid aging at an earlier date than its neighbors.[3] A graying population combined with established entitlement programs that confer defined benefits set the stage for a surge in social insurance spending.[4] Expenditures on insurance have continued to rise since the population has not stopped aging; in 2019, almost 30 percent of the population was sixty-five or older, the highest percentage in the world.[5] Nonetheless, Japan's old age security system resembles those of its regional peers in that the government has not established a minimum income level for seniors; in other words, its noncontributory pillar falls short of providing adequate protection for the least well off.

East Asian nations exhibit mostly similar labor market policies and wage trends. Earnings, especially for low-skill workers, have risen slowly over the last two decades in all countries but only after enjoying a prolonged period of fast growth. The exception is China, where wages continued to soar as the country sustained its rapid economic modernization. The education wage premium has expanded in all countries, widening the pay gap between low- and high-skill workers, excluding Taiwan. In Taiwan, the massification of tertiary education led to an oversupply of college-educated workers that lowered the returns on educational achievement. As in most developed nations, salaries in the region have not kept pace with improvements in labor productivity resulting in a significant decline in labor's share of national output. This phenomenon is a marked change from the pre-2000 era, when productivity and wages rose at comparable rates, a circumstance that was hailed as one of the hallmarks of shared growth.

Yet, East Asian governments have done little to boost the earnings of low-skill workers. They have implemented few income support measures apart from minimum wages (which are often set very low), made little use of ALMPs, and have rolled out passive labor market policies (PLMPs) with minimal coverage and benefit levels. Singapore has stood out for creating an active labor policy (the Progressive Wage Model) aimed at improving the standard of living of some (but not all) low-skill workers. Nevertheless, it does not have a minimum wage and still relies heavily on migrant workers to fill many low-paying jobs. In contrast to other economies in the region, labor's share of national income in Singapore has been stable.

Child maltreatment is a serious problem in all of East Asia, and government responses to this tragedy have not slowed its rise or addressed its consequences adequately. Incidents of maltreatment have surged, but public officials have not deemed this issue to be a national priority, and the agencies entrusted with designing remedies have received little funding. Government initiatives have focused on the reporting of cases as opposed to prevention or assisting victims or rehabilitating perpetrators. Legal frameworks for the protection of children are weak, so reporting tends to be inconsistent and incomplete and perpetrators are often sanctioned lightly. China probably has the highest levels of maltreatment, yet its government has done the least to address the growing problem. Large internal migration has fueled a sharp rise in cases, in both rural and urban areas, because the children of migrants are often left unprotected or find themselves living in harsh conditions.

The scarcity of affordable housing has emerged as a major issue in East Asian cities as home prices have soared at the same time household income has stagnated. These trends have forced many urban residents to move farther away from their jobs or live in substandard flats closer to work. Among other problems, these developments have led to higher levels of child maltreatment since unsatisfactory and inconvenient living conditions may fuel parental neglect, frustration, and resentment. Hong Kong has experienced the most grievous difficulties and currently has the world's most expensive housing, but Taipei and Seoul are not far behind. Facing similar but less severe initial circumstances as Hong Kong, Singapore has garnered accolades globally for its success in supplying affordable housing to a majority of the population. This achievement is largely due to policies implemented over a half-century ago, notably, the decision to use the Central Provident Fund as a means of financing the construction and purchase of homes. Japan, pursuing a strategy focused on private markets, has also fared better, even though housing costs in its major cities are not low. In large part, greater affordability in Japan is attributable to less restrictive land use and zoning policies that have allowed housing supply to increase in line with demand.

General Strategy

East Asian nations are more alike than different with respect to overall social welfare strategy. As the preceding section and chapters have shown, they have adopted remarkably similar social policies in most critical dimensions. All have featured highly dualistic social welfare systems that channeled the bulk of benefits to the nonpoor instead of the poor (table 1.6). The pattern of focusing on the nonpoor was most pronounced in the case of China and South Korea, but nowhere in the region did expenditures on the poor exceed 30 percent of total social protection spending. In addition, coverage rates for social assistance programs in 2015, which usually target low-income groups, were extremely low—8.3 to 19.5 percent (table 1.7). In contrast, those for social insurance, which typically favor the nonpoor, were far higher—67.8 to 85.3 percent. Coverage for insurance programs rose in all nations from 2009 to 2015, but it actually dropped for assistance in Japan and Singapore. Policymakers in some countries have actively discouraged eligible recipients from applying for means-tested benefits, contributing to low coverage.[6]

All governments in the region spent far more on social insurance than assistance, which is usually the case in other developed countries as well (table 1.3). Nonetheless, the disparity in favor of insurance was notably greater, especially in Japan and Taiwan. Hong Kong exhibited a more balanced approach, but only because it expended comparatively little on insurance. Levels of social assistance themselves were very low in the entire region, especially in the case of welfare assistance, which is the type of spending most focused on the poor (table 1.5). In the period 2010 to 2019, all nations expanded insurance more than assistance, with the exception of Hong Kong (table 1.12). Most raised social assistance outlays only slightly or not at all, but Hong Kong and especially South Korea had substantial increases.

Human capital development has been impressive in all East Asian economies. The achievements were not based on elevated levels of public investment, as is often assumed, however. Government spending on education (except in China) was lower than the OECD average, and nations relied heavily on private funding to attain strong results (table 1.10). Moreover, public expenditures on education have generally decreased since 2000; only China has increased its outlays as it ramped up its efforts to upgrade its economy. Likewise, East Asian nations had comparable levels of spending on health care, with only Japan and Singapore constituting contrasting outliers (table 1.4). No country had significant expenditures on ALMPs until 2019, when China raised its spending in this category considerably (table 1.12).

In sum, the passage of time has not led to significant divergence in the composition of social welfare policies in the region, reflecting the persistence of well-established priorities, but it has contributed to differences—seemingly growing—in the overall level of social protection. In chapter 1, we reviewed Ito Peng and Joseph Wong's claim that East Asian nations could be divided into two groups: (1) Japan, South Korea, and Taiwan, and (2) China, Hong Kong, and

Singapore. This classification offers a useful framework for exploring the variance that we have identified. Do East Asian countries in fact separate into these two groups and, if so, are the dissimilarities between them likely to deepen?

Peng and Wong were correct in identifying Japan and South Korea (but not Taiwan, at least for the moment) as distinct from their East Asian peers. South Korea may at some point join Japan in becoming a liberal welfare state, adding to the ranks of Ireland, the United Kingdom, and United States, though that is far from certain. It raised expenditures on social protection by 56 percent from 2010 to 2019 (table 1.12), and its rapid aging is likely to keep up the pressure to increase spending on insurance. Taiwan's social protection disbursements, however, have risen far more slowly—15.5 percent over the same decade—and they now total far less than South Korea's, even though it spent more than that country in 2010. Furthermore, there is little indication that its expenditures are likely to accelerate as South Korea's have.

Their predictions have not panned out in other respects. This group's policies did not have a more redistributive or universal character as those authors anticipated they would. Most of their social spending went to the nonpoor and not the poor, in part because it was so heavily skewed toward insurance, especially in Japan and Taiwan. Although South Korea has increased spending on social assistance the most of any East Asian society, it dedicated the least funds to welfare schemes, which is significant because these programs are expressly designed to target disbursements toward low-income individuals. Coverage rates for insurance programs greatly exceeded those for assistance; in fact, the rates for social assistance in Japan and South Korea were less than those in China and Singapore (table 1.7).

In the second group of countries, Hong Kong and Singapore continued to resemble one another in most respects. They undertook similarly large increases in social expenditures, 40.9 and 33.3 percent, respectively, from 2010 to 2019, but their absolute levels of spending remained very low. China experienced a somewhat larger increase—43 percent—and has overtaken Taiwan as the third largest spender in the region. The rapid expansion of its insurance programs, driven in large part by an aging population, hints that it may too increase social protection to Western levels. Nevertheless, chances are it will skew its spending toward the nonpoor even more than Japan and South Korea. As chapter 6 showed, the vast majority of its old age security expenditures go to urban regular workers and neglect migrants and rural residents. At this point, a sensible conclusion is that Taiwan resembles China, Hong Kong, and Singapore, more than Japan and South Korea.

Notwithstanding these differences, it bears repeating that all six countries remain fundamentally alike in maintaining a dualistic welfare system and prioritizing human capital development. What is the basis of this surprising continuity of social policy in East Asia? Is it a consequence of path dependency, reflecting the difficulty policymakers face generally in altering the basic features of social welfare systems once they are established? Is it due to successive generations of policymakers opting to preserve productivism, perhaps based on ideology, political strategy, or financial calculus? Or have powerful private interest groups thwarted reform-minded policymakers from pursuing a more generous and inclusive social welfare approach?

Our findings tentatively point to the conclusion that the durability of the productivist approach is the result of a deliberate choice. We could reasonably expect the four powerful trends analyzed in this volume—globalization and technical change, urbanization, demographic shifts, and changing family structures—to result in an expansion of social protection, as they have in most European countries. Moreover, the growing wealth of East Asian populations has increased demand for a greater range and depth of social services and given governments the means to enlarge the supply of social goods accordingly. Policymakers have responded to this demand but only in a highly selective fashion. They have expanded social insurance for the nonpoor but mostly resisted calls for wider and more generous safety nets. They have disguised this bias by building policy façades that incorporate minor reforms that give the appearance of addressing the social problems that affect citizens with greatest need most severely. Time and time again, they have stuck with this cynical strategy despite unambiguous evidence that social crises are severe and will not abate without more energetic state intervention. We cannot say whether these decisions are primarily driven by policymakers' ideological or political preferences or by their efforts to cater to key constituencies who wish to retain the advantages they have enjoyed in the status quo. Further research on this topic would not only generate a better understanding of the inertia East Asian nations have exhibited toward social policy but also of the roles and influence of private actors, state institutions, ideology, and public officials in their policymaking process.

Democratization, Growth, and Social Welfare in Japan, South Korea, and Taiwan

Social policy in Japan, South Korea, and Taiwan has received more attention than elsewhere in the region. Japan has greatly outspent other East Asian nations and, in many respects, is a harbinger of trends that are now just emerging in its neighbors.[7] It created its social welfare state long before the others and was the first to begin facing macro-level challenges, like an aging population and intense urbanization. South Korea and Taiwan underwent democratization starting in the mid-1980s, a process that several scholars suggested would lead to greater social spending and sensitivity to redistributive issues. Japan also adopted new electoral rules intended to move the country toward a two-party system and end the dominance of the Liberal Democratic Party. They gave political parties an incentive to appeal to a broader electorate through more universal policies, as opposed to targeting benefits toward narrow constituencies.[8]

Japan's social protection spending has risen steadily over the last few decades, and its current level places it solidly in the middle of the OECD pack. Specifically, the country has transformed into a liberal welfare state rather than a social democratic or Bismarckian one. The strongest evidence for this categorization comes from a reexamination of Japan based on the concept of decommodification. Decommodification is defined as "the extent to which welfare state benefits provide 'de-commodified' social rights of citizenship. In effect, what this amounts to is a measure, not of the size of aggregate state spending, but of the eligibility criteria by which individuals qualify as beneficiaries of the welfare state and the generosity with which these individuals are treated."[9] Recent empirical work using a decommodification index determined that Japan fit comfortably among other countries associated with the liberal model.[10]

Nevertheless, Japan has not altered the composition of its spending significantly as its welfare system matured. The bulk of its outlays are for social insurance and it expends very little on social assistance or labor programs to help workers under duress, like retraining or unemployment compensation. This pattern of expenditures persists even though some authors expected its 1994 electoral reforms to result in an expansion of inclusive as opposed to targeted social policies.[11] Social protection retains a highly dualistic character that favors the nonpoor and places the poor on the back burner. In this regard, Japan resembles both productivist and some liberal welfare states, particularly the United States, demonstrating that it straddles the two categories. In other work, we argue that the productivist and liberal welfare models can be conceived as different points on a continuum, separated mainly by their total level of social spending.[12]

South Korea expanded social protection spending the most in East Asia in the 2010s. This outcome is in line with the predictions of scholars like Yeon-Myung Kim and Wong, who anticipated that democratization would eventually push the country's social expenditures up to levels similar to Japan's and reorient social programs toward greater redistribution of income toward disadvantaged groups and rural areas.[13] In this view, South Korea lags behind Japan largely because it started building its social welfare system at a much later date. These authors claimed that the introduction of universal health care in 1989 was a significant step toward the transformation of the country's social welfare system. The National Health Insurance was rolled out in 1977 and public spending on health care spiked, rising by a startling 10.1 percent on a per capita basis annually from 1981 to 2002.[14]

Achieving universal healthcare was a major feat that should not be minimized. Whether the impetus was political or due to other factors is difficult to determine, however. Randall Jones found that a large portion of the spending increase can be attributed to the effects of rising incomes and the aging of the population. The degree of social protection afforded by expanded health care was also less than it appeared at first glance. Jones noted that the private sector bore roughly 50 percent of the cost of supporting the new system through high copayments and restricted benefits. In contrast, private expenditures accounted for only 28 percent of health spending in OECD countries on average in this period.[15] This heavy burden has resulted in varying degrees of access to quality healthcare services based on the ability to pay.

South Korea also created a public pension system in 1988 coinciding with the start of democratization. Some authors placed great significance on the flat rate component of the main pension program (the National Pension Service [NPS]), which they pointed out has a redistributive impact by generating higher replacement rates for low earners. This feature, along with high maximum replacement rates, seemed to promise a more solidaristic approach to social welfare. As chapter 2 detailed, however, this early promise has not panned out. Policymakers have reduced the maximum replacement rate sharply and the functioning of the system has not led to adequate old age security for all older adults. Specifically, outcomes have reflected the fundamental labor market divide between insiders and outsiders that encompasses both regular versus nonregular workers and employees of large versus small firms. Regular workers who have long earnings histories take far more out of the system than the large population of nonregular workers, and employees of large firms have access to corporate welfare in addition to public benefits. Consequently, South Korea has an exceptionally high elderly relative poverty rate, and nearly two-fifths of the generation that helped produce its economic miracle must scramble desperately to make ends meet.

More generally, the primary beneficiaries of increased social spending in South Korea have been the middle class, not the poor, indicating that the country's dualistic approach to social welfare has persisted (only China's expenditures have been more skewed). Legislators implemented several new programs to expand the safety net but often failed to fund them at levels that would represent a notable change in the nation's welfare approach. The coverage rate of assistance programs was a scant 13 percent in 2015, only a small jump from 9.5 percent in 2009 (table 1.6). Furthermore, South Korea spent a meager 0.3 percent of gross domestic product (GDP) on welfare assistance, which was the lowest amount in East Asia and well below the OECD average of 0.9 (table 1.5).[16] Consequently, the country's degree of redistribution, as measured by the difference between its before and after Gini coefficients, was extremely small and typical of other East Asian, not Western nations (table 1.8).

Unlike South Korea, Taiwan has increased social protection spending only slightly over the last three decades despite its transition to democracy. The International Labour Organization (ILO) reported that social expenditures increased from 8.0 to 9.9 percent of GDP from 1990 to 2000, possibly as a consequence of greater political competition. They peaked in 2005, however, and declined to 9.7 percent in 2010, indicating that whatever momentum democratization had initially created for expansion of the welfare system had already begun to ebb.[17]

As in South Korea, a significant social policy achievement was the creation of a universal health system, which provides excellent care (a judgment borne out by Taiwan's superb handling of the COVID-19 pandemic). Nonetheless, to an even greater extent than in South Korea, policymakers have failed to allocate adequate funding to the other new social programs they introduced starting in the 1980s. Outlays on social insurance have grown moderately over time, but those on assistance, already at levels below those of most other East Asian countries, remained unchanged from 2010 to 2019 at a mere 1 percent of GDP. As chapter 3 showed, labor market policies did not expand or shift priorities in response to democratization either. The government made large investments in human capital development through its massification of tertiary education but it failed to provide adequate support for struggling low-skill workers. Altogether, Taiwan's pattern of social expenditures has contributed to the least income redistribution of any East Asian nation (along with China) as seen in table 1.8. There are few if any signs that the country's social spending priorities will change any time soon.

What are the implications of these findings for our understanding of the relationship between economic growth, democratization, and social welfare? The conventional wisdom in comparative politics is that economic growth and democratization are critical factors for understanding the birth and evolution of the welfare state.[18] Economic development permits greater expenditures on social issues as constraints on government revenue and spending are eased. In addition, citizens demand greater social protection to cushion the disruptive effects associated with economic modernization. Democracy expands the scope and level of social spending because politicians must consider the interests of newly empowered groups, including disadvantaged ones, in order to gain and remain in power. One consequence is believed to be greater efforts to redistribute income and design universal policies that contain strong solidaristic elements.

This has not been the case in East Asia. Social welfare expenditures rose as economies developed, but only at a slow pace and in an uneven fashion across the region despite similar rates of growth. Democratic transitions in South Korea and Taiwan during the 1980s gave rise to a moderate expansion of some portions of the welfare state, particularly in the former. The dualistic nature of their social welfare system, however, did not change significantly, even after the opposition won elections. For its part, Japan has maintained a minimal safety net despite an electoral reform in 1994 that was designed to incentivize politicians to appeal to broader constituencies. Looking back further, the country's democratic and economic advances prior to 1945 impeded rather than aided the development of a robust safety net because they augmented the power of antiredistributive agrarian and urban economic elites.[19] Similarly, economic growth in some Western countries, for instance, the United States, arguably has increased rather than decreased the economic insecurity of large segments of the population.[20] These observations imply that the expansion of social protection systems in countries undergoing sustained growth does not necessarily proceed in either an additive or cumulative fashion.

The "misery beneath the miracle" paradox suggests that the relationship between economic growth and social welfare may be characterized by mutual causality. The theoretical literature has concentrated primarily on how the former affects the latter. Yet, the reverse causal relationship deserves equal attention. As we have stressed throughout this volume, the extreme imbalance between growth and social protection strategies that has prevailed in East Asia is likely to hinder rather than promote growth in the long run by, among other things, damaging the stock and quality of human capital. A thorough examination of the ways and extent to which this reverse effect matters in different political institutional and societal contexts would take us closer to comprehending the complex coevolution of industrial capitalism, democracy, and social protection in both the East and the West.[21]

East Meets West in Social Welfare Systems Analysis

East Asian nations (excluding China) have income levels that are comparable to those found in OECD members in Europe and North America. Some scholars have predicted that rapid economic modernization—and, in some cases, democratization—would lead to the expansion of social protection in the region and before long at least some nations would resemble their OECD peers in terms of policies and outcomes.[22] Convergence toward the West would mark the end of the productivist era or even indicate that the conception of East Asian social welfare states as being inherently different from other advanced industrial nations was incorrect in the first place. In the latter case, East Asia could be seen as following the same historical evolution in the development of robust social welfare systems as Western countries before them; earlier authors simply had mistaken what were in reality the opening phases of this process as evidence of a distinct East Asian model.[23]

To assess these claims, we begin by examining the level and composition of aggregate social spending. The data show that despite similar income levels, governments in East Asia were smaller, as measured by public spending as a percentage of GDP, and (except Japan) dedicated fewer resources to social protection (see table C.1). This determination indicates that lower expenditures on social protection in the region were not merely a function of limits imposed by constraints on public spending. Policymakers chose to commit a smaller portion of government outlays to protection, signifying that it was less of a priority than other objectives.

In one respect, it is surprising that governments in East Asia are small and have such low levels of social expenditures compared with those in the West. A sizable literature has demonstrated that advanced industrial nations with open economies usually develop bigger public sectors than those with closed economies and frequently feature higher social expenditures, including those on safety nets. Dani Rodrik contended that social spending protects against external shocks and helps generate political support for greater integration into the world economy.[24] David Cameron argued that large public sectors allow policymakers in open economies to implement stabilizers that help to manage business cycles and create mechanisms that facilitate the economy's adjustment to changing international conditions.[25] This need is even more pronounced for small states, which have a greater reliance on trade due to the limited size of their domestic

TABLE C.1 Government spending ratios for East Asia and OECD, 2019

	GOVERNMENT/GDP	SOCIAL PROTECTION/TOTAL
China	24.2	41.3
Hong Kong	21.4	28.0
Japan	38.8	58.8
South Korea	33.9	36.3
Singapore	14.7	42.2
Taiwan	15.4	26.9
OECD average	42.5	47.3
OECD-18 average	44.7	52.1

Sources: OECD, *Government at a Glance, 2021* (Paris: OECD Publishing, 2021), and "Social Expenditure – Aggregated Data," OECD Social and Welfare Statistics, 2023; Republic of China, National Bureau of Statistics, "Statistical Yearbook (2022); Hong Kong, Census and Statistics Department, "Hong Kong Annual Digest of Statistics 2022 Edition," October 2022; Republic of Singapore, "eBook of Statistics," 2023; Taiwan (ROC), Statistics Bureau, "Net Government Expenditures of All Levels," 2023

markets.[26] Hong Kong, Singapore, and Taiwan fit the description of small, open nations very well.[27] Most of their economic activities involve cross-border transactions and over the years they have had to adjust frequently and rapidly to the changing international division of labor. Only Japan and China are relatively closed economies, though the latter is more open than one might expect given its status as a very large, populous country with sizable domestic markets.[28] In short, a powerful force that has prodded other developed nations to expand levels of social protection—integration into the global economy—has not had the same impact in East Asia.[29]

As table C.2 shows, the only East Asian nation that had levels of overall social spending on par with OECD and OECD-18 countries (an average of 20.1 percent and 23.3 percent of GDP, respectively) in 2019 was Japan (22.8 percent), and this was solely due to its very high expenditures on social insurance (20.5 percent). All governments in the region devoted a much larger proportion of their outlays to social insurance than assistance, and this proportion was generally higher than the OECD average. No consistent pattern emerged across the region of favoring pensions over health care as OECD countries did, as table C.3 indicates. In all of East Asia, policymakers apportioned significantly fewer resources to social assistance than OECD and OECD-18 nations (an average of 2.9 percent and 3.5 percent of GDP, respectively), although Japan and especially South Korea increased their expenditures after 2015 (see table 1.12).

Compared to its Western peers, social policy in East Asia was more dualistic and resulted in less redistribution toward lower income groups (tables 1.6 and 1.8).[30] Analogous data on the breakdown of social protection spending are not available for the OECD, but several studies on social assistance have indicated that the bias in favor of the nonpoor was less pronounced. In OECD and OECD-18 countries, an average of 23.4 and 25.4 percent, respectively, of public cash transfers to working-age individuals went to the lowest quintile, whereas 19.3 and 18.2 percent, respectively, went to the highest quintile in 2015.[31] In Japan and South Korea, 18.5 and 22.4 percent, respectively, were allocated to the lowest quintile, and 18.2 and 21.3, percent, respectively, to the highest quintile. Willem Adema, Pauline Fron, and Maxime Ladaique devised a more sophisticated measure of the distribution of such benefits called "gross public transfers."[32] The lowest quintile's share of gross public transfers was 4.7 percent on average in the OECD compared to just 1.2 percent in South Korea and 3.3 percent in Japan in 2009. Another study found that the lowest two income deciles received 50 percent or more of total public spending on families in at least half of OECD countries.[33]

Coverage rates were also higher in OECD countries. Take-up rates for social assistance and housing programs, which ranged from 40 to 80 percent, were up to four times higher than in East Asia, and government efforts to reach

TABLE C.2 Social protection in East Asia and the OECD (as a % of GDP), 2019

	TOTAL SOCIAL PROTECTION	SOCIAL INSURANCE	SOCIAL ASSISTANCE	ALMP
China*	10.0	8.4	0.9	0.6
Hong Kong	6.0	4.1	1.9	n/a
Japan	22.8	20.5	2.1	0.2
South Korea	12.3	9.4	2.5	0.4
Singapore*	6.2	5.3	0.6	0.3
Taiwan	9.7	8.7	1.0	n/a
Germany	25.6	21.9	3.1	0.6
Sweden	25.1	20.8	4.5	0.2
United States	18.3	16.6	1.4	0.1
OECD average	20.1	16.6	2.9	0.6
OECD-18 average	23.3	19.2	3.5	0.6

* China: 2018; Singapore: 2018

Sources: OECD, "Social Expenditure—Aggregated Data"; Hong Kong, Census and Statistics Department, "Annual Digest of Statistics 2022"; Taiwan (ROC), Statistical Bureau, "Social Protection Expenditure"; OECD, Society at a Glance: Asia/Pacific 2022 (Paris: OECD Publishing, 2022)

TABLE C.3 Social insurance in East Asia and the OECD (as a % of GDP), 2019

	TOTAL INSURANCE	PENSIONS	HEALTH CARE	OTHER
China*	8.4	5.3	2.9	0.2
Hong Kong	4.1	1.4	2.5	0.2
Japan	20.5	8.4	9.6	2.5
South Korea	9.4	3.1	4.8	1.5
Singapore*	5.3	0.0	2.4	2.9
Taiwan	8.7	4.9	3.3	0.5
Germany	21.9	8.7	8.3	4.9
Sweden	20.8	9.7	6.6	4.5
United States	16.6	6.6	8.4	1.7
OECD average	16.6	7.4	5.8	3.4
OECD-18 average	19.2	8.7	6.4	4.1

* China: 2018; Singapore: 2018

Sources: OECD, "Social Expenditure—Aggregated Data"; Hong Kong, Census and Statistics Department, "Annual Digest of Statistics 2022"; Taiwan (ROC), Statistical Bureau, "Social Protection Expenditure," 2023; OECD, Society at a Glance: Asia/Pacific 2022

underserved populations were frequently extensive.[34] Using a different metric, the ILO found that in OECD and OECD-18 countries an average of 65.4 and 81.4 percent of all vulnerable individuals, respectively, received noncontributory cash benefits.[35] Social insurance in the average OECD country has also gone disproportionately to the nonpoor, but in all likelihood the poor have received a significantly higher portion of this spending than in East Asia because many programs are means tested.[36]

East Asian nations have less extensive labor market policies than their Western peers. They only began to use ALMPs in the past decade, and China alone spends at a level similar to OECD countries (table 1.12). PLMPs have been in place somewhat longer, but they are generally poorly funded, have low replacement rates, and insure only a small percentage of eligible participants.[37] Average spending on PLMPs in OECD and OECD-18 countries was 0.67 and 0.91 percent of GDP, respectively, versus 0.16 and 0.47 in Japan and South Korea, respectively, in 2019.[38] Net replacement rates for unemployment insurance in Japan and Korea were considerably lower than in most Western nations in the period from 2001 to 2015.[39] Finally, the number of eligible workers covered by unemployment benefits in 2020 only exceeded 25 percent in South Korea (where it was 45.4 percent); the average in OECD and OECD-18 countries was 53.4 and 70.4, respectively.[40]

In summary, East Asian governments dedicate sizable resources to social protection but have opted to exclude large segments of their populations from enjoying the phenomenal economic success they have achieved. Unlike their Western peers, they persist in eschewing policies that would create a safety net for the working poor, disabled, and other disadvantaged groups. They have implemented policy façades instead, even as social problems are exacerbated by macro-level forces such as technical change, heightening the demand for programs to mitigate elevated economic risk. Western nations have varied in the extent and quality of their response to the need for social protection but, as a group, they have undoubtedly fared better overall. They are certainly not free of social problems but they generally—with the notable exception of the United States—provide better care to the elderly, have less working poverty, possess a greater supply of affordable housing, and offer superior protection of children.[41]

Extending the Dynamic Integrated Approach

East Asia, like the rest of the world, has confronted a myriad of challenging new developments in the last decade that affect the ability of social welfare systems to protect citizens, but two stand out: the COVID-19 pandemic and climate change. Public health and climate crises raise additional risks for the economic security and quality of life of citizens that are likely to intensify the region's misery and magnify the pitfalls of productivism. More generally, we believe that these issue areas ought to be included in the portfolio of large-scale, transformative processes that will have significant impacts on welfare outcomes in the future. The dynamic integrated approach is a useful tool for connecting public health and climate concerns with the ability of social welfare systems to function effectively.[42]

East Asian governments largely failed to buffer the negative effects of the pandemic on vulnerable citizens, leaving them to fend for themselves, yet again. In South Korea, for example, most local government programs and civil society initiatives that had filled gaps in the nation's safety net for the elderly were retrenched substantially. Volunteer operations that delivered food to older adults—especially those living alone—were put on hold. Incheon, the third largest city in South Korea, temporarily suspended 97 percent of the government jobs that it sets aside for struggling seniors due to health concerns.[43] Many of them returned to work once social distancing rules were lifted out of sheer necessity—they could not retire because of insufficient pension benefits. This was in sharp contrast with the mass exodus of older workers—who had the option to stop working—from the labor force in many Western nations.[44] Worries also mounted over the rising degree of social isolation, number of suicides, and occurrence of mental illness among low-income seniors as the pandemic wore on.

Japan's child maltreatment crisis worsened during the pandemic, as some risk factors for abuse and neglect, namely, elevated levels of stress and economic insecurity, intensified. Measures to control the spread of COVID-19 also kept children at home, making detection of abuse and neglect cases more difficult. Other related and disquieting trends brought on by the crisis were soaring incidents of female suicide—a shocking increase of more than 80 percent—and domestic violence.[45]

The pandemic also elevated the risk of child maltreatment in Hong Kong, especially among families residing in crowded, poor living conditions in both private and public housing. For many residents, the fear of contracting the coronavirus added to an already long list of threats to their well-being. Some dwellers of tiny, subdivided flats chose homelessness, sleeping outdoors in cardboard boxes in order to avoid the cramped conditions that spread the disease; for others, Hong Kong's quarantine centers became a welcome refuge from their normal living quarters.[46]

Finally, East Asia's inadequate unemployment insurance schemes and public employment training programs stood out conspicuously amidst the distress that hit labor markets. Policymakers in some nations were forced to include cash payments to workers in the unprecedented stimulus packages they implemented to prop up their economies. These benefits were one-offs and did little to address ongoing social welfare crises, which will require multipronged, long-term government interventions to make a difference. What the massive contingency outlays did do was raise public expenditures to levels that some public officials immediately found uncomfortable (e.g., in South Korea and Hong Kong) or increased already high levels of public debt (e.g., in Japan). These developments may precipitate a movement to retrench social spending or freeze it at current levels. Other measures adopted during the pandemic could also hurt the long-term solvency of entitlement programs. In China, for instance, the government temporarily exempted struggling firms from making their contributions to provincial social insurance funds. This directive helped companies to survive but compromised the funds' capacity to make pension and unemployment payments in the future.[47]

Like COVID-19, climate change has affected nearly every individual and community across the globe. East Asia is no exception. Extreme heat, typhoons, and floods have abounded across the region, shattering long-standing records and imposing high human and fiscal costs. Yet climate-related disasters are projected to become even more pervasive and severe, which could make some parts of East Asia virtually uninhabitable and result in the massive displacement of persons. Low-income households are particularly vulnerable to climate change risks, which include injuries, illness (e.g., respiratory and heart diseases), homelessness, and mental health issues (e.g., depression and posttraumatic stress disorder), because they reside in areas that have inferior physical and social infrastructure, feature poor quality and easily damaged housing, and are most exposed to weather events or pollution (e.g., floodplains or dense urban centers). East Asia's threadbare safety nets are not equipped to provide adequate support if emergencies arise, especially when they end up having long-term consequences. Despite the high stakes, scholars have shown little interest in analyzing the links between climate change and social welfare; on the few occasions they are discussed, the focus tends to be on other regions (namely, Europe), and they are treated as a specialty not mainstream topic.[48]

The dynamic, integrated approach furnishes the tools required to identify the larger social welfare impacts of the pandemic and climate change in East Asia and elsewhere. In the case of public health, for example, using an integrated, dynamic approach to identify system effects highlights the importance of two closely related issues, mental health and suicides, for understanding developments in multiple issue areas, notably, education, child welfare, old age security, and elderly care. If a public health crisis leads to a deterioration of mental health or raises the number of suicides, affected families will find it harder to care for elders or save sufficient funds for their children's education or own retirement. We believe that this is likely to occur in South Korea in the aftermath of COVID-19 given the country's high rate of elderly poverty and low fertility rate. Employing a dual micro–macro lens reveals that a public health crisis is likely to have distinct impacts on different groups of individuals. For example, COVID-19 forced more women than men out of the job market in Japan and the United

States, contributing to a disproportionate surge in cases of depression and even suicides among women.[49] This observation alarmed public health professionals and has sparked calls to consider gender criteria when formulating mental health policies in response to public health emergencies.

Integrating climate change into welfare studies also adds a dynamic element to the analysis of social welfare models. First, national welfare systems have the potential to provide adaptive protection against climate change-induced uncertainties and risks. According to Ian Gough, extending welfare state studies to construct ecosocial policy analyses is warranted because "institutionalized comprehensive social policy is an important precautionary climate strategy in its own right."[50] Second, potential policy solutions for climate change are likely to have progressive or regressive effects on the distribution of income over time. For instance, some localities in China have pursued the dual objectives of decarbonizing the energy supply and mitigating poverty by allowing residents to harvest solar power, thereby reducing their energy bills and generating income through the sale of surpluses. South Korea's Green New Deal policy (also known as the K-New Deal), which seeks to reduce carbon emissions by deploying radical conservation measures and investing in renewable energy, aims to boost employment in new green sectors. Rapid decarbonization, however, may worsen inequality by impacting the finances of low-income households negatively. For example, measures to increase carbon prices or implement environmental taxes (on energy use, pollution, or private transportation) would impose disproportionate costs on low-income households, whose food and transportation consumption is typically carbon intensive.[51] Well designed social welfare policies could contribute to an ecosocial policy that strikes a viable balance between sustainability and equity goals.[52]

More broadly, finding ways to better integrate public health and climate change into comparative social welfare analysis will generate new questions for comparative research. Treating public health policy as an additional type of social protection, for instance, would draw more attention to the capacity of different types of welfare systems to respond to crises like pandemics.[53] Will differences in social welfare systems lead to diverse patterns in the quantity or quality of protection afforded to vulnerable populations, like children and the elderly, when a pandemic strikes? Examining public health policy through the prism of social welfare systems can also yield new insights into the relationship between national-level institutions, programs, and actors, on the one hand, and their local government counterparts, on the other. In his book on the COVID-19 crisis in Japan, Takenaka Harukata argued that the pandemic exposed the limits on the national government's ability to care for its citizens; local officials were forced to step up and play critical roles in protecting their residents.[54] In a similar vein, several global cities have devised more equitable and efficient climate change mitigation strategies than others, raising the effectiveness of local government spending in a variety of policy areas, including social welfare.[55] How might such strategies be adapted for implementation at the regional and national levels?

Final Thoughts

This book has explored the pitfalls of the East Asian welfare model using a methodology that we call dynamic integrated social welfare analysis. In doing so, it has endeavored to shift the focus of scholarly attention away from conventional views of East Asia as the birthplace of an economic miracle to one that acknowledges the social misery lying beneath it. The region is beset by social crises that threaten the well-being of its citizens and jeopardize the continuity of its economic success. We argue that this deterioration is the product of a social welfare strategy—productivism—that propelled rapid growth in the past but is now holding back progress in the region.

This concluding chapter has sought to open up a badly needed dialogue between the siloed academic work on social welfare policy in East Asia and the West. The social policies of the two groupings remain far apart in some respects, with two notable exceptions. Japan's social policies now bear a striking resemblance to those of the United States, a leading liberal welfare state, and South Korea has moved some ways toward the liberal model though its overall spending remains much lower. This conclusion points to the need to explore the sources of uniformity and diversity in social welfare systems across advanced industrial countries and open up avenues of research into the origins and evolution of welfare states by bringing in new cases whose relevancy is indisputable. A new line of research similar to our own identifies additional common features among East Asian countries and the United States and has sought to explain the root causes behind the shared characteristics.[56]

Our findings also suggest that the relationship between economic growth, democratic reforms, and social welfare development is even more complex than once believed. East Asian nations achieved some of the same objectives prized by Western states, such as sustained growth and improvements in human development indicators, without constructing sizable welfare states. And their rapid growth, coupled with democratization in some countries, generally has not led to an expansion of social protection along the lines that it did in Europe. But evidence is mounting that the decision to maintain a productivist approach by erecting policy façades in the face of powerful trends like technical change and aging populations is beginning to hinder economic performance and inflict deep and lasting damage on its citizens. These observations offer important lessons for policymakers in other developed countries who are pondering the question of whether to retrench or reconfigure their welfare states and those in emerging market and developing countries who are just starting to construct their own. This line of research has become more urgent as the COVID-19 pandemic and climate-related disasters have ratcheted up the need to provide social protection to vulnerable populations by adding new layers of economic and social insecurity to an already extensive mix.

Notes

INTRODUCTION

1. *Parasite*, directed by Bong Joon-ho (2019; Seoul: Barunson E&A).

2. Jaewon Kim, "No Country for Old Koreans: Moon Faces Senior Poverty Crisis," *Nikkei Asian Review*, January 19, 2019; "Humans in Cages: Hong Kong's Shoebox Housing," *Radio Free Europe, Radio Liberty*, March 9, 2015; "Record 219,000 Cases of Child Abuse Logged in Japan in Fiscal '22," *Japan Times*, September 7, 2023; "Long Hours and Low Pay Will Become the Norm in Taiwan," *Asia One*, September 23, 2013; and Lijia Zhang, "Left-Behind Children a Poignant Reminder of the Cost of China's Development," *South China Morning Post*, May 26, 2018.

3. Hong Kong was once a British colony and is now a special administrative region of the Republic of China. Hong Kong enjoyed considerable autonomy, including in the sphere of social policy, under the "one country, two systems" principle until approximately 2020, when mainland China exerted greater control over the city's affairs. The status of Taiwan is hotly disputed, with Beijing claiming it is a province of China that has no independent standing. Nonetheless, Taiwan has managed its own affairs for decades and certainly has formulated and implemented its own social policies. Hong Kong and Taiwan are sometimes but not always found in international data sets compiled by organizations such as the International Labour Organization and World Bank. For ease of exposition, we include Hong Kong and Taiwan in the groupings East Asian countries and nations in this volume.

4. A good overview of these categories is OECD, *Growing Unequal? Income Distribution and Poverty in OECD Countries* (Paris: OECD Publishing, 2008). Chapter 2 discusses the components and features of these policy areas at length.

5. Singapore is included because it shares many of the same baseline characteristics as our other nations and has struggled with similar social problems. It has enjoyed far greater success in supplying affordable housing—providing an important contrast with its neighbors (chapter 5)—and has experimented with an innovative approach to raising wages for low-skill workers—unlike other East Asian nations (chapter 3).

6. In the next chapter and conclusion, we take a closer look at Japan's social welfare approach and specify that although the strategy it pursued during its high growth period fell under the rubric of productivism—and continues to exhibit several of its features—it currently falls more accurately into the category of what Esping-Anderson has labeled liberal welfare states. Gosta Esping-Andersen, *The Three Worlds of Welfare Capitalism* (Princeton, NJ: Princeton University Press, 1990).

7. For instance, see José Edgardo Campos and Hilton L. Root, *The Key to the Asian Miracle: Making Shared Growth Credible* (Washington, DC: Brookings, 2001); and World Bank, *The East Asian Miracle: Economic Growth and Public Policy* (New York: Oxford University Press, 1993).

8. For example, Joseph Wong, *Healthy Democracies: Welfare Politics in Taiwan and South Korea* (Ithaca, NY: Cornell University Press, 2004); and Yeon-Myung Kim, "Beyond East Asian Welfare Productivism in South Korea," *Policy and Politics* 36, no. 1 (2008): 109–25.

9. A major work by a historian that reached this conclusion is Peter Lindert, *Growing Public: Social Spending and Economic Growth since the Eighteenth Century*, 2nd ed. (New York: Cambridge University Press, 2004). The varieties of capitalism literature has claimed that social welfare policy evolves to be complementary to a country's capitalist system. Peter Hall and David Soskice, eds., *Varieties of Capitalism: The Institutional Foundations of Comparative Advantage* (New York: Oxford University Press, 2003).

10. See for example, Ye Yuan, Judy Major-Girardin, and Steven Brown, "Storytelling Is Intrinsically Mentalistic: A Functional Magnetic Resonance Imaging Study of Narrative Production across Modalities," *Journal of Cognitive Neuroscience* 30, no. 9 (2018): 1298–314.

11. Zoë McElhinney and Catherine Kennedy, "Enhancing the Collective, Protecting the Personal: The Valuable Role of Composite Narratives in Medical Education Research," *Perspectives on Medical Education* 11, no. 4 (2022): 220–27; and Paul Atkinson, "The Contested Terrain of Narrative Analysis—An Appreciative Response," *Sociology of Health & Illness* 32, no. 4 (2010): 661–62.

12. Andrea L. Campbell, *Trapped in America's Safety Net: One Family's Struggle* (Chicago: Chicago University Press, 2014); Jacob S. Hacker, *The Great Risk Shift: The New Economic Insecurity and the Decline of the American Dream*, 2nd ed. (New York: Oxford University Press, 2008); and Matthew Desmond, *Poverty, by America* (New York: Crown, 2023).

13. Andrew Gelman and Thomas Basbøll, "When Do Stories Work? Evidence and Illustration in the Social Sciences," *Sociological Methods & Research* 43, no. 4 (2014): 548–49

14. Thomas B. Newman, "The Power of Stories over Statistics," *British Medical Journal* 327, no. 7429 (2002): 1424–27; and Rebecca Willis, "The Use of Composite Narratives to Present Interview Findings," *Qualitative Research* 19, no. 4 (2019): 471–80.

15. Sarah Rose Cavanagh, *The Spark of Learning* (Morgantown: West Virginia University Press, 2016), 36.

16. Lani Peterson, "The Science behind the Art of Storytelling," *Harvard Business Publishing*, November 14, 2017.

17. Zaretta Hammond, *Culturally Responsive Teaching and the Brain* (Thousand Oaks, CA: Corwin, 2015), 48.

18. Patricia Gercik, *On Track with the Japanese* (Bloomington, IN: AuthorHouse, 2011).

1. THE PROMISE AND PERILS OF PRODUCTIVISM

1. Steven Durlauf, Paul Johnson, and Jonathan Temple, "Growth Econometrics," in *Handbook of Economic Growth*, ed. Philippe Aghion and Steven N. Durlauf, vol. 1 (Amsterdam: Elsevier, 2005), 555–667.

2. As noted in the introduction, we include Hong Kong and Taiwan in the groupings East Asian countries, nations, and societies for ease of exposition.

3. A commonly used definition of a system effect is found in the seminal work of Robert Jervis, who posited that system effects exist when "(a) a set of units or elements is interconnected so that changes in some elements or their relations produce changes in other parts of the system, and (b) the entire system exhibits properties and behaviors that are different from those of the parts." Robert Jervis, *Systems Effects: Complexity in Political and Social Life* (Princeton, NJ: Princeton University Press, 1997), 6.

4. All data in this paragraph are from Surjit Bhalla, *Imagine There's No Country: Poverty, Inequality and Growth in the Era of Globalization* (Washington, DC: Institute for International Economics, 2002), chapter 2.

5. World Bank, *The East Asian Miracle: Economic Growth and Public Policy* (New York: Oxford University Press, 1993). For a fascinating updated discussion of development models in East and Southeast Asia, see T. J. Pempel, *A Region of Regimes: Prosperity & Plunder in the Asia-Pacific* (Ithaca, NY: Cornell University Press, 2021). The following analysis concentrates on the common features in economic strategy among the countries we study; there are, of course, important differences as well, as noted in following chapters. Chapter 6 analyzes the case of China, whose experience diverges in several important respects from the others.

6. Scholars have disagreed about the nature of the autonomy enjoyed by East Asian policymakers, but most now recognize that an analysis of their links to key societal groups is required to explain their effectiveness. A key work in this literature is Peter Evans, *Embedded Autonomy: States and Industrial Transformation* (Princeton, NJ: Princeton University Press, 1995).

7. Three examples are Alice Amsden, *Asia's Next Giant: South Korea and Late Industrialization* (New York: Oxford University Press, 1989); Chalmers Johnson, *MITI and the Japanese Miracle: The Growth of Industrial Policy 1925–1975* (Stanford, CA: Stanford University Press, 1982); and Robert Wade, *Governing the Market: Economic Theory and the Role of Government in East Asia's Industrialization* (Princeton, NJ: Princeton University Press, 1990). In contrast, Hong Kong achieved high, sustained growth by following a truly lassiez-faire approach, with very little government involvement in the economy and virtually no protectionist barriers. Singapore also pursued a relatively free trade policy though the government intervened extensively in the economy in other ways.

8. The concept of the developmental state originated with Johnson, *MITI and the Japanese Miracle*. For a variety of perspectives on the concept, see Meredith Woo-Cumings, ed., *The Developmental State* (Ithaca, NY: Cornell University Press, 1999). A comparative analysis of the state's role in developing countries is Atul Kohli, *State-Directed Development: Political Power and Industrialization in the Global Periphery* (New York: Cambridge University Press, 2004).

9. Paul Krugman, "Targeted Industrial Policies: Theory and Evidence," Proceedings—Economic Policy Symposium—Jackson Hole, Federal Reserve Bank of Kansas City, August 24–26, 1983; and Arvid Lukauskas, "Financial Restriction and the Developmental State in East Asia: Toward a More Complex Political Economy," *Comparative Political Studies* 35, no. 4 (2002): 379–412.

10. Time series data on Gini coefficients for all East Asian countries based on the same methodology and data sources do not exist. Table 1.1 separates the available data into two periods: 1965 to 1970 and 1980 to 2015. Data for the former are drawn from specific country studies only and are not strictly comparable. Statistics for the latter are derived from two longitudinal databases (OECD and Luxembourg), as well as country-specific sources for nations not included in those collections; once again, these figures may not be entirely comparable, but their methodologies are sufficiently similar to make reasonable comparisons. The Standardized World Income Inequality Database website developed by Frederik Solt was essential for compiling the data for 1965 to 1970. Frederick Solt, "Measuring Income Inequality across Countries and over Time: The Standardized World Income Inequality Database," *Social Science Quarterly* 101, no. 3 (2022): 1183–99.

11. This is true for China as well. Inequality in China was low and fairly constant until 1979 when economic and political reforms precipitated an increase in inequality. The figure for 1980—0.310—is, therefore, surely representative of Gini coefficients in the 1960s. Redistributive policies in South Korea and Taiwan were minimal in this time period, so their reported after taxes and transfers coefficients were likely quite close to before taxes and transfers measures.

12. OECD, "Income Distribution," OECD Social and Welfare Statistics, 2023. Gini coefficients in Latin America clustered around 0.50 in the same period. Facundo Alvaredo, François Bourguignon, Francisco Ferreira, and Nora Lustig, "Seventy-Five Years of Measuring Income Inequality in Latin America," IDB Working Paper Series no. IDB-WP-01521, October 2023.

13. Both OECD averages are from OECD, "Income Distribution."

14. Richard Grabowski, "East Asia, Land Reform and Economic Development," *Canadian Journal of Development Studies / Revue Canadienne d'études du Développement* 23, no. 1 (2002): 105–26.

15. José Edgardo Campos and Hilton L. Root, *The Key to the Asian Miracle: Making Shared Growth Credible* (Washington, DC: Brookings, 2001). See also World Bank, *East Asian Miracle*, chapter 4.

16. Worker unrest was not tolerated anywhere in the region, but labor policies were hardly uniform across East Asian countries. Frederic C. Deyo, "State and Labor: Modes of Political Exclusion in East Asian Development," in *The Political Economy of the New Asian Industrialism*, ed. Frederic C. Deyo (Ithaca, NY: Cornell University Press, 1987), 182–202.

17. Some of the most important works in this voluminous literature are Harold Wilensky and Charles N. Lebeaux, *Industrial Society and Social Welfare* (New York: Russell Sage Foundation, 1958); Ramesh Mishra, "Welfare and Industrial Man: A Study of Welfare in Western Industrial Societies in Relation to a Hypothesis of Convergence," *Sociological Review* 21, no. 4 (1973): 535–60; and Robert J. Barro, "A Cross-Country Study of Growth, Saving, and Government," in *National Savings and Economic Performance*, ed. Douglas Bernheim and John B. Shoven (Chicago: Chicago University Press, 1991), 271–304.

18. Gøsta Esping-Andersen, *The Three Worlds of Welfare Capitalism* (Princeton, NJ: Princeton University Press, 1990). For in-depth descriptions of the three models, see Daniel Béland, Kimberly J. Morgan, Herbert Obinger, and Christopher Pierson, eds., *The Oxford Handbook of the Welfare State*, 2nd Edition (New York: Oxford University Press, 2021). In what follows, we identify Denmark, Finland, Norway, and Sweden as social democratic; France, Germany, Italy, Luxembourg, and Switzerland as Bismarckian; and Australia, Canada, Ireland, New Zealand, the UK, and the US as liberal. Several states, for instance, Austria, Belgium, and the Netherlands, appear under different categories depending on the study, so they are excluded in the averages that follow. Greece, Portugal, and Spain are often not included in typologies under the three main models (sometimes appearing on their own as Southern Europe), so we excluded them in the averages as well. Data are drawn from OECD, "Social Expenditure—Aggregated Data," OECD Social and Welfare Statistics, 2023.

19. Huck-ju Kwon, "An Overview of the Study: The Developmental Welfare State and Policy Reforms in East Asia," in *Transforming the Developmental Welfare State in East Asia*, ed. Huck-ju Kwon (London: Palgrave MacMillian, 2005), 1–23. One important exception is Gregory Kasza's study of Japan. He found that "Japan is no more unique than the other advanced welfare states but sits comfortably within the general parameters of the species." Gregory J. Kasza, *One World of Welfare: Japan in Comparative Perspective* (Ithaca, NY: Cornell University Press, 2006), 140.

20. Ian Holliday, "Productivist Welfare Capitalism: Social Policy in East Asia," *Political Studies* 48, no. 4 (2000): 706–23.

21. In East Asia, this task was facilitated by higher initial levels of educational achievement than in other countries with similar per capita incomes. Anne Booth, "Initial Conditions and Miraculous Growth: Why Is Southeast Asia Different from Taiwan and South Korea?" *World Development* 27, no. 2 (1999): 301–21. Several multilateral organizations, notably, the World Bank, have attributed a significant portion of the region's success to

investment in human capital and referenced this experience in encouraging other nations to allocate more resources to education in particular.

22. Holliday, "Productivist Welfare Capitalism," 715.

23. Holliday, "Productivist Welfare Capitalism." Wong argued that social spending was also used by authoritarian development states to co-opt key constituencies. Joseph Wong, *Healthy Democracies: Welfare Politics in Taiwan and South Korea* (Ithaca, NY: Cornell University Press, 2004), x.

24. Ito Peng and Joseph Wong, "East Asia," in *The Oxford Handbook of the Welfare State*, ed. Francis G. Castles, Stephan Leibfried, Jane Lewis, Herbert Obinger, and Christopher Pierson (New York: Oxford University Press, 2010), 656–70.

25. Yumiko Shimabukuro and Arvid Lukauskas, "Building an Inegalitarian Welfare State: The Impact of Dualistic Coordinated Capitalism & Elite-Made Democracy in Japan" (unpublished manuscript, September 1, 2023).

26. Francis Castles, "What Welfare States Do: A Disaggregated Expenditure Approach," *Journal of Social Policy* 38, no. 1 (2008): 45–62; Lyle Scruggs and James P. Allan, "Welfare-State Decommodification in 18 OECD Countries: A Replication and Revision," *Journal of European Social Policy* 16, no. 1 (2006): 55–72; and Clare Bambra, "Decommodification and the Worlds of Welfare Revisited," *Journal of European Social Policy* 16, no. 1 (2006): 73–80.

27. A good overview is OECD, *Growing Unequal? Income Distribution and Poverty in OECD Countries* (Paris: OECD Publishing, 2008).

28. The data on social protection spending in this section are from the OECD, the Asian Development Bank (ADB), and national government sources for Hong Kong and Taiwan. We use the ADB for comparisons within East Asia because it offers data on the composition of social assistance spending, coverage rates for social insurance and assistance programs, and the distribution of benefits to the poor versus the non-poor using an innovative methodology. The ADB data cover four East Asian societies—China, Japan, South Korea and Singapore—but not Hong Kong and Taiwan and are only available for 2009 and 2015. Asian Development Bank, *The Social Protection Indicator for Asia: Assessing Progress* (Mandaluyong City, Philippines: Asian Development Bank, 2019). The statistics for Hong Kong and Taiwan are from our own calculations applying ADB methodology to official government data. Comparisons involving Western countries also draw upon various OECD databases.

29. Singapore (6), Hong Kong (18), Japan (25), Taiwan (27), South Korea (30), and China (62) were ranked among the top major countries in nominal GDP per capita in 2023. OECD and OECD-18 average income would be ranked twenty-fourth and twelfth, respectively, if they were included as such in this list. International Monetary Fund, "GDP Per Capita, Current Prices," 2023.

30. We focus on 2015 in tables 1.3 and 1.4, in which we compare social spending in East Asia and the OECD, using OECD figures for Japan and South Korea (data from 2019 are analyzed later in this chapter and in the concluding chapter). The discrepancies between the ADB and OECD data sets are small for Japan but substantial for Korea. For instance, total social protection spending for Japan is 21.2 percent (ADB) versus 21.9 percent (OECD) of GDP, but in Korea it is 8.4 percent (ADB) versus 9.6 percent (OECD) of GDP. The relative magnitude of Japan's expenditures on health and old age differs as well; in the ADB data, Japan spent more on pensions than health, whereas the OECD indicates the opposite. In reporting statistics on social assistance and insurance we apply ADB methodology to OECD data since the latter does not aggregate its data into these broad categories. This is not always a straightforward exercise. For instance, the OECD supplies data on "incapacity related" outlays but does not separate expenditures on disability insurance from disability benefits; this is significant because the former is a type of

social insurance, and the latter is social assistance. The OECD also reports only one figure for health spending that includes outlays on both insurance and assistance. The ADB separates data into insurance and assistance in both instances. We insert notes to explain how we have handled difficulties of this sort wherever pertinent.

31. The eighteen are Austria, Belgium, Canada, Denmark, Finland, France, Germany, Greece, Ireland, Italy, Luxembourg, Netherlands, Norway, Spain, Sweden, Switzerland, United Kingdom, and the United States. This group includes most but not all of the original members of the OECD.

32. Of the expenditure categories employed by the OECD, "family" (2 percent), "housing" (0.3 percent), and "other social areas" (0.5 percent) are types of social assistance spending. "Health," "incapacity," and "old age" contain a mix of social insurance and assistance expenditures. Social assistance makes up a small portion of health (5.3 percent) but a significant part of old age (7.0 percent) and incapacity (1.9 percent) outlays. Thus, it is likely that our figures slightly understate social assistance and overstate social insurance spending in OECD countries.

33. International Labour Organization, *World Social Protection Report 2017–2019: Universal Social Protection to Achieve Sustainable Development Goals* (Geneva: International Labour Office, 2017), table B.17. The ILO does not supply data for the other elements of welfare assistance, which are likely to be smaller but still significant. The OECD does not disaggregate social assistance spending into welfare, elderly, child welfare, health, and disability assistance.

34. OECD, "Income Distribution."

35. Masayoshi Hayashi, "Chihō zaisei to Seikatsu Hogo" [Local finance and the Daily Life Security]. In *Seikatsu Hogo no keizai bunseki* [Economic analysis of the Daily Life Security], ed. Abe Aya, Kunieda Shigeki, Suzuki Wataru, and Hayashi Masayoshi (Tokyo: Tokyo Daigaku Shuppankai, 2008), 239–68.

36. Margarita Estevez-Abe, *Welfare and Capitalism in Postwar Japan* (New York: Cambridge University Press, 2008); and Dokyun Kim, "The Development of Functional Equivalents to the Welfare State in Post-war Japan and South Korea," in *The Small Welfare State: Rethinking Welfare in the US, Japan and South Korea*, ed. Jae-jin Yang (Cheltenham, UK: Edward Elgar Publishing, 2020), 163–89. Hong Kong public officials have also argued that spending on education, health, and housing should be considered as a form of social protection and be counted as such. Health care expenditures are well captured in standard reporting of social insurance outlays, and education is not usually conceptualized as a form of social insurance or assistance. The claim that social protection data do not reflect the social protection supplied by high spending on public housing, however, merits closer attention. Hong Kong spent 32.5 billion Hong Kong dollars on public housing, which represented 5 percent of total government expenditure or 1.1 percent of GDP in 2018. It is important to note, however, that other countries also dedicate sizable (but fewer) resources to housing policy.

37. Megumi Naoi, "Voting with the Wallet: Consumers, Income-Earners and the New Politics of Globalization Backlash" (unpublished book manuscript, 2020).

38. Saito Jun, *Jimintō chōki seiken no seiji keizaigaku* [The political economy of the LDP regime] (Tokyo: Keisō Shobō, 2010).

39. Among the many works with a generally favorable assessment are Campos and Root, *Key to the Asian Miracle*; Holliday, "Productivist Welfare Capitalism"; and Catherine Jones, "The Pacific Challenge: The Confucian Welfare States," in *New Perspectives on the Welfare State in Europe*, ed. Catherine Jones (New York: Routledge, 1993), 192–210.

40. Peter Lindert, *Growing Public: Social Spending and Economic Growth since the Eighteenth Century*, 2nd ed. (New York: Cambridge University Press, 2004).

41. The data reported here are for spending per each intended beneficiary and, hence, differ from the figures found in tables 1.3 and 1.4. For details on this methodology, see Asian Development Bank, *Social Protection Indicator*. The ADB did not furnish these data for Hong Kong and Taiwan and we were unable to replicate their methodology to do our own calculations.

42. Relative poverty rates are defined as the percentage of the population earning 50% or below of median income. In 2020, the relative poverty rate was 15.7 in Japan, 15.3 in South Korea, and 24.7 in China (2019), compared to the OECD average of 11.5. China does not report a poverty rate based on a relative measure. The rate we provide here used a poverty line of USD6.85 per day, which is the World Bank's level for an upper middle-income country (which China now is). OECD, "Income Distribution"; and World Bank, "Poverty and Inequality Platform," 2023.

43. Coverage rates are defined as the percentage of eligible individuals who actually receive benefits. Rates above 100 percent in South Korea and Singapore indicate that some individuals received benefits from more than one program. For details on this methodology, see Asian Development Bank, *Social Protection Indicator*. The ADB does not supply these data for Hong Kong and Taiwan.

44. Sheldon Garon, "Japanese Policies toward Poverty and Public Assistance: A Historical Perspective," World Bank Institute Working Papers no. 37200, 2002; and Masayoshi, "Chihō zaisei."

45. Hong Kong, which has flat income and corporate taxes, has the least progressive tax system in East Asia, whereas Japan has the most. Tax policy in Japan tends to redistribute income primarily from the working population to the aged, not across income deciles. Zheng Jian and Daniel Jeongjae Lee, "Prospects for Progressive Tax Reforms in Asia and the Pacific," Working Paper Series, Macroeconomic Policy and Financing for Development Division WP/17/08, United Nations ESCAP 2017, April 2017.

46. The OECD only reported Gini coefficients for China for the year 2010, so these figures were used for consistency. China's National Bureau of Statistics reported an after taxes and transfers coefficient of 0.462 for 2015, down from 0.481 in 2010; it did not provide data on before taxes and transfers. See Juzhong Zhuang and Li Shi, "Understanding Recent Trends in Income Inequality in the People's Republic of China," ADB Economics Working Paper Series no. 489, July 2016. Governments in China, Singapore, and Taiwan do not report relative poverty rates. Chapter 2 offers estimates of their relative poverty rates.

47. The statistics presented here were calculated using the "Private (mandatory and voluntary)" indicator from OECD, "Social Expenditure—Aggregated Data." Japan and Korea are the only East Asian countries included in this database.

48. In Japan, the ratio was virtually equal to the OECD but not the OECD-18 average in 2010.

49. For example, see World Bank, *East Asian Miracle*. Efforts to improve human capital involve supplying both education and health services. Spending is only a rough measure of quality or the significance that governments place on education and health, since other factors also influence outcomes.

50. A classic statement on the effects of globalization is Dani Rodrik, *Has Globalization Gone Too Far?* (Washington, DC: Institute for International Economics, 1997).

51. Global cities also attract high-skill migrants in sectors like finance and technology. These individuals tend to improve the productivity of resident workers in their sectors and do not depress their wages.

52. The sum of imports and exports as a percentage of GDP in 2018 was 38 percent for China, 377 percent for Hong Kong, 37 percent for Japan, 83 percent for South Korea, 326 percent for Singapore, and 105 percent for Taiwan. The world average was 59 percent.

Data for Taiwan are from Taiwan (ROC), Ministry of Foreign Affairs, "Taiwan.gov.tw: Economy"; for all other countries, they are from World Bank, "Trade (% of GDP)," World Development Indicators, 2023. China is at the heart of several global supply chains and receives high levels of foreign direct investment, so its exposure to international forces is higher than suggested by the figure above.

53. Among the first works to recognize and analyze this transformation was Saskia Sassen, *The Global City: New York, London, Tokyo* (Princeton, NJ: Princeton University Press, 2001).

54. Willem Thorbecke and Namesh Salike, "Understanding Foreign Direct Investment in East Asia," ADBI Working Paper Series no. 290, June 2011; and Min-Hua Chiang and Lafaye de Micheaux, "China's Outward Foreign Direct Investment in Southeast Asia: Analyzing the Chinese State's Strategies and Potential Influence," *Thunderbird International Business Review* 64, no. 6 (2022): 581–93.

55. UNCTAD, *World Investment Report 2023* (New York: United Nations Publications, 2023). Outward FDI from China alone amounted to USD146.5 billion.

56. Nir Jaimovich and Henry E. Siu, "The Trend Is the Cycle: Job Polarization and Jobless Recoveries," NBER Working Paper no. 18334, August 2012.

57. International Monetary Fund, *World Economic Outlook: Seeking Sustainable Growth. Short-Term Recovery, Long-Term Challenges* (Washington, DC: International Monetary Fund, 2017), chapter 2.

58. David H. Autor, Lawrence F. Katz, and Melissa S. Kearney, "The Polarization of the U.S. Labor Market," *American Economic Review* 98, no. 2 (2006): 189–94. See also Leonard Schoppa, "Globalization and the Squeeze on the Middle Class: Does Any Version of the Postwar Social Contract Meet the Challenge?," in *Social Contracts Under Stress: The Middle Classes of America, Europe, and Japan at the Turn of the Century*, ed. Olivier Zunz, Leonard Schoppa, and Nobuhiro Hiwatari (New York: Russell Sage, 2002), 319–44.

59. Jacob S. Hacker and Paul Pierson, *Winner-Take-All Politics: How Washington Made the Rich Richer—and Turned Its Back on the Middle Class* (New York: Simon & Schuster, 2010).

60. David Autor, Lawrence F. Katz and Melissa S. Kearney, "Trends in U.S. Wage Inequality: Revising the Revisionists," *Review of Economics and Statistics* 90, no. 2 (2008): 300–23.

61. Tokyo shares some characteristics with these cities but has significantly lower income inequality because of the long-lasting effects of the bursting of Japan's bubble economy. See "The Secure v the Poor," *Economist*, February 12, 2015.

62. Government of the Hong Kong Special Administrative Region, "Hong Kong Poverty Situation Report 2020," November 2021; and Eurostat, "In-Work at-Risk-of-Poverty Rate by Group of Citizenship (Population Aged 18 and Over)," 2023.

63. The figures for Japan and Korea are for 2018. In-work poverty among young Korean workers (nineteen to thirty-five) was particularly high at 37.1 percent in 2015. Hwangbo Yon, "Around One-Third of Young South Koreans Experience Working Poverty," *Hankyoreh*, March 5, 2017. On Japan, see Zhiyong An and Kohei Asao, "Options to Strengthen the Social Safety Net in Japan," IMF Selected Issues Papers SIP/2023/033, March 2023.

64. Hernando de Soto, *The Other Path: The Economic Answer to Terrorism* (New York: Basic Books, 2002); and Edward Glaeser, *Triumph of the City: How Our Greatest Invention Makes Us Richer, Smarter, Greener, Healthier, and Happier* (London: Penguin Books, 2011).

65. United Nations, Department of Economic and Social Affairs, Population Dynamics, "World Urbanization Prospects 2018: Country Profiles," 2018.

66. World Bank, "Urban Population Growth (Annual %)." World Development Indicators, 2023.

67. Karen Eggleston, Jean C. Oi, and Yiming Wang, eds., *Challenges in the Process of China's Urbanization* (Palo Alto, CA: Shorenstein Asia-Pacific Research Center, 2017).

68. The literature is reviewed in Paul Puschmann and Arne Solli, "Household and Family during Urbanization and Industrialization: Efforts to Shed New Light on an Old Debate," *History of the Family* 19, no. 1 (2014): 1–12.

69. World Population Review, "Largest Metro Areas in the World," 2023.

70. Bertrand Renaud, Kyung-Hwan Kim, and Man Cho, *Dynamics of Housing in East Asia* (Chichester, UK: John Wiley & Sons, 2016), chapter 10.

71. Fang Zhao, Juha Erkki, Antero Hamalaienen, and Honglin L. Chen, "Child Protection in China: Changing Policies and Reactions from the Field of Social Work," *International Journal of Social Welfare* 26 (2017): 334.

72. Ming-Hsuan Lee, "Migration and Children's Welfare in China: The Schooling and Health of Children Left Behind," *Journal of Developing Areas* 44, no. 2 (2011): 165–82.

73. The age dependency ratio is the number of dependents aged sixty-five and older divided by the working age population, ages fifteen to sixty-four.

74. Cumulative labor force growth in Japan was a mere 1 percent over the period 2000 to 2018; it was 15.9 percent in Hong Kong (2000–16), 26.5 percent in Korea (2000–18), and 21.4 percent in Taiwan (2000–18). Singapore is excluded here because its heavy use of migrant workers has resulted in volatile labor force growth with no clear trend.

75. World Bank, *Live Long and Prosper: Aging in East Asia and Pacific* (Washington, DC: World Bank, 2016).

76. David E. Bloom, David Canning, and Günther Fink, "Implications of Population Ageing for Economic Growth," *Oxford Review of Economic Policy* 26, no. 4 (2010): 583–612; and Thai Than Dang, Pablo Antolin, and Oxley Howard, "Fiscal Implications of Ageing: Projections of Age-Related Spending," OECD Economics Department Working Papers no. 305, September 2001.

77. David Drakakis-Smith, Elspeth Graham, Peggy Teo, and Ooi Giok Ling, "Singapore: Reversing the Demographic Transition to Meet Labour Needs," *Scottish Geographical Magazine* 109, no. 3 (1993): 153–63.

78. James M. Raymo, Hyunjoon Park, Yu Xie, and Wei-Jun Jean Yeung, "Marriage and Family in East Asia: Continuity and Change," *Annual Review of Sociology* 41 (2015): 471–92.

79. Gavin W. Jones, "Changing Family Sizes, Structures and Functions in Asia," *Asia-Pacific Population Journal* 27, no. 1 (2012): 95; and Elisabeth Schroder-Butterfill and Philip Kreager, "Actual and De Facto Childlessness in Old Age: Evidence and Implications from East Java, Indonesia," *Population and Development Review* 31, no. 1 (2005): 19–55.

80. The ratio of senile or bed-ridden seniors to non-working women ages forty to forty-nine, the largest group of elderly care givers, is expected to rise from 14 percent in 2000 to 50 percent in 2025. Naohiro Ogawa, "Population Aging and Policy Options for a Sustainable Future: The Case of Japan," *Genus* 61, no. 3/4 (2005): 389–91.

81. This policy was part of the Abenomics package of economic reforms and reflected concern over Japan's shrinking workforce.

82. Jones, "Changing Family Sizes." The extent of this trend varies by nation and even subregion across East Asia. It is important to note that these bonds remain strong in comparative perspective; the percentage of people aged sixty or older living with a child or grandchild is considerably higher than in Western societies.

83. The number of individuals living in public units decreased by 600,000 from 1990 to 2016 despite an increase of 150,000 units. Richard Wong, "Demography, Housing, and the Economic Future of Hong Kong," presentation at the Hong Kong CSB Advanced Leadership Enhancement Programme for Directorate Officials, December 1, 2017. On the demographics behind this trend, see Richard Wong, *Hong Kong Land for Hong Kong*

People: Fixing the Failures of Our Housing Policy (Hong Kong: Hong Kong University Press, 2015).

84. Government of Hong Kong, Housing Authority, "At a Glance," 2023.

85. Rebecca A. Colman and Cathy Spatz Widom, "Childhood Abuse and Neglect and Adult Intimate Relationships: A Prospective Study," *Child Abuse & Neglect* 28, no. 11 (2004): 1133–51.

86. See Mason M. S. Kim, *Comparative Welfare Capitalism in East Asia: Productivist Models of Social Policy* (Basingstoke, UK: Palgrave MacMillian, 2016); and Peng and Wong, "East Asia."

87. Data on the breakdown of benefits going to the poor and non-poor are not available for 2019.

88. The surplus in 2022 was 1.0 of GDP, down from a high of 5.6 percent of GDP in 2017. The government's reserves in 2022 were sufficient to cover 1.3 years of expenditures; in some previous years, reserves were sufficient to cover more than two years of expenditures. Hong Kong Special Administrative Region, "Hong Kong Annual Digest of Statistics 2022 Edition," October 2022.

89. On the US case, see Christopher Howard, *The Welfare State Nobody Knows: Debunking Myths about U.S. Social Policy* (Princeton, NJ: Princeton University Press, 2008).

90. Ichiro Wada and Ataru Igarashi, "The Social Costs of Child Abuse in Japan," *Children and Youth Services Review* 46 (2014): 72.

91. Minoru Matsutani, "S. Korea's Economy and the Elderly: Declining Workforce, Graying of Society Severely Burdens Welfare Programs," *Japan Times*, May 11, 2014.

92. Brian Keely, *Income Inequality: The Gap between Rich and Poor* (Paris: OECD Publishing, 2015).

93. For policy responses to declining fertility rates in Japan, which has the lowest labor force growth in East Asia, see Schoppa, "Globalization and the Squeeze on the Middle Class."

94. In Singapore, the government established the Family Planning and Population Board in 1967 to advocate for smaller families and introduced several policies to stem births. Lim Keak Cheng, "Post-Independence Population Planning and Social Development in Singapore," *GeoJournal* 18, no. 2 (1989): 163–74. China introduced its one-child policy in 1979 to slow population growth as a key element of broader economic reforms. Therese Hesketh, Li Lu, and Zhu Wei Xing, "The Effect of China's One-Child Family Policy after 25 Years," *New England Journal of Medicine* 353 (2005): 1171–76.

95. Jones, "Changing Family Sizes."

96. Kuan-lin Liu, Ku Chuan, and Yu Hsiao-han, "Student Groups Demand an Increase in Minimum Wage," *Focus Taiwan News Channel*, May 24, 2018; and Sean Lin, "Groups Protest Council 'Coercing' Labor Ministry," *Taipei Times*, January 20, 2019.

2. MISERY IN THE GOLDEN YEARS

1. This chapter's synthetic narrative is based on the authors' field research in Seoul, as well as journalistic accounts. We have also incorporated the valuable insights of social entrepreneur Hoyoung Lee, the founder and CEO of Tenthroom (Sib-si-il-bang) and CRO of Impact Research Lab, who has dedicated his academic and professional career to ameliorating food insecurity and poor housing conditions among the elderly poor in Seoul. The suicide of Kim Joo-hyun, an actual worker at a Samsung factory, occurred in 2011. Jeon Jin-sik, "Following Worker Suicide, Samsung Reluctantly Pledges Change," *Hankyoreh*, April 18, 2011.

2. For an overview of South Korea's economic transformation, see Byung Nak Song, *The Rise of the Korean Economy* (New York: Oxford University Press, 1997).

3. *Chaebol* refers to a large industrial conglomerate usually owned by a single family.

4. OECD, "Social Expenditure—Aggregated Data," OECD Social and Welfare Statistics (database), 2023.

5. Hagen Koo, "Engendering Civil Society: The Role of the Labor Movement," in *Korean Society: Civil Society, Democracy and the State*, ed. Charles Armstrong (New York: Routledge, 2007), 73–94.

6. Beneficiaries of the government's industrial policies were expected to make contributions to politicians (*jun jo-seh*) as a sign of gratitude. Over time "a racketeering state became the flip side of the developmentalist state." Jung-en Woo, *Race to the Swift: State and Finance in Korean Industrialization* (New York: Columbia University Press, 1991), 200.

7. The OECD sets the poverty line at 50 percent of the national median equalized household income. The governments of Singapore and Taiwan do not provide official relative poverty data for the elderly or total population. Some scholars have calculated these rates, and we discuss their estimates in a later section. China only supplies data on levels of absolute poverty; see chapter 6 for more details.

8. In 2020, the Hong Kong government revised how it reports after taxes and transfers poverty, leading to dramatically lower rates. Rates previously reported for past years were also revised downward. For instance, the total poverty rate originally provided for 2019 (which we show here) was 15.8 percent, but it dropped to only 9.3 percent in the latest government report. Government of the Hong Kong Special Administrative Region, Census and Statistics Department, Office of the Government Economist Financial Secretary's Office, "Hong Kong Poverty Situation Report 2020," November 2021.

9. Inohe Ku and Chang-o Kim, "Decomposition Analyses of the Trend in Poverty among Older Adults: The Case of South Korea," *Journals of Gerontology: Series B* 75, no. 3 (2020), 684–93.

10. In Japan, seniors' average income was 75 percent of the average household income. Hye Yeong Seong, "Yeongeum poreom gyeo-ul-ho: Hanguk, Miguk, Ilbon Roh-in eui gagu sobi jichul bigyo" [Pension Forum Winter Edition: Comparing the Expenditure Level of the Elderly Household in Korea, United States, and Japan], *National Pension Research Institute* 60 (2015): 49–55; and OECD, *Pensions at a Glance 2017: OECD and G20 Indicators* (Paris: OECD Publishing, 2017).

11. "Korea's Elderly Has Smallest Disposable Income among OECD Members," *Dong-a Ilbo*, December 6, 2022; OECD, *Working Better with Age: Korea* (Geneva: OECD Publishing, 2018); and Cynthia Kim, "The Jobs—and Ageing Faces—Behind South Korea's Record Low Unemployment Numbers," *Reuters*, March 24, 2022.

12. Jiseob Kim, "Structural Weakness of Debt Held by Senior Householders," *KDI*, December 9, 2015.

13. Kim Min-Jeung and Cho Hye-Jin, "Boochae boyoo euntaeja gagu eui jaejung sangtae meet boochae sanghwan ganeungsung: Euntae saenghwal jageum eul koryohan boonseok" [Financial status and debts repayment possibility of retirement households that have debts], *Consumer Policy and Education Review* 9 (2013): 41–62; Park Myung Hee and Paik Il Woo, "Hankuk sa-gyo-yook sijang jeongae eui yeoksawha euimi" [The history of Korean private tutoring market development and its implication], *Educational Research for Tomorrow* 29, no. 2 (2016): 23–50.

14. Korea, National Police Agency, "Kyungchal beomjae tongkei" [Police Crime Statistics], 2019.

15. Bryan Harris and Kang Buseong, "South Korea's Penniless Pensioners Face Final Years in Crisis," *Financial Times*, November 27, 2017; and Lee Ho Sun, "Roh-in eul daesang-euiro haneun seongmaemae pihye yeosung yeonkoo: Bacchus azumma siltae chosa meet roh-in sangdam jeopgeun" [The old women prostitutes serving old men: Research

on the actual condition of 'Bacchus azumma' and the basic setting of the elderly counseling process], *Journal of the Korean Gerontological Society* 31, no. 3 (2011): 489–503.

16. OECD, "Suicide Rates," 2023.

17. OECD, *Society at a Glance 2019* (Paris: OECD Publishing, 2019).

18. The rates were 15.1 percent for the 65 to 69 age group, 18.2 percent for 70 to 74, 23.6 percent for 75 to 79, 30.7 percent for 80 to 84, and 33.1 percent for 85 and above. Jung Bum Kim and Taesuck Kihl, "Suicidal Ideation Associated with Depression and Social Support: A Survey-Based Analysis of Older Adults in South Korea," *BMC Psychiatry* 21 (2021): 409.

19. United Nations, Department of Economic and Social Affairs. Population Division, "World Population Prospects," 2022.

20. Korea, Statistical Information Service, "Projected Population by Age Group," 2021.

21. "Korea Extends Natural Population Fall as Fertility Rate Falls to 0.7," *Korea Times*, August 30, 2023; and World Bank, "Life Expectancy at Birth, Total (Years)," Databank/World Development Indicators, 2023.

22. Nasreen Khan, Shereen Khan, Olivia Tan Swee Leng, Tan Booi Chen, and Rossane Gale Vergara, "Explore the Factors that Influence Elderly Poverty," *Journal of Southeast Asian Research* 2017 (2017): 1–13.

23. Luca Ventura, "Household Savings Rates 2021," *Global Finance*, January 25, 2021. The gross national savings rate was 34 percent of GDP, reflecting large government surpluses and corporate savings.

24. "Poverty Worsening among South Korea's Aged People," *Nation*, July 8, 2012.

25. Many parents are also burdened by their children's extravagant weddings.

26. OECD, *Education at a Glance 2022* (Paris: OECD Publishing, 2022), 277. Private spending on education surged after the COVID-19 pandemic, reaching a recorded high of USD20 billion in 2022. Park Jun-hee, "Spending on Private Education Surpasses W26tr in 2022," *Korea Herald*, March 7, 2023.

27. OECD, *Education at a Glance, Korea*, 8; Park and Paik, "Hankuk sa-gyo-yook"; and Jeyup S. Kwaak, "South Korea's $18 Billion Education Problem," *Wall Street Journal*, August 28, 2014.

28. Byeong Cheol Oh, Ji-Yoon Yeon, Hyo-Sang Lee, Doo Woong Lee, and Eun-Cheol Park, "Correlation between Private Education Costs and Parental Depression in South Korea," *BMC Public Health* 20 (2020): 972.

29. World Bank, "Urban Population Growth (Annual %)," World Development Indicators, 2023.

30. Economist Intelligence Unit, "Worldwide Cost of Living Survey 2021," December 2021; and Kyung-Hwan Kim and Miseon Park, "Housing Policy in the Republic of Korea," ADBI Working Paper Series no. 570, Asian Development Bank, April 2016.

31. Erin Hye-Won Kim and Philip J. Cook, "The Continuing Importance of Children in Relieving Elder Poverty: Evidence from Korea," *Ageing and Society* 31, no. 6 (2011): 953–76.

32. Claire Lee, "Fewer Koreans Feel Responsible for Aging Parents," *Korea Herald*, May 8, 2016.

33. Sun Jae Lee, "Poverty amongst the Elderly in South Korea: The Perception, Prevalence, and Causes and Solutions," *International Journal of Social Science and Humanity* 4, no. 3 (2014): 242–45.

34. The number of such deaths rose from 682 in 2011 to over 1,000 in 2014. Choe Sang-Hun, "A Lonely End for South Koreans Who Cannot Afford to Live, or Die," *New York Times*, November 1, 2015.

35. Seong Sook Kim, "Pension Reform Options in Korea" (paper presentation, IMF International Conference, Tokyo, Japan, January 2013).

36. About two-thirds of those aged fifty-five to sixty-four left their career jobs before they reached the pensionable age. OECD, *Economic Surveys: Korea 2022* (Geneva: OECD Publishing, 2022), 74–75. Another study found that 76 percent of early retirements were nonvoluntary, 60 percent wanted to find new jobs, only 26 percent of retirees were able to do so, and 80 percent of those who found work ended up accepting low-paying positions. Hoyoung Lee, Haeun Kim, and Hyun Shin, "Tackling Involuntary Retirement in South Korea," *Stanford Social Innovation Review*, October 20, 2021.

37. OECD, *Reviews of Pension Systems: Korea* (Paris: OECD Publishing, 2022), 35–36.

38. Thomas R. Klassen, "New Policies for Korea's Aging Labor Force: The Role of Contractual Mandatory Retirement," Korea Labor Institute, September 2011; Accordingly, countries such as the United States, Canada, and United Kingdom gradually have abolished the practice of contractual mandatory retirement. The rationales for a legal ban also included ending age discrimination, promoting workplace equal opportunity, and human rights protection. C. T. Gillin and Thomas R. Klassen, "Age Discrimination and Early Retirement Policies: A Comparison of Labor Market Regulation in Canada and the United States," *Journal of Aging & Social Policy* 7, no. 1 (1995): 85–102.

39. Two-thirds of individuals aged 55 to 64 were employed, and one-third held low-paying temporary positions (compared to the OECD average of only 8 percent). OECD, *Working Better with Age: Korea* (Geneva: OECD Publishing, 2018), 45.

40. Jiyeun Lee, "'Silver Service' Jobs Help Korea's Pensioners Survive," *Bloomberg*, December 13, 2016.

41. OECD, *Working Better with Age: Korea*, 33.

42. Thomas Klassen and Kun-ha Yu, "Introduction to Retirement in Korea," in *Korea's Retirement Predicament*, ed. Thomas R. Klassen and Yunjeong Yang (New York: Routledge, 2013), 1–20.

43. This system is named after the German chancellor Otto von Bismarck, who introduced the world's first contribution-based old age social insurance program in 1889. On the various types of old age security programs, see Karl Hinrichs and Julia F. Lynch, "Old-Age Pensions," in *The Oxford Handbook of the Welfare State*, ed. Francis G. Castles, Stephan Leibfried, Jane Lewis, Herbert Obinger, and Christopher Pierson (New York: Oxford University Press, 2012), 353–66.

44. William Henry Beveridge was a British economist and pioneering social reformer who proposed a flat rate universal contribution and benefit scheme in the groundbreaking Beveridge Report (officially, Social Insurance and Allied Services) in 1942.

45. Asghar Zaidi, "Poverty Risks for Older People in EU Countries—An Update," European Centre for Social Welfare Policy and Research, Policy Brief, January 2010, 1.

46. OECD, *Reviews of Pension Systems: Korea*, 38.

47. Most employees choose lump-sum severance payments over a portable individual retirement account, a decision which contributes to lower income levels in retirement.

48. International Labour Organization, *World Social Protection Report 2020–22: Social Protection at the Crossroads—In Pursuit of a Better Future* (Geneva: International Labour Organization, 2021), table A4.3. The OECD reported higher expenditures for Korea, equal to 3.4 percent of GDP. OECD, "Social Expenditure—Detailed Data," OECD Social and Welfare Statistics, 2023.

49. OECD, "Social Expenditure—Detailed Data."

50. The social insurance system began with targeted, small-scale old age security programs for government workers (1960), military officials (1963), and private school teachers (1975).

51. OECD, *Reviews of Pension Systems: Korea*, 48, 66–67. The baseline for the flat payment is "the average wage of all contributors over the three years prior to retirement, updated for inflation."

52. Salaried workers contributed for an average of 8.4 years and the self-employed a mere four years. Hanam Phang, "National Pension, Labour Market and Retirement in Korea: Institutional Mismatch and Policy Alternatives," in *Korea's Retirement Predicament*, ed. Thomas R. Klassen and Yunjeong Yang (New York: Routledge, 2013), 96–111.

53. Sun-Jae Hwang, "Public Pensions as the Great Equalizer? Decomposition of Old-Age Income Inequality in South Korea, 1998–2010," *Journal of Aging & Social Policy* 28, no. 2 (2016): 81–97.

54. Hyungpyo Moon, "Demographic Changes and Pension Reform in the Republic of Korea," ADBI Working Paper Series no. 135, April 2009.

55. The replacement rate was set at 50 percent in 2008 and is being lowered by 0.5 percent each year until 2028, when it will reach 40 percent.

56. The rate for a full career low earner is 46 percent, which reflects the redistributive element built into pension distributions through the NPS's flat rate component. OECD, *Reviews of Pension Systems: Korea*, 67–68.

57. OECD, *Reviews of Pension Systems: Korea*, 72–76.

58. OECD, *Working Better with Age: Korea*, 39.

59. Hwang, "Public Pensions as the Great Equalizer?"

60. The percentage of employees in large companies who enjoy retirement allowances (93.7 percent), extra sources of income such as bonuses (91.4 percent), and overtime pay (82.3 percent) is very high. Jae-jin Yang, "The Welfare State and Income Security for the Elderly in Korea." In *Korea's Retirement Predicament*, ed. Thomas R. Klassen and Yunjeong Yang (New York: Routledge, 2013), 39–52.

61. OECD, *Working Better with Age: Korea*, 13, 33.

62. Yang, "Welfare State and Income Secutity."

63. The benefit was equivalent to only 5 percent of the NPS participant's average monthly income, which amounted to approximately USD80 for a single-member household.

64. Although the BLSP covers the poor in general, more than one-fourth of the beneficiaries are elderly.

65. Republic of Korea, Ministry of Health and Welfare, "Basic Livelihood Security Program: Benefit Recipients & Payment," 2017.

66. Choi Sung-jin, "Basic Pension Coming on July 1, but Tangled in Bureaucratic Complications," *Hankyoreh*, June 24, 2014.

67. OECD, *Working Better with Age: Korea*, 114.

68. OECD, *Working Better with Age: Korea*, 117.

69. For an excellent history of the evolution of labor relations in South Korea, see Yoonkyung Lee, *Militants or Partisans: Labor Unions and Democratic Politics in Korea and Taiwan* (Palo Alto, CA: Stanford University Press, 2011).

70. Yang, "Welfare State and Income Secutity," 44–45.

71. Klassen and Yu, "Introduction."

72. Yang, "Welfare State and Income Security," 44. Korea's legislature is a unicameral body of 300 seats. A total of 253 are chosen through single-member districts, and forty-seven are selected through proportional representation.

73. Yongman Cho, "Legal Foundations of Mandatory Retirement," 60.

74. Eunhee Choi, "Older Workers and Federal Work Programs," 308–24.

75. Jesook Song, *South Koreans in the Debt Crisis*.

76. Yeon Kyung Chee, "Elder Care in Korea."

77. Wan He, Daniel Goodkind and Paul Kowal, "Asia Aging."

78. He, Goodkind and Kowal, "Asia Aging." UN estimates for 2050 indicate even more pronounced aging: China (36.5 percent), Hong Kong (40.9 percent), Japan (42.5 percent),

South Korea (41.5 percent), Singapore (40.4 percent), and Taiwan (38.2 percent). United Nations, "World Population Prospects: 2015 Revision," 27-30.

79. OECD, "Income Distribution," OECD Social and Welfare Statistics, 2023.

80. Yoshie Sano and Saori Yasumoto, "Policy Responses to Population-Declining Society: Development and Challenges of Family Policies in Japan," in *Handbook of Family Policies Across the Globe*, ed. Mihaela Robila (New York: Springer Science & Business Media, 2013), 327; and Matthew Bremner, "The Lonely End." *Slate*, June 26, 2015.

81. Japan, National Police Agency, "Reiwa 4 nenchū ni okeru jisatsu no jōkyō" [Suicide trends in 2022], March 14, 2023.

82. Ankit Panda, "What's Behind Japan's Rise in Senior Citizen Crime?," *Japan Times*, November 25, 2016; and "Why Some Japanese Pensioners Want to Go to Jail," *BBC News*, January 31, 2019.

83. OECD, "Net Pension Replacement Rates," 2023.

84. Pernille Rudlin, "Retirement Systems in Japan—Under Revision but Lacking Clarity," Rudlin Consulting, August 2022.

85. Japan, Ministry of Health Labour and Welfare, "2016 teinensei nado" [2016 system of mandatory retirement], 2016.

86. OECD, *Working Better with Age: Japan* (Paris: OECD Publishing, 2018).

87. Daniel Leussink, "Japan's Elderly Workers, Once Key to Abenomics, Suffer as Pandemic Closes Businesses," *Reuters*, May 21, 2020.

88. Irene Y. H. Ng, "Definitions and Measurements of Poverty," *SSR Snippet* 4 (2020): 2–9. Ng set the poverty line at 50 percent of median national income. Comparing her finding with poverty rates in other countries must be done with caution, but it does suggest that total and elderly poverty in Singapore are extensive.

89. Kane Cunico, Yvonne Lim, and Jade Han, "Ploughing On: The Faces and Insecurities of Singapore's Elderly Working Poor," *Channel News Asia*, May 7, 2017.

90. The Housing Development Board oversees public housing in Singapore. Chapter 5 analyzes that country's public housing system in more detail.

91. For details, see Republic of Singapore, Ministry of Social and Family Development, "ComCare Long Term Assistance," 2023. The government also offers various types of in-kind benefits, including the Pioneer Generation Package (e.g., subsidies for medications and clinic fees), Senior Citizen Concession Card (e.g., discounts on transportation), and levy concessions on foreign domestic workers.

92. For details, see Republic of Singapore, Ministry of Manpower, "Silver Support Scheme," 2023.

93. Chan Ho-him, "In the Shadow of Hong Kong's Skyscrapers, the Poor Scavenge for Cardboard," *Financial Times*, December 22, 2021.

94. Government of the Hong Kong Special Administrative Region, Census and Statistics Department, Office of the Government Economist Financial Secretary's Office, "Hong Kong Poverty Situation Report 2020," November 2021.

95. The Mandatory Provident Fund (MPF) resembles the CPF in Singapore. It was created in 2000, so it does not cover current retirees. The MPF has a lower contribution rate and provides smaller pensions than the CPF.

96. Fiona Sun, "Hong Kong Government to Give Eligible Elderly Receiving Allowances an Extra HK$995 a Month from September 1," *South China Morning Post*, June 20, 2022.

97. Jeffie Lam, "Policy Address: CY Leung Abolishes Controversial 'Bad Son Statement' and Announces Means-Tested Pensions," *South China Morning Post*, January 19, 2017.

98. Gru Erde, "Tackling the Growing Income Gap in Taiwan," *Think China*, February 15, 2023.

99. See for example, Steven Pressman, "Cross-National Comparisons of Poverty and Income Inequality," in *The Economics of Inequality, Poverty, and Discrimination in the 21st Century*, ed. Robert S. Rycroft (Santa Barbara, CA: ABC-CLIO, 2013), 27. Some journalistic accounts have reported on terrible living conditions for seniors, including those who are officially above the poverty line. For example, see Woon Wei Jong, "Growing Old Alone: Elderly Poor Want Better Housing, Better Care in Taiwan," *Think China*, February 16, 2022.

100. Pensions Funds Online, "Pension System in Taiwan," 2023.

101. Workers have been able to choose between the new and old pension schemes since 2014. See Taiwan (ROC), Ministry of Labor, Bureau of Labor Insurance, "The New Labor Pension System is not the Old-Age Benefits of the Labor Insurance Program," August 2021, for details.

102. Social Security Administration, "Social Security Programs throughout the World: Asia and the Pacific, 2018," 2018.

103. Chen Po-Chien, "Impoverishment of Elderly People," *Taipei Times*, September 17, 2016.

3. BROKEN PROMISES

1. See the introduction to a special issue of the *Journal of Asian Public Policy* dedicated to this topic. Jan-Der Lue and Chan-ung Park, "Beyond Productivist Social Policy: The East Asian Welfare–Work Nexus in Transition," *Journal of Asian Public Policy* 6, no. 1 (2013): 1–9. Two articles from this volume on individual country experiences are cited in this chapter.

2. This narrative is based on the authors' field research in Kaohsiung, Taichung, and the Taipei metropolitan area, as well as journalistic and scholarly accounts of recent business and labor market trends in Taiwan.

3. Seventy-three members are elected from single-member constituencies drawn from Special Municipalities, cities, and counties; thirty-four are chosen through a nationwide proportional representation system; and two aboriginal constituencies select three members each.

4. Robert Wade, *Governing the Market: Economic Theory and the Role of Government in East Asia's Industrialization* (Princeton, NJ: Princeton University Press, 1990); and World Bank, *The East Asian Miracle: Economic Growth and Public Policy* (New York: Oxford University Press, 1993).

5. Taiwan (ROC), Statistical Bureau, "Social Protection Expenditure," 2023.

6. Cindy Sui, "Changing Times Force Taiwan to Raise Welfare Spending," *BBC News*, April 24, 2013.

7. Real wages are nominal wages adjusted for inflation. Standard microeconomic theory posits that real wages should grow in line with the marginal product of labor. On wages, see Shu-shiuan Lu, "East Asian Growth Experience Revisited from the Perspective of a Neoclassical Model," *Review of Economic Dynamics* 15, no. 3 (2012): 359–76. On GDP and labor productivity, see Noriyoshi Oguchi, "Productivity Trends in Asia since 1980," *International Productivity Monitor* 10 (2005): 69–78.

8. Real wages grew at an annual rate of 1 percent in the period 2020 to 2022, whereas labor productivity increased by 4.1 percent, continuing the trend of productivity improvements surpassing wage growth by a wide margin. Taiwan (ROC), Statistical Bureau, "Average Monthly Earnings," 2023.

9. Paulina Restrepo-Echavarria and Brian Reinbold, "Measuring Labor Share of the Asian Tigers," Federal Reserve Bank of St. Louis, January 11, 2018.

10. U.S. Bureau of Labor Statistics, "Employed Full Time. Median Usual Weekly Real Earnings. Wage and Salary Workers. 16 Years and Over [LES1252881600Q]," FRED, Federal Reserve Bank of St. Louis, September 2023.

11. International Labour Organization, *Global Wage Report 2022/23: The Impact of Inflation and COVID-19 on Wages and Purchasing Power* (Geneva: International Labour Organization, 2022); and OECD, "Average Wages," 2023.

12. Trading Economics, "Taiwan Minimum Monthly Wage," 2023; and OECD, "Earnings: Real Minimum Wages," OECD Employment and Labour Market Statistics, 2023.

13. Starting wages for college- and junior college–educated individuals were about 20 percent lower in 2012 than in 2000, while those of high school-educated workers were roughly the same. Sheng-Ju Chan and Chi-Hua Yang, "The Employment of the College Graduate: Changing Wages in Mass Higher Education," in *Mass Higher Education Development in East Asia: Strategy, Quality and Challenges*, ed. Jung Cheol Shin, Gerard A. Postiglione, and Futao Huang (New York: Springer, 2015), 301, 303.

14. Meng-Feng Yen, "The Wage Premium and Market Structure: The Case of South Korea and Taiwan" (paper presentation, Agriculture and Applied Economics Association Annual Meeting, Washington, DC, August 4–6, 2013). Yen noted that the decline was still continuing the year before he published his study (2012). See also James P. Vere, "Education, Development, and Wage Inequality: The Case of Taiwan," *Economic Development and Cultural Change* 53, no. 3 (2005): 711–35.

15. Lok Sang Ho, Xiangdong Wei, and Wai Chung Wong, "The Effect of Outward Processing Trade on Wage Inequality: The Hong Kong Case," *Journal of International Economics* 67, no. 1 (2005): 241–57.

16. Julián Messina and Joana Silva, *Wage Inequality in Latin America: Understanding the Past to Prepare for the Future* (Washington, DC: World Bank, 2018). In the United States, the education premium has flattened in recent years and even declined during the COVID-19 pandemic. Leila Bengali, Marcus Sander, Robert G. Valletta, and Cindy Zhao, "Falling Wage Premiums by Race and Ethnicity," FRBSF Economic Letter 2023–22, August 2023.

17. See table 1.1 for details. Taiwan's before taxes and transfers coefficient was well below the average for OECD countries (0.478), but its posttax and transfers coefficient was very similar (0.314). This indicates that OECD nations used government policy to redistribute far more income than Taiwan and ultimately obtained a similar level of inequality.

18. Pan-Long Tsai and Chao-Hsi Huang, "Openness, Growth and Poverty: The Case of Taiwan," *World Development* 35, no. 11 (2007): 1858–71.

19. Jen-Der Lue, "Promoting Work: A Review of Active Labour Market Policies in Taiwan," *Journal of Asian Public Policy* 6, no. 1 (2013): 81–98.

20. For example, see Judy Lin, "Taiwan's Low-Income Group to Be Exempted from Taxes," *Taiwan News*, April 16, 2017. The monthly minimum wage in 2017, when Lin's article was written, was NTD22,000 (about USD720).

21. Taiwan (ROC), Statistical Bureau, "Average Monthly Earnings."

22. In 2013, the average social assistance payment was about USD140 per month. Sui, "Changing Times."

23. Chang Wen-po, "Pay Raises Alone Cannot Solve Low Wages," *Taipei Times*, January 23, 2018.

24. Sophia Yang, "Taiwan Ministry of Labor Unveils Average Starting Wage across Different Sectors," *Taiwan News*, June 19, 2022.

25. Various student groups, for example, rallied for an increase in the minimum wage in May 2018. Kuan-lin Liu, Ku Chuan, and Yu Hsiao-han, "Student Groups Demand an Increase in Minimum Wage," *Focus Taiwan News Channel*, May 24, 2018.

26. Ji-Ping Lin, "Tradition and Progress: Taiwan's Evolving Migration Reality," *Migration Information Source*, January 24, 2012.

27. Statista, "Number of Taiwanese People Living Overseas as of 2021, by Continent (in 1,000s)," August 2023. No data are available on the employment or skill level of the emigrants or why they chose to leave Taiwan.

28. Nicola Smith, "Taiwan Is Suffering from a Massive Brain Drain and the Main Beneficiary is China," *Time*, August 21, 2017; and Keoni Everington, "China Poaches 3,000 Chip Engineers, but Taiwan Winning from Trade War," *Taiwan News*, December 3, 2019.

29. Evelyn Kao, "Low Salary Problems," *Focus Taiwan News Channel*, December 21, 2015.

30. Valerie Kincade Oppenheimer, "A Theory of Marriage Timing," *American Journal of Sociology* 94, no. 3 (1988): 563–91; and Matthijs Kalmijn, "The Influence of Men's Income and Employment on Marriage and Cohabitation: Testing Oppenheimer's Theory in Europe," *European Journal of Population* 27, no. 3 (2011): 269–93.

31. United Nations, Department of Economic and Social Affairs, "Can Pro-Natalist Policies Reverse the Fertility Decline in Taiwan Province of China?," United Nations Expert Group Meeting on Policy Responses to Low Fertility Policy Brief no. 17, November 2015.

32. Taiwan (ROC), National Development Council, "Strengthening Population and Immigration Policies," 2023. On fertility rates in other countries see World Population Review, "Fertility Rate by Country," 2023.

33. United Nations, Department of Economic and Social Affairs, "Can Pro-Natalist Policies Reverse the Fertility Decline?"; and Yu-Hua Chen, "Trends in Low Fertility and Policy Responses in Taiwan," *Japanese Journal of Population* 10, no. 1 (2012): 78–88.

34. The survey polled office workers with college degrees over the age of twenty. The results were cited in Duncan DeAeth, "Low Salaries, Long Work Hours to Blame for Taiwan's Low Birthrate: Survey," *Taiwan News*, April 2, 2018.

35. David H. Autor, Lawrence F. Katz and Melissa S. Kearney, "Trends in U.S. Wage Inequality: Revising the Revisionists," *Review of Economics and Statistics* 90, no. 2 (2008): 300–23.

36. Taiwan (ROC), Statistical Bureau, "Earnings and Productivity, Labor Productivity by Value Added," 2023.

37. Huang Tien-lin, "The Facts about Wage Stagnation," *Taipei Times*, December 13, 2012.

38. The majority (91 percent) of Taiwan's offshore production was carried out in mainland China after the removal of restrictions. Timothy Sturgeon and Ji-Ren Lee, "Industry Co-Evolution: A Comparison of Taiwan and North American Electronics Contract Manufacturers," in *Global Taiwan: Building Competitive Strengths in a New International Economy*, ed. Richard K. Lester and Suzanne Berger (New York: Routledge, 2005), 33–75. Since 2020, some Taiwanese firms have moved operations from the mainland in response to China's zero-COVID policy, to avoid US trade restrictions, and to diversify supply chains. Matthew Fulco, "Amid a Changing World Economy, Taiwanese Manufacturers Return Home," American Chamber of Commerce in Taiwan, February 9, 2021.

39. Meng-Wen Tsou, Jin-Tan Liu, James K. Hammitt, and Ching-Fu Chang, "The Impact of Foreign Direct Investment in China on Employment Adjustments in Taiwan: Evidence from Matched Employer–Employee Data," *Japan and the World Economy* 25–26 (2013): 68–79.

40. Alex Jiang, "Firms Mull Moving Production from China to Taiwan," *Focus Taiwan News Channel*, June 11, 2010.

41. In November 2011, Taiwan was home to 420,000 foreign contract workers. Industry employed 222,000, and the service sector employed 198,000. Foreign workers came mainly from Indonesia, Vietnam, the Philippines, and Thailand. Lin, "Tradition and

Progress"; and Hong-Zen Wang, "Immigration Trends and Policy Changes in Taiwan," *Asian and Pacific Migration Journal* 20, no. 2 (2011): 169–94.

42. Statista, "Annual Net Migration from and to Taiwan from 1990 to 2022," August 2023; and "Foreign Workers First Included as Factor of Lower Wages in Study," *China Post*, January 14, 2016.

43. Chin-Chun Yi and Wen-Yin Chien, "The Linkage Between Work and Family: Female's Employment Patterns in Three Chinese Societies," *Journal of Comparative Family Studies* 33, no. 3 (2002): 451–74.

44. Roger Mark Selya, "Taiwan as a Service Economy," *Geoforum* 25, no. 3 (1994): 305–22.

45. Andres Maroto and Luis Rubalcaba, "Services Productivity Revisited," *Service Industries Journal* 28, no. 3 (2008): 337–53; and John C. Haltiwanger, Julia I. Lane, and James R. Spletzer, "Productivity Differences across Employers: The Roles of Employer Size, Age, and Human Capital," *American Economic Review* 89, no. 2 (1999): 94–98.

46. Kao, "Low Salary Problems."

47. Taiwan (ROC), Ministry of Education, "Education Statistical Indicators," 2019. The numbers declined to 55,000 and 3,500 in master's and doctoral programs, respectively, in 2016.

48. For an overview of massification, see Ka Ho Mok, "After Massification: The Quest for Entrepreneurial Universities and Technological Advancement in Taiwan," *Journal of Higher Education Policy and Management* 35, no. 3 (2013): 264–79.

49. Chuing Prudence Chou, "Education in Taiwan: Taiwan's Colleges and Universities," *Brookings*, November 12, 2014.

50. Elizabeth Weise, "Taiwan's Problem? Too Many College Graduates, Too Few Machinists," *USA Today*, May 7, 2015.

51. Chen Dorothy I-ru, "Higher Education Reform in Taiwan and Its Implications on Equality," *Chinese Education and Society* 45, no. 5–6 (2012): 134–51.

52. The quantity of resources available to universities declined causing the amount of money spent on each student to fall. Universities spent an average of NTD213,401(about USD8,145) per student in 1996, but only NTD175,263 (about USD5,480) in 2006. See I-ru, "Higher Education Reform." Institutions began to compete for a decreasing number of students due to low birth rates and, more recently, a lower demand for degrees. The university acceptance rate increased from around 20 percent before 1970, to 49 percent in 1996, and to over 90 percent since 2006, one of the highest rates in Asia. Chou, "Education in Taiwan."

53. David Ashton, Francis Green, Johnny Sung, and Donna James, "The Evolution of Education and Training Strategies in Singapore, Taiwan and S. Korea: A Development Model of Skill Formation," *Journal of Education and Work* 15, no. 1 (2002): 5–30.

54. See the summary of a study in Chinese cited in Hao Chen and Hsin-Hsien Fan, "Education in Taiwan: The Vision and Goals of the 12-Year Curriculum," *Brookings*, November 11, 2014.

55. Taiwan (ROC), National Development Council, "Industry's Talent Shortages: The Current Situation and Policy Response," January 2019.

56. On the general issues involved in matching skill sets to the type of labor firms need and the problems if this fails to occur, see Ulrich Teichler, "Higher Education and the World of Work: Conceptual Frameworks, Comparative Perspectives, Empirical Findings," in *Mass Higher Education Development in East Asia: Strategy, Quality and Challenges*, ed. Jung Cheol Shin, Gerard A. Postiglione, and Futao Huang (New York: Springer, 2015), 269–88.

57. Numerous studies concluded that an oversupply of university graduates caused the drop in the education wage premium. For examples, see T. H. Gindling and Way Sun,

"Higher Education Planning and the Wages of Workers with Higher Education in Taiwan," *Economics of Education Review* 21, no. 2 (2002): 153–69; and Yih-chyi Chuang and Wei-wen Lai, "Heterogeneity, Comparative Advantage, and Return to Education: The Case of Taiwan," *Economics of Education Review* 29, no. 5 (2010): 804–12.

58. Claudia Goldin and Lawrence Katz, *The Race Between Education and Technology* (Cambridge, MA: Belknap Press of Harvard University Press, 2008).

59. Jessica Magaziner, "Education in Taiwan," *World Education News + Reviews*, June 7, 2016.

60. Chou, "Education in Taiwan."

61. See Chen and Fan, "Education in Taiwan." An early assessment of this plan is Blansefloer Coudenys, Gina Strohbach, Tammy Tang, and Rachel Udabe, "On the Path toward Life-long Learning: An Early Analysis of Taiwan's 12-year Basic Education Reform," in *Education to Build Back Better: What Can We Learn from Education Reform for a Post-Pandemic World*, ed. Fernando M. Reimers, Uche Amaechi, Alysha Banerji, and Margaret Wang (Cham, Switzerland: Springer, 2022), 75–98.

62. For an overview of ALMPs, see Herwig Immervoll and Stefano Scarpetta, "Activation and Employment Support Policies in OECD Countries. An Overview of Current Approaches," *IZA Journal of Labor Policy* 1, no. 9 (2012).

63. On income support policies, see Sarah Marchal, Ive Marx, and Gerlinde Verbist, "Income Support Policies for the Working Poor," IZA Institute of Labor Economics, Discussion Paper Series IZA DP no. 10665, March 2017.

64. A good overview is OECD, *Employment Outlook 2015* (Paris: OECD Publishing, 2015).

65. For instance, see Ramon Peña-Casas and Mia Latta, *Working Poor in the European Union* (Dublin: Office for Official Publications of the European Communities, 2004); and OECD, "LMP Interventions for the Long-Term Unemployed: An Initial Assessment," March 2019.

66. Spending on PLMPs usually exceeds that on either income support policies or ALMPs. PLMPs typically cover most workers in the formal sector and are not designed to target low-income workers in particular. Methodologies for calculating spending on PLMPs differ across sources, complicating efforts to make cross-regional comparisons. The ADB, whose data are used extensively in this volume, includes PLMPs in their social insurance measure. It only reports spending on unemployment insurance, omitting several related types of expenditures—generally small—that the OECD incorporates. For an overview of these methodological issues, see Clemente Pignatti and Eva Van Belle, "Better Together: Active and Passive Labour Market Policies in Developed and Developing Economies," International Labour Office, Research Department Working Paper no. 37, December 2018.

67. For overviews, see Michael Hill and Yaun-shie Hwang, "Taiwan: What Kind of Social Policy Regime?," in *East Asian Welfare Regimes in Transition: From Confucianism to Globalization*, ed. Alan Walker and Chack-Kie Wong (Bristol, UK: Policy Press, 2005), 145–64; and M. Ramesh, *Social Policy in East and Southeast Asia: Education, Health, Housing and Income Maintenance* (New York: Routledge, 2004), especially chapter 7.

68. Kim Won Sub and Shih-Jiunn Shi, "Emergence of New Welfare States in East Asia? Domestic Social Changes and the Impact of 'Welfare Internationalism' in South Korea and Taiwan (1945–2012)," *International Journal of Social Quality* 3, no. 2 (2013): 113.

69. Joseph Wong, *Healthy Democracies: Welfare Politics in Taiwan and South Korea* (Ithaca, NY: Cornell University Press, 2004).

70. These initiatives included the Multifaceted Job Creation Program, Public Sector Temporary Employment Creation Program, wage subsidy programs, and on-plant job training programs. Lue, "Promoting Work"; and Shi-Jiunn Shi, "Shifting Dynamics of the

Welfare Politics in Taiwan: From Income Maintenance to Labour Protection," *Journal of Asian Public Policy* 5, no. 1 (2012): 82–96.

71. The main PLMP is unemployment insurance, but reemployment, vocational training, parental leave allowances, and a national health insurance premium subsidy for unemployed workers and dependents also provide limited benefits. Inohe Ku and Chango Kim, "Decomposition Analyses of the Trend in Poverty Among Older Adults: The Case of South Korea." *Journals of Gerontology: Series B* 75, no. 3 (2018): 106–7.

72. Shi, "Shifting Dynamics," 88.

73. Taiwan (ROC), Ministry of Labor, "Insurance Benefits," August 2022; Taiwan (ROC), Statistical Bureau, "Social Protection Expenditure"; and Ku and Kim, "Decomposition Analyses." 112.

74. International Labour Organization, *World Social Protection Report 2020–22: Social Protection at the Crossroads—In Pursuit of a Better Future* (Geneva: International Labour Organization, 2021).

75. Ku and Kim, "Decomposition Analyses," 115–16.

76. Eunju Chi and Hyeok Yong Kwon, "Unequal New Democracies in East Asia: Rising Inequality and Government Responses in South Korea and Taiwan," *Asian Survey* 52, no. 5 (2012): 913–14.

77. Government of the Hong Kong Special Administrative Region, Census and Statistics Department, "Real Wage Indices for Employees up to Supervisory Level by Industry Section (September 1992 = 100)," 2023; and Government of the Hong Kong Special Administrative Region, Census and Statistics Department, "Labour Productivity Index (Year 2015 = 100)," 2023. Real wages decreased by 1.7 percent between 2018 and 2022. Hong Kong Special Administrative Region, Census and Statistics Department, "Hong Kong Annual Digest of Statistics 2022 Edition," October 2022.

78. Ho, Wei and Wong, "Effect of Outward Processing Trade on Wage Inequality," 243.

79. Hong Kong's Gini coefficient has risen steadily since the 1970s and was 0.539 in 2016, the highest among developed countries. See table 1.1.

80. Government of the Hong Kong Special Administrative Region, Census and Statistics Department, Office of the Government Economist Financial Secretary's Office, "Hong Kong Poverty Situation Report 2020," November 2021, table A.2.3. The average rate of in-work poverty across twenty-eight European countries in 2013 was 9.2 percent. Henning Lohmann, "The Concept and Measurement of In-Work Poverty," in *Handbook on In-Work Poverty*, ed. Henning Lohmann and Ive Marx (Cheltenham, UK: Edward Elgar Publishing, 2018), 7–25.

81. The SFS includes the Active Employment Assistance and the Community Work Programmes. Hung Wong found that these schemes had limited impact on the employment of recipients. Hung Wong, "Impact of Active Labour Market Policies and Statutory Minimum Wage on Welfare Recipients in Hong Kong" (paper presentation, 19th FISS International Research Seminar on "Challenges for Social Protection," June 19, 2012).

82. Raymond K. K. Chan and Chris K. C. Chan, "The Shifting Boundary between Work and Welfare: A Review of Active Labour Market Policies in Hong Kong," *Journal of Asian Public Policy* 6, no. 1 (2013): 26–41. The authors provided an overview of ALMPs and concluded that they were generally effective in job placements.

83. Hugo Horta, "The Declining Scientific Wealth of Hong Kong and Singapore," *Scientometrics* 117, no. 1 (2018): 427–47.

84. Michael O'Sullivan and Michael Yat-him Tsang, "Educational Inequalities in Higher Education in Hong Kong," *Inter-Asia Cultural Studies* 16, no. 3 (2015): 454–69.

85. Republic of Singapore, Department of Statistics, "Labour, Employment, Wages and Productivity," 2023.

86. The wages of those at the twentieth percentile of the income distribution grew at annual rate of 4.8 percent from 2015 to 2022, whereas those at the fiftieth percentile grew at 3.5 percent. Republic of Singapore, Department of Statistics, "Labour, Employment, Wages and Productivity."

87. OECD, "Average Wages."

88. Restrepo-Echavarria and Reinbold, "Measuring Labor Share." The average for OECD countries in this period was roughly 60 percent. See International Labour Organization and OECD, "The Labour Share in G20 Economies," (report, G20 Employment Working Group, Antalya, Turkey, February 26–27, 2015).

89. These were the requirements in 2023. Workforce Income Supplement payments are made in the form of 40 percent cash and 60 percent Central Provident Fund contributions. Republic of Singapore, Central Provident Fund Board, "Workfare Income Supplement," 2023.

90. Irene Y. H. Ng, Yi Ying Ng, and Lee Poh Choo, "Singapore's Restructuring of Low-Wage Work: Have Cleaning Job Conditions Improved?," *Economic and Labour Relations Review* 29, no. 3 (2018): 308–27.

91. Cleaners (SD1,700 or USD1,250) and security guards (SD1,870 or USD1,380) were among the lowest paid workers in Singapore in 2023.

92. Republic of Singapore, Department of Statistics, "Household Income," 2023.

93. The PAP won a record low 61 percent of the vote in the July 2020 elections. The Worker's Party picked up ten of ninety-three seats, its best showing ever. "Singapore Ruling PAP Party Wins Elections, but Support Falls," *BBC News*, July 10, 2020.

94. Yasmine Yahya, "Helping Low-Wage Workers in Singapore: What More Can Be Done?," *Straits Times*, June 24, 2018.

95. OECD, "Annual Average Wage Growth," 2023.

96. Annual productivity improvements in the manufacturing and service sectors were 0.1 percent and 0 percent, respectively, in the same time period. Japan Productivity Center, "Productivity Statistics: Manufacturing and Non-Manufacturing," 202.

97. Restrepo-Echavarria and Reinbold, "Measuring Labor Share."

98. Japan, Statistics Bureau, "Labor Force Survey: Employee (by Age Group and Type of Employment)," June 2019.

99. Japan, Ministry of Health, Labour and Welfare, Office of Counsellor for Labour Policy Planning, "Analysis of Japan's Labor Economy 2017," *Japan Labor Issues* 2, no. 7 (2018): 1–12.

100. Takao Kato, *Productivity, Wages and Unions in Japan* (Geneva: International Labour Organization, 2016).

101. Japan Productivity Center, "Productivity Statistics": and Kyoji Fukao, "Productivity in the Service Sector: Reforming Japan's GDP Statistics Is Urgently Needed for More Accuracy," Research Institute of Economy, Trade and Industry, February 2017.

102. Yasuhiro Kamimura and Naoko Soma, "Active Labour Market Policies in Japan: A Shift Away from the Company-Centered Model?," *Journal of Asian Public Policy* 6, no. 1 (2013): 42–59.

103. "Average Minimum Wage in Japan Set to Exceed ¥1,000 for First Time," *Nippon.com*, August 15, 2023.

104. OECD, "Social Expenditure—Detailed Data," OECD Social and Welfare Statistics, 2023.

105. Wages rose by 1.8 percent from 2019 to 2022. OECD, "Annual Average Wage Growth."

106. Much of the decline occurred from 1970 to 2000. Restrepo-Echavarria and Reinbold, "Measuring Labor Share."

107. OECD, *Working Better with Age: Korea* (Geneva: OECD Publishing, 2018), 33.

108. Korea, Statistical Information Service, "Index of Income Distribution," 2023; and Korea, Minimum Wage Commission, "Minimum Wage Review," December 2021.

109. OECD, *Economic Surveys: Korea 2020* (Geneva: OECD Publishing, 2020), 69.

110. Song Jung-a, "Seoul Faces Backlash over Rise in Minimum Wage," *Financial Times*, February 26, 2018. Increasing the minimum wage to 10,000 won would have fixed it at 70 percent of the country's median wage. Kyung-ho Kim, "Debate Rages on Impact of Minimum Wage Hikes," *Korea Herald*, February 7, 2018.

111. Korea, Minimum Wage Commission, "Minimum Wage System," September 2023. The minimum wage in 2023 was USD7.20.

112. International Labour Organization, *World Social Protection Report 2017–2019: Universal Social Protection to Achieve Sustainable Development Goals* (Geneva: International Labour Office, 2017), table B6; and OECD, *Economic Surveys: Korea*, 85.

113. OECD, Surveys: Korea, 87. For details on workforce policies in Korea, see Dong-chul Jung and Chan-ung Park, "A New Direction in the Welfare-Work Nexus in South Korea," *Journal of Asian Public Policy* 6, no. 1 (2013): 60–80.

114. OECD, *Towards Better Social and Employment Security in Korea* (Geneva: OECD Publishing, 2018), 52.

115. The OECD defines the employment gap for disadvantaged groups as "the average difference in the prime age men's employment rate and the rates for five disadvantaged groups (mothers with children, youth who are not in full-time education or training, workers aged 55–64, non-natives, and persons with disabilities; % of the prime-age men's rate)." OECD, *Surveys: Korea*, 64.

116. OECD, *Towards Better Social and Employment Security*.

117. OECD, *Economic Surveys: Korea*, 95, 104.

118. For details on these policies and their effectiveness, see OECD, *Economic Surveys: Korea*. The administration of Yoon Suk-Yeol has launched additional initiatives.

119. Unmet training needs among seniors are considered to be the largest among OECD countries. OECD, *Economic Surveys, Korea*, 76.

4. ABUSED AND NEGLECTED

1. The narrative of the tragic lives of Megumi and Takeshi is based on a real child maltreatment fatality case that took place in Osaka, Japan in the summer of 2010. "Mom: No Remorse for Kids' Deaths," *Japan Times*, August 1, 2010.

2. Yumiko Shimabukuro, "Democratization and the Development of Japan's Uneven Welfare State" (Ph.D. diss., MIT, 2012).

3. Richard J. Samuels, *Machiavelli's Children: Leaders and Their Legacies in Italy and Japan* (Ithaca, NY: Cornell University Press, 2003), 80.

4. Yumiko Shimabukuro and Arvid Lukauskas, "Building an Inegalitarian Welfare State: The Impact of Dualistic Coordinated Capitalism & Elite-Made Democracy in Japan" (unpublished manuscript, September 1, 2023).

5. Andy Baker and Ethan Scheiner, "Electoral System Effects and Ruling Party Dominance in Japan: A Counterfactual Simulation Based on Adaptive Parties," *Electoral Studies* 26, no. 2 (2007): 477–91.

6. The MMD/SNTV system intensified intraparty competition and placed the burden of campaign financing on individual candidates rather than parties. In addition, the system gave candidates an incentive to target narrow groups because they needed to secure only a relatively small share of votes to win a seat. See for example, Jean-Marie Bouissou, "Organizing One's Support Base." The development of a universalistic social welfare system was also hindered by a lack of a centralized working-class movement. Ronald F. Dore, *British Factory, Japanese Factory: The Origins of National Diversity in Industrial Relations* (Los Angeles: University of California Press, 1973), 412.

7. A total of 295 out of 475 Lower House Diet seats are now chosen by plurality, and 180 are selected through proportional representation. Frances McCall Rosenbluth and Michael F. Thies, *Japan Transformed: Political Change and Economic Restructuring* (Princeton, NJ: Princeton University Press, 2010).

8. Masayoshi Hayashi, "Chihō zaisei to seikatsu hogo" [Local finance and the Daily Life Security], in *Seikatsu Hogo no keizai bunseki* [Economic analysis of the Daily Life Security], ed. Abe Aya, Kunieda Shigeki, Suzuki Wataru, and Hayashi Masayoshi (Tokyo: Tokyo Daigaku Shuppankai, 2008), 239–68.

9. An excellent overview of the evolution of child maltreatment discourse is Roger Goodman, "The 'Discovery' and 'Rediscovery' of Child Abuse (jidō gyakutai) in Japan," in *A Sociology of Japanese Youth: From Returnees to NEETs*, ed. Roger Goodman, Yuki Imoto, and Tuukka Toivonen (London: Routledge, 2012), 111.

10. "Couple Arrested over Death of 5-Year-Old Daughter Who Police Allege Was Abused and Denied Food," *Japan Times*, June 6, 2018.

11. Justin McCurry, "Japan PM Vows to Fight Child Abuse after 'Heart-Wrenching' Death of Girl, 10," *Guardian*, February 7, 2019.

12. Eri Niiya, "Harrowing Child Neglect Case Shines Light on Chains of Abuse," *Asahi Shimbun*, February 10, 2022.

13. Karin Kaneko and Kanako Takahara, "Johnny's Replaces President as It Admits to Abuse by Late Founder," *Japan Times*, September 7, 2023.

14. Japan, Ministry of Justice, "Japanese Law Translation Database System, Act on the Prevention, etc. of Child Abuse," March 4, 2014. The 2019 revision also banned all forms of corporal punishment.

15. Japan, Children and Families Agency, "Reiwa 4 nendo jidō sōdanjo de no jidō gyakutai sōdan taiō kensū" [The number of child abuse incidents the child consultation centers handled in FY2022], September 2023.

16. Aya Goto, Seiji Yasumura, Junko Yabe, and Michael R Reich, "Addressing Japan's Fertility Decline: Influences of Unintended Pregnancy on Child Rearing," *Reproductive Health Matters* 14, no. 27 (2006): 193.

17. One of the few cross-national collaborative studies is the World Studies of Abuse in the Family Environment (WorldSAFE) project, which gauged incidents of parental discipline behaviors using the Parent–Child Conflict Tactics Scale.

18. This concern was echoed in Ichiro Wada and Ataru Igarashi, "The Social Costs of Child Abuse in Japan," *Children and Youth Services Review* 46 (2014): 72–77; and Iida Kanae, "'Yūaikai Sōdōmei' nendō ni okeru minshushugi to shakaishugi" [The democratic movement and socialism in the Friendly Society General Labor Federation], *Mita Gakkai Zasshi* 71, no. 3 (1978): 303–21. See also Japan, Prime Minister's Office, "Jidō gyakutai bōshi taisaku ni kansuru kankei kakuryō kaigi" [Relevant ministerial meetings on the strategies to prevent child abuse], March 19, 2019.

19. Fuhua Zhai and Qin Gao, "Child Maltreatment among Asian Americans: Characteristics and Explanatory Framework," *Child Maltreatment* 14, no. 2 (2009): 207–24.

20. Ruth Gilbert, Cathy Spatz Widom, Kevin Browne, David Fergusson, Elspeth Webb, and Staffan Janson, "Burden and Consequences of Child Maltreatment in High-Income Countries," *Lancet* 373, no. 9657 (2009): 68–81.

21. Japan, Ministry of Health Labour and Welfare, "Kodomo gyakutai ni yoru shibō jirei tō no kenshō kekka" [Results from Examining Cases of Child Abuse–Related Deaths], August 2017; and Sakai Seiji, *Kodomo gyakutai e no chōsen: Iryō, fukushi, shinri, shihō no renkei wo mezashite* [Tackling child abuse: Aiming toward linking the medical, welfare, psychology, and judiciary] (Tokyo: Seishin Shobō, 2013), 3–4.

22. The Japan Pediatric Society's findings were reported in "Gyakutaishi, nen 350nin no kanōsei—Kokushūkei no sanbaichō" [Child abuse deaths, possibility of 350 people per year—more than three times the national total], *Nihon Keizai Shimbun*, April 8, 2016.

23. Raymond H. Starr, Jr., and David A. Wolfe, *The Effects of Child Abuse and Neglect: Issues and Research* (New York: Guilford Press, 1991); and M. Angeles Cerezo and Dolores Frias, "Emotional and Cognitive Adjustment in Abused Children," *Child Abuse & Neglect* 18, no. 11 (1994): 923–32.

24. For comparative research on this topic, see Sue Gerhardt, *Why Love Matters: How Affection Shapes a Baby's Brain* (London: Routledge, 2004); and Daniel J. Siegel, *The Developing Mind: How Relationships and the Brain Interact to Shape Who We Are* (New York: Guilford Press, 2015).

25. NHK Supesharu Kieta Kodomo Tachi Shuppan Han, *Rupo kieta kodomotachi: Gyakutai kankin no shinsō ni semaru* [Report on the vanished children: Closing in on the truth surrounding abusive confinement] (Tokyo: NHK Shuppan, 2015), 74.

26. Yamada Kana, "Gyakutai de shōgai, kenmei ni ikiru tōzakaru oya, mimamoru shisetsu shokuin" [Disabled because of abuse, working hard to live amid parental withdrawal, facility staff provides care], *Asahi Shimbun*, October 20, 2016.

27. Karsten I. Paul and Klaus Moser, "Unemployment Impairs Mental Health: Meta-Analyses," *Journal of Vocational Behavior* 74, no. 3 (2009): 264–82.

28. NHK Supesharu Kieta Kodomo Tachi Shuppan Han, *Rupo kieta kodomotachi*. The link between child maltreatment and criminal activity garnered attention because Japanese prison and juvenile detention centers have become the second home for child abuse victims. A 2014 case involving a seventeen-year-old in Saitama Prefecture illustrates this point. The young man had suffered years of physical and verbal abuse from his parents who barred him from attending school. He became known as one of the vanished children (*kieta kodomo tachi*) by virtue of being outside the purview of public institutions. His tumultuous and violent upbringing contributed to his murdering his grandparents after they turned him away. Yamadera Kaoru, *Dare mo boku wo miteinai: Naze 17sai no shōnen wa sofubo wo satsugai shitanoka* [Nobody is watching me: Why did the 17-year-old murder his grandparents?] (Tokyo: Popurasha, 2017).

29. Yamadera, *Dare mo boku wo miteinai*.

30. David S. Zielinski, "Child Maltreatment and Adult Socioeconomic Well-Being," *Child Abuse & Neglect* 33, no. 10 (2009): 666–78.

31. Wada and Igarashi, "Social Costs of Child Abuse in Japan," 72, 74. Building on Wada and Igarashi's research, a later study found that the costs of child abuse in residential care facilities for children with disabilities alone were an additional USD648 million annually. Naruhisa Nakane and Ichiro Wada, "Estimating the Social Costs of Child Abuse in Residential Care for Children with Disabilities Using the Japanese Survey on the Interactions of Adverse and Positive Childhood Experiences toward Adulthood," *International Journal of Environmental Research and Public Health* 19, no. 24 (2022): 16476.

32. Samuel X. Radbill, "A History of Child Abuse and Infanticide," in *The Battered Child*, ed. Ray E. Helfer and C. Henry Kempe (Chicago: University of Chicago Press, 1968), 3–17.

33. Stephen J. Pfohl, "The 'Discovery' of Child Abuse," *Social Problems* 24, no. 3 (1977): 314.

34. The government enacted the 1933 Child Abuse Prevention Law to curb child beggars and prostitutes; the legislation did not signal a shift in its hands-off approach to child protection. See Masako Ishii-Kuntz, "Child Abuse: History and Current State in Japanese Context," in *Family Violence in Japan: A Life Course Perspective*, ed. Fumie Kumagai and Masako Ishii-Kuntz (Singapore: Springer, 2016), 49–78.

35. Takenaka Tetsuo, "Kodomo gyakutai wa ima" [Child abuse today]. In *Kodomo gyakutai to enjo* [Child abuse and support], ed. Takenaka Tetsuo, Hasegawa Masato, Asakura Keiichi, and Kita Kazunori (Kyoto: Mineruva Shobō, 2002), 3.

36. A genealogy of the child abuse literature is found in Christopher Spencer Greeley, "The Evolution of the Child Maltreatment Literature," *Pediatrics* 130, no. 2 (2012): 347–48.

37. C. Henry Kempe, Frederic N. Silverman, Brandt F. Steele, William Droegemueller, and Henry K. Silver, "The Battered-Child Syndrome," *JAMA* 181, no. 1 (1962): 17–24.

38. John Caffey, "The Whiplash Shaken Infant Syndrome: Manual Shaking by the Extremities with Whiplash-Induced Intracranial and Intraocular Bleedings, Linked with Residual Permanent Brain Damage and Mental Retardation," *Pediatrics* 54, no. 4 (1974): 396.

39. UNICEF, "Fact Sheet: A Summary of the Rights under the Convention on the Rights of the Child," accessed 2018.

40. David Gough, "Child Abuse in Japan," *Child Psychology and Psychiatry Review* 1 (1996): 13.

41. Sakai, *Kodomo gyakutai e no chōsen*, 81.

42. Sakai, *Kodomo gyakutai e no chōsen*, 32–33; and Roger Goodman, "Child Abuse in Japan: 'Discovery' and the Development of Policy," in *Family and Social Policy in Japan: Anthropological Approaches*, ed. Roger Goodman (Cambridge, UK: Cambridge University Press, 2002), 144.

43. Most of the budget increase in the early 2000s surrounding the CAPL went to new programs to raise public awareness and enhance coordination among various civil society actors across the country. Goodman, "'Discovery' and 'Rediscovery' of Child Abuse," 112–13.

44. In 2016, the Japanese government also overhauled the seventy-year-old Child Welfare Law in an effort to improve the quality of institutionalized care for children. Makiko Okuyama, "Child Abuse in Japan: Current Problems and Future Perspectives," *Japan Medical Association Journal* 49, no. 11–12 (2006): 372.

45. Vicky N. Albert and Richard P. Barth, "Predicting Growth in Child Abuse and Neglect Reports in Urban, Suburban, and Rural Counties," *Social Service Review* 70, no. 1 (1996): 72.

46. Jay Belsky, a renowned child psychologist, was one of the first scholars to advance an ecological approach to child maltreatment. Jay Belsky, "Etiology of Child Maltreatment: A Developmental-Ecological Analysis," *Psychological Bulletin* 114, no. 3 (1993): 413.

47. James Garbarino, "The Human Ecology of Child Maltreatment: A Conceptual Model for Research," *Journal of Marriage and Family* 39, no. 4 (1977): 721–35.

48. A comprehensive analysis is found in Sachiko Bamba and Wendy L. Haight, *Child Welfare and Development: A Japanese Case Study* (New York: Cambridge University Press, 2011).

49. Jill E. Korbin, *Child Abuse and Neglect: Cross-Cultural Perspectives* (Oakland: University of California Press, 1982); and Darran Yates, "The Stress of City Life," *Nature Reviews Neuroscience* 12 (2011): 430.

50. NHK Supesharu Kieta Kodomo Tachi Shuppan Han, *Rupo kieta kodomotachi*, 102–3. A study of 119 child abuse cases in Hokkaido determined that nearly 40 percent of them involved parents or guardians who suffered from mental illness. Another study discovered that between 50 and 70 percent of parents who abused their children had a mental illness. This study is discussed in Sawada Izumi, "Yōikusha ga mentaru herusu mondai wo kakaeru gyakutai kazoku e no shien" [Aid for the caretakers from abusive families that have mental health issues]. In *Kodomo gyakutai to kazoku: 'Kasanari au furi' to shakai teki shien*" [Child abuse and the family: The "cumulative disadvantages" and societal support], ed. Matsumoto Ichirō (Tokyo: Akaishi Shoten, 2013), 78. Research has shown that poor mental health is not a sufficient condition for negative childrearing outcomes. Other factors, such as poverty, social isolation, and urbanization, contribute to the abusive behavioral pattern.

51. Garbarino, "Human Ecology of Child Maltreatment."

52. United Nations, Department of Economic and Social Affairs, "World Urbanization Prospects 2018: Country Profiles," 2018.

53. Ronald Inglehart, C. Haerpfer, A. Moreno, C. Welzel, K. Kizilova, J. Diez-Medrano, M. Lagos, P. Norris, E. Ponarin, and B. B. Puranen, "World Values Survey: Round Four—Country-Pooled Datafile Version," J. D. Systems Institute, 2014.

54. Japan, Children and Families Agency, "Reiwa 4 nendo."

55. Ishikawa Yūki, *Rupo kyosho fumei jidō: Kieta kodomotachi* [Report on children whose whereabouts are unknown: The children who vanished] (Tokyo: Chikuma Shinsho, 2015), 212–13.

56. The most comprehensive study of the link between income inequality and child abuse and neglect in the United States is John Eckenrode, Elliott G. Smith, Margaret E. McCarthy, and Michael Dineen, "Income Inequality and Child Maltreatment in the United States," *Pediatrics* 133, no. 3 (2014): 454–61.

57. Laurence D. Steinberg, Ralph Catalano and David Dooley, "Economic Antecedents of Child Abuse and Neglect," *Child Development* 52, no. 3 (1981): 975–85.

58. For example, see Aya Isumi, Takeo Fujiwara, Nobutoshi Nawa, Manami Ochi, and Tsuguhiko Kato, "Mediating Effects of Parental Psychological Distress and Individual-Level Social Capital on the Association between Child Poverty and Maltreatment in Japan," *Child Abuse & Neglect* 83 (2018): 142–50.

59. Japan, Ministry of Health, and Welfare, Labor, "Reiwa 3 nendo Jidō Sōdanjo deno jidō gyakutai sōdan taiō kensū" [Number of Child Abuse Consultations Handled at Child Guidance Centers in 2021], 2022.

60. This study is described in Matsumoto Ichirō, "Kodomo, kazoku ga chokumen suru fukugō teki konnan" [The complex difficulties that children and families face]. In *Kodomo gyakutai to kazoku: 'Kasanari au furi' to shakai teki shien* [Child abuse and the family: The "cumulative disadvantages" and societal support], ed. Matsumoto Ichirō (Tokyo: Akaishi Shoten, 2013), 23.

61. Wada and Igarashi, "Social Costs of Child Abuse in Japan."

62. The report is cited in Yoshiaki Nohara, "Children of Poor, Jobless Single Moms Have Become an Underclass in Japan," *Japan Times*, June 26, 2018.

63. A rise in the local unemployment rate has been shown to increase child maltreatment that may even result in death (due to neglect). Masato Oikawa, Akira Kawamura, Cheolmin Kang, Zentaro Yamagata, and Haruko Noguchi, "Do Macroeconomic Shocks in the Local Labor Market Lead to Child Maltreatment and Death? Empirical Evidence from Japan," *Child Abuse & Neglect* 124 (2022): 105430.

64. Joanne N. Wood, Sheyla P. Medina, Chris Feudtner, Xianqun Luan, Russell Localio, Evan S. Fieldston, and David M. Rubin, "Local Macroeconomic Trends and Hospital Admissions for Child Abuse, 2000–2009," *Pediatrics* 130, no. 2 (2012): e358.

65. For an extended discussion on various poverty indicators in Japan, see Shimabukuro, "Democratization and Development."

66. Ishikawa, *Rupo kyosho fumei*, 14–15.

67. James L. Spearly and Michael Lauderdale, "Community Characteristics and Ethnicity in the Prediction of Child Maltreatment Rates," *Child Abuse & Neglect* 7, no. 1 (1983): 91–105; and Carol Coohey, "Child Maltreatment: Testing the Social Isolation Hypothesis," *Child Abuse & Neglect* 20, no. 3 (1996): 241–54.

68. Japan, Ministry of Health, Labor and Welfare, "Reiwa 3 nendo zenkoku hitori oya setaitō chōsa kekka no gaiyō" [Summary of the 2021 national single-parent household survey results], December 2022.

69. The OECD and the Japanese government define single-parent poverty as the proportion of single-parent households with children who earn less than 50 percent of the median income. "Survey: Almost Half of Homes with One Parent Live in Poverty," *Asahi Shimbun*, July 5, 2023. Single mothers living with their parents may not fare much better as their parents are also likely to be poor. Sawako Shirahase and James M. Raymo, "Single

Mothers and Poverty in Japan: The Role of Intergenerational Coresidence," *Social Forces* 93, no. 2 (2014): 545–69.

70. Spearly and Lauderdale, "Community Characteristics."
71. Japan, Ministry of Health, "Reiwa 3 nendo zenkoku."
72. Goto et al., "Addressing Japan's Fertility Decline," 195.
73. Aya Goto, Seiji Yasumura, Michael R Reich, and Akira Fukao, "Factors Associated with Unintended Pregnancy in Yamagata, Japan," *Social Science & Medicine* 54, no. 7 (2002): 1065–79.
74. Japan, Ministry of Health, Labor and Welfare, "Reiwa 3 nendo 'shussei ni kansuru tōkei' no gaiyō" [Summary of 2021 "birth statistics"], July 2021.
75. Jean M. Twenge and W. Keith Campbell, *The Narcissism Epidemic: Living in the Age of Entitlement* (New York: Simon and Schuster, 2009).
76. Hosaka Tōru, "Kodomo to kazoku wo meguru mondai" [The Problem Surrounding a Child and Family]. In *Nihon no kodomo gyakutai: Sengo Nihon no "kodomo no kikiteki jōkyō" ni kansuru shinri shakai teki bunseki* [Japan's child abuse: A psychosocial analysis of postwar Japan's "child crisis situation"], ed. Tōru Hosaka (Tokyo: Fukumura Shuppan, 2007), 361–74.
77. Takahashi Shigehiro, *Boshi shinjū no jittai to kazoku kankei no kenkōka—Hoken fukushi gakuteki apurōchi ni yoru kenkyū* [The reality of mother-child suicides and the health improvement of family relations—an academic study based on the social insurance approach] (Tokyo: Kawashima Shoten, 1987).
78. For an influential piece on the historical evolution of the concept of childhood, see Philippe Aries, *Centuries of Childhood: A Social History of Family Life* (New York: Random House, 1962).
79. Dan Kiley, *The Peter Pan Syndrome: Men Who Have Never Grown Up* (New York: Avon Books, 1995). For example, in the 2010 Osaka starvation case that formed the basis of the chapter's opening narrative, the young mother found basic chores, such as disposing of trash, bathing children, and cooking, to be bothersome so she stopped doing them and later proceeded to confine and starve her children to death. A similar incident took place in South Korea. A twenty-two-year-old father was arrested for the death of his two-year old son after leaving him alone for ten days to play video games. Jeyup S. Kwaak, Gamer Arrested after Death of Neglected Child," *Wall Street Journal*, April 14, 2014.
80. Hiroshi Wagatsuma, "Child Abandonment and Infanticide: A Japanese Case," in *Child Abuse and Neglect: Cross-Cultural Perspectives*, ed. Jill E. Korbin (Berkeley: University of California Press, 1981), 120–38.
81. Ishii-Kuntz, "Child Abuse."
82. Chisato Tanaka, "Two Girls' Deaths after Alleged Abuse Expose Shortcomings in Japan's Child-Protection Services," *Japan Times*, March 25, 2019.
83. Masuzawa Takashi and Ishikura Yōko, "1990 nendai ikō no shakai, kazoku, kodomo wo meguru jōkyō" [Post-1990 state of society, family, and children], in *Nihon no kodomo gyakutai: Sengo Nihon no "kodomo no kikiteki jōkyō" ni kansuru shinri shakai teki bunseki* [Japan's child abuse: A psychosocial analysis of postwar Japan's "child crisis situation"], ed. Hosaka Tōru (Tokyo: Fukumura Shuppan, 2007), 175–88.
84. Goodman, "Child Abuse in Japan," 136.
85. Penalties for child abuse and neglect are low, even in the context of the country's general prison sentencing guidelines. This leniency is based on the presumption that parents or caretakers meant to harm, not murder, the child.
86. Although whistleblowers have legal protection and authorities are no longer required to disclose their names, the fear of retaliation by parents (e.g., violence or defamation lawsuits) discourages many from reporting.

87. Fumie Kumagai, "Introduction: Toward a Better Understanding of Family Violence in Japan," in *Family Violence in Japan: A Life Course Perspective*, ed. Fumie Kumagai and Masako Ishii-Kuntz (Singapore: Springer, 2016), 1–48.

88. James M. Raymo, Hyunjoon Park, Miho Iwasawa, and Yanfei Zhou, "Single Motherhood, Living Arrangements, and Time with Children in Japan," *Journal of Marriage and Family* 76, no. 4 (2014): 843–61.

89. Japan, Ministry of Health, Labor and Welfare, "Reiwa 3 nendo zenkoku."

90. Akiko S. Oishi, "Child Support and the Poverty of Single-Mother Households in Japan," National Institute of Population and Social Security Research Paper Series no. 2013–E01, August 2013.

91. See Kathryn E. Goldfarb, "Family at the Margins: State, Welfare and Well-being in Japan," *Japanese Studies* 36, No. 2 (2016): 151–54.

92. NHK Supesharu Kieta Kodomo Tachi Shuppan Han, *Rupo kieta kodomotachi*.

93. Spearly and Lauderdale, "Community Characteristics."

94. Nishizawa Satoru, *Kodomo gyakutai* [Child abuse] (Tokyo: Kōdansha, 2010).

95. Japan, Ministry of Health, Labor and Welfare, "Reiwa 3 nendo jidō."

96. Hosaka Tōru and Masuzawa Takashi, "2000nen ikō no aratana dōkō" [New Developments after 2000], in *Nihon no kodomo gyakutai: Sengo Nihon no "kodomo no kikiteki jōkyō" ni kansuru shinri shakai teki bunseki* [Japan's child abuse: A psychosocial analysis of postwar Japan's "child crisis situation"], ed. Hosaka Tōru (Tokyo: Fukumura Shuppan, 2007), 428–29.

97. "Prosecutors Seek 20-Year Sentence for Man Who Let 5-Year-Old Son Starve to Death," *Japan Today*, October 10, 2015.

98. "Prosecutors Seek 20-year Sentence."

99. McCurry, "Japan PM Vows to Fight Child Abuse."

100. "Girl Dies in Mie after AI Suggested Not Taking Her into Custody," *Japan Times*, July 12, 2023; and Tomohiro Yamamoto, "AI Put 39% Need for Protective Custody of Girl Who Later Died," *Asahi Shimbun*, July 11, 2023.

101. The lack of government efforts to combat child maltreatment can also be seen in the dearth of facilities. Unlike the Unites States, where the vast majority of children who enter state care live in foster homes, 90 percent of Japanese children reside in government-regulated childcare institutions (*yōgo shisetsu*). There are nearly six hundred of these institutions throughout the country and they generally operate at maximum capacity. Bamba and Haight, *Child Welfare and Development*, 16–17.

102. According to a 2011 government survey, 34.1 percent of local government officials who handled child abuse cases were part-time workers. Yamadera, *Dare mo boku wo miteiinai*, 230–31.

103. Hosaka and Masuzawa, "2000nen ikō"; and Sakai, *Kodomo gyakutai e no chōsen*.

104. The Child Rearing Allowance was amended in May 2016 to double the payments for second and third children to the current levels of 10,000 yen (USD100) and 6,000 yen (USD60), respectively. The benefit calculation is based on a sliding scale that is capped at an annual income of 3.65 million yen (USD36,000).

105. Sheldon Garon, "Japanese Policies toward Poverty and Public Assistance: A Historical Perspective," World Bank Institute Working Papers no. 37200, 2002.

106. Yamadera, *Dare mo boku wo miteinai*, 230–31.

107. For an excellent account of how high private savings in Japan facilitated private investment in education and housing, see Sheldon Garon, *Beyond Our Means: Why America Spends While the World Saves* (Princeton, NJ: Princeton University Press, 2012).

108. Expenditures amounted to 0.2 percent in Hong Kong, 1.9 percent in Japan, 1.2 percent in Korea, and 0.4 percent in Singapore. No data were reported for China and Taiwan. International Labour Organization, *World Social Protection Report 2020–22:*

Social Protection at the Crossroads—In Pursuit of a Better Future (Geneva: International Labour Organization, 2021), table A4.3.

109. Serim Lee, Jieun Lee and Jongserl Chun, "The Child Abuse Reporting Guideline Compliance in Korean Newspapers," *Child Youth Service Review* 151 (2023): 107037.

110. Jun Sung Hong, Na Youn Lee, Hye Joon Park, and Kathleen Coulborn Faller, "Child Maltreatment in South Korea: An Ecological Systems Analysis," *Children and Youth Services Review* 33, no. 7 (2011): 1058–66.

111. Sonam Yang, "Cane of Love: Parental Attitudes towards Corporal Punishment in Korea," *British Journal of Social Work* 39, no. 8 (2009): 1542.

112. Yiyoon Chung, Haksoon Ahn and T. J. Lah, "Child Welfare Policy and Services in Korea," *International Journal of Social Welfare* 31, no. 1 (2022): 33–44.

113. Chung Ah-young, "Child Abuse Is Society's Dirty Secret," *Korea Times*, January 20, 2016.

114. There are dramatically different estimates of the number of annual child maltreatment cases in Taiwan, ranging from as high as 82,000 to somewhere between 10,000 and 17,000 in the period after 2012. Lanying Huang, Yi-Fen Lu, Yi-Chun Yu, Chuen-Jim Sheu, "Collaborating to Safeguard Children in Taiwan: Systemic Transformation," *Journal of Community Safety and Well-Being* 8, No. 4 (2023): 205-10. Anecdotal evidence suggests that child maltreatment is widespread and increasing. Huang-Chi Ho, "Taiwan's Rising Child Abuse Cases Raise Concern," *TVBS*, November 23, 2023.

115. Chien-Chung Hsu, "A Study of Non-Government Child Welfare Services in Taiwan Focused on Children in Need of Child Welfare Service Intervention" (PhD diss., The University of Queensland, 2016); Chih-Tsai Chen, Nan-Ping Yang and Pesus Chou, "Child Maltreatment in Taiwan for 2004–2013: A Shift in Age Group and Forms of Maltreatment," *Child Abuse & Neglect* 52 (2016): 169–76; and David Y. H. Wu, "Child Abuse in Taiwan," in *Child Abuse and Neglect: Cross-Cultural Perspectives*, ed. Jill E. Korbin (Berkeley: University of California Press, 1981), 139–140.

116. Duncan DeAeth, "Child Abuse in N. Taiwan: Three Year Old Boy Restrained, Starved, and Beaten," *Taiwan News*, September 23, 2018.

117. "Horror in Taiwan: Parents Charged over Abuse, Deaths of Three Young Siblings," *South China Morning Post*, October 19, 2017.

118. Lee I-chia, "Child Abuse Ignored as Deaths Mount: Doctor," *Taipei Times*, April 25, 2018.

119. Shermaine Ang, "Child Abuse Cases in Singapore Continue to Rise after Hitting Decade-High in 2020," *Straits Times*, April 11, 2022.

120. For more information on Montfort Care and Big Love, see http://www.montfortcare.org.sg.

121. Shermaine Ang, "New Child Protection Centre Opens in Bedok to Deal with Rising Abuse Cases," *Straits Times*, March 21, 2022.

122. Alice Wu, "Be a Better Neighbor, Don't Ignore Signs of Child Abuse in Hong Kong," *South China Morning Post*, January 21, 2018.

123. Hong Kong Special Administrative Region, Social Welfare Department, "Statistics on Newly Registered Child Protection, Newly Reported Spouse/Cohabitant Battering and Sexual Violence Cases in 2022," June 2023.

124. The findings were reported in Margaret Fung-Yee Wong, "Multidisciplinary Response in Domestic Violence: How We Started and Where We Are Heading," in *Preventing Family Violence: A Multidisciplinary Approach*, ed. Ko-Ling Chan (Hong Kong: University of Hong Kong Press, 2012), 324.

125. Kahon Chan, "Hong Kong Police Record 29 Per Cent Rise in Child Abuse Cases, as Return to School Campuses Brings Incidents to Light," *South China Morning Post*, August 23, 2023.

126. Ernest Kao and Peace Chiu, "Hong Kong Welfare Minister Pledges Action on Child Abuse after Shocking Death of Girl, 5," *South China Morning Post*, January 14, 2018.

127. Government of the Hong Kong Special Administrative Region, Central Policy Unit, "A Study on Epidemiology of Child Abuse and Its Geographic Distribution in Hong Kong: An Important Social Indicator of Different Districts and Communities," March 2013; and Claudia J. Coulton, Francisca Richter, Seok-Joo Kim, Robert Fischer, and Youngmin Cho, "Temporal Effects of Distressed Housing on Early Childhood Risk Factors and Kindergarten Readiness," *Children and Youth Services Review* 68 (2016): 59–72.

128. Peace Chiu, "In Hong Kong, Most Child Abuse Victims Suffer at Hands of Parents," *South China Morning Post*, January 15, 2018.

5. IN THE SHADOW OF VICTORIA PEAK

1. This narrative is based on journalistic accounts, government and nongovernmental organization reports, and the authors' field research and interviews with residents.

2. Stan Hok-Wui Wong, *Electoral Politics in Post-1997 Hong Kong: Protest, Patronage, and the Media* (Singapore: Springer, 2015).

3. Steven Durlauf, Paul Johnson, and Jonathan Temple, "Growth Econometrics," in *Handbook of Economic Growth*, ed. Philippe Aghion and Steven N. Durlauf, vol. 1 (Amsterdam: Elsevier, 2005), 555–667.

4. World Bank, "GDP Growth (Annual %)," World Development Indicators, 2023.

5. OECD, "Social Expenditure—Aggregated Data," OECD Social and Welfare Statistics, 2023.

6. Jeff Larrimore and Jenny Schuetz, "Assessing the Severity of Rent Burden on Low-Income Families," FEDS Notes, Board of Governors of the Federal Reserve System, December 2017.

7. They increased a further 18 percent from 2017 to 2021. Hong Kong Special Administrative Region, Census and Statistics Department, "Hong Kong Annual Digest of Statistics 2022 Edition," October 2022.

8. Government of the Hong Kong Special Administrative Region, Rating and Valuation Department, "Property Market Statistics: Private Domestic—Rental Indices by Class (Territory-wide) (from 1979)," 2023. The real estate market cooled considerably during the COVID-19 pandemic and prices and rents declined in 2022.

9. Kate Evert-Allen, "How Much Property Will $US1 Million Buy You across the World?," Knight Frank, March 1, 2023. Hong Kong was the fourth most expensive city in the world in 2021. Economist Intelligence Unit, "Worldwide Cost of Living Survey 2021," December 2021.

10. Urban Reform Institute and the Frontier Centre for Public Policy, "Demographia International Housing Affordability," 2023.

11. Wendell Cox, "Hong Kong's Decentralizing Commuting Patterns," *Newgeography*, December 12, 2012. In contrast, average commuting times in New York and Paris were less than thirty minutes.

12. Hong Kong, Census and Statistics Department, "Annual Digest 2022," chapter 9.

13. Government of Hong Kong Special Administrative Region, Housing Authority, "At a Glance," 2023.

14. Government of Hong Kong, Housing Authority, "At a Glance."

15. "Destined for Life in Tiny Cage Homes," *South China Morning Post*, April 7, 2011.

16. Lindsay Wilson, "How Big Is a House? Average House Size by Country—2023," Shrink that Footprint, 2023.

17. Government of Hong Kong, Housing Authority, "At a Glance"; and Government of the Hong Kong Special Administrative Region, Housing Bureau, "Housing in Figures 2022," August 31, 2022.

18. Government of Hong Kong, Housing Authority, "At a Glance."

19. The documentary *Once upon a Rooftop* details the daily life of a community living in a Hong Kong rooftop slum. See Sybil Wendler, *Once upon a Rooftop*, CAAM, 2011.

20. Hong Kong Special Administrative Region, Census and Statistics Department, "Thematic Household Survey Report—Report no. 60—Housing Conditions of Sub-Divided Units in Hong Kong," March 2016. A more recent estimate is that 220,000 people lived in 101,000 subdivided flats in 2022. Brian Wong, "As Hong Kong Marks 25 Years of British Handover, Its 'Cage Homes' Remain a Stark Reminder of Its Inequities," *Time Magazine*, June 30, 2022.

21. Elizabeth Cheung and Fanny W. Y. Fung, "Hong Kong Tenants Living in Subdivided Flats Pay More of Their Earnings to Live in Smaller Units," *South China Morning Post*, June 25, 2015.

22. Corine S.M. Wong, W. C. Chan, Linda C. W. Lam, W. Y. Law, W. Y. Tang, T. Y. Wong, and Eric Y. H. Chen, "Living Environment and Psychological Distress in the General Population of Hong Kong," *Procedia Environmental Sciences* 36 (2016): 78–81. The literature on the influence of housing on mental and physical health is expansive. For examples, see Joanne C. Sandberg, Jennifer W. Talton, Sara A. Quandt, Haiying Chen, Maria Weir, Walkiria R. Doumani, Arjun B. Chatterjee, and Thomas A. Arcury, "Association between Housing Quality and Individual Health Characteristics on Sleep Quality among Latino Farmworkers," *Journal of Immigrant and Minority Health* 16, no. 2 (2014): 265–72; and Gary W. Evans, "Housing Quality and Mental Health," *Journal of Consulting and Clinical Psychology* 68, no. 3 (2000): 526–30.

23. Peace Chiu, "How Can Hong Kong's Poor Beat Poverty When Work Doesn't Pay?," *South China Morning Post*, January 4, 2019.

24. Government of the Hong Kong Special Administrative Region, Central Policy Unit, "A Study on Epidemiology of Child Abuse and its Geographic Distribution in Hong Kong: An Important Social Indicator of Different Districts and Communities," March 2013. The findings are broadly consistent with those of other studies that have concluded that the quality of housing and child abuse are negatively correlated. Claudia J. Coulton, Francisca Richter, Seok-Joo Kim, Robert Fischer, and Youngmin Cho, "Temporal Effects of Distressed Housing on Early Childhood Risk Factors and Kindergarten Readiness," *Children and Youth Services Review* 68 (2016): 59–72.

25. Government of the Hong Kong Special Administrative Region, Census and Statistics Department, "2016 Population By-Census, Thematic Report—Household Income Distribution in Hong Kong," 2017. The government has changed its methodology for calculating income inequality (and relative poverty, see later in this chapter) in a way that lowered Gini coefficients significantly, both for the most current year and past years. Thus, we are unable to extend the time series beyond 2016. The new methodology is reflected in Government of the Hong Kong Special Administrative Region, Census and Statistics Department, "2021 Population Census, Thematic Report—Household Income Distribution in Hong Kong," 2023. There is little reason to believe income inequality has declined to the extent reported. One publication noted that the richest decile earned 47.3 times more than the poorest in 2022. Oxfam Hong Kong, "Hong Kong Poverty Report: Poverty and Employment during the Pandemic," October 2022.

26. Relative poverty is defined as an income equal to or less than 50 percent of the national median. The before taxes and transfers poverty rate reached 23.6 percent in 2020, signifying that 1.65 million Hong Kong residents lived in poverty. The after taxes and transfers poverty rate averaged around 9 percent in the 2010s. It declined to 7.9 percent in 2020 despite a sharp drop in household income because the government provided extensive one-off measures to supplement incomes (such as a cash payout of HKD10,000 or USD1,250). Government of the Hong Kong Special Administrative Region, Census and

Statistics Department, Office of the Government Economist Financial Secretary's Office, "Hong Kong Poverty Situation Report 2020," November 2021, chapter 2. Hong Kong's after taxes and transfers measure is not consistent with the OECD's so it is difficult to make cross country comparisons. For instance, Hong Kong's reported rate would be lower than most European countries, including Sweden, in 2020. As noted previously, the government has altered the way it calculates the impact of government programs on income distribution and poverty. For a blistering critique of Hong Kong's poverty statistics, see Victor Apps, "Hong Kong's Distorted Poverty Statistics are Misleading," *China Daily*, November 24, 2020.

27. Some organizations have claimed that old-age poverty is close to 40 percent. Oxfam Hong Kong, "Poverty Report."

28. The average rate of working poverty in the OECD was about 7 percent. Government of Hong Kong, Census and Statistics Department, "Hong Kong Poverty Situation Report 2020," table A.2.3.

29. Richard Wong, *Fixing Inequality in Hong Kong* (Hong Kong: Hong Kong University Press, 2017), chapter 6.

30. In more technical terms, the income elasticity of demand for housing is greater than one.

31. R. Sean Craig and Changchun Hua, "Determinants of Property Prices in Hong Kong SAR: Implications for Policy," IMF Working Paper no. 11/277, November 2011. The authors concluded that the real interest rate and an index of construction costs had weaker effects and level of real domestic credit had the smallest impact.

32. Buyers from mainland China accounted for 51 percent of all residential property sales in the third quarter of 2011.

33. As the Hong Kong currency is pegged to the US dollar, monetary policymakers have little control over the cost of credit. US interest rates were unusually low during the past few decades until the Federal Reserve began to raise rates aggressively in 2022.

34. The role of migration in driving up housing prices in Hong Kong is also observed in the parallel case of Chinese cities. See Yingchao Lin, Zhili Ma, Ke Zhao, Weiyan Hu, and Jing Wei, "The Impact of Population Migration on Urban Housing Prices: Evidence from China's Major Cities," *Sustainability* 10 (2018): 3169.

35. On the demographics behind this trend, see Richard Wong, *Hong Kong Land for Hong Kong People: Fixing the Failures of Our Housing Policy* (Hong Kong: Hong Kong University Press, 2015).

36. Richard Wong, "Demography, Housing, and the Economic Future of Hong Kong" (presentation, Hong Kong CSB Advanced Leadership Enhancement Programme for Directorate Officials, December 1, 2017). The data were drawn from Housing Authority and Census and Statistics Department publications that are no longer available online.

37. Wong, *Fixing Inequality*, 44–45.

38. Wong, "Demography." In 2016, 22 percent of the population lived in private rental units, up from 16 percent in 2006.

39. Hong Kong, Legislative Council Secretariat. Research Office, "Land Utilization in Hong Kong," Statistical Highlights ISSH04/16–17, October 24, 2016. Parklands and nature reserves alone make up 40 percent of all land area.

40. Hong Kong, Legislative Council Secretariat, "Land Utilization in Hong Kong." The government has identified several new sites with potential for reclamation. The most notable example would entail constructing an artificial island between Hong Kong and Lantau Islands that would create around 600 to 800 hectares of land.

41. Wong, *Fixing Inequality*, chapter 25.

42. Peggy Sito, "Hong Kong is Third Most Expensive Place for Building Costs, According to Global Survey," *South China Morning Post*, July 2, 2015.

43. Robin Harding, "Why Tokyo Is the Land of Rising Home Construction But Not Prices," *Financial Times*, August 3, 2016.

44. This categorization of housing policy stages is adapted from Rebecca L. H. Chiu, "The Transferability of Hong Kong's Public Housing Policy," *International Journal of Housing Policy* 10, no. 3 (2010): 301–23. See also Fung Ping Yan, "Public Housing in Hong Kong Past, Present and Future," 2006; and Wong, *Fixing Inequality*, chapters 2–4.

45. Wong, *Fixing Inequality*, 27–28.

46. For details on the HOS, see Adrienne La Grange and Frederik Pretorius, "Ontology, Policy and the Market: Trends to Home-Ownership in Hong Kong," *Urban Studies* 37, no. 9 (2000): 1561–82.

47. La Grange and Pretorius, "Ontology, Policy and the Market."

48. Chiu, "Transferability of Hong Kong's Public Housing Policy," 306.

49. A 2002 landmark government study provided the basis for the new approach. Hong Kong Special Administrative Region, "Review of the Institutional Framework of Public Housing: The Report," June 2002.

50. Donald Tsang, "Statement on 5 June 2002 by the Chief Secretary for Administration on Home Ownership Scheme Policy," CB (1) 2100/01–02(01), June 5, 2002.

51. Peggy Sito, Denise Tsang, and Lam Ka-sing, "Developers' Cosy Ties with Politics May Explain Hong Kong's Biggest Woe: Widening Income Gap in the Least Affordable City on Earth," *South China Morning Post*, September 2, 2019.

52. The special stamp duty was imposed on residential properties resold within twenty-four months of purchase; this tax was levied in addition to an existing stamp duty of 4.25 percent.

53. Craig and Hua, "Determinants of Property Prices in Hong Kong SAR."

54. The government asked the Long-Term Housing Strategy Steering Committee to conduct a comprehensive review of public and private housing demand and formulate a new long-run housing strategy. The Committee was also tasked with assessing the medium- and long-term housing needs of different social strata and groups as well as setting priorities. It published a lengthy and detailed public consultation paper in September 2013. Hong Kong, Long Term Housing Strategy Steering Committee, "Building Consensus, Building Homes: Long Term Housing Strategy Consultation Document," September 2013.

55. "Destined for Life in Tiny Cage Homes."

56. After years of controversy, the government announced in 2023 that it would build 12,000 new apartments on the Fanling Golf Course, the oldest links course in Greater China. Shawna Kwan, "Hong Kong Is Building Public Housing on a Golf Course in a Snub to the Old Elite," *Bloomberg*, August 31, 2023.

57. Tom Holland, "Just Enforcing the Rules Could End HK's Housing Shortage," *South China Morning Post*, October 31, 2013.

58. Wong, *Fixing Inequality*, 44–45.

59. The problem has persisted to this day. About 4 percent of public housing residents had income or wealth above the maximum allowed in 2023 and speculation involving public flats was still common. Edith Lin, "Stricter Rules Proposed to Weed out Wealthy in Hong Kong Public Rental Flats and Protect Those Most in Need of Housing," *South China Morning Post*, May 23, 2023.

60. HOS units may be sold on the open market subject to a resale restriction period (which has been reduced from ten to two years) and the return of the subsidy received when the unit was purchased to the Housing Authority. The subsidy repayment is generally very large, providing owners with little incentive to sell their units. See Wong, *Hong Kong Land*, chapter 12.

61. Hong Kong Special Administrative Region, "The Chief Executive's 2018 Policy Address: Striving Ahead, Rekindling Hope," 2018.

62. Holmes Chan, "Six New Housing Policies, Including Vacancy Tax, Announced by Hong Kong's Chief Exec. Carrie Lam," *Hong Kong Free Press*, June 29, 2018. The vacancy tax was the most popular of the proposed measures.

63. Charles Ka Yui Leung, Joe Cho Yiu Ng and Edward Chi Ho Tang, "Why Is the Hong Kong Housing Market Unaffordable? Some Stylized Facts and Estimations," Globalization Institute Working Paper no. 380, Federal Reserve Bank of Dallas, April 2020; and Hong Kong, Census and Statistics Department, "Annual Digest 2022."

64. David Tweed, "New Hong Kong Housing Policies Will Bring Focus, Carrie Lam Says," *Bloomberg*, June 30, 2018.

65. Hong Kong, Legislative Council Secretariat, Legislative Council Panel on Housing, "Housing-Related Initiatives in the Chief Executive's 2022 Policy Address," LC Paper no. CB(1)730/2022(03), November 7, 2022.

66. Inclusionary zoning would take the form of reserving a percentage of units for low- and middle-income households in private residential developments in exchange for subsidies or tax breaks. One such scheme was the Pilot Scheme on Private Developer Participation in Subsidised Housing Development. The newly developing Northern Metropolis (part of the Greater Bay Area) was identified as one of the priority zones for new residential projects. Simon Quail, Steve Lewis and Wai-duen Lee, "What Are the Options to Improve Housing Affordability in Hong Kong?," EY, March 31, 2023.

67. The Legco's primary functions are to enact, amend or repeal laws, approve budgets, and monitor government performance. Voters in five geographic constituencies elect thirty-five Legco seats directly, but functional constituencies choose the other thirty-five. This has guaranteed that nonestablishment parties are underrepresented. In the September 2016 election, for example, democratic parties won the majority of votes cast and seats elected by geographical constituencies but still ended up with fewer seats in Legco than establishment parties, twenty-nine to forty (one seat went to a nonaligned independent party).

68. Leung, Ng and Tang, "Why Is the Hong Kong Housing Market Unaffordable?"

69. Hong Kong, Census and Statistics Department, "Annual Digest 2022." The government has run fiscal surpluses since 2005 with the exception of 2019 (a small deficit) and 2020 (a sizable deficit due to COVID-19).

70. Hong Kong, Census and Statistics Department, "Annual Digest 2022."

71. Hong Kong's five largest developers have built 45 percent of all residential property in the territory. Sito, Tsang, and Ka-sing, "Developers' Cosy Ties."

72. Peggy Sito and Sandy Li, "How Hong Kong Land Policies Help Fuel City's Ever-Rising Property Prices," *South China Morning Post*, December 23, 2017.

73. Yvonne Liu and Joyce Ng, "Land Application List Scrapped in Bid to Control Supply," *South China Morning Post*, March 1, 2013. From 1999 to 2002, the application list system coexisted with regular auctions. A downturn in property prices in 2002 led the government to use the list system exclusively until 2010 when it reintroduced regular auctions.

74. Sito and Li, "How Hong Kong Land Policies."

75. Holmes Chan, "Ex-Hong Kong Leader CY Leung Defends Controversial 1990s Housing Policy, Says Crisis Could Have Been Averted," *Hong Kong Free Press*, June 13, 2018.

76. Asian Development Bank, "Low-Income Housing Policies: Lessons from International Experience," February 2009.

77. The government initiated the CPF in 1955 in order to avoid creating an extensive state-sponsored social security program. The pension program first became an important element in housing policy in 1968 when the Home Ownership Scheme permitted CPF funds to be used for housing expenses.

78. Singapore overtook Hong Kong as the most expensive private housing market in East Asia in 2023.

79. Alexandra Stevenson, "A High-End Property Collapse in Singapore," *New York Times*, February 17, 2015.

80. Mimi Kirk, "The Peculiar Inequality of Singapore's Famed Public Housing," *City Lab*, June 9, 2015.

81. Most of the approximately 400,000 Malaysian workers commute into Singapore daily, but they are allowed to rent HDB flats.

82. Junija Ye, "Migrant Landscapes: A Spatial Analysis of South Asian Male Migrants in Singapore," in *Changing Landscapes of Singapore: Old Tensions, New Discoveries*, ed. Elaine Lyn-Ee Ho, Chih Yuan Woon, and Kamalini Ramadas (Singapore: National University of Singapore Press, 2013), 142–57. Clara Lee and Darrelle Ng, "Construction Firms Grapple with Workers' Housing as Dorm Rental Rates Soar," *Channel News Asia*, September 21, 2023.

83. Ye, "Migrant Landscapes."

84. Charlotte Glennie, "Singapore Is Keeping an Eye on its Migrant Workers," *BBC News*, April 14, 2015.

85. "Singapore PM Promises Safety of Foreign Workers," *India TV News*, December 15, 2013.

86. The government has also facilitated the creation of super dorms. The Tuas View Dormitory, the nation's largest, boasts 16,800 beds and houses workers from multiple sectors, including construction, marine, processing, and manufacturing. It offers many onsite amenities and facilities, such as health clinics, food courts, gymnasiums, barber shops, grocery stores, and movie theaters.

87. Yosuke Hirayama, "Housing and State Strategy in Post-War Japan," in *Housing and the New Welfare State: Perspectives from East Asia and Europe*, ed. Richard Groves, Alan Murie, and Christopher Watson (Aldershot, UK: Ashgate, 2007), 101–28.

88. Hangtian Xu and Yiming Zhou, "Public Housing Provision and Housing Vacancies in Japan," *Journal of the Japanese and International Economies* 53 (2019): 101038.

89. OECD, "PH4.2 Social Rental Housing Stock," OECD Affordable Housing, March 2022.

90. Shin-Young Park, "The State and Housing Policy in Korea," in *Housing and the New Welfare State: Perspectives from East Asia and Europe*, ed. Richard Groves, Alan Murie, and Christopher Watson (Aldershot, England: Ashgate, 2007), 75–100.

91. OECD, "PH4.2 Social Rental Housing Stock."

92. In the *jeonse* system, renters obtain a two-year lease by putting up a large deposit—averaging 40 to 60 percent of the cost of the unit (typically about USD200,000). The renter lives rent-free for the duration of the lease, while the landlord uses the deposit as an interest free loan.

93. Michelle Ye Hee Lee and Min Joo Kim, "How Seoul Failed Its Most Vulnerable, Flooded in Their Basement Homes," *Washington Post*, August 12, 2022.

94. Ock Hyun-ju, "Seoul to Improve Living Conditions in Semi-Basement Apartments Depicted in 'Parasite,'" *Korea Herald*, February 18, 2020.

95. Justin McMurry, "Seoul to Phase Out Parasite-Style Semi-Basement Flats after Storm Deaths," *Guardian*, August 11, 2022.

96. For details on the various initiatives, see Chunil Kim and Jinsoo Ko, "Unintended Consequences of Housing Policies: Evidence from South Korea," *Sustainability* 15, no. 4 (2023): 3407.

97. Jennifer Ahn, "South Korea's Real Estate Policy and the Presidential Election," Council on Foreign Relations, February 7, 2022.

98. Dong-eun Kim and Minu Kim, "Korean Government to Ease Regulations to Supply 2.7 Million New Houses by 2027," *Pulse*, August 17, 2022.

99. Yi-Ling Chen, "The Factors and Implications of Rising Housing Prices in Taiwan," *Brookings*, July 15, 2015.

100. A key event was the formation of a minority government by the Democratic Progressive Party (DPP) in 1990. Pui Yee Connie Tang, "Taiwan's Housing Policy in the Context of East Asian Welfare Models," in *Housing and the New Welfare State: Perspectives from East Asia and Europe*, ed. Richard Groves, Alan Murie, and Christopher Watson (Aldershot, UK: Ashgate, 2007), 159–82.

101. The last year the Survey reported figures for both cities was 2015. A 2023 article placed Taiwan among the top ten most expensive housing markets in the world. Roy Ngerng, "Taiwan's Housing Crisis (Part 1): Taiwan's Housing Prices Are among the Highest Globally But Wages Are One of the Lowest among Advanced Countries," *News Lens*, March 22, 2023.

102. The vacancy rate in Taipei was 13.4 percent in 2016. Low transaction and property taxes that made it inexpensive to purchase and hold a property in anticipation of large capital gains were one cause of high vacancies.

103. Katherine Wei, "Taiwan Boosts Affordable Social Housing by Converting Hotels to Homes," *Straits Times*, January 11, 2022; and Chen Chun-hua and Kay Liu, "New Housing Market, Police-Related Schemes Set to Take Effect," *Focus Taiwan News Channel*, June 27, 2023.

6. LEFT BEHIND

1. Anton Cheremukhin, Mikhail Golosov, Sergei Guriev, and Aleh Tsyvinski, "The Economy of People's Republic of China from 1953," NBER Working Paper no. 21397, July 2015.

2. Robert Ash, "Squeezing the Peasants: Grain Extraction, Food Consumption and Rural Living Standards in Mao's China," *China Quarterly* 188 (2006): 959–98.

3. Cheremukhin et al., "Economy of the People's Republic of China."

4. Barry Naughton, *The Chinese Economy: Transformation and Growth* (Cambridge, MA: MIT Press, 2007).

5. Justin Yifu Lin, *Demystifying the Chinese Economy* (Cambridge, UK: Cambridge University Press, 2012).

6. Scholars of transition economies use the term marketize to describe the process of preparing firms to compete in free markets. In the Chinese case, it meant allowing firm managers to make production and pricing decisions and operate on a profit-loss basis as well as converting workers into contractual employees. Gary H. Jefferson and Thomas G. Rawski, "Enterprise Reform in Chinese Industry," *Journal of Economic Perspectives* 8, no. 2 (1994): 47–70.

7. Guocang Huan, "China's Open Door Policy, 1978–1984," *Journal of International Affairs* 39, no. 2 (1986): 1–18.

8. Congressional Research Service, "China's Economic Rise: History, Trends, Challenges, and Implications for the United States," June 2019.

9. Cheremukhin et al., "Economy of the People's Republic of China"; and Eswar S. Prasad, "China's Growth Model: Choices and Consequences," in *Emerging Giants: China and India in the World Economy*, ed. Barry Eichengreen, Poonam Gupta, and Rajiv Kumar (New York: Oxford University Press, 2010), 227–42. Net exports, surprisingly, did not make a significant contribution to rapid growth.

10. Zongcai Wei and Rebecca L. H. Chiu, "Livability of Subsidized Housing Estates in Marketized China: An Institutional Interpretation," *Cities* 83 (2018): 108–17.

11. Ken Wills, "Seeking Balance: China Strives to Adapt Social Protection to the Needs of a Market Economy," *Finance and Development* 55, no. 4 (2018): 20–23. Data on social protection spending in China are discussed later in this section.

12. Tiejun Cheng and Mark Selden, "The Origins and Social Consequences of China's Hukou System," *China Quarterly* 139 (1994): 647–48.

13. Wills, "Seeking Balance."

14. Nara Dillion, *Radical Inequalities: China's Revolutionary Welfare State in Comparative Perspective*. (Cambridge, MA: Harvard University Press, 2015).

15. Qin Gao, *Welfare, Work and Poverty: Social Assistance in China* (New York: Oxford University Press, 2018); and John Dixon, *The Chinese Welfare System, 1949–1979* (New York: Praeger Publishers, 1981).

16. Edward Steinfeld, *Forging Reform in China: The Fate of State-Owned Industry* (New York: Cambridge University Press, 1998); and Elisabeth J. Croll, "Social Welfare Reform: Trends and Tensions," *China Quarterly* 159 (1999): 684–99.

17. Croll, "Social Welfare Reform," 685.

18. Dixon, *Chinese Welfare System*.

19. China also accumulated huge foreign exchange reserves as the result of its huge trade surpluses. They have exceeded USD3 trillion since 2010, an amount which is equivalent to between 30 and 50 percent of its GDP. Salvatore Babones, "China Is Sitting on $3 Trillion in Currency Reserves, But Is That Enough?," *Forbes*, May 24, 2018. These reserves could be used to increase government spending, but this would probably entail abandoning its currency peg.

20. The figures are current yuan converted to USD. Republic of China, National Bureau of Statistics, "China Statistical Yearbook," 2017; and Republic of China, National Bureau of Statistics, "China Statistical Yearbook," 2022.

21. Asian Development Bank, *The Social Protection Indicator for Asia: Assessing Progress* (Mandaluyong City, Philippines: Asian Development Bank, 2019). See also Philippe Windgender, "Intergovernmental Fiscal Reform in China," IMF Working Paper WP/18/88, April 2018.

22. OECD, *Society at a Glance: Asia/Pacific 2022* (Paris: OECD Publishing, 2022). The figures indicated here are not strictly comparable to those reported earlier for 2015, as they are drawn from different sources—the ADB for 2015 and the OECD for 2019. The OECD tends to report higher social spending than the ADB.

23. David Rosser Phillips and Zhixin Feng, "Challenges for the Aging Family in the People's Republic of China," *Canadian Journal on Aging* 34, no. 3 (2015): 290–304.

24. Croll, "Social Welfare Reform"; and Rita Jing-Ann Chou, "Filial Piety by Contract? The Emergence, Implementation, and Implications of the 'Family Support Agreement' in China," *The Gerontologist* 51, no. 1 (2011): 3–16.

25. On the expansion of tertiary education, see Qiao Wen, "Estimating Education and Labor Market Consequences of China's Higher Education Expansion," *Sustainability* 14 (2022): 1–25; and World Bank, "Government Expenditure on Education, Total (% of GDP)," World Development Indicators, 2023. Expenditures have leveled out in the last decade.

26. In-depth looks at the origins of the *hukou* system are Tiejun Cheng and Mark Selden, "The Origins and Social Consequences of China's Hukou System"; and Zhiqiang Liu, "Institution and Inequality: The Hukou System in China," *Journal of Comparative Economics* 33, no. 1 (2005): 133–57.

27. On the rationales behind excluding migrant workers and their offspring, see Kam Wing Chan, "The Household Registration System and Migrant Labor in China: Notes on a Debate," *Population and Development Review* 36, no. 2 (2010): 357–64.

28. Edward Glaeser, *Triumph of the City: How Our Greatest Invention Makes Us Richer, Smarter, Greener, Healthier, and Happier* (London: Penguin Books, 2011).

29. An excellent overview of urban versus rural benefits is Croll, "Social Welfare Reform."
30. Cheng and Selden, "Origins and Social Consequences."
31. Croll, "Social Welfare Reform."
32. Kam Wing Chan, "Internal Migration in China: Integrating Migration with Urbanization Policies and Hukou Reform," KNOMAD Policy Brief 16, November 2021.
33. Chan, "Internal Migration in China," 5.
34. Windgender, "Intergovernmental Fiscal Reform in China."
35. Windgender, "Intergovernmental Fiscal Reform in China."
36. Karen Eggleston, Jean C. Oi, and Yiming Wang, eds., *Challenges in the Process of China's Urbanization* (Palo Alto, CA: Shorenstein Asia-Pacific Research Center, 2017).
37. Steinfeld, *Forging Reform in China*.
38. Wen, "Estimating Education and Labor Market Consequences."
39. See table 1.1. On rural and urban inequality, see Sonali Jain-Chandra, Niny Khor, Rui Mano, Johanna Schauer, Philippe Wingender, and Juzhong Zhuang. "Inequality in China—Trends, Drivers and Policy Remedies." IMF Working Paper WP/18/127, June 2018. The country's Gini coefficient has leveled off or even declined slightly since 2010, as we discuss later in this chapter.
40. World Bank, "Fertility Rate, Total (Births Per Woman)," World Development Indicators, 2023.
41. Harsher measures were also used. Local and provincial officials, without the approval of the national government, forced hundreds of millions of women to undergo abortions or sterilization. Adam Taylor, "The Human Suffering Caused by China's One-Child Policy," *Washington Post*, October 29, 2015.
42. "As much as three-quarters of the decline in fertility since 1970 occurred before the launching of the one-child policy; fertility levels fluctuated in China after the policy was launched; and most of the further decline in fertility since 1980 can be attributed to economic development, not coercive enforcement of birth limits." Martin King Whyte, Wang Feng, and Yong Cai, "Challenging Myths about China's One-Child Policy," *China Journal* 74 (2015): 144.
43. At the same time, the government fined single women that bore children but prevented them from using reproductive technologies. To this day, the government still sanctions parents who have more than the permitted number of children. Sui-Lee Wee and Steven Lee Myers, "China's Birthrate Hits Historic Low, in Looming Crisis for Beijing," *New York Times*, January 17, 2020.
44. United Nations, Department of Economic and Social Affairs, "World Population Prospects, 2022."
45. To keep this in perspective, this ratio is still much lower than what is anticipated in Japan (77.8) and South Korea (72.4). Data for China are from United Nations, Department of Economic and Social Affairs, "World Population Prospects, 2022." Data for Japan and South Korea are from OECD, *Pensions at a Glance 2017: OECD and G20 Indicators* (Paris: OECD Publishing, 2017), 123.
46. Statista, "Degree of Urbanization in China from 1980 to 2022," August 2023.
47. Republic of China, National Bureau of Statistics, "Main Data of the Seventh National Population Census," May 11, 2021l. Almost 125 million people had moved to another province.
48. China Labour Bulletin, "Migrant Workers and Their Children," September 6, 2023.
49. Wills, "Seeking Balance." The objectives were to increase China's percentage of urban residents to be more in line with developed countries, boost domestic consumption, and improve the delivery of services. The 2020 census indicated that there had been an increase of 236.4 million people in the urban population and a decrease of 164.4 million

people in the rural population since 2010. Republic of China, National Bureau of Statistics, "Main Data."

50. Fang Zhao, Juha Erkki, Antero Hamalaienen, and Honglin L. Chen. "Child Protection in China: Changing Policies and Reactions from the Field of Social Work," *International Journal of Social Welfare* 26 (2017): 334.

51. On the general decline in child welfare due to parental migration, see Ming-Hsuan Lee, "Migration and Children's Welfare in China: The Schooling and Health of Children Left Behind," *Journal of Developing Areas* 44, no. 2 (2011): 165–82.

52. Xiaoyan Lei, John Strauss, Meng Tian, and Yaohui Zhao, "Living Arrangements of the Elderly in China: Evidence from the CHARLS National Baseline," *China Economic Journal* 8, no. 3 (2015): 191–214.

53. Chau-Kiu Cheung and Alex Yui-Huen Kwan, "The Erosion of Filial Piety by Modernisation in Chinese Cities," *Ageing and Society* 29, no. 2 (2009): 179–98; and Chou, "Filial Piety by Contract?"

54. Zhixin Feng, "Childlessness and Vulnerability of Older People in China," *Age and Ageing* 47, no. 2 (2017): 1–6.

55. Figures are in constant 2011 dollars adjusted for purchasing power parity. Indermit Gill, "Deep-Sixing Poverty in China." *Brookings*, January 25, 2021. Gill noted that China's poverty line is set just above the level the World Bank recommended for countries with per capita income below USD1,000, that is, USD1.90.

56. Jinquan Gong, Gewei Wang, Yafeng Wang, and Yaohui Zhao, "Consumption and Poverty of Older Chinese: 2011–2020," *Journal of the Economics of Ageing* 23 (2022): 1–12.

57. Björn Gustafsson and Ding Sai, "Growing into Relative Income Poverty: Urban China, 1988–2013," *Social Indicators Research* 147 (2020): 73–94.

58. Jeanette Wang, "One in 4 Elderly Chinese Living Below Poverty Line, Landmark Study Finds," *South China Morning Post*, May 31, 2013. For an in-depth analysis, see Quanbao Jiang, Shucai Yang, and Jesus J. Sánchez-Barricarte, "Can China Afford Rapid Aging?," *Springerplus* 5, no. 1 (2016): 1107.

59. Educational expenses jumped from 2 percent of household income in 1990 to over 10 percent after 2000. Individuals also paid far more for medical services, with out-of-pocket expenses climbing from 20 percent of the cost of care in 1978 to as high as 60 percent in 2000. Longmei Zhang, Ray Brooks, Ding Ding, Haiyan Ing, Hui He, Jing Lu, and Rui Mano, "China's High Savings: Drivers, Prospects, and Policies," IMF Working Paper WP/18/277, December 2018.

60. "At 54, China's Average Retirement Age Is Too Low," *Economist*, June 24, 2021. The official retirement ages are sixty for men, fifty-five for white-collar women, and fifty for women factory workers.

61. World Bank, "Urban Population Growth (Annual %)," World Development Indicators, 2023. The government has announced plans to slowly increase the retirement age starting in late 2023. Farah Master, "China to Raise Retirement Age to Deal with Aging Population—Media," *Reuters*, March 14, 2023.

62. Qiushi Feng, Wei-Jun Jean Yeung, Zhenglian Wang, and Yi Zeng, "Age of Retirement and Human Capital in an Aging China, 2015–2050," *European Journal of Population* 35 (2019): 29–62.

63. Wei Bai, Yan-Li Lee, Jingyi Liao, Lusi Wu, Mei Xie, and Tao Zhou, "The Gender Pay Gap in China: Insights from a Discrimination Perspective," *arXiv*, 2022; and Republic of China, National Bureau of Statistics, "China Statistical Yearbook," 2022.

64. Wills, "Seeking Balance."

65. OECD, *Pensions at a Glance 2015: OECD and G20 Indicators* (Paris: OECD Publishing, 2015), 233. Civil servants had their own pension scheme initially, but it was merged with the Basic Pension in 2015. The average income replacement rate for urban workers

(pension benefits expressed as a percentage of pre-retirement earnings) declined sharply from about 80 percent in the mid-1990s to a little below 50 percent after 2010.

66. China Labour Bulletin, "China's Social Security System," August 18, 2021; and "In Milestone Move, China Launches Private Pension Scheme," *Reuters*, April 21, 2022.

67. Li Yang, "Towards Equity and Sustainability? China's Pension System Reform Moves Center Stage," World Inequality Lab no. 2021/13, April 2021, figure 4.

68. Zongyuan Zoe Liu, "China's Pensions System Is Buckling under an Aging Population," *Foreign Policy*, June 29, 2023.

69. Starting in 2017, the government has made contributions into the fund for 60 million poor people. China Labour Bulletin, "China's Social Security System."

70. Liu, "China's Pensions System Is Buckling"; and Yang, "Towards Equity and Sustainability?" The replacement ratio in URRPS was less than one-third that of the BOAI.

71. Yang, "Towards Equity and Sustainability?," 12.

72. Phillips and Feng, "Challenges for the Aging Family," 296; and China Labour Bulletin, "Migrant Workers." Other forms of social protection were also lacking; for instance, just 27 percent of migrants had access to work-related injury compensation and only 17 percent had unemployment insurance.

73. Saijun Zhang, Qinying Ci and Min Zhan, "Public Assistance in Urban and Rural China: A Tale of Two Stories," *International Journal of Social Welfare* 26 (2017): 303–13; and Gao, *Welfare, Work and Poverty*.

74. Jennifer Pan, *Welfare for Autocrats: How Social Assistance in China Cares for its Rulers* (New York: Oxford University Press, 2020).

75. Emily Rauhala, "He Was One of Millions of Chinese Seniors Growing Old Alone. So He Put Himself Up for Adoption," *Washington Post*, May 2, 2018.

76. Liu, "China's Pensions System Is Buckling." The average age of migrant workers jumped from 34 to 42.3 between 2009 and 2022, while that of all Chinese workers increased from 36.8 to 39 (in the period 2009–20).

77. Frank Tang, "China's State Pension Fund to Run Dry by 2035 as Workforce Shrinks Due to Effects of One-Child Policy, Says Study," *South China Morning Post*, April 12, 2019. The central government has already had to supply funds to several provinces with older populations that have run deficits. President Xi also ordered several large SOEs to transfer 10 percent of their stock to the pension funds to shore up their finances.

78. Yang, "Towards Equity and Sustainability?," 20.

79. Junsen Zhang, Yaohui Zhao, Albert Park, and Xiaoqing Song, "Economic Returns to Schooling in Urban China, 1988 to 2001," *Journal of Comparative Economics* 33 (2005): 730–52.

80. Hongben Li, Lei Li, Binzhen Wu, and Yan Yan Xiong, "The End of Cheap Chinese Labor," *Journal of Economic Perspectives* 26, no. 4 (2012): 57–74.

81. Official government data cover only 70 percent of urban employment. They do not include informal sector and self-employed workers in urban settings, as well as laborers in rural areas. See Dmitriy Plekhanov, "Is China's Era of Cheap Labor Really Over?," *Diplomat*, December 13, 2017.

82. Republic of China, National Bureau of Statistics, "China's Statistical Yearbook." One author reported annual real wage growth of only 0.1 percent from 1978 to 1997, but these data are based on constant USD, not local currency. Li et al., "End of Cheap Labor"

83. Jain-Chandra et al., "Inequality in China," 6.

84. Jun Zhang and Xiaofeng Liu, "The Evolving Pattern of the Wage-Labor Productivity Nexus in China: Evidence from Manufacturing Firm-Level Data," *Economic Systems* 37, no. 3 (2013): 354–68. The authors determined that increases in labor productivity exceeded gains in wages in the 1990s and 2000s.

85. Chong-En Bai and Zhenjie Qian, "The Factor Income Distribution in China: 1978–2007," *China Economic Review* 21 (2010): 650–70. These figures were based on

official data. Bai and Qian claimed that these data overstated the decline of labor's share and estimated it to be closer to 7.2 percent.

86. Weining Hu, "China's Labor Market: Gaining Insights into HR Trends," *China Briefing*, January 18, 2017.

87. Zhang et al., "Economic Returns to Schooling."

88. Lijia Guo, Jiashun Huang, and You Zhang, "Education Development in China: Education Return, Quality, and Equity," *Sustainability* 11 (2019): 3750, reviewed several studies that examined returns to education.

89. Le Wang, "Economic Transition and College Premium in Urban China," *China Economic Review* 23, no. 2 (2012): 238–52.

90. Xinyang Chang, "Analysis of Education Wage Premium in Several Provinces of China," *Modern Economy* 6 (2015): 862–70.

91. Xiaohua Feng, "Effect of Intra-Industry Trade on Skill Premium in Manufacturing in China," *China Economic Review* 47 (2018): 206–18.

92. Wen, "Estimating Education and Labor Market Consequences."

93. Stella Qiu and Elias Glenn, "China Goes on Tech-Hiring Binge and Wages Soar, Closing Gap with Silicon Valley," *Reuters*, January 24, 2018.

94. Jain-Chandra et al., "Inequality in China," 5.

95. Kevin Lin, "Rising Inequality and its Discontents in China," *New Labor Forum* 25, no. 3 (2016): 66–74. Labor unrest due to wage cuts, layoffs, and unpaid salaries is substantial: 830 labor strikes or protests took place in 2022 and 1,300 were projected by the end of 2023. Marrian Zhou, "Factory Strikes Flare Up in China as Economic Woes Deepen," *Nikkei Asia*, August 28, 2023. In the past, labor unrest of this magnitude unsettled national leaders and sparked vigorous efforts to suppress reports of incidents, block the emergence of labor movements, and arrest organizers, instead of bringing about major reforms. Javier C. Hernandez, "Workers' Activism Rises as China's Economy Slows. Xi Aims to Rein Them In," *New York Times*, February 6, 2019. The government's decision to abandon its COVID-19 policy after mass protests indicate that it is sometimes responsive to citizen dissatisfaction.

96. Policymakers first introduced ALMPs to help create employment opportunities for workers displaced by reform of SOEs. For details, see Chris K. C. Chan and Yujian Zhai, "Active Labour Market Policies in China: Towards Improved Labour Protection?," *Journal of Asian Public Policy* 6, no. 1 (2013): 10–25.

97. The Employment First initiative also provides employment services and technical training to recent college graduates.

98. Liu, "China's Pensions System Is Buckling."

99. China Labour Bulletin, "China's Social Security System."

100. Chunbing Xing and Jianwei Xu, "Regional Variation of the Minimum Wages in China," *IZA Journal of Labor & Development* 5, no. 8 (2016). Shanghai had one of the highest minimum wages in the country in 2023, at approximately USD3.30. WageIndicator, "Minimum Wage Updated in Shanghai, China from 01 July 2023—July 03, 2023," 2023.

101. Xing and Xu, "Regional Variation."

102. Shi-Chang Yang, Ying-Li Zhang, Dong-Jun Zhang, Li-Juan Shen, and Gui-Ying Yao, "Meta-Analysis of Incidence Rate of Child Abuse in China," *Chinese Journal of School Health* 9 (2014): 1346–48.

103. Hanlin Fu, Tiejian Feng, Jiabi Qin, Tingting Wang, Xiaobing Wu, Yuamo Cai, Lina Lan, and Tubao Yang, "Reported Prevalence of Childhood Maltreatment among Chinese College Students: A Systematic Review and Meta-Analysis," *PLoS One* 13, no. 10 (2018), e0205808. Similarly, research conducted in Zhejiang province determined that over 80% of college students had been physically and psychologically abused. Yanyan Ni

and Therese Hesketh, "Child Maltreatment in China: A Cross-Sectional Study of Prevalence and Attitudes among Young Adults," *Lancet* 386, no. S52 (2015).

104. Jing Hua, Zhe Mu, Bright Nwaru, Guixiong Gu, Wei Meng, and Zhuochun Wu, "Child Neglect in One-Child Families from Suzhou City of Mainland China," *BMC International Health and Human Rights* 14, no. 8 (2014): 1–9; Xin Xia, Joe Xiang, Jianbo Shao, Gary A. Smith, Chuanhua Yu, Huiping Zhu, and Huiyun Xiang, "Characteristics and Trends of Hospitalized Pediatric Abuse Head Trauma in Wuhan, China 2002," *International Journal of Environmental Research and Public Health* 9 (2012): 4187–96; and Catherine So-kum Tang, "The Rate of Physical Child Abuse in Chinese Families: A Community Survey in Hong Kong," *Child Abuse & Neglect* 22, no. 5 (1998): 381–91.

105. Recent news stories have spotlighted civil society efforts to counter child abuse. See "China Steps up Efforts to Counter Child Abuse," *Xinhua News*, November 20, 2019. From 2013 to 2015, the Chinese media reported 968 cases of sexual abuse of children involving 1,790 victims. "A Horror Confronted: Sexual Abuse of Children," *Economist*, August 27, 2016; and Ailin Tang and Keith Bradhser, "A Billionaire's Fall Spotlights Child Sexual Abuse in China," *New York Times*, July 9, 2019.

106. Costs are defined as disability-adjusted life years due to mental health disorders and health-risk behaviors. Xiangming Fang, Deborah A Fry, Kai Ji, David Finkelhor, Jingqi Chen, Patricia Lannene, and Michael P. Dunne, "The Burden of Child Maltreatment in China: A Systematic Review," *Bull World Health Organ* 93, no. 3 (2015): 176–85.

107. Hua et al., "Child Neglect in One-Child Families."

108. Ian Katz, Xiaoyuan Shang, and Yahua Zhang, "Missing Elements of a Child Protection System in China: The Case of LX," *Social Policy and Society* 10, no. 1 (2010): 96–97; and Qiao Dongping and Chan Yuk-chung, "Myths of Child Abuse in China: Findings Based on a Qualitative Study in Beijing," *China Journal of Social Work* 1, no. 3 (2008): 270.

109. Kane Zhang and Lynn Xu, "Surging Child Sex Abuse Cases in China: Recent Efforts Are Just a Bandaid on a Festering Wound Caused by Communism, Say Experts," *Epoch Times*, July 18, 2023.

110. Out-of-wedlock children were denied *hukou* until the 2016 reform. Their social rights are still far from secure as gaining access to provincial level services often requires a marriage certificate and detailed information regarding the father. Mandy Zuo, "Single Mum in Legal Fight for China's Unmarried Mothers," *South China Morning Post*, September 14, 2019.

111. Chan, "Internal Migration in China."

112. China Labour Bulletin, "Migrant Workers." The total population of migrant children—138 million—represented 46.4 percent of all children in China. Parental migration from city to city in search of employment has also created a large pool of left-behind urban children, estimated to number 8.7 million. Lian Tong, Qiong Yan, and Ichiro Kawachi, "The Factors Associated with Being Left-Behind Children in China: Multilevel Analysis with Nationally Representative Data," *PLoS One* 14, no. 11 (2019).

113. "Horror Confronted."

114. China Labour Bulletin, "Migrant Workers," from the section titled "Family Support."

115. China Labour Bulletin, "Migrant Workers."

116. Chen Tingting and Lv Pu, "Safeguarding Children against Domestic Violence in China," Asia Foundation, March 1, 2017.

117. " Left-Behind Girls Vulnerable to Sexual Assault: Report," *Xinhua News*, September 13, 2013.

118. Feng Wang, Jingjing Lu, Lin Leesa, and Xudong Zhou, "Mental Health and Risk Behaviors of Children in Rural China with Different Patterns of Parental Migration: A Cross-Sectional Study," *Child and Adolescent Psychiatry and Mental Health* 13, no. 39

(2019); and Xue Zhao, Jian Chen, Ming-Chun Chen, Xiao-Ling Lv, Yu-Hong Jiang, and Ye-Huan Sun, "Left-Behind Children in Rural China Experience Higher Levels of Anxiety and Poorer Living Conditions," *Acta Paediatrica* 103 (2014): 665–70.

119. Tingting and Pu, "Safeguarding Children."

120. "Left-Behind Girls Vulnerable."

121. Tang, "Rate of Physical Child Abuse in Chinese Families."

122. Karoline Kan, "My Secret Life as a Forbidden Second Child in China," *Foreign Policy*, February 4, 2016.

123. Kyung-Sup Chang, "The Confucian Family Instead of the Welfare State? Reform and Peasant Welfare in Post-Mao China," *Asian Perspective* 17, no. 1 (1993): 178.

124. International Labour Organization, *World Social Protection Report 2017–2019: Universal Social Protection to Achieve Sustainable Development Goals* (Geneva: International Labour Office, 2017); and Katz, Shang, and Zhang, "Missing Elements of a Child Protection System."

125. X. Li, Q. Yue, S. Wang, H. Wang, J. J Jiang, L. Gong, W. Liu, X. Huang, and Tao Xu, "Knowledge, Attitudes, and Behaviours of Healthcare Professionals Regarding Child Maltreatment in China," *Child Care Health and Development* 43, no. 6 (2017): 869–75.

126. International Labour Organization, *World Social Protection Report 2020–22: Social Protection at the Crossroads—In Pursuit of a Better Future* (Geneva: International Labour Organization, 2021), table A4.2.

127. Victor Shaw, "Urban Housing Reform in China," *Habitat International* 21, no. 2 (1997): 199–212; and Ya Ping Wang, "From Social Welfare to Support of Home Ownership: The Experience of China," in *Housing and the New Welfare State: Perspectives from East Asia and Europe*, ed. Richard Groves, Alan Murie, and Christopher Watson (Aldershot, UK: Ashgate, 2007), 129–58.

128. Fulong Wu, "Housing and the State in China," in *International Encyclopedia of Housing and Home*, ed. Susan J. Smith, Maria Elsinga, Lorna Fox O'Mahony, Ong Seow Eng, Susan Wachter, and Chris Hamnett, vol. 3 (Oxford, UK: Elsevier, 2012), 323–29; and Joyce Yanyum Man, Siqi Zheng, and Rongrong Ren, "Housing Policy and Housing Markets: Trends, Patterns, and Affordability," in *China's Housing Reform and Outcomes*, ed. Joyce Yanyum Man (Cambridge, MA: Lincoln Institute of Land Policy, 2011), 3–18.

129. Commodity housing consists of dwellings that are constructed on urban land that is leased from a municipal government and sold on the open market at prevailing prices.

130. Man, Zheng, and Ren, "Housing Policy and Housing Markets"; and Wei Shi, Jie Chen, and Hongwei Wang, "Affordable Housing Policy in China: New Developments and New Challenges," *Habitat International* 54 (2016): 224–33.

131. Weiping Wu, "Sources of Migrant Housing Disadvantage in Urban China," *Environment and Planning A* 36 (2004): 1285–304.

132. In 2014, the public rental housing program was merged with cheap rental housing; the latter is now intended solely for low-income households. Shi, Chen, and Wang, "Affordable Housing Policy in China."

133. Tong, Yan, and Kawachi, "Factors Associated with Being Left-Behind Children"; and Junhua Chen, Ying Wu, and Huijia Li, "Vocational Status, Hukou and Housing Migrants in the New Century: Evidence from a Multi-City Study of Housing Inequality," *Social Indicators Research* 139 (2018): 309–25.

134. Ya Ping Wang and Alan Murie, "The Process of Commercialization of Urban Housing in China," *Urban Studies* 33, no. 6 (1996): 971–89.

135. Wang, "From Social Welfare to Support of Home Ownership."

136. Wu, "Housing and the State in China."

137. The HPF allows contributors to use their accounts for home purchases and maintenance and offers access to subsidized mortgages. It resembles the MPF in Singapore in that contributions not used for housing can be redeemed in retirement. Public sector workers and SOE employees were the primary users of the HPF initially, but the pool of contributors now includes employees of private and foreign-owned firms. The total enrollment was 153 million in 2020. China Labour Bulletin, "China's Social Security System."

138. Yingchao Lin, Zhili Ma, Ke Zhao, Weiyan Hu, and Jing Wei, "The Impact of Population Migration on Urban Housing Prices: Evidence from China's Major Cities," *Sustainability* 10, no. 9 (2018): 3169. Housing prices in 2014 were 1.6 and 3.2 times higher than in 1999 and 2008, respectively. Cities with the most immigration, for example, Shanghai, experienced the largest price increases. Shi, Chen, and Wang, "Affordable Housing Policy in China," 226.

139. The lack of options for savers in China has contributed to this trend. Affordable housing must be occupied and cannot be purchased as an investment. Residents must live in their unit for a fixed number of years before being permitted to sell it.

140. Zhang Jie, "Housing Occupancy Rate in 28 Chinese Cities at 12%: Report," *Asian News Network - China Daily*, August 8, 2022.

141. Chi Lo, "China's Structural Reform Policy: This Time Is It for Real?," *International Economy* 24, no. 3 (2010): 36–39; and Shi, Chen, and Wang, "Affordable Housing Policy in China."

142. Youqin Huang, "Low-Income Housing in Chinese Cities: Policies and Practices," *China Quarterly* 212 (2012): 941–64.

143. Wei Shi, Jie Chen, and Hongwei Wang, "Affordable Housing Policy in China: New Developments and New Challenges," *Habitat International* 54, part 3 (2016): 224–33.

144. Jing Zhou and Richard Ronald, "The Resurgence of Public Housing Provision in China: The Chongqing Programme," *Housing Studies* 32, no. 4 (2017): 428–48. In 2012, central and local governments allocated 413 billion yuan to public housing projects and raised an additional 467 billion though corporate bonds, bank loans, and other instruments.

145. Yonghua Zou, "Contradictions in China's Affordable Housing Policy: Goals vs. Structure," *Habitat International* 41 (2014): 8–16.

146. Xiao Wang and Richard Herd found that nontax sources accounted for somewhat less than 30 percent of total government revenue. Xiao Wang and Richard Herd, "The System of Revenue Sharing and Fiscal Transfers in China," OECD Economics Department Working Papers no. 1030, February 201.

147. Fox Z. Y. Hu and Jiwei Qian, "Land-Based Finance, Fiscal Autonomy and Land Supply for Affordable Housing in Urban China: A Prefecture-Level Analysis," *Land Use Policy* 69 (2017): 454–60; Zhou and Ronald, "Resurgence of Public Housing Provision in China"; and "29% of Chinese Fiscal Revenues Derived from Land Sales," *China Banking News*, January 21, 2019.

148. Local government debt was 17.9 trillion yuan in mid 2013, up from negligible levels in 2007. The state pushed subnational governments to undertake a sharp increase in spending after the US financial crisis in order to maintain a high level of economic growth. Carlos Tejada, "China Places Cap on Local Government Debt," *Wall Street Journal*, August 30, 2015.

149. Winni Zhou and Kevin Yao, "China Audit Uncovers Misuse of Affordable Housing Funds," *Reuters*, August 17, 2015.

150. Wei and Chiu, "Livability of Subsidized Housing Estates"; and Wen Zeng, Philip Rees, and Lili Xiang, "Do Residents of Affordable Housing Communities in China Suffer from Relative Accessibility Deprivation? A Case Study of Nanjing," *Cities* 90 (2019): 141–56.

151. Yunxiao Dang, Zhilin Liu, and Wenzhong Zhang, "Land-Based Interests and the Spatial Distribution of Affordable Housing Development: The Case of Beijing, China," *Habitat International* 44 (2014): 137–45; and Zuopeng Ma, Chenggu Liu, and Jing Zhang, "Affordable Housing Brings about Socio-Spatial Exclusion in Changchun, China: Explanation in Various Economic Motivations of Local Governments," *Habitat International* 76 (2018): 40–47.

152. Zan Yang, Chengdong Yi, Wei Zhang, and Chun Zhang, "Affordability of Housing and Accessibility of Public Services: Evaluation of Housing Programs in Beijing," *Journal of Housing and the Built Environment* 29 (2014): 521–40; and Wei and Chiu, "Livability of Subsidized Housing Estates."

153. Yaquiang Wang and Xin Dong, "Housing Policies for Rural Migrant Workers in China," in *Urban Inequality and Segregation in Europe and China*, ed. Gwilym Pryce, Ya Ping Wang, Yu Chen, Jingjing Shan, and Houkai Wei (Cham, Switzerland: Springer, 2021), 181–203. In 2016, 62.4 percent of rural migrant workers lived in rental units. Sixty-one percent of these individuals lived in private flats, and 13.4 percent resided in apartments provided by work units or employers.

154. Helen Roxburgh, "China's Radical Plan to Limit the Populations of Beijing and Shanghai," *Guardian*, March 19, 2018.

155. Wade Shepard, *Ghost Cities of China: The Story of Cities without People in the World's Most Populated Country* (London: Zed Books, 2015). Ghost cities are typically the result of developers being obligated to build housing upon being granted land. They are not permitted to wait until demand is sufficient to make construction financially viable. Housing units may remain unoccupied for long periods if housing prices drop or companies provide dormitory accommodations.

156. Jie Chen, Qianjin Hao, and Mark Stephens, "Assessing Housing Affordability in Post-Reform China: A Case Study of Shanghai," *Housing Studies* 25, no. 6 (2010): 877–901; and Ya Ping Wang and Alan Murie, "The New Affordable and Social Housing Provision System in China: Implications for Comparative Housing Studies," *International Journal of Housing Policy* 11, no. 3 (2011): 237–54.

157. Huang, "Low-Income Housing in Chinese Cities."

158. Fitch Ratings, "China Property Watch—January 2023: Public Housing Initiative to Stabilise Private Property Market," January 31, 2023.

159. Kristy Hung and Lisa Zhou, "China Could Base Housing Model on Singapore Instead of Hong Kong," *Bloomberg Intelligence*, February 23, 2023.

160. Brad W. Setser, "The IMF's China Problem," Council on Foreign Relations, September 28, 2017.

CONCLUSION

1. This neglect only seems to be worsening. The first edition of the *Oxford Handbook of the Welfare State* contained a brief chapter on East Asian welfare systems. It has been eliminated from the second. Daniel Béland, Kimberly J. Morgan, Herbert Obinger, and Christopher Pierson, eds., *The Oxford Handbook of the Welfare State*, 2nd ed. (New York: Oxford University Press, 2021).

2. The governments of Singapore and Taiwan do not supply official poverty data for the elderly or total population. Some scholars have calculated these rates, and we discussed their estimates in the sections dedicated to those nations in chapter 2.

3. Japan spent 12.1 percent of GDP on programs for the elderly, compared to 3.7 percent, 1.6 percent, 2.7 percent, 0.7 percent, and 4.7 percent for China, Hong Kong, South Korea, Singapore, and Taiwan, respectively, in 2017 (or latest year). International Labour Organization, *World Social Protection Report 2017–2019: Universal Social Protection*

to Achieve Sustainable Development Goals (Geneva: International Labour Organization, 2017), 86, figure 4.8. Japan's age profile began to shift quickly in the 1990s, whereas the graying of neighboring populations commenced at least a decade later.

4. Naohiro Yashiro, "Aging of the Population in Japan and Its Implications to the Other Asian Countries," *Journal of Asian Economics* 8, no. 2 (1997): 245–61.

5. The next closest major country is Italy at 24.1 percent. The world average is 9.8 percent. See World Bank, "Population Estimates and Projections," Databank/World Development Indicators, 2023.

6. Masayoshi Hayashi, "Chihō zaisei to Seikatsu Hogo" [Local finance and the Daily Life Security], in *Seikatsu Hogo no keizai bunseki* [Economic analysis of the Daily Life Security], ed. Abe Aya, Kunieda Shigeki, Suzuki Wataru, and Hayashi Masayoshi (Tokyo: Tokyo Daigaku Shuppankai, 2008), 239–68.

7. Phillip Lipscy, "Japan: The Harbinger State," *Japanese Journal of Political Science* 24, no. 1 (2023): 80–97.

8. Japan abolished its single nontransferable voting system with multimember districts and adopted a mixed electoral system consisting of single-member districts with plurality voting and a party list system with proportional representation in 1994. For more on this topic, see Frances McCall Rosenbluth and Michael F. Thies, *Japan Transformed: Political Change and Economic Restructuring* (Princeton, NJ: Princeton University Press, 2010).

9. Francis Castles, "What Welfare States Do: A Disaggregated Expenditure Approach," *Journal of Social Policy* 38, no. 1 (2008): 46.

10. For example, see Lyle Scruggs and James P. Allan, "Welfare-State Decommodification in 18 OECD Countries: A Replication and Revision," *Journal of European Social Policy* 16, no. 1 (2006): 55–72; and Clare Bambra, "Decommodification and the Worlds of Welfare Revisited," *Journal of European Social Policy* 16, no. 1 (2006): 73–80. Using a different approach, Mari Miura reaches a similar conclusion. Mari Miura, *Welfare through Work: Conservative Ideas, Partisan Politics, and Social Protection in Japan* (Ithaca, NY: Cornell University Press, 2012).

11. Margarita Estevez-Abe, *Welfare and Capitalism in Postwar Japan* (New York: Cambridge University Press, 2008).

12. Yumiko Shimabukuro and Arvid Lukauskas, "Building an Inegalitarian Welfare State: The Impact of Dualistic Coordinated Capitalism & Elite-Made Democracy in Japan" (unpublished manuscript, September 1, 2023).

13. Yeon-Myung Kim, "Beyond East Asian Welfare Productivism in South Korea," *Policy and Politics* 36, no. 1 (2008): 109–25; and Joseph Wong, *Healthy Democracies: Welfare Politics in Taiwan and South Korea* (Ithaca, NY: Cornell University Press, 2004). Kim argued that the move toward greater social protection was supported by the emergence of new cross-class welfare alliances and the blossoming of civic culture under democracy.

14. Randall S. Jones, "Public Social Spending in Korea in the Context of Rapid Population Ageing," OECD Economics Department Working Papers no. 615, OECD Publishing, May 2008, 28. See also OECD, "Social Expenditure Update 2019: Public Social Spending is High in Many OECD Countries," January 2019. A detailed study of the expansion of health care in South Korea is Wong, *Healthy Democracies*.

15. Jones, "Public Social Spending in Korea," 27–29.

16. On the OECD, see ILO, *World Social Protection Report 2017–2019*, table B.17.

17. We were unable to find social expenditure levels in Taiwan prior to 2010 using the sources referenced elsewhere in this volume. Caution is needed in comparing data from those sources and the ILO statistics. For the single year covered by both—2010—the ILO figure is significantly higher (9.7 percent vs. 8.4 percent). Here we are concerned with the trend in spending over the period 1990 to 2010, not the absolute values.

18. An insightful assessment of prominent studies that argue that democracy leads to public policy favorable to the poor is Michael Ross, "Is Democracy Good for the Poor?," *American Journal of Political Science* 50, no. 4 (2006): 860–74. On the link between economic advancements and social welfare development see Harold Wilensky and Charles N. Lebeaux, *Industrial Society and Social Welfare* (New York: Russell Sage Foundation, 1958); and Gregory J. Kasza, *One World of Welfare: Japan in Comparative Perspective* (Ithaca, NY: Cornell University Press, 2006).

19. Shimabukuro and Lukauskas, "Building an Inegalitarian Welfare State."

20. Jacob S. Hacker, *The Great Risk Shift: The New Economic Insecurity and the Decline of the American Dream*, 2nd edition (New York: Oxford University Press, 2008); and Matthew Desmond, *Poverty, by America* (New York: Crown, 2023).

21. A valuable effort to examine the co-evolution of these variable is Torben Iversen and David Soskice, *Democracy and Prosperity: Reinventing Capitalism through a Turbulent Century* (Princeton, NJ: Princeton University Press, 2019).

22. Stephan Haggard and Robert R. Kaufman, *Development, Democracy, and Welfare States: Latin America, East Asia, and Eastern Europe* (Princeton, NJ: Princeton University Press, 2008); Kasza, *One World of Welfare*; Yeon-Myung Kim, "Towards a Comprehensive Welfare State in South Korea: Institutional Features, New Socio-Economic and Political Pressures, and the Possibility of the Welfare State," Asia Research Centre Working Paper no. 14 (2006); Kim, "Beyond East Asian Welfare Productivism"; and Wong, *Healthy Democracies*.

23. A good example of this claim is Kim, "Beyond East Asian Welfare Productivism," 111.

24. Dani Rodrik, "Why Do More Open Economies Have Bigger Governments?," *Journal of Political Economy* 106, no. 5 (1998): 998.

25. "Governments in small open economies have tended to provide a variety of income supplements in the form of social security schemes, health insurance, unemployment benefits, job training, employment subsidies to firms, and even investment capital." David Cameron, "The Expansion of the Public Economy: A Comparative Analysis." *American Political Science Review* 72, no. 4 (1978): 1260.

26. Peter Katzenstein, *Small States in World Markets: Industrial Policy in Europe* (Ithaca, NY: Cornell University Press, 1985). The quintessential examples are small European states.

27. As measured by the ratio of trade (exports + imports) to GDP, Hong Kong (384 percent), Singapore (337 percent) and Taiwan (127 percent) were among the most open economies in the world in 2022. South Korea (97 percent) was also more open than the world average (57 percent). Data are from World Bank, "Trade (% of GDP)," World Development Indicators, 2023. The exception to this is for Taiwan, whose data comes from Statista, "Share of International Trade of Goods and Services in Nominal GDP in Taiwan in Selected Quarters from 4th Quarter 2018 to 4th Quarter 2022," August 2023.

28. Nevertheless, China (38 percent) and Japan (37 percent) relied on export-led growth during their periods of rapid development. China's level of openness is high compared to other large economies. In the United States, for example, trade as a percentage of GDP is 25 percent. World Bank, "Trade."

29. Alícia Adserà and Carles Boix hypothesized that leaders in authoritarian regimes, even those in small, open states, might choose to liberalize trade but opt for a limited public sector in order to keep taxes low, confident that their political dominance would enable them to suppress the demands for social insurance or compensatory spending. This argument may help to explain the existence of small public sectors in East Asian nations with authoritarian regimes in their early years, but not their limited size since democratization. The authors noted that Southern European countries with open economies, like Spain and

Portugal, raised spending markedly after they transitioned from authoritarian to democratic regimes in the 1970s. As already discussed, democratic transitions resulted in only minimal increases in social spending in Taiwan and moderate expansion in South Korea. Alícia Adserà and Carles Boix, "Trade, Democracy, and the Size of the Public Sector: The Political Underpinnings of Openness," *International Organization* 56, no. 2 (2002): 229–62.

30. The Asian Development Bank (ADB) has not updated its breakdown on the recipients of social protection expenditures beyond 2015.

31. OECD, *Society at a Glance 2019* (Paris: OECD Publishing, 2019). Comparing OECD and ADB figures must be done with caution. First, in the OECD measure discussed here, public cash transfers received by working-age individuals is only one component of social assistance. Second, the ADB figures use each nation's official poverty line—typically 50 percent of median income—to demarcate the poor population, whereas the OECD data refers to the lowest income quintile.

32. Willem Adema, Pauline Fron, and Maxime Ladaique, "How Much Do OECD Countries Spend on Social Protection and How Redistributive Are Their Tax/Benefit Systems?," *International Social Security Review* 67, no. 1 (2014): 16–19.

33. OECD, "Social Expenditure Update 2019: Public Social Spending is High in Many OECD Countries," January 2019, 4.

34. Virginia Hernanz, Franck Malherbert, and Michele Pellizzari, "Take-Up of Welfare Benefits in OECD Countries: A Review of the Evidence," OECD Social, Employment and Migration Working Papers, no. 17 OECD, 2004. The OECD study did not include take-up rates in East Asia. Our conclusion is based on comparing the OECD and ADB data, so this finding is only suggestive.

35. ILO, *World Social Protection Report 2017–2019*, table B.3. Our calculations are based on countries for which statistics are provided for 2015.

36. Comprehensive data on the distribution of social insurance spending across income groups in OECD countries are not available. The ILO noted that a significant percentage of insurance benefits in OECD countries were means tested. International Labour Organization, *World Social Protection Report 2017–2019*.

37. Details on unemployment programs in China, Japan, South Korea, and Taiwan are found in Gyu-Jin Hwang, "How Fair Are Unemployment Benefits? The Experience of East Asia," *International Social Security Review* 72, no. 2 (2019): 49–73. Hwang also noted that benefits in these countries were of short duration.

38. OECD, "Public Expenditure and Participant Stocks on LMP," 2023. Comparisons between East Asia and the OECD are confined to Japan and South Korea because of data limitations. By all accounts, other East Asian nations spent even less.

39. Hwang, "How Fair Are Unemployment Benefits?," 65.

40. ILO, *World Social Protection Report 2017–2019*, table B.6.

41. The OECD publishes a comprehensive overview of social conditions around the globe on an annual basis. The latest version is OECD, *Society at a Glance 2019*.

42. A further extension of the approach would be to incorporate transnational sources of social protection for migrants into the analysis. Peggy Levitt, Erica Dobbs, Ken Chih-Yan Sun, and Ruxandra Paul, *Transnational Social Protection: Social Welfare across National Borders* (New York: Oxford University Press, 2023).

43. "Noin iljari saeob jungdan janggihwa—noin 97% iljari hyueob" [Prolonged suspension of senior job positions—97% of senior jobs suspended], *Yonhap News*, March 15, 2020.

44. Gwynn Guilford and Sarah Chaney Cambon, "Covid Shrinks the Labor Market, Pushing Out Women and Baby Boomers," *Wall Street Journal*, December 3, 2020.

45. "Jūgatsu ni jisatsu shita hito josei nijūdai to yonjūdai ga kyonen no dōjiki yori nibai ijō ni" [Two times as many women in their twenties and forties committed suicide in October than one year ago], *NHK News*, November 24, 2020.

46. Laura Westbrook, "Coronavirus Crisis Exposes Harsh Existence of Hong Kong's Poorest Households," *South China Morning Post*, March 14, 2020.

47. Cheng Siwei and Guo Yingzhe, "Provincial Pension Funds Face New Squeeze as Government Waives Contributions," *Caixin Global*, March 4, 2020.

48. Mi Ah Schoyen and Bjorn Hvinden, "Climate Change as a Challenge for European Welfare States," in *Handbook of European Social Policy*, ed. Patricia Kennett and Noemi Lendvai-Bainton (Northampton, MA: Edward Elgar Publishing, 2017), 371–85.

49. Gwynn Guilford and Sarah Chaney Cambon, "Covid Shrinks the Labor Market"; Catherine K. Ettman, Salma M. Abdalla, Gregory H. Cohen, Laura Sampson, Patrick M. Vivier, and Sandro Galea, "Prevalence of Depression Symptoms in US Adults before and during the COVID-19 Pandemic," *JAMA Network* 3, no. 9 (2020): e2019686; and Lucy Craft, "Soaring Female Suicide Rate amid COVID Crisis in Japan Could Be a Warning to the World," *CBS News*, December 1, 2020.

50. Ian Gough, "From Welfare States to Planetary Well-Being," in *The Oxford Handbook of the Welfare State*, ed. Daniel Béland, Kimberly J. Morgan, Herbert Obinger, and Christopher Pierson, 2nd ed. (New York: Oxford University Press, 2021), 902.

51. Gough warned of the potential for negative distributional impacts of climate mitigation programs: "This clash between social need, unequal incomes, and the market pricing of energy can lead to 'energy poverty' or 'fuel poverty.'" Gough, "From Welfare States," 906.

52. Gough, "From Welfare States," 907.

53. We might also be able to discover important differences among nations with similar models. For instance, public health responses to the COVID-19 diverged across liberal welfare states. Canada centralized decision-making and pursued redistributive policies that largely succeeded in slowing the pandemic, whereas the United States defaulted to a decentralized approach and implemented a set of regressive measures that largely failed. Tracey Lindeman, "What Canada's COVID Response Can Teach the U.S. about Social Safety Nets," *Fortune*, October 23, 2020.

54. Takenaka Harukata, *Korona kiki no seiji—Abe seiken vs. chiji* [Politics under the COVID crisis—Abe government vs. mayors] (Tokyo: Chūkō Shinsho, 2020).

55. Delfina Grinspan, John-Rob Pool, Ayushi Trivedi, James Anderson, and Mathilde Bouyé, "Green Space: An Underestimated Tool to Create More Equal Cities," World Resources Institute, September 29, 2020.

56. See Jae-Jin Yang, ed., *The Small Welfare State: Rethinking Welfare in the US, Japan, and South Korea* (Northampton, MA: Edward Elgar Publishing, 2020).

Bibliography

"A Horror Confronted: Sexual Abuse of Children." *Economist*, August 27, 2016. https://www.economist.com/china/2016/08/25/a-horror-confronted.

Adema, Willem, Pauline Fron, and Maxime Ladaique. "How Much Do OECD Countries Spend on Social Protection and How Redistributive Are Their Tax/Benefit Systems?" *International Social Security Review* 67, no. 1 (2014): 1–25. https://doi.org/10.1111/issr.12028.

Adserà, Alícia, and Carles Boix. "Trade, Democracy, and the Size of the Public Sector: The Political Underpinnings of Openness." *International Organization* 56, no. 2 (2002): 229–62. https://doi.org/10.1162/002081802320005478.

Ah-young, Chung. "Child Abuse Is Society's Dirty Secret." *Korea Times*, January 20, 2016. http://www.koreatimes.co.kr/www/news/nation/2016/01/116_195909.html.

Ahn, Jennifer. "South Korea's Real Estate Policy and the Presidential Election." Council on Foreign Relations, February 7, 2022. https://www.cfr.org/blog/south-koreas-real-estate-policy-and-presidential-election.

Albert, Vicky N., and Richard P. Barth. "Predicting Growth in Child Abuse and Neglect Reports in Urban, Suburban, and Rural Counties." *Social Service Review* 70, no. 1 (1996): 58–82. doi.org/10.1086/604165.

Alvaredo, Facundo, François Bourguignon, Francisco Ferreira, and Nora Lustig. "Seventy-Five Years of Measuring Income Inequality in Latin America." IDB Working Paper Series No. IDB-WP-01521, October 2023. https://publications.iadb.org/en/seventy-five-years-measuring-income-inequality-latin-america.

Amsden, Alice. *Asia's Next Giant: South Korea and Late Industrialization*. New York: Oxford University Press, 1989.

An, Zhiyong, and Kohei Asao. "Options to Strengthen the Social Safety Net in Japan." IMF Selected Issues Papers SIP/2023/033, March 2023. https://www.imf.org/-/media/Files/Publications/Selected-Issues-Papers/2023/English/SIPEA2023033.ashx.

Ang, Shermaine. "Child Abuse Cases in Singapore Continue to Rise after Hitting Decade-High in 2020." *Straits Times*, April 11, 2022. https://www.straitstimes.com/singapore/child-abuse-cases-in-spore-continue-to-rise-after-hitting-decade-high-in-2020.

Ang, Shermaine. "New Child Protection Centre Opens in Bedok to Deal with Rising Abuse Cases." *Straits Times*, March 21, 2022. https://www.straitstimes.com/singapore/community/new-child-protection-centre-opens-in-bedok-to-deal-with-rising-abuse-cases.

Apps, Victor. "Hong Kong's Distorted Poverty Statistics Are Misleading." *China Daily*, November 24, 2020. https://www.chinadaily.com.cn/a/202011/24/WS5fbc7801a31024ad0ba96164.html.

Aries, Philippe. *Centuries of Childhood: A Social History of Family Life*. New York: Random House, 1962.

Ash, Robert. "Squeezing the Peasants: Grain Extraction, Food Consumption and Rural Living Standards in Mao's China." *China Quarterly* 188 (2006): 959–98. https://doi.org/10.1017/S0305741006000518.

Ashton, David, Francis Green, Johnny Sung, and Donna James. "The Evolution of Education and Training Strategies in Singapore, Taiwan and S. Korea: A Development Model of Skill Formation." *Journal of Education and Work* 15, no. 1 (2002): 5–30. https://psycnet.apa.org/doi/10.1080/13639080120106695.

Asian Development Bank. *The Social Protection Index: Assessing Results for Asia and the Pacific*. Mandaluyong City, Philippines: Asian Development Bank, 2013. https://www.adb.org/publications/social-protection-index-assessing-results-asia-and-pacific.

Asian Development Bank. *The Social Protection Indicator for Asia: Assessing Progress*. Mandaluyong City, Philippines: Asian Development Bank, 2019. https://dx.doi.org/10.22617/TCS190257-2.

Asian Development Bank. "Low-Income Housing Policies: Lessons from International Experience." February 2009. https://www.adb.org/sites/default/files/publication/29341/os-low-income-housing-policies.pdf.

"At 54, China's Average Retirement Age Is Too Low." *Economist*, June 24, 2021. https://www.economist.com/china/2021/06/22/chinas-average-retirement-age-is-ridiculously-low-54.

Atkinson, Paul. "The Contested Terrain of Narrative Analysis—An Appreciative Response." *Sociology of Health & Illness* 32, no. 4 (2010): 661–62. https://doi.org/10.1111/j.1467-9566.2010.01240_1.x.

Autor, David H., Lawrence F. Katz, and Melissa S. Kearney. "The Polarization of the U.S. Labor Market." *American Economic Review* 98, no. 2 (2006): 189–94. https://doi.org/10.1257/000282806777212620.

Autor, David H., Lawrence F. Katz, and Melissa S. Kearney. "Trends in U.S. Wage Inequality: Revising the Revisionists." *Review of Economics and Statistics* 90, no. 2 (2008): 300–23. https://doi.org/10.1162/rest.90.2.300.

"Average Minimum Wage in Japan Set to Exceed ¥1,000 for First Time." *Nippon.com*, August 15, 2023. https://www.nippon.com/en/japan-data/h01751/.

Babones, Salvatore. "China Is Sitting on $3 Trillion in Currency Reserves, But Is That Enough?," *Forbes*, May 24, 2018. https://www.forbes.com/sites/salvatorebabones/2018/05/24/china-is-sitting-on-3-trillion-in-currency-reserves-but-is-that-enough/#416755515fce.

Bai, Chong-En, and Zhenjie Qian. "The Factor Income Distribution in China: 1978–2007." *China Economic Review* 21 (2010): 650–70. https://doi.org/10.1016/j.chieco.2010.08.004.

Bai, Wei, Yan-Li Lee, Jingyi Liao, Lusi Wu, Mei Xie, and Tao Zhou. "The Gender Pay Gap in China: Insights from a Discrimination Perspective." *arXiv*, 2022. https://arxiv.org/pdf/2206.09306.

Baker, Andy, and Ethan Scheiner. "Electoral System Effects and Ruling Party Dominance in Japan: A Counterfactual Simulation Based on Adaptive Parties." *Electoral Studies* 26, no. 2 (2007): 477–91. https://doi.org/10.1016/j.electstud.2007.03.002.

Bamba, Sachiko, and Wendy L. Haight. *Child Welfare and Development: A Japanese Case Study*. New York: Cambridge University Press, 2011.

Bambra, Clare. "Decommodification and the Worlds of Welfare Revisited." *Journal of European Social Policy* 16, no. 1 (2006): 73–80. https://doi.org/10.1177/0958928706059835.

Barro, Robert J. "A Cross-Country Study of Growth, Saving, and Government." In *National Savings and Economic Performance*, edited by Douglas Bernheim and John B. Shoven, 271–304. Chicago: University of Chicago Press, 1991.

Béland, Daniel, Kimberly J. Morgan, Herbert Obinger, and Christopher Pierson, eds. *The Oxford Handbook of the Welfare State*. 2nd ed. New York: Oxford University Press, 2021.

Belsky, Jay. "Etiology of Child Maltreatment: A Developmental-Ecological Analysis." *Psychological Bulletin* 114, no. 3 (1993): 413–34. https://doi.org/10.1037/0033-2909.114.3.413.

Bengali, Leila, Marcus Sander, Robert G. Valletta, and Cindy Zhao. "Falling Wage Premiums by Race and Ethnicity." FRBSF Economic Letter 2023-22, August 2023. https://www.frbsf.org/economic-research/publications/economic-letter/2023/august/falling-college-wage-premiums-by-race-and-ethnicity/.

Bhalla, Surjit. *Imagine There's No Country: Poverty, Inequality and Growth in the Era of Globalization*. Washington, DC: Institute for International Economics, 2002.

Bloom, David E., David Canning, and Günther Fink. "Implications of Population Ageing for Economic Growth." *Oxford Review of Economic Policy* 26, no. 4 (2010): 583–612. https://doi.org/10.1093/oxrep/grq038.

Booth, Anne. "Initial Conditions and Miraculous Growth: Why Is Southeast Asia Different from Taiwan and South Korea?" *World Development* 27, no. 2 (1999): 301–21. https://doi.org/10.1016/S0305-750X(98)00126-0.

Bouissou, Jean-Marie. "Organizing One's Support Base under the SNTV: The Case of the Japanese Kōenkai." In *Elections in Japan, Korea, and Taiwan under the Single Non-Transferable Vote*, edited by Bernard N. Grofman, Sung-Chull Lee, Edwin Winckler, and Brian Woodall, 87–120. Ann Arbor: Michigan University Press, 2002.

Bremner, Matthew. "The Lonely End." *Slate*, June 26, 2015. https://matthewembremner.com/2017/12/07/the-lonely-end-slate-magazine/.

Caffey, John. "The Whiplash Shaken Infant Syndrome: Manual Shaking by the Extremities with Whiplash Induced Intracranial and Intraocular Bleedings, Linked with Residual Permanent Brain Damage and Mental Retardation." *Pediatrics* 54, no. 4 (1974): 396–403. https://doi.org/10.1542/peds.54.4.396.

Cameron, David. "The Expansion of the Public Economy: A Comparative Analysis." *American Political Science Review* 72, no. 4 (1978): 1243–61. https://doi.org/10.2307/1954537.

Campbell, Andrea L. *Trapped in America's Safety Net: One Family's Struggle*. Chicago: Chicago University Press, 2014.

Campos, José Edgardo, and Hilton L. Root. *The Key to the Asian Miracle: Making Shared Growth Credible*. Washington, DC: Brookings, 2001.

Castles, Francis. "What Welfare States Do: A Disaggregated Expenditure Approach." *Journal of Social Policy* 38, no. 1 (2008): 45–62. https://doi.org/10.1017/S0047279408002547.

Cavanagh, Sarah Rose. *The Spark of Learning*. Morgantown: West Virginia University Press, 2016.

Cerezo, M. Angeles, and Dolores Frias. "Emotional and Cognitive Adjustment in Abused Children." *Child Abuse & Neglect* 18, no. 11 (1994): 923–32. https://doi.org/10.1016/S0145-2134(05)80003-1.

Chan, Chris K. C., and Yujian Zhai. "Active Labour Market Policies in China: Towards Improved Labour Protection?" *Journal of Asian Public Policy* 6, no. 1 (2013): 10–25. https://doi.org/10.1080/17516234.2013.765181.

Chan, Holmes. "Six New Housing Policies, Including Vacancy Tax, Announced by Hong Kong's Chief Exec. Carrie Lam." *Hong Kong Free Press*, June 29, 2018. https://www.hongkongfp.com/2018/06/29/six-new-housing-policies-including-vacancy-tax-announced-hong-kongs-chief-exec-carrie-lam/.

Chan, Holmes. "Ex-Hong Kong Leader CY Leung Defends Controversial 1990s Housing Policy, Says Crisis Could Have Been Averted." *Hong Kong Free Press*, June 13, 2018. https://hongkongfp.com/2018/06/13/ex-hong-kong-leader-cy-leung-defends-controversial-1990s-housing-policy-says-crisis-averted/.

Chan, Kahon. "Hong Kong Police Record 29 Per Cent Rise in Child Abuse Cases, as Return to School Campuses Brings Incidents to Light." *South China Morning Post*, August 23, 2023. https://www.scmp.com/news/hong-kong/law-and-crime/article/3232078/hong-kong-police-record-29-cent-rise-child-abuse-cases-return-school-campuses-brings-incidents-light.

Chan, Kam Wing. "The Household Registration System and Migrant Labor in China: Notes on a Debate." *Population and Development Review* 36, no. 2 (2010): 357–64. https://doi.org/10.1111/j.1728-4457.2010.00333.x.

Chan, Kam Wing. "Internal Migration in China: Integrating Migration with Urbanization Policies and Hukou Reform." KNOMAD Policy Brief 16, November 2021. https://www.knomad.org/sites/default/files/publication-doc/policy_brief_16_internal_migration_in_china-integrating_migration_with_urbanization_policies_and_hukou_reform-nov_21.pdf.

Chan, Raymond K. K, and Chris K. C. Chan. "The Shifting Boundary between Work and Welfare: A Review of Active Labour Market Policies in Hong Kong." *Journal of Asian Public Policy* 6, no. 1 (2013): 26–41. https://doi.org/10.1080/17516234.2013.765178.

Chan, Sheng-Ju, and Chi-Hua Yang. "The Employment of the College Graduate: Changing Wages in Mass Higher Education." In *Mass Higher Education Development in East Asia: Strategy, Quality and Challenges*, edited by Jung Cheol Shin, Gerard A. Postiglione, and Futao Huang, 289–306. New York: Springer, 2015.

Chang, Kyung-Sup. "The Confucian Family Instead of the Welfare State? Reform and Peasant Welfare in Post-Mao China." *Asian Perspective* 17, no. 1 (1993): 169–200. http://www.jstor.org/stable/42704015.

Chang, Xinyang. "Analysis of Education Wage Premium in Several Provinces of China." *Modern Economy* 6 (2015): 862–70. https://dx.doi.org/10.4236/me.2015.68081.

Chee, Yeon Kyung. "Elder Care in Korea: The Future Is Now." *Ageing International* 26, no. 1/2 (2000): 25–37. https://doi.org/10.1007/s12126-000-1002-1.

Chen, Chih-Tsai, Nan-Ping Yang, and Pesus Chou. "Child Maltreatment in Taiwan for 2004–2013: A Shift in Age Group and Forms of Maltreatment." *Child Abuse & Neglect* 52 (2016): 169–76. https://doi.org/10.1016/j.chiabu.2015.10.029.

Chen, Hao, and Hsin-Hsien Fan. "Education in Taiwan: The Vision and Goals of the 12-Year Curriculum." *Brookings*, November 11, 2014. https://www.brookings.edu/opinions/education-in-taiwan-the-vision-and-goals-of-the-12-year-curriculum/.

Chen, Jie, Qianjin Hao, and Mark Stephens. "Assessing Housing Affordability in Post-Reform China: A Case Study of Shanghai." *Housing Studies* 25, no. 6 (2010): 877–901. https://doi.org/10.1080/02673037.2010.511153.

Chen, Junhua, Ying Wu, and Huijia Li. "Vocational Status, Hukou and Housing Migrants in the New Century: Evidence from a Multi-City Study of Housing Inequality." *Social Indicators Research* 139 (2018): 309–25. https://doi.org/10.1007/s11205-017-1562-z.

Chen, Yi-Ling. "The Factors and Implications of Rising Housing Prices in Taiwan." *Brookings*, July 15, 2015. https://www.brookings.edu/opinions/the-factors-and-implications-of-rising-housing-prices-in-taiwan/.

Chen, Yu-Hua. "Trends in Low Fertility and Policy Responses in Taiwan." *Japanese Journal of Population* 10, no. 1 (2012): 78–88. http://www.ipss.go.jp/webj-ad/webjournal.files/population/2012_Vol.10/Web%20Journal_Vol.10_04.pdf.

Cheng, Lim Keak. "Post-Independence Population Planning and Social Development in Singapore." *GeoJournal* 18, no. 2 (1989): 163–74. https://doi.org/10.1007/BF01207090.

Cheng, Tiejun, and Mark Selden. "The Origins and Social Consequences of China's Hukou System." *China Quarterly* 139 (1994): 644–88. https://doi.org/10.1017/S0305741000043083.

Cheremukhin, Anton, Mikhail Golosov, Sergei Guriev, and Aleh Tsyvinski. "The Economy of People's Republic of China from 1953." NBER Working Paper No. 21397, July 2015. https://www.nber.org/papers/w21397.

Cheung, Chau-Kiu, and Alex Yui-Huen Kwan. "The Erosion of Filial Piety by Modernisation in Chinese Cities." *Ageing and Society* 29, no. 2 (2009): 179–98. https://doi.org/10.1017/S0144686X08007836.

Cheung, Elizabeth, and Fanny W. Y. Fung. "Hong Kong Tenants Living in Subdivided Flats Pay More of Their Earnings to Live in Smaller Units." *South China Morning Post*, June 25, 2015. https://www.scmp.com/news/hong-kong/hong-kong-economy/article/1826382/hong-kong-tenants-living-subdivided-flats-pay-more.

Chi, Eunju, and Hyeok Yong Kwon. "Unequal New Democracies in East Asia: Rising Inequality and Government Responses in South Korea and Taiwan." *Asian Survey* 52, no. 5 (2012): 900–23. https://dx.doi.org/10.1525/as.2012.52.5.900.

Chiang, Min-Hua, and Lafaye de Micheaux. "China's Outward Foreign Direct Investment in Southeast Asia: Analyzing the Chinese State's Strategies and Potential Influence." *Thunderbird International Business Review* 64, no. 6 (2022): 581–93. https://doi.org/10.1002/tie.22311.

Chiew Tong, Goh. "Singapore Overtakes Hong Kong as the Most Expensive Asia-Pacific City for Private Homes." *CNBC*, May 31, 2023. https://www.cnbc.com/2023/06/01/singapore-overtakes-hong-kong-as-most-costly-apac-city-for-private-homes.html.

China Labour Bulletin. "China's Social Security System." August 18, 2021. https://clb.org.hk/en/content/china's-social-security-system.

China Labour Bulletin. "Migrant Workers and Their Children." September 6, 2023. https://clb.org.hk/en/content/migrant-workers-and-their-children.

"China Steps up Efforts to Counter Child Abuse." *Xinhua News*, November 20, 2019. http://www.xinhuanet.com/english/2019-11/20/c_138570474.htm.

Chiu, Peace. "How Can Hong Kong's Poor Beat Poverty When Work Doesn't Pay?" *South China Morning Post*, January 4, 2019. https://www.scmp.com/news/hong-kong/society/article/2180568/how-can-hong-kongs-poor-beat-poverty-when-work-doesnt-pay.

Chiu, Peace. "In Hong Kong, Most Child Abuse Victims Suffer at Hands of Parents." *South China Morning Post*, January 15, 2018. https://www.scmp.com/news/hong-kong/law-crime/article/2128210/when-care-turns-cruelty-hong-kong-most-child-abuse-victims.

Chiu, Rebecca L. H. "The Transferability of Hong Kong's Public Housing Policy." *International Journal of Housing Policy* 10, no. 3 (2010): 301–23. https://doi.org/10.1080/14616718.2010.506746.

Cho, Yongman. "The Legal Foundations of Mandatory Retirement in Korea." In *Korea's Retirement Predicament*, edited by Thomas R. Klassen and Yunjeong Yang, 53–64. New York: Routledge, 2013.

Choi, Eunhee. "Older Workers and Federal Work Programs: The Korean Senior Employment Program (KSEP)." *Journal of Aging & Social Policy* 28, no. 4 (2016): 308–24. https://doi.org/10.1080/08959420.2016.1153993.

Chou, Chuing Prudence. "Education in Taiwan: Taiwan's Colleges and Universities." *Brookings*, November 12, 2014. https://www.brookings.edu/opinions/education-in-taiwan-taiwans-colleges-and-universities/.

Chou, Rita Jing-Ann. "Filial Piety by Contract? The Emergence, Implementation, and Implications of the 'Family Support Agreement' in China." *The Gerontologist* 51, no. 1 (2011): 3–16. https://doi.org/10.1093/geront/gnq059.

Chuang, Yih-chyi, and Wei-wen Lai. "Heterogeneity, Comparative Advantage, and Return to Education: The Case of Taiwan." *Economics of Education Review* 29, no. 5 (2010): 804–12. https://doi.org/10.1016/j.econedurev.2010.03.003.

Chun-hua, Chen, and Kay Liu. "New Housing Market, Police-Related Schemes Set to Take Effect." *Focus Taiwan News Channel*, June 27, 2023. https://focustaiwan.tw/business/202306270004.

Chung, Yiyoon, Haksoon Ahn, and T. J. Lah. "Child Welfare Policy and Services in Korea." *International Journal of Social Welfare* 31, no. 1 (2022): 33–44. https://doi.org/10.1111/ijsw.12478.

Colman, Rebecca A., and Cathy Spatz Widom. "Childhood Abuse and Neglect and Adult Intimate Relationships: A Prospective Study." *Child Abuse & Neglect* 28, no. 11 (2004): 1133–51. https://doi.org/10.1016/j.chiabu.2004.02.005.

Congressional Research Service. "China's Economic Rise: History, Trends, Challenges, and Implications for the United States." June 2019. https://fas.org/sgp/crs/row/RL33534.pdf.

Coohey, Carol. "Child Maltreatment: Testing the Social Isolation Hypothesis." *Child Abuse & Neglect* 20, no. 3 (1996): 241–54. https://doi.org/10.1016/S0145-2134(95)00143-3.

Coudenys, Blansefloer, Gina Strohbach, Tammy Tang, and Rachel Udabe. "On the Path toward Life-long Learning: An Early Analysis of Taiwan's 12-year Basic Education Reform." In *Education to Build Back Better: What Can We Learn from Education Reform for a Post-pandemic World*, edited by Fernando M. Reimers, Uche Amaechi, Alysha Banerji, and Margaret Wang, 75–98. Cham, Switzerland: Springer, 2022. https://doi.org/10.1007/978-3-030-93951-9.

Coulton, Claudia J., Francisca Richter, Seok-Joo Kim, Robert Fischer, and Youngmin Cho. "Temporal Effects of Distressed Housing on Early Childhood Risk Factors and Kindergarten Readiness." *Children and Youth Services Review* 68 (2016): 59–72. https://doi.org/10.1016/j.childyouth.2016.06.017.

"Couple Arrested over Death of 5-Year-Old Daughter Who Police Allege Was Abused and Denied Food." *Japan Times*, June 6, 2018. https://www.japantimes.co.jp/news/2018/06/06/national/crime-legal/couple-arrested-death-5-year-old-daughter-police-allege-abused-denied-food/.

Cox, Wendell. "Hong Kong's Decentralizing Commuting Patterns." *Newgeography*, December 12, 2012. https://www.newgeography.com/content/003300-hong-kong-s-decentralizing-commuting-patterns.

Craft, Lucy. "Soaring Female Suicide Rate amid COVID Crisis in Japan Could Be a Warning to the World." *CBS News*, December 1, 2020. https://www.cbsnews.com/news/female-suicide-surge-japan-covid-pandemic-could-be-warning-world-womens-mental-health/.

Craig, R. Sean, and Changchun Hua. "Determinants of Property Prices in Hong Kong SAR: Implications for Policy." IMF Working Paper No. 11/277, November 2011. https://www.imf.org/external/pubs/ft/wp/2011/wp11277.pdf.
Croll, Elisabeth J. "Social Welfare Reform: Trends and Tensions." *China Quarterly* 159 (1999): 684–99. https://doi.org/10.1017/s030574100000343x.
Cunico, Kane, Yvonne Lim, and Jade Han. "Ploughing On: The Faces and Insecurities of Singapore's Elderly Working Poor." *Channel News Asia*, May 7, 2017. https://www.channelnewsasia.com/news/cnainsider/ploughing-on-the-faces-and-insecurities-of-singapore-s-elderly-8824490.
Dang, Thai Than, Pablo Antolin, and Oxley Howard. "Fiscal Implications of Ageing: Projections of Age-Related Spending." OECD Economics Department Working Papers No. 305, September 2001. https://www.oecd-ilibrary.org/economics/fiscal-implications-of-ageing_503643006287.
Dang, Yunxiao, Zhilin Liu, and Wenzhong Zhang. "Land-Based Interests and the Spatial Distribution of Affordable Housing Development: The Case of Beijing, China." *Habitat International* 44 (2014): 137–45. https://doi.org/10.1016/j.habitatint.2014.05.012.
De Soto, Hernando. *The Other Path: The Economic Answer to Terrorism*. New York: Basic Books, 2002.
DeAeth, Duncan. "Child Abuse in N. Taiwan: Three Year Old Boy Restrained, Starved, and Beaten." *Taiwan News*, September 23, 2018. https://www.taiwannews.com.tw/en/news/3536455.
DeAeth, Duncan. "Low Salaries, Long Work Hours to Blame for Taiwan's Low Birthrate: Survey." *Taiwan News*, April 2, 2018. https://www.taiwannews.com.tw/en/news/3396578.
Desmond, Matthew. *Poverty, by America*. New York: Crown, 2023.
"Destined for Life in Tiny Cage Homes." *South China Morning Post*, April 7, 2011. https://www.scmp.com/article/964357/destined-life-tiny-cage-homes.
Deyo, Frederic C. "State and Labor: Modes of Political Exclusion in East Asian Development." In *The Political Economy of the New Asian Industrialism*, edited by Frederic C. Deyo, 182–202. Ithaca, NY: Cornell University Press, 1987.
Dillon, Nara. *Radical Inequalities: China's Revolutionary Welfare State in Comparative Perspective*. Cambridge, MA: Harvard University Press, 2015.
Dixon, John. *The Chinese Welfare System, 1949–1979*. New York: Praeger Publishers, 1981.
Dongping, Qiao, and Chan Yuk-chung. "Myths of Child Abuse in China: Findings Based on a Qualitative Study in Beijing." *China Journal of Social Work* 1, no. 3 (2008): 266–78. https://doi.org/10.1080/17525090802404856.
Dore, Ronald F. *British Factory, Japanese Factory: The Origins of National Diversity in Industrial Relations*. Los Angeles: University of California Press, 1973.
Drakakis-Smith, David, Elspeth Graham, Peggy Teo, and Ooi Giok Ling. "Singapore: Reversing the Demographic Transition to Meet Labour Needs." *Scottish Geographical Magazine* 109, no. 3 (1993): 153–63. https://doi.org/10.1080/00369229318736895.
Durlauf, Steven, Paul Johnson, and Jonathan Temple. "Growth Econometrics." In *Handbook of Economic Growth*, edited by Philippe Aghion and Steven N. Durlauf. Vol. 1, 555–667. Amsterdam: Elsevier, 2005.
Eckenrode, John, Elliott G. Smith, Margaret E. McCarthy, and Michael Dineen. "Income Inequality and Child Maltreatment in the United States." *Pediatrics* 133, no. 3 (2014): 454–61. https://doi.org/10.1542/peds.2013-1707.
Economist Intelligence Unit. "Worldwide Cost of Living Survey 2021." December 2021. https://www.eiu.com/n/campaigns/worldwide-cost-of-living-2021/.

Eggleston, Karen, Jean C. Oi, and Yiming Wang, eds. *Challenges in the Process of China's Urbanization*. Palo Alto, CA: Shorenstein Asia-Pacific Research Center, 2017.
Erde, Gru. "Tackling the Growing Income Gap in Taiwan." *Think China*, February 15, 2023. https://www.thinkchina.sg/tackling-growing-income-gap-taiwan.
Esping-Andersen, Gosta. *The Three Worlds of Welfare Capitalism*. Princeton, NJ: Princeton University Press, 1990.
Estevez-Abe, Margarita. *Welfare and Capitalism in Postwar Japan*. New York: Cambridge University Press, 2008.
Ettman, Catherine K., Salma M. Abdalla, Gregory H. Cohen, Laura Sampson, Patrick M. Vivier, and Sandro Galea. "Prevalence of Depression Symptoms in US Adults Before and During the COVID-19 Pandemic." *JAMA Network* 3, no. 9 (2020): e2019686. https://doi.org/10.1001/jamanetworkopen.2020.19686.
Eurostat. "In-Work at-Risk-of-Poverty Rate by Group of Citizenship (Population Aged 18 and Over)." 2023. https://ec.europa.eu/eurostat/databrowser/view/ilc_iw15/default/table?lang=en.
Evans, Gary W. "Housing Quality and Mental Health." *Journal of Consulting and Clinical Psychology* 68, no. 3 (2000): 526–30. https://doi.org/10.1037//0022-006x.68.3.526.
Evans, Peter. *Embedded Autonomy: States and Industrial Transformation*. Princeton, NJ: Princeton University Press, 1995.
Everington, Keoni. "China Poaches 3,000 Chip Engineers, But Taiwan Winning from Trade War." *Taiwan News*, December 3, 2019. https://www.taiwannews.com.tw/en/news/3829558.
Evert-Allen, Kate. "How Much Property Will $US1 Million Buy You across the World?" Knight Frank, March 1, 2023. https://www.knightfrank.com/research/article/2023-03-01-where-are-the-most-expensive-cities-in-the-world.
Fang, Xiangming, Deborah A Fry, Kai Ji, David Finkelhor, Jingqi Chen, Patricia Lannene, and Michael P. Dunne. "The Burden of Child Maltreatment in China: A Systematic Review." *Bull World Health Organ* 93, no. 3 (2015): 176–85. https://doi.org/10.2471%2FBLT.14.140970.
Feng, Qiushi, Wei-Jun Jean Yeung, Zhenglian Wang, and Yi Zeng. "Age of Retirement and Human Capital in an Aging China, 2015–2050." *European Journal of Population* 35 (2019): 29–62. https://doi.org/10.1007/s10680-018-9467-3.
Feng, Xiaohua. "Effect of Intra-Industry Trade on Skill Premium in Manufacturing in China." *China Economic Review* 47 (2018): 206–18. https://doi.org/10.1016/j.chieco.2017.08.011.
Feng, Zhixin. "Childlessness and Vulnerability of Older People in China." *Age and Ageing* 47, no. 2 (2017): 1–6. https://doi.org/10.1007%2Fs10823-021-09427-x.
Fitch Ratings. "China Property Watch—January 2023: Public Housing Initiative to Stabilise Private Property Market." January 31, 2023. https://www.fitchratings.com/research/corporate-finance/china-property-watch-january-2023-public-housing-initiative-to-stabilise-private-property-market-31-01-2023.
"Foreign Workers First Included as Factor of Lower Wages in Study." *China Post*, January 14, 2016.
Fu, Hanlin, Tiejian Feng, Jiabi Qin, Tingting Wang, Xiaobing Wu, Yuamo Cai, Lina Lan, and Tubao Yang. "Reported Prevalence of Childhood Maltreatment among Chinese College Students: A Systematic Review and Meta-Analysis." *PLoS One* 13, no. 10 (2018), e0205808. https://doi.org/10.1371%2Fjournal.pone.0205808.
Fukao, Kyoji. "Productivity in the Service Sector: Reforming Japan's GDP Statistics Is Urgently Needed for More Accuracy." Research Institute of Economy, Trade

and Industry, February 2017. https://www.rieti.go.jp/en/papers/contribution/fukao/11.html.
Fulco, Matthew. "Amid a Changing World Economy, Taiwanese Manufacturers Return Home." *Taiwan Business Topics*, February 9, 2021. https://topics.amcham.com.tw/2021/02/changing-world-economy-taiwanese-manufacturers-return/.
Gao, Qin. *Welfare, Work and Poverty: Social Assistance in China*. New York: Oxford University Press, 2018.
Gao, Xuwen, Wenquan Liang, Ahmed Mushfiq Mobarak, and Ran Song. "Migration Restrictions Can Create Gender Inequality: The Story of China's Left-Behind Children." NBER Working Paper No. 30990, February 2023. https://doi.org/10.3386/w30990.
Garbarino, James. "The Human Ecology of Child Maltreatment: A Conceptual Model for Research." *Journal of Marriage and Family* 39, no. 4 (1977): 721–35. https://doi.org/10.2307/350477.
Garon, Sheldon. "Japanese Policies toward Poverty and Public Assistance: A Historical Perspective." World Bank Institute Working Papers No. 37200, 2002. http://documents.worldbank.org/curated/en/194971468774912987/Japanese-policies-towards-poverty-and-public-assistance-a-historical-perspective.
Garon, Sheldon. *Beyond Our Means: Why America Spends while the World Saves*. Princeton, NJ: Princeton University Press, 2012.
Gelman, Andrew, and Thomas Basbøll. "When Do Stories Work? Evidence and Illustration in the Social Sciences." *Sociological Methods & Research* 43, no. 4 (2014): 547–70. https://doi.org/10.1177/0049124114526377.
Gercik, Patricia. *On Track with the Japanese*. Bloomington, IN: AuthorHouse, 2011.
Gerhardt, Sue. *Why Love Matters: How Affection Shapes a Baby's Brain*. London: Routledge, 2004.
Gilbert, Ruth, Cathy Spatz Widom, Kevin Browne, David Fergusson, Elspeth Webb, and Staffan Janson. "Burden and Consequences of Child Maltreatment in High-Income Countries." *Lancet* 373, no. 9657 (2009): 68–81. https://doi.org/10.1016/S0140-6736(08)61706-7.
Gill, Indermit. "Deep-Sixing Poverty in China." *Brookings*, January 25, 2021. https://www.brookings.edu/articles/deep-sixing-poverty-in-china/.
Gillin, C. T., and Thomas R. Klassen. "Age Discrimination and Early Retirement Policies: A Comparison of Labor Market Regulation in Canada and the United States." *Journal of Aging & Social Policy* 7, no. 1 (1995): 85–102. https://doi.org/10.1300/j031v07n01_06.
Gindling, T. H., and Way Sun. "Higher Education Planning and the Wages of Workers with Higher Education in Taiwan." *Economics of Education Review* 21, no. 2 (2002): 153–69. https://doi.org/10.1016/S0272-7757(00)00049-2.
"Girl Dies in Mie after AI Suggested Not Taking Her into Custody." *Japan Times*, July 12, 2023. https://www.japantimes.co.jp/news/2023/07/12/national/ai-assessment-mie-girl-dies/.
Glaeser, Edward. *Triumph of the City: How Our Greatest Invention Makes Us Richer, Smarter, Greener, Healthier, and Happier*. London: Penguin Books, 2011.
Glennie, Charlotte. "Singapore Is Keeping an Eye on Its Migrant Workers." *BBC News*, April 14, 2015. https://www.bbc.com/news/business-32297860.
Goldin, Claudia, and Lawrence Katz. *The Race between Education and Technology*. Cambridge, MA: Belknap Press of Harvard University Press, 2008.
Goldfarb, Kathryn E. "Family at the Margins: State, Welfare and Well-Being in Japan." *Japanese Studies* 36, no. 2 (2016): 151–54. https://doi.org/10.1080/10371397.2016.1209730.

Gong, Jinquan, Gewei Wang, Yafeng Wang, and Yaohui Zhao. "Consumption and Poverty of Older Chinese: 2011–2020." *Journal of the Economics of Ageing* 23 (2022): 1–12. https://doi.org/10.1016/j.jeoa.2022.100410.

Goodkind, Daniel. "The Astonishing Population Averted by China's Birth Restrictions: Estimates, Nightmares, and Reprogrammed Ambitions." *Demography* 54 (2017): 1375–400. https://doi.org/10.1007/s13524-017-0595-x.

Goodman, Roger. "Child Abuse in Japan: 'Discovery' and the Development of Policy." In *Family and Social Policy in Japan: Anthropological Approaches*, edited by Roger Goodman, 131–55. Cambridge, UK: Cambridge University Press, 2002.

Goodman, Roger. "The 'Discovery' and 'Rediscovery' of Child Abuse (Jidō Gyakutai) in Japan." In *A Sociology of Japanese Youth: From Returnees to NEETs*, edited by Roger Goodman, Yuki Imoto, and Tuukka Toivonen, 98–121. London: Routledge, 2012.

Goto, Aya, Seiji Yasumura, Michael R. Reich, and Akira Fukao. "Factors Associated with Unintended Pregnancy in Yamagata, Japan." *Social Science & Medicine* 54, no. 7 (2002): 1065–79. https://doi.org/10.1016/S0277-9536(01)00081-8.

Goto, Aya, Seiji Yasumura, Junko Yabe, and Michael R. Reich. "Addressing Japan's Fertility Decline: Influences of Unintended Pregnancy on Child Rearing." *Reproductive Health Matters* 14, no. 27 (2006): 191–200. https://doi.org/10.1016/S0968-8080(06)27233-1.

Gough, David. "Child Abuse in Japan." *Child Psychology and Psychiatry Review* 1 (1996): 12–18. https://doi.org/10.1111/j.1475-3588.1996.tb00003.x.

Gough, Ian. "From Welfare States to Planetary Well-Being." In *The Oxford Handbook of the Welfare State*, edited by Daniel Béland, Kimberly J. Morgan, Herbert Obinger, and Christopher Pierson, 2nd ed., 901–20. New York: Oxford University Press, 2021.

Government of the Hong Kong Special Administrative Region. Census and Statistics Department. "Labour Productivity Index (Year 2015 = 100)." 2023. https://www.censtatd.gov.hk/en/web_table.html?id=103#.

Government of the Hong Kong Special Administrative Region. Census and Statistics Department. "Real Wage Indices for Employees up to Supervisory Level by Industry Section (September 1992 = 100)." 2023. https://www.censtatd.gov.hk/en/web_table.html?id=220-19002#.

Government of the Hong Kong Special Administrative Region. Census and Statistics Department. "2016 Population By-Census, Thematic Report—Household Income Distribution in Hong Kong." 2017. https://www.bycensus2016.gov.hk/data/16BC_Income_Report.pdf.

Government of the Hong Kong Special Administrative Region. Census and Statistics Department. "2021 Population Census, Thematic Report—Household Income Distribution in Hong Kong." 2023. https://www.censtatd.gov.hk/en/data/stat_report/product/B1120108/att/B11201082021XXXXB0100.pdf.

Government of the Hong Kong Special Administrative Region. Census and Statistics Department. "2014/15 Household Expenditure Survey and the Rebasing of the Consumer Price Indices." April 2016. https://www.statistics.gov.hk/pub/B10600082015XXXXB0100.pdf.

Government of the Hong Kong Special Administrative Region. Census and Statistics Department. "2019/20 Household Expenditure Survey and the Rebasing of the Consumer Price Indices." June 2021. https://www.censtatd.gov.hk/en/data/stat_report/product/B1060003/att/B10600082020XXXXB0100.pdf.

Government of the Hong Kong Special Administrative Region. Census and Statistics Department. Office of the Government Economist Financial Secretary's

Office. "Hong Kong Poverty Situation Report 2018." December 2019. https://www.commissiononpoverty.gov.hk/eng/pdf/Hong_Kong_Poverty_Situation_Report_2018(2019.12.13).pdf.

Government of the Hong Kong Special Administrative Region. Census and Statistics Department. Office of the Government Economist Financial Secretary's Office. "Hong Kong Poverty Situation Report 2020." November 2021. https://www.censtatd.gov.hk/en/data/stat_report/product/B9XX0005/att/B9XX0005E2020AN20E0100.pdf.

Government of the Hong Kong Special Administrative Region. Central Policy Unit. "A Study on Epidemiology of Child Abuse and its Geographic Distribution in Hong Kong: An Important Social Indicator of Different Districts and Communities." March 2013. https://www.cepu.gov.hk/doc/en/research_reports/CPU%20research%20report%20-%20epidemiology_of_child_abuse_and_its_geographic_distribution_in_hong_kong.pdf.

Government of Hong Kong Special Administrative Region. Housing Authority. "At a Glance." 2023. https://www.housingauthority.gov.hk/en/at-a-glance/index.html.

Government of the Hong Kong Special Administrative Region. Housing Bureau. "Housing in Figures 2022." August 31, 2022. https://www.hb.gov.hk/eng/publications/housing/HIF2022.pdf.

Government of the Hong Kong Special Administrative Region. Rating and Valuation Department. "Property Market Statistics: Private Domestic—Rental Indices by Class (territory-wide) (from 1979)." 2023. https://www.rvd.gov.hk/en/publications/property_market_statistics.html.

Grabowski, Richard. "East Asia, Land Reform and Economic Development." *Canadian Journal of Development Studies / Revue Canadienne d'études du Développement* 23, no. 1 (2002): 105–26. https://doi.org/10.1080/02255189.2002.9668856.

Greeley, Christopher Spencer. "The Evolution of the Child Maltreatment Literature." *Pediatrics* 130, no. 2 (2012): 347–48. https://doi.org/10.1542/peds.2012-1442.

Grinspan, Delfina, John-Rob Pool, Ayushi Trivedi, James Anderson, and Mathilde Bouyé. "Green Space: An Underestimated Tool to Create More Equal Cities." World Resources Institute, September 29, 2020. https://www.wri.org/insights/green-space-underestimated-tool-create-more-equal-cities.

Guilford, Gwynn, and Sarah Chaney Cambon. "Covid Shrinks the Labor Market, Pushing Out Women and Baby Boomers." *Wall Street Journal*, December 3, 2020. https://www.wsj.com/articles/covid-shrinks-the-labor-market-pushing-out-women-and-baby-boomers-11607022074.

Guo, Lijia, Jiashun Huang, and You Zhang. "Education Development in China: Education Return, Quality, and Equity." *Sustainability* 11 (2019): 3750. https://doi.org/10.3390/su11133750.

Gustafsson, Björn, and Ding Sai. "Growing into Relative Income Poverty: Urban China, 1988–2013." *Social Indicators Research* 147 (2020): 73–94. https://doi.org/10.1007/s11205-019-02155-3.

"Gyakutaishi, nen 350nin no kanōsei—Kokushūkei no sanbaichō" [Child abuse deaths, possibility of 350 people per year—more than three times the national total]. *Nihon Keizai Shimbun*, April 8, 2016. https://www.nikkei.com/article/DGXLASDG08H05_Y6A400C1CR0000/.

Hacker, Jacob S. *The Great Risk Shift: The New Economic Insecurity and the Decline of the American Dream*. 2nd ed. New York: Oxford University Press, 2008.

Hacker, Jacob S., and Paul Pierson. *Winner-Take-All Politics: How Washington Made the Rich Richer—and Turned Its Back on the Middle Class*. New York: Simon & Schuster, 2010.

Haggard, Stephan, and Robert R. Kaufman. *Development, Democracy, and Welfare States: Latin America, East Asia, and Eastern Europe.* Princeton, NJ: Princeton University Press, 2008.

Hall, Peter, and David Soskice, eds. *Varieties of Capitalism: The Institutional Foundations of Comparative Advantage.* New York: Oxford University Press, 2003.

Haltiwanger, John C., Julia I. Lane, and James R. Spletzer. "Productivity Differences across Employers: The Roles of Employer Size, Age, and Human Capital." *American Economic Review* 89, no. 2 (1999): 94–98. https://doi.org/10.1257/aer.89.2.94.

Hammond, Zaretta. *Culturally Responsive Teaching and the Brain.* Thousand Oaks, CA: Corwin, 2015.

Harding, Robin. "Why Tokyo Is the Land of Rising Home Construction But Not Prices." *Financial Times*, August 3, 2016. https://www.ft.com/content/023562e2-54a6-11e6-befd-2fc0c26b3c60.

Harris, Bryan, and Kang Buseong. "South Korea's Penniless Pensioners Face Final Years in Crisis." *Financial Times*, November 27, 2017. https://www.ft.com/content/cf73149a-6542-11e7-9a66-93fb352ba1fe.

Hayashi, Masayoshi. "Chihō zaisei to Seikatsu Hogo" [Local finance and the Daily Life Security], in *Seikatsu Hogo no keizai bunseki* [Economic analysis of the Daily Life Security], edited by Abe Aya, Kunieda Shigeki, Suzuki Wataru, and Hayashi Masayoshi, 239–68. Tokyo: Tokyo Daigaku Shuppankai, 2008.

He, Wan, Daniel Goodkind, and Paul Kowal. "Asia Aging: Demographic, Economic, and Health Transitions." U.S. Census Bureau, International Population Reports P95/22–1, June 2022. https://www.census.gov/content/dam/Census/library/publications/2022/demo/p95-22-1.pdf.

Hernandez, Javier C. "Workers' Activism Rises as China's Economy Slows. Xi Aims to Rein Them In." *New York Times*, February 6, 2019. https://www.nytimes.com/2019/02/06/world/asia/china-workers-protests.html?module=inline.

Hernanz, Virginia, Franck Malherbert, and Michele Pellizzari. "Take-Up of Welfare Benefits in OECD Countries: A Review of the Evidence." OECD Social, Employment and Migration Working Papers, No. 17 OECD, 2004. https://www.oecd.org/els/soc/30901173.pdf.

Hesketh, Therese, Li Lu, and Zhu Wei Xing. "The Effect of China's One-Child Family Policy after 25 Years." *New England Journal of Medicine* 353 (2005): 1171–76. https://doi.org/10.1056/nejmhpr051833.

Hill, Michael, and Yaun-shie Hwang. "Taiwan: What Kind of Social Policy Regime?" In *East Asian Welfare Regimes in Transition: From Confucianism to Globalization*, edited by Alan Walker and Chack-Kie Wong, 145–64. Bristol, UK: Policy Press, 2005.

Hinrichs, Karl, and Julia F. Lynch. "Old-Age Pensions." In *The Oxford Handbook of the Welfare State*, edited by Francis G. Castles, Stephan Leibfried, Jane Lewis, Herbert Obinger, and Christopher Pierson, 353–66. New York: Oxford University Press, 2012.

Hirayama, Yosuke. "Housing and State Strategy in Post-War Japan." In *Housing and the New Welfare State: Perspectives from East Asia and Europe*, edited by Richard Groves, Alan Murie, and Christopher Watson, 101–28. Aldershot, UK: Ashgate, 2007.

Ho, Huang-Chi. "Taiwan's Rising Child Abuse Cases Raise Concern." *TVBS*, November 23, 2023. https://news.tvbs.com.tw/english/2314783.

Ho, Lok Sang, Xiangdong Wei, and Wai Chung Wong. "The Effect of Outward Processing Trade on Wage Inequality: The Hong Kong Case." *Journal of International Economics* 67, no. 1 (2005): 241–57. https://doi.org/10.1016/j.jinteco.2004.09.005.

Ho-him, Chan. "In the Shadow of Hong Kong's Skyscrapers, the Poor Scavenge for Cardboard." *Financial Times*, December 22, 2021. https://www.ft.com/content/9e653b9e-c729-4240-80a5-c1cc483cfe02.

Holland, Tom. "Just Enforcing the Rules Could End HK's Housing Shortage." *South China Morning Post*, October 31, 2013. https://www.scmp.com/business/article/1343953/just-enforcing-rules-could-end-hong-kongs-housing-shortage.

Holliday, Ian. "Productivist Welfare Capitalism: Social Policy in East Asia." *Political Studies* 48, no. 4 (2000): 706–23. https://doi.org/10.1111/1467-9248.00279.

Hong Kong. Legislative Council Secretariat. Legislative Council Panel on Housing. "Housing-Related Initiatives in the Chief Executive's 2022 Policy Address." LC Paper No. CB(1)730/2022(03), November 7, 2022. https://www.legco.gov.hk/yr2022/english/panels/hg/papers/hg20221107cb1-730-3-e.pdf.

Hong Kong. Legislative Council Secretariat. Research Office. "Land Utilization in Hong Kong." Statistical Highlights ISSH04/16–17, October 24, 2016. https://www.legco.gov.hk/research-publications/english/1617issh04-land-utilization-in-hong-kong-20161024-e.pdf.

Hong Kong. Long Term Housing Strategy Steering Committee. "Building Consensus, Building Homes: Long Term Housing Strategy Consultation Document." September 2013. https://www.hb.gov.hk/eng/policy/housing/policy/lths/lthb_consultation_doc_201309.pdf.

Hong Kong Special Administrative Region. "The Chief Executive's 2018 Policy Address: Striving Ahead, Rekindling Hope." 2018. https://www.policyaddress.gov.hk/2018/eng/pdf/PA2018.pdf.

Hong Kong Special Administrative Region. "Review of the Institutional Framework of Public Housing: The Report." June 2002. https://www.hb.gov.hk/eng/policy/housing/issues/rifphreport.pdf.

Hong Kong Special Administrative Region. Census and Statistics Department. "Hong Kong Annual Digest of Statistics 2009 Edition." November 2009. https://www.censtatd.gov.hk/en/data/stat_report/product/B1010003/att/B10100032009AN09B0700.pdf.

Hong Kong Special Administrative Region. Census and Statistics Department. "Hong Kong Annual Digest of Statistics 2012 Edition." November 2012. https://www.statistics.gov.hk/pub/B10100032012AN12B0100.pdf.

Hong Kong Special Administrative Region. Census and Statistics Department. "Hong Kong Annual Digest of Statistics 2017 Edition." October 2017. https://www.censtatd.gov.hk/en/data/stat_report/product/B1010003/att/B10100032017AN17B0100.pdf.

Hong Kong Special Administrative Region. Census and Statistics Department. "Hong Kong Annual Digest of Statistics 2019 Edition." October 2019. https://www.statistics.gov.hk/pub/B10100032019AN19B0100.pdf.

Hong Kong Special Administrative Region. Census and Statistics Department. "Hong Kong Annual Digest of Statistics 2022 Edition." October 2022. https://www.censtatd.gov.hk/en/data/stat_report/product/B1010003/att/B10100032022AN22B0100.pdf.

Hong Kong Special Administrative Region. Census and Statistics Department. "Thematic Household Survey Report—Report No. 60—Housing Conditions of

Sub-Divided Units in Hong Kong." March 2016. https://www.statistics.gov.hk/pub/B11302602016XXXXB0100.pdf.

Hong Kong Special Administrative Region. Census and Statistics Department. "2016 Population By-Census, Thematic Report: Household Income Distribution in Hong Kong." June 2017. https://www.bycensus2016.gov.hk/data/16BC_Income_Report.pdf.

Hong Kong Special Administrative Region. Social Welfare Department. "Statistics on Newly Registered Child Protection, Newly Reported Spouse/Cohabitant Battering and Sexual Violence Cases in 2022." June 2023. https://www.swd.gov.hk/vs/index_e.html#s3.

Hong, Jun Sung, Na Youn Lee, Hye Joon Park, and Kathleen Coulborn Faller. "Child Maltreatment in South Korea: An Ecological Systems Analysis." *Children and Youth Services Review* 33, no. 7 (2011): 1058–66. https://doi.org/10.1016/j.childyouth.2011.01.012.

"Horror in Taiwan: Parents Charged over Abuse, Deaths of Three Young Siblings." *South China Morning Post*, October 19, 2017. https://www.scmp.com/news/china/society/article/2116023/horror-taiwan-parents-indicted-over-abuse-deaths-three-young.

Horta, Hugo. "The Declining Scientific Wealth of Hong Kong and Singapore." *Scientometrics* 117, no. 1 (2018): 427–47. https://doi.org/10.1007/s11192-018-2845-0.

Hosaka, Tōru. "Kodomo to kazoku wo meguru mondai" [The problem surrounding a child and family]. In *Nihon no kodomo gyakutai: Sengo Nihon no "kodomo no kikiteki jōkyō" ni kansuru shinri shakai teki bunseki* [Japan's child abuse: A psychosocial analysis of postwar Japan's "child crisis situation"], edited by Tōru Hosaka, 361–74. Tokyo: Fukumura Shuppan, 2007.

Hosaka, Tōru, and Masuzawa Takashi. "2000nen ikō no aratana dōkō" [New developments after 2000]. In *Nihon no kodomo gyakutai: Sengo Nihon no "kodomo no kikiteki jōkyō" ni kansuru shinri shakai teki bunseki* [Japan's child abuse: A psychosocial analysis of post-war Japan's "child crisis situation"], edited by Hosaka Tōru, 427–32. Tokyo: Fukumura Shuppan, 2007.

Howard, Christopher. *The Welfare State Nobody Knows: Debunking Myths about U.S. Social Policy*. Princeton, NJ: Princeton University Press, 2008.

Hsu, Chien-Chung. "A Study of Non-Government Child Welfare Services in Taiwan Focused on Children in Need of Child Welfare Service Intervention." PhD diss., University of Queensland, 2016.

Hu, Fox Z. Y., and Jiwei Qian. "Land-Based Finance, Fiscal Autonomy and Land Supply for Affordable Housing in Urban China: A Prefecture-Level Analysis." *Land Use Policy* 69 (2017): 454–60. https://doi.org/10.1016/j.landusepol.2017.09.050.

Hu, Weining. "China's Labor Market: Gaining Insights into HR Trends." *China Briefing*, January 18, 2017. https://www.china-briefing.com/news/chinas-labor-market-hr-trends/.

Hua, Jing, Zhe Mu, Bright Nwaru, Guixiong Gu, Wei Meng, and Zhuochun Wu. "Child Neglect in One-Child Families from Suzhou City of Mainland China." *BMC International Health and Human Rights* 14, no. 8 (2014): 1–9. https://doi.org/10.1186/1472-698X-14-8.

Huan, Guocang. "China's Open Door Policy, 1978–1984." *Journal of International Affairs* 39, no. 2 (1986): 1–18. https://www.jstor.org/stable/24356571.

Huang, Lanying, Yi-Fen Lu, Yi-Chun Yu, and Chuen-Jim Sheu, "Collaborating to Safeguard Children in Taiwan: Systemic Transformation." *Journal of Community Safety and Well-Being* 8, No. 4 (2023): 205-10. http://dx.doi.org/10.35502/jcswb.334.

Huang, Youqin. "Low-Income Housing in Chinese Cities: Policies and Practices." *China Quarterly* 212 (2012): 941–64. https://doi.org/10.1017/S0305741012001270.

"Humans in Cages: Hong Kong's Shoebox Housing." *Radio Free Europe, Radio Liberty*, March 9, 2015. https://www.rferl.org/a/china-hong-kong-housing/26872808.html.

Hung, Kristy, and Lisa Zhou. "China Could Base Housing Model on Singapore Instead of Hong Kong." *Bloomberg Intelligence*, February 23, 2023. https://www.bloomberg.com/professional/blog/china-could-base-housing-model-on-singapore-instead-of-hong-kong/#:~:text=Singapore%20could%20be%20a%20role,country%27s%20households%2C%20according%20to%20Singapore.

Hwang, Gyu-Jin. "How Fair Are Unemployment Benefits? The Experience of East Asia." *International Social Security Review* 72, no. 2 (2019): 49–73. https://doi.org/10.1111/issr.12202.

Hwang, Sun-Jae. "Public Pensions as the Great Equalizer? Decomposition of Old-Age Income Inequality in South Korea, 1998–2010." *Journal of Aging & Social Policy* 28, no. 2 (2016): 81–97. https://doi.org/10.1080/08959420.2016.1145503.

Hyun-ju, Ock. "Seoul to Improve Living Conditions in Semi-Basement Apartments Depicted in 'Parasite.'" *Korea Herald*, February 18, 2020. http://www.koreaherald.com/view.php?ud=20200218000706.

I-chia, Lee. "Child Abuse Ignored as Deaths Mount: Doctor." *Taipei Times*, April 25, 2018. http://www.taipeitimes.com/News/taiwan/archives/2018/04/25/2003691960.

Iida, Kanae. "'Yūaikai sōdōmei' undō ni okeru minshushugi to shakaishugi" [The democratic movement and socialism in the Friendly Society General Labor Federation]. *Mita Gakkai Zasshi* 71, no. 3 (1978): 303–21. https://doi.org/10.14991/001.19780601–0001.

I-ru, Chen Dorothy. "Higher Education Reform in Taiwan and Its Implications on Equality." *Chinese Education and Society* 45, no. 5–6 (2012): 134–51. https://doi.org/10.2753/CED1061-1932450510.

Immervoll, Herwig, and Scarpetta, Stefano. "Activation and Employment Support Policies in OECD Countries. An Overview of Current Approaches." *IZA Journal of Labor Policy* 1, no. 9 (2012). https://doi.org/10.1186/2193-9004-1-9.

"In Milestone Move, China Launches Private Pension Scheme." *Reuters*, April 21, 2022. https://www.reuters.com/world/china/china-unveils-private-pension-plan-ageing-population-2022-04-21/.

Inglehart, Ronald, C. Haerpfer, A. Moreno, C. Welzel, K. Kizilova, J. Diez-Medrano, M. Lagos, P. Norris, E. Ponarin, and B. B. Puranen. "World Values Survey: Round Four—Country-Pooled Datafile Version." J. D. Systems Institute, 2014. http://www.worldvaluessurvey.org/WVSDocumentationWV4.jsp.

International Labour Organization. *Global Wage Report 2022/23: The Impact of Inflation and COVID-19 on Wages and Purchasing Power*. Geneva: International Labour Organization, 2022. https://www.ilo.org/wcmsp5/groups/public/---ed_protect/---protrav/---travail/documents/publication/wcms_862569.pdf.

International Labour Organization. *World Social Protection Report 2017–2019: Universal Social Protection to Achieve Sustainable Development Goals*. Geneva: International Labour Organization, 2017. https://www.ilo.org/wcmsp5/groups/public/---dgreports/---dcomm/---publ/documents/publication/wcms_604882.pdf.

International Labour Organization. *World Social Protection Report 2020–22: Social Protection at the Crossroads—In Pursuit of a Better Future*. Geneva: International Labour Organization, 2021. https://www.ilo.org/wcmsp5/groups/public/---ed_protect/---soc_sec/documents/publication/wcms_817572.pdf.

International Labour Organization and OECD. "The Labour Share in G20 Economies." Antalya, Turkey: G20 Employment Working Group, 2015. https://www.oecd.org/g20/topics/employment-and-social-policy/The-Labour-Share-in-G20-Economies.pdf.

International Monetary Fund. "GDP Per Capita, Current Prices." 2023. https://www.imf.org/external/datamapper/NGDPDPC@WEO/OEMDC/ADVEC/WEOWORLD/EST/AND.

International Monetary Fund. *World Economic Outlook: Seeking Sustainable Growth. Short-Term Recovery, Long-Term Challenges*. Washington, DC: International Monetary Fund, 2017. https://www.imf.org/en/Publications/WEO/Issues/2017/09/19/world-economic-outlook-october-2017.

Ishii-Kuntz, Masako. "Child Abuse: History and Current State in Japanese Context." In *Family Violence in Japan: A Life Course Perspective*, edited by Fumie Kumagai and Masako Ishii-Kuntz, 49–78. Singapore: Springer, 2016.

Ishikawa, Yūki. *Rupo kyosho fumei jidō: Kieta kodomotachi* [Report on children whose whereabouts are unknown: The children who vanished]. Tokyo: Chikuma Shinsho, 2015.

Isumi, Aya, Takeo Fujiwara, Nobutoshi Nawa, Manami Ochi, and Tsuguhiko Kato. "Mediating Effects of Parental Psychological Distress and Individual-Level Social Capital on the Association between Child Poverty and Maltreatment in Japan." *Child Abuse & Neglect* 83 (2018): 142–50. https://doi.org/10.1016/j.chiabu.2018.07.005.

Iversen, Torben, and David Soskice. *Democracy and Prosperity: Reinventing Capitalism through a Turbulent Century*. Princeton, NJ: Princeton University Press, 2019.

Jaewon, Kim. "No Country for Old Koreans: Moon Faces Senior Poverty Crisis." *Nikkei Asian Review*, January 19, 2019. https://asia.nikkei.com/Spotlight/Asia-Insight/No-country-for-old-Koreans-Moon-faces-senior-poverty-crisis.

Jaimovich, Nir, and Henry E. Siu. "The Trend Is the Cycle: Job Polarization and Jobless Recoveries." NBER Working Paper No. 18334, August 2012. https://www.nber.org/papers/w18334.pdf.

Jain-Chandra, Sonali, Niny Khor, Rui Mano, Johanna Schauer, Philippe Wingender, and Juzhong Zhuang. "Inequality in China—Trends, Drivers and Policy Remedies." IMF Working Paper WP/18/127, June 2018. https://www.imf.org/en/Publications/WP/Issues/2018/06/05/Inequality-in-China-Trends-Drivers-and-Policy-Remedies-45878.

Japan. Children and Family Agency. "Reiwa 4 nendo jidō sōdanjo de no jidō gyakutai sōdan taiō kensū" [The number of child abuse incidents the child consultation centers handled in FY2022]. September 2023. https://www.cfa.go.jp/assets/contents/node/basic_page/field_ref_resources/a176de99-390e-4065-a7fb-fe569ab2450c/12d7a89f/20230401_policies_jidougyakutai_19.pdf.

Japan. Ministry of Health, Labour and Welfare. "Kodomo gyakutai ni yoru shibō jirei tō no kenshō kekka" [Results from examining cases of child abuse related deaths]. August 2017. https://www.mhlw.go.jp/stf/seisakunitsuite/bunya/0000173329.html.

Japan. Ministry of Health, Labour and Welfare. "Reiwa 3 nendo jidō sōdanjo deno jidō gyakutai sōdan taiō kensū" [Number of child abuse consultations handled at Child Guidance Centers in 2021]. 2022. https://www.cfa.go.jp/assets/contents/node/basic_page/field_ref_resources/a176de99-390e-4065-a7fb-fe569ab2450c/1cdcbd45/20230401_policies_jidougyakutai_07.pdf.

Japan. Ministry of Health, Labour and Welfare. "Reiwa 3 nendo 'shussei ni kansuru tōkei' no gaiyō" [Summary of 2021 "birth statistics"]. July 2021. https://www.mhlw.go.jp/toukei/saikin/hw/jinkou/tokusyu/syussyo07/dl/gaikyou.pdf.

Japan. Ministry of Health, Labour and Welfare. "Reiwa 3 nendo Zenkoku Hitori Oya Setaitō Chōsa Kekka no gaiyō" [Summary of 2021 National Single-Parent Household Survey Results]. December 2022. https://www.cfa.go.jp/assets/contents/node/basic_page/field_ref_resources/f1dc19f2-79dc-49bf-a774-21607026a21d/9ff012a5/20230725_councils_shingikai_hinkon_hitorioya_6TseCaln_05.pdf.

Japan. Ministry of Health, Labour and Welfare. "2016 teinensei nado" [2016 system of mandatory retirement]. 2016. https://www.mhlw.go.jp/toukei/itiran/roudou/jikan/syurou/16/dl/gaiyou02.pdf.

Japan. Ministry of Health, Labour and Welfare. Office of Counsellor for Labour Policy Planning. "Analysis of Japan's Labor Economy 2017." *Japan Labor Issues* 2, no. 7 (2018): 1–12. https://www.jil.go.jp/english/jli/documents/2018/007-02.pdf.

Japan. Ministry of Internal Affairs and Communication. Statistics Bureau. "Statistical Handbook of Japan." 2022. https://www.stat.go.jp/english/data/handbook/pdf/2022all.pdf.

Japan. Ministry of Justice. "Japanese Law Translation, Act on the Prevention, etc. of Child Abuse." March 4, 2014. https://www.japaneselawtranslation.go.jp/en/laws/view/2221/en.

Japan. National Police Agency. "Reiwa 4 nenchū ni okeru jisatsu no jōkyō" [Suicide trends in 2022]. March 14, 2023. https://www.mhlw.go.jp/content/R4kakutei01.pdf.

Japan. Prime Minister's Office. "Jidō gyakutai bōshi taisaku ni kansuru kankei kakuryō kaigi" [Relevant ministerial meetings on the strategies to prevent child abuse]. March 19, 2019. https://www.kantei.go.jp/jp/98_abe/actions/201903/19jido_gyakutai.html.

Japan. Statistics Bureau. "Labor Force Survey: Employee (by Age Group and Type of Employment)." June 2019. https://www.stat.go.jp/english/data/roudou/results/annual/ft/index.html.

Japan Productivity Center. "Productivity Statistics: Manufacturing and Non-Manufacturing." 2023. https://jpc.jpc-net.jp/eng/stats/index.html#:~:text=%E3%83%BBLabor%20productivity%20index%20of%20Manufacturing,rate%20was%20down%20%2D1.4%25.

Jefferson, Gary H., and Thomas G. Rawski. "Enterprise Reform in Chinese Industry." *Journal of Economic Perspectives* 8, no. 2 (1994): 47–70. https://doi.org/10.1257/jep.8.2.47.

Jervis, Robert. *Systems Effects: Complexity in Political and Social Life*. Princeton, NJ: Princeton University Press, 1997.

Jian, Zheng, and Daniel Jeongjae Lee. "Prospects for Progressive Tax Reforms in Asia and the Pacific." Working Paper Series, Macroeconomic Policy and Financing for Development Division WP/17/08, United Nations ESCAP 2017, April 2017. https://www.unescap.org/sites/default/files/publications/WP-17-08_Prospects%20Progressive%20Tax%20Reform.pdf.

Jiang, Alex. "Firms Mull Moving Production from China to Taiwan." *Focus Taiwan News Channel*, June 11, 2010. http://focustaiwan.tw/news/aeco/201006110044.aspx.

Jiang, Quanbao, Shucai Yang, and Jesus J. Sánchez-Barricarte. "Can China Afford Rapid Aging?" *Springerplus* 5, no. 1 (2016): 1107. https://doi.org/10.1186/s40064-016-2778-0.

Jie, Zhang. "Housing Occupancy Rate in 28 Chinese Cities at 12%: Report." *Asian News Network - China Daily*, August 8, 2022. https://asianews.network/

housing-occupancy-rate-in-28-chinese-cities-at-12-report/#:~:text=The%20 report%20said%20that%20the,vacancy%20rate%2C%20said%20the%20 report.
Jin-sik, Jeon. "Following Worker Suicide, Samsung Reluctantly Pledges Change." *Hankyoreh*, April 18, 2011. http://www.hani.co.kr/arti/english_edition/e_national/473516.html.
Johnson, Chalmers. *MITI and the Japanese Miracle: The Growth of Industrial Policy 1925–1975*. Stanford, CA: Stanford University Press, 1982.
Jones, Catherine. "The Pacific Challenge: The Confucian Welfare States." In *New Perspectives on the Welfare State in Europe*, edited by Catherine Jones, 192–210. New York: Routledge, 1993.
Jones, Gavin W. "Changing Family Sizes, Structures and Functions in Asia." *Asia-Pacific Population Journal* 27, no. 1 (2012): 83–102. https://doi.org/10.18356/91819ae8-en.
Jones, Randall S. "Public Social Spending in Korea in the Context of Rapid Population Ageing." OECD Economics Department Working Papers No. 615, OECD Publishing, May 2008. https://doi.org/10.1787/241545746547.
Jong, Woon Wei. "Growing Old Alone: Elderly Poor Want Better Housing, Better Care in Taiwan." *Think China*, February 16, 2022. https://www.thinkchina.sg/growing-old-alone-elderly-poor-want-better-housing-better-care-taiwan.
Joon-ho, Bong, dir. *Parasite*. 2019; Seoul: Barunson E&A.
Jung-a, Song. "Seoul Faces Backlash over Rise in Minimum Wage." *Financial Times*, February 26, 2018. https://www.ft.com/content/1138bc54-0d5e-11e8-8eb7-42f857ea9f09.
Jung, Dongchul, and Chan-ung Park. "A New Direction in the Welfare-Work Nexus in South Korea." *Journal of Asian Public Policy* 6, no. 1 (2013): 60–80. https://doi.org/10.1080/17516234.2013.767417.
"Jūgatsu ni jisatsu shita hito josei nijūdai to yonjūdai ga kyonen no dōjiki yori nibai ijō ni" [Two times as many women in their 20s and 40s committed suicide in October than one year ago]. *NHK News*, November 24, 2020. https://www3.nhk.or.jp/news/html/20201124/k10012728391000.html.
Kalmijn, Matthijs. "The Influence of Men's Income and Employment on Marriage and Cohabitation: Testing Oppenheimer's Theory in Europe." *European Journal of Population* 27, no. 3 (2011): 269–93. https://doi.org/10.1007/s10680-011-9238-x.
Kamimura, Yasuhiro, and Naoko Soma. "Active Labour Market Policies in Japan: A Shift Away from the Company-Centered Model?" *Journal of Asian Public Policy* 6, no. 1 (2013): 42–59. https://doi.org/10.1080/17516234.2013.767420.
Kan, Karoline. "My Secret Life as a Forbidden Second Child in China." *Foreign Policy*, February 4, 2016. https://foreignpolicy.com/2016/02/04/china-one-child-policy-birth-control-population-secret-life-forbidden-child/.
Kaneko, Karin, and Kanako Takahara. "Johnny's Replaces President as It Admits to Abuse by Late Founder." *Japan Times*, September 7, 2023. https://www.japantimes.co.jp/news/2023/09/07/japan/society/johnnys-new-president/.
Kang, Seoghoon. "Globalization and Income Inequality in Korea: An Overview." Paper presented at the FDI, Human Capital and Education in Developing Countries FDI Technical Meeting, Paris, December 2001. https://web-archive.oecd.org/2012-06-15/161353-2698445.pdf.
Kao, Ernest, and Peace Chiu. "Hong Kong Welfare Minister Pledges Action on Child Abuse after Shocking Death of Girl, 5." *South China Morning Post*, January 14,

2018. https://www.scmp.com/news/hong-kong/community/article/2128209/hong-kong-welfare-minister-pledges-action-child-abuse-after.
Kao, Evelyn. "Low Salary Problems." *Focus Taiwan News Channel*, December 21, 2015. https://focustaiwan.tw/business/201512210007.
Kasza, Gregory J. *One World of Welfare: Japan in Comparative Perspective*. Ithaca, NY: Cornell University Press, 2006.
Kato, Takao. *Productivity, Wages and Unions in Japan*. Geneva: International Labour Organization, 2016.
Katz, Ian, Xiaoyuan Shang, and Yahua Zhang. "Missing Elements of a Child Protection System in China: The Case of LX." *Social Policy and Society* 10, no. 1 (2010): 93–102. https://doi.org/10.1017/S1474746410000424.
Katzenstein, Peter. *Small States in World Markets: Industrial Policy in Europe*. Ithaca, NY: Cornell University Press, 1985.
Keely, Brian. *Income Inequality: The Gap between Rich and Poor*. Paris: OECD Publishing, 2015.
Kempe, C. Henry, Frederic N. Silverman, Brandt F. Steele, William Droegemueller, and Henry K. Silver. "The Battered-Child Syndrome." *JAMA* 181, no. 1 (1962): 17–24. https://doi.org/10.1001/jama.1962.03050270019004.
Khan, Nasreen, Shereen Khan, Olivia Tan Swee Leng, Tan Booi Chen, and Rossane Gale Vergara. "Explore the Factors that Influence Elderly Poverty." *Journal of Southeast Asian Research* 2017 (2017): 1–13. https://doi.org/10.5171/2017.938459.
Kiley, Dan. *The Peter Pan Syndrome: Men Who Have Never Grown Up*. New York: Avon Books, 1995.
Kim, Chunil, and Jinsoo Ko. "Unintended Consequences of Housing Policies: Evidence from South Korea." *Sustainability* 15, no. 4 (2023): 3407. https://doi.org/10.3390/su15043407.
Kim, Cynthia. "The Jobs—and Ageing Faces—Behind South Korea's Record Low Unemployment Numbers." *Reuters*, March 24, 2022. https://www.reuters.com/world/asia-pacific/jobs-ageing-faces-behind-south-koreas-record-low-employment-numbers-2022-03-23/#:~:text=Although%20the%20drift%20to%20low,for%20the%20peer%20group%20average.
Kim, Dong-eun, and Minu Kim. "Korean Government to Ease Regulations to Supply 2.7 Million New Houses by 2027." *Pulse*, August 17, 2022. https://pulsenews.co.kr/view.php?year=2022&no=725762.
Kim, Dokyun. "The Development of Functional Equivalents to the Welfare State in Post-war Japan and South Korea." In *The Small Welfare State: Rethinking Welfare in the US, Japan and South Korea*, edited by Jae-jin Yang, 163–89. Cheltenham, UK: Edward Elgar Publishing, 2020.
Kim, Erin Hye-Won, and Philip J. Cook. "The Continuing Importance of Children in Relieving Elder Poverty: Evidence from Korea." *Ageing and Society* 31, no. 6 (2011): 953–76. https://doi.org/10.1017/S0144686X10001030.
Kim, Jiseob. "Structural Weakness of Debt Held by Senior Householders." *KDI*, December 9, 2015. https://www.kdi.re.kr/eng/research/analysisView?art_no=2675.
Kim, Jung Bum, and Taesuck Kihl. "Suicidal Ideation Associated with Depression and Social Support: A Survey-Based Analysis of Older Adults in South Korea." *BMC Psychiatry* 21 (2021): 409. https://doi.org/10.1186%2Fs12888-021-03423-8.
Kim, Kyung-ho. "Debate Rages on Impact of Minimum Wage Hikes." *Korea Herald*, February 7, 2018. http://www.koreaherald.com/view.php?ud=20180207000568.

Kim, Kyung-Hwan, and Miseon Park. "Housing Policy in the Republic of Korea." ADBI Working Paper Series No. 570, Asian Development Bank (April 2016). https://www.adb.org/sites/default/files/publication/183281/adbi-wp570.pdf.

Kim, Mason M. S. *Comparative Welfare Capitalism in East Asia: Productivist Models of Social Policy*. Basingstoke, UK: Palgrave MacMillian, 2016.

Kim, Min-Jeung, and Hye-Jin Cho, "Boochae euntaeja gagu eui jaejung sangtae meet boochae sanghwan ganeungsung: Euntae saenghwal jageum eul koryohan boonseok" [Financial status and debts repayment possibility of retirement households that have debts]. *Consumer Policy and Education Review* 9 (2013): 41–62. https://www.earticle.net/Article/A200268.

Kim, Seong Sook. "Pension Reform Options in Korea." Paper presented at the IMF International Conference, Tokyo, Japan, January 2013. https://www.imf.org/external/np/seminars/eng/2013/oapfad/pdf/kim_ppr.pdf.

Kim, Yeon-Myung. "Beyond East Asian Welfare Productivism in South Korea." *Policy and Politics* 36, no. 1 (2008): 109–25. https://doi.org/10.1332/030557308783431652.

Kim, Yeon-Myung. "Towards a Comprehensive Welfare State in South Korea: Institutional Features, New Socio-Economic and Political Pressures, and the Possibility of the Welfare State." Asia Research Centre Working Paper No. 14 (2006). https://eprints.lse.ac.uk/25195/1/ARCWorkingPaper14Yeon-MyungKIMJan2006.pdf.

Kirk, Mimi. "The Peculiar Inequality of Singapore's Famed Public Housing." *City Lab*, June 9, 2015. https://www.citylab.com/equity/2015/06/the-peculiar-inequality-of-singapores-famed-public-housing/395411/.

Klassen, Thomas R., and Kun-ha Yu. "Introduction to Retirement in Korea." In *Korea's Retirement Predicament*, edited by Thomas R. Klassen and Yunjeong Yang, 1–20. New York: Routledge, 2013.

Klassen, Thomas R. "New Policies for Korea's Aging Labor Force: The Role of Contractual Mandatory Retirement." Korea Labor Institute, September 2011. https://kdevelopedia.org/Resources/view/04201601260143181.do.

Kohli, Atul. *State-Directed Development: Political Power and Industrialization in the Global Periphery*. New York: Cambridge University Press, 2004.

Koo, Hagen. "Engendering Civil Society: The Role of the Labor Movement." In *Korean Society: Civil Society, Democracy and the State*, edited by Charles Armstrong, 73–94. New York: Routledge, 2007.

Korbin, Jill E. *Child Abuse and Neglect: Cross-Cultural Perspectives*. Oakland: University of California Press, 1982.

Korea. Minimum Wage Commission. *Minimum Wage Review*. December 2021. https://www.minimumwage.go.kr/file/downloadSeq.do?bultnId=4070&fileSeq=1.

Korea. Minimum Wage Commission. *Minimum Wage System*. September 2023. https://www.minimumwage.go.kr/english/introduce/minWage.do.

Korea. National Police Agency. "Kyungchal beomjae tongkei" [Police crime statistics]. 2019. http://kosis.kr/index/index.do.

Korea. Statistical Information Service. "Index of Income Distribution." 2023. https://kosis.kr/statHtml/statHtml.do?orgId=101&tblId=DT_1HDLF05&vw_cd=MT_ETITLE&list_id=C2_1_40&scrId=&language=en&seqNo=&lang_mode=en&obj_var_id=&itm_id=&conn_path=MT_ETITLE&path=%252Feng%252FstatisticsList%252FstatisticsListIndex.do.

Korea. Statistical Information Service. "Projected Population by Age Group." 2021. http://kosis.kr/eng/statisticsList/statisticsListIndex.do?menuId=M_01_01

&vwcd=MT_ETITLE&parmTabId=M_01_01&statId=1994044&themaId=#Sele ctStatsBoxDiv.

"Korea Extends Natural Population Fall as Fertility Rate Falls to 0.7." *Korea Times*, August 30, 2023. https://www.koreatimes.co.kr/www/nation/2023/11/113_358114.html.

"Korea's Elderly Has Smallest Disposable Income among OECD Members." *Dong-a Ilbo*, December 6, 2022. https://www.donga.com/en/article/all/20221206/3806539/1.

Krugman, Paul. "Targeted Industrial Policies: Theory and Evidence." Proceedings—Economic Policy Symposium—Jackson Hole, Federal Reserve Bank of Kansas City, August 24–26, 1983. https://econpapers.repec.org/RePEc:fip:fedkpr:y:1983:p:123-176.

Ku, Inohe, and Chang-O Kim. "Decomposition Analyses of the Trend in Poverty among Older Adults: The Case of South Korea." *Journals of Gerontology: Series B* 75, no. 3 (2020), 684–93. https://doi.org/10.1093/geronb/gby047.

Kumagai, Fumie. "Introduction: Toward a Better Understanding of Family Violence in Japan." In *Family Violence in Japan: A Life Course Perspective*, edited by Fumie Kumagai and Masako Ishii-Kuntz, 1–48. Singapore: Springer, 2016.

Kwaak, Jeyup S. "Gamer Arrested after Death of Neglected Child." *Wall Street Journal*, April 14, 2014. https://blogs.wsj.com/korearealtime/2014/04/14/gamer-arrested-after-death-of-neglected-child/.

Kwaak, Jeyup S. "South Korea's $18 Billion Education Problem." *Wall Street Journal*, August 28, 2014. https://blogs.wsj.com/korearealtime/2014/08/28/south-koreas-18-billion-education-problem/.

Kwan, Shawna. "Hong Kong Is Building Public Housing on a Golf Course in a Snub to the Old Elite." *Bloomberg*, August 31, 2023. https://www.bloomberg.com/news/articles/2023-08-31/hong-kong-building-public-housing-on-fanling-golf-course-in-snub-to-old-elite.

Kwon, Huck-ju. "An Overview of the Study: The Developmental Welfare State and Policy Reforms in East Asia." In *Transforming the Developmental Welfare State in East Asia*, edited by Huck-ju Kwon, 1–23. London: Palgrave MacMillian, 2005.

La Grange, Adrienne, and Frederik Pretorius. "Ontology, Policy and the Market: Trends to Home-Ownership in Hong Kong." *Urban Studies* 37, no. 9 (2000): 1561–82. https://doi.org/10.1080/00420980020080261.

Lam, Jeffie. "Policy Address: CY Leung Abolishes Controversial 'Bad Son Statement' and Announces Means-Tested Pensions." *South China Morning Post*, January 19, 2017. https://www.scmp.com/news/hong-kong/education-community/article/2063272/policy-address-cy-leung-abolishes-controversial.

Larrimore, Jeff, and Jenny Schuetz. "Assessing the Severity of Rent Burden on Low-Income Families." FEDS Notes, Board of Governors of the Federal Reserve System, December 2017. https://www.federalreserve.gov/econres/notes/feds-notes/assessing-the-severity-of-rent-burden-on-low-income-families-20171222.html.

Lee, Claire. "Fewer Koreans Feel Responsible for Aging Parents." *Korea Herald*, May 8, 2016. https://www.koreaherald.com/view.php?ud=20160508000359.

Lee, Clara, and Darrelle Ng. "Construction Firms Grapple with Workers' Housing as Dorm Rental Rates Soar." *CNA*, September 21, 2023. https://www.channelnewsasia.com/singapore/construction-foreign-workers-dormitories-rental-soar-alternative-housing-ctq-3788066.

Lee, Ho Sun. "Roh-in eul daesang-euiro haneun seongmaemae pihye yeosung yeonkoo: Bacchus azumma siltae chosa meet roh-in sangdam jeopgeun" [The old women prostitutes serving old men: Research on the actual condition of

"Bacchus azumma" and the basic setting of the elderly counseling process]. *Journal of the Korean Gerontological Society* 31, no. 3 (2011): 489–503.

Lee, Hoyoung, Haeun Kim, and Hyun Shin. "Tackling Involuntary Retirement in South Korea." *Stanford Social Innovation Review*, October 20, 2021. https://ssir.org/articles/entry/tackling_involuntary_retirement_in_south_korea.

Lee, Jiyeun. "'Silver Service' Jobs Help Korea's Pensioners Survive." *Bloomberg*, December 13, 2016. https://www.bloomberg.com/news/articles/2016-12-13/silver-delivery-services-redefine-retirement-for-aging-korea.

Lee, Michelle Ye Hee, and Min Joo Kim. "How Seoul Failed Its Most Vulnerable, Flooded in Their Basement Homes." *Washington Post*, August 12, 2022. https://www.washingtonpost.com/world/2022/08/12/seoul-floods-banjiha-basement-south-korea/.

Lee, Ming-Hsuan. "Migration and Children's Welfare in China: The Schooling and Health of Children Left Behind." *Journal of Developing Areas* 44, no. 2 (2011): 165–82. https://www.jstor.org/stable/23215246.

Lee, Serim, Jieun Lee, and Jongserl Chun. "The Child Abuse Reporting Guideline Compliance in Korean Newspapers." *Child Youth Service Review* 151 (2023): 107037. https://doi.org/10.1016/j.childyouth.2023.107037.

Lee, Sun Jae. "Poverty amongst the Elderly in South Korea: The Perception, Prevalence, and Causes and Solutions." *International Journal of Social Science and Humanity* 4, no. 3 (2014): 242–45. https://doi.org/10.7763/IJSSH.2014.V4.355.

Lee, Yoonkyung. *Militants or Partisans: Labor Unions and Democratic Politics in Korea and Taiwan*. Palo Alto, CA: Stanford University Press, 2011.

"Left-Behind Girls Vulnerable to Sexual Assault: Report." *Xinhua News*, September 13, 2013. http://en.people.cn/90882/8400335.html.

Lei, Xiaoyan, John Strauss, Meng Tian, and Yaohui Zhao. "Living Arrangements of the Elderly in China: Evidence from the CHARLS National Baseline." *China Economic Journal* 8, no. 3 (2015): 191–214. https://doi.org/10.1080%2F17538963.2015.1102473.

Leung, Charles Ka Yui, Joe Cho Yiu Ng, and Edward Chi Ho Tang. "Why Is the Hong Kong Housing Market Unaffordable? Some Stylized Facts and Estimations." Globalization Institute Working Paper No. 380, Federal Reserve Bank of Dallas, April 2020. https://www.dallasfed.org/~/media/documents/research/international/wpapers/2020/0380.pdf.

Leussink, Daniel. "Japan's Elderly Workers, Once Key to Abenomics, Suffer as Pandemic Closes Businesses." *Reuters*, May 21, 2020. https://www.reuters.com/article/us-health-coronavirus-japan-elderly-unem/japans-elderly-workers-once-key-to-abenomics-suffer-as-pandemic-closes-businesses-idUSKBN22Y06G.

Levitt, Peggy, Erica Dobbs, Ken Chih-Yan Sun, and Ruxandra Paul. *Transnational Social Protection: Social Welfare across National Borders*. New York: Oxford University Press, 2023.

Li, Hongben, Lei Li, Binzhen Wu, and Yan Yan Xiong. "The End of Cheap Chinese Labor." *Journal of Economic Perspectives* 26, no. 4 (2012): 57–74. https://doi.org/10.1257/jep.26.4.57.

Li, X., Q. Yue, S. Wang, H. Wang, J. J Jiang, L. Gong, W. Liu, X. Huang, and Tao Xu. "Knowledge, Attitudes, and Behaviours of Healthcare Professionals Regarding Child Maltreatment in China." *Child Care Health and Development* 43, no. 6 (2017): 869–75. https://doi.org/10.1111/cch.12503.

Lin, Edith. "Stricter Rules Proposed to Weed out Wealthy in Hong Kong Public Rental Flats and Protect Those Most in Need of Housing." *South China Morning Post*, May 23, 2023. https://www.scmp.com/news/hong-kong/hong-kong-economy/

article/3221565/stricter-rules-proposed-weed-out-wealthy-public-rental-flats-and-protect-those-most-need-housing.

Lin, Ji-Ping. "Tradition and Progress: Taiwan's Evolving Migration Reality." *Migration Information Source*, January 24, 2012. https://www.migrationpolicy.org/article/tradition-and-progress-taiwans-evolving-migration-reality.

Lin, Judy. "Taiwan's Low-Income Group to Be Exempted from Taxes." *Taiwan News*, April 16, 2017. https://www.taiwannews.com.tw/en/news/3142152.

Lin, Justin Yifu. *Demystifying the Chinese Economy*. Cambridge, UK: Cambridge University Press, 2012.

Lin, Kevin. "Rising Inequality and its Discontents in China." *New Labor Forum* 25, no. 3 (2016): 66–74. https://doi.org/10.1177/1095796016661160.

Lin, Sean. "Groups Protest Council 'Coercing' Labor Ministry." *Taipei Times*, January 20, 2019. http://www.taipeitimes.com/News/taiwan/archives/2019/01/20/2003708288.

Lin, Yingchao, Zhili Ma, Ke Zhao, Weiyan Hu, and Jing Wei. "The Impact of Population Migration on Urban Housing Prices: Evidence from China's Major Cities." *Sustainability* 10, no. 9 (2018): 3169. https://doi.org/10.3390/su10093169.

Lindeman, Tracey. "What Canada's COVID Response Can Teach the U.S. about Social Safety Nets." *Fortune*, October 23, 2020. https://fortune.com/2020/10/23/canada-unemployment-cerb-economy-growth-coronavirus/.

Lindert, Peter. *Growing Public: Social Spending and Economic Growth since the Eighteenth Century*. 2nd ed. New York: Cambridge University Press, 2004.

Lipscy, Phillip. "Japan: The Harbinger State." *Japanese Journal of Political Science* 24, no. 1 (2023): 80–97. https://doi.org/10.1017/S1468109922000329.

Liu, Kuan-lin, Ku Chuan, and Yu Hsiao-han. "Student Groups Demand an Increase in Minimum Wage." *Focus Taiwan News Channel*, May 24, 2018. http://focustaiwan.tw/news/aipl/201805240012.aspx.

Liu, Yvonne, and Joyce Ng. "Land Application List Scrapped in Bid to Control Supply." *South China Morning Post*, March 1, 2013. https://www.scmp.com/news/hong-kong/article/1163971/land-application-list-scrapped-bid-control-supply.

Liu, Zhiqiang. "Institution and Inequality: The Hukou System in China." *Journal of Comparative Economics* 33, no. 1 (2005): 133–57. https://doi.org/10.1016/j.jce.2004.11.001.

Liu, Zongyuan Zoe. "China's Pensions System Is Buckling under an Aging Population." *Foreign Policy*, June 29, 2023. https://foreignpolicy.com/2023/06/29/china-pensions-aging-demographics-economy/#cookie_message_anchor.

Lo, Chi. "China's Structural Reform Policy: This Time Is It for Real?" *International Economy* 24, no. 3 (2010): 36–39. http://www.international-economy.com/TIE_Su10_Lo.pdf.

Lohmann, Henning. "The Concept and Measurement of In-Work Poverty." In *Handbook on In-Work Poverty*, edited by Henning Lohmann and Ive Marx, 7–25. Cheltenham, UK: Edward Elgar Publishing, 2018.

"Long Hours and Low Pay Will Become the Norm in Taiwan." *Asia One*, September 23, 2013. https://www.asiaone.com/long-hours-and-low-pay-become-norm-taiwan-observer.

Lu, Shu-shiuan. "East Asian Growth Experience Revisited from the Perspective of a Neoclassical Model." *Review of Economic Dynamics* 15, no. 3 (2012): 359–76. https://doi.org/10.1016/j.red.2012.04.002.

Lue, Jen-Der. "Promoting Work: A Review of Active Labour Market Policies in Taiwan." *Journal of Asian Public Policy* 6, no. 1 (2013): 81–98. https://doi.org/10.1080/17516234.2013.765184.

Lue, Jen-Der and Chan-ung Park, "Beyond Productivist Social Policy: The East Asian Welfare–Work Nexus in Transition. *Journal of Asian Public Policy* 6, no. 1 (2013): 1–9. https://doi.org/10.1080/17516234.2013.765182.

Lukauskas, Arvid. "Financial Restriction and the Developmental State in East Asia: Toward a More Complex Political Economy." *Comparative Political Studies* 35, no. 4 (2002): 379–412. https://doi.org/10.1177/0010414002035004001.

Luxembourg Income Study. "Luxembourg Income Study Database." 2023. https://www.lisdatacenter.org/our-data/lis-database/.

Ma, Zuopeng, Chenggu Liu, and Jing Zhang. "Affordable Housing Brings about Socio-Spatial Exclusion in Changchun, China: Explanation in Various Economic Motivations of Local Governments." *Habitat International* 76 (2018): 40–47. https://doi.org/10.1016/j.habitatint.2018.05.003.

Magaziner, Jessica. "Education in Taiwan." *World Education News + Reviews*, June 7, 2016. https://wenr.wes.org/2016/06/education-in-taiwan.

Man, Joyce Yanyum, Siqi Zheng, and Rongrong Ren. "Housing Policy and Housing Markets: Trends, Patterns, and Affordability." In *China's Housing Reform and Outcomes*, edited by Joyce Yanyum Man, 3–18. Cambridge, MA: Lincoln Institute of Land Policy, 2011.

Marchal, Sarah, Ive Marx, and Gerlinde Verbist. "Income Support Policies for the Working Poor." IZA Institute of Labor Economics, Discussion Paper Series IZA DP No. 10665, March 2017. http://ftp.iza.org/dp10665.pdf.

Maroto, Andres, and Luis Rubalcaba. "Services Productivity Revisited." *Service Industries Journal* 28, no. 3 (2008): 337-53. https://doi.org/10.1080/02642060701856209.

Master, Farah. "China to Raise Retirement Age to Deal with Aging Population—Media." *Reuters*, March 14, 2023. https://www.reuters.com/world/china/china-raise-retirement-age-deal-with-aging-population-media-2023-03-14/.

Masuzawa, Takashi, and Ishikura Yōko. "1990 nendai ikō no shakai, kazoku, kodomo wo meguru jōkyō" [Post-1990 state of Society, Family, and children]. In *Nihon no kodomo gyakutai: Sengo Nihon no "kodomo no kikiteki jōkyō" ni kansuru shinri shakai teki bunseki* [Japan's Child Abuse: A Psychosocial Analysis of postwar Japan's "child crisis situation"], edited by Hosaka Tōru, 175–88. Tokyo: Fukumura Shuppan, 2007.

Matsumoto, Ichirō. "Kodomo, kazoku ga chokumen suru fukugō teki konnan" [The complex difficulties that children and families face]. In *Kodomo gyakutai to kazoku: "Kasanari au furi" to shakai teki shien* [Child abuse and the family: The "cumulative disadvantages" and societal support], edited by Matsumoto Ichirō, 20–36. Tokyo: Akaishi Shoten, 2013.

Matsutani, Minoru. "S. Korea's Economy and the Elderly: Declining Workforce, Graying of Society Severely Burdens Welfare Programs." *Japan Times*, May 11, 2014. https://www.japantimes.co.jp/news/2014/05/11/business/s-koreas-economy-elderly/#.XQxUCi2ZO8o.

McCurry, Justin, "Japan PM Vows to Fight Child Abuse after 'Heart-Wrenching' Death of Girl, 10." *Guardian,* February 7, 2019. https://www.theguardian.com/world/2019/feb/07/japan-pm-vows-to-fight-child-abuse-after-heart-wrenching-death-of-girl-10.

McElhinney, Zoë, and Catherine Kennedy. "Enhancing the Collective, Protecting the Personal: The Valuable Role of Composite Narratives in Medical Education Research." *Perspectives on Medical Education* 11, no. 4 (2022): 220–27. https://doi.org/10.1007/s40037–022–00723-x.

McMurry, Justin. "Seoul to Phase Out Parasite-Style Semi-Basement Flats after Storm Deaths." *Guardian*, August 11, 2022. https://www.theguardian.com/world/2022/aug/11/seoul-phase-out-parasite-semi-basement-flats-storm-deaths.

Messina, Julián, and Joana Silva. *Wage Inequality in Latin America: Understanding the Past to Prepare for the Future*. Washington, DC: World Bank, 2018. https://doi.org/10.1596/978-1-4648-1039-8.

Mishra, Ramesh. "Welfare and Industrial Man: A Study of Welfare in Western Industrial Societies in Relation to a Hypothesis of Convergence." *Sociological Review* 21, no. 4 (1973): 535–60. https://doi.org/10.1111/j.1467–954X.1973.tb00496.x.

Miura, Mari. *Welfare through Work: Conservative Ideas, Partisan Politics, and Social Protection in Japan*. Ithaca, NY: Cornell University Press, 2012.

Mok, Ka Ho. "After Massification: The Quest for Entrepreneurial Universities and Technological Advancement in Taiwan." *Journal of Higher Education Policy and Management* 35, no. 3 (2013): 264–79. https://doi.org/10.1080/1360080X.2013.786857.

"Mom: No Remorse for Kids' Deaths." *Japan Times*, August 1, 2010. https://www.japantimes.co.jp/news/2010/08/01/national/mom-no-remorse-for-kids-deaths/#.XSYdTC3MzLY.

Moon, Hyungpyo. "Demographic Changes and Pension Reform in the Republic of Korea." ADBI Working Paper Series No. 135, April 2009. https://www.econstor.eu/dspace/bitstream/10419/53659/1/604640897.pdf.

Nakane, Naruhisa, and Ichiro Wada. "Estimating the Social Costs of Child Abuse in Residential Care for Children with Disabilities Using the Japanese Survey on the Interactions of Adverse and Positive Childhood Experiences toward Adulthood." *International Journal of Environmental Research and Public Health* 19, no. 24 (2022): 16476. https://doi.org/10.3390/ijerph192416476.

Naoi, Megumi. "Voting with the Wallet: Consumers, Income-Earners and the New Politics of Globalization Backlash." Unpublished manuscript, 2020.

Naughton, Barry. *The Chinese Economy: Transformation and Growth*. Cambridge, MA: MIT Press, 2007.

Newman, Thomas B. "The Power of Stories over Statistics." *British Medical Journal* 327, no. 7429 (2002): 1424–27. https://doi.org/10.1136/bmj.327.7429.1424.

Ng, Irene Y. H. "Definitions and Measurements of Poverty." *SSR Snippet*, no. 4 (2020): 2–9. https://fass.nus.edu.sg/ssr/wp-content/uploads/sites/8/2020/11/Snippet_Issue4_Poverty_Poor_Work_2020.pdf.

Ng, Irene Y. H., Yi Ying Ng, and Lee Poh Choo. "Singapore's Restructuring of Low-Wage Work: Have Cleaning Job Conditions Improved?" *Economic and Labour Relations Review* 29, no. 3 (2018): 308–27. https://doi.org/10.1177/1035304618782558.

Ngerng, Roy. "Taiwan's Housing Crisis (Part 1): Taiwan's Housing Prices Are among the Highest Globally but Wages Are One of the Lowest Among Advanced Countries." *News Lens*, March 22, 2023. https://international.thenewslens.com/article/182910.

NHK Supesharu Kieta Kodomo Tachi Shuppan Han. *Rupo kieta kodomotachi: Gyakutai kankin no shinsō ni semaru* [Report on the vanished children: Closing in on the truth surrounding abusive confinement]. Tokyo: NHK Shuppan, 2015.

Ni, Yanyan, and Hesketh, Therese. "Child Maltreatment in China: A Cross-Sectional Study of Prevalence and Attitudes among Young Adults." *Lancet* 386, S52 (2015). https://doi.org/10.1016/S0140–6736(15)00633–9.

Niiya, Eri. "Harrowing Child Neglect Case Shines Light on Chains of Abuse." *Asahi Shimbun*, February 10, 2022. https://www.asahi.com/ajw/articles/14545492.
Nishizawa, Satoru. *Kodomo gyakutai* [Child abuse]. Tokyo: Kōdansha, 2010.
Nohara, Yoshiaki. "Children of Poor, Jobless Single Moms Have Become an Underclass in Japan." *Japan Times*, June 26, 2018. https://www.japantimes.co.jp/news/2018/06/26/national/social-issues/children-poor-jobless-single-moms-become-underclass-japan/#.XSf-BS3Myt8.
"Noin iljari saeob jungdan janggihwa—noin 97% iljari hyueob" [Prolonged suspension of the senior job positions—97% of senior jobs suspended]. *Yonhap News*, March 15, 2020.
O'Sullivan, Michael, and Michael Yat-him Tsang. "Educational Inequalities in Higher Education in Hong Kong." *Inter-Asia Cultural Studies* 16, no. 3 (2015): 454–69. https://doi.org/10.1080/14649373.2015.1069007.
OECD. "Annual Average Wage Growth." 2023. https://stats.oecd.org.
OECD. "Average Wages." 2023. https://doi.org/10.1787/cc3e1387-en.
OECD. "Earnings: Real Minimum Wages." OECD Employment and Labour Market Statistics, 2023. https://doi.org/10.1787/data-00656-en.
OECD. *Economic Surveys: Korea 2020*. Geneva: OECD Publishing, 2020. https://doi.org/10.1787/374630b6-en.
OECD. *Economic Surveys: Korea 2022*. Geneva: OECD Publishing, 2022. https://doi.org/10.1787/20bf3d6e-en.
OECD. *Education at a Glance 2003*. Paris: OECD Publishing, 2003. https://doi.org/10.1787/19991487.
OECD. *Education at a Glance 2019: Country Note—Korea*. Paris: OECD Publishing, 2019. https://doi.org/10.1787/66684527-en.
OECD. *Education at a Glance 2022: OECD Indicators*. Paris: OECD Publishing, 2022. https://doi.org/10.1787/3197152b-en.
OECD. *Education at a Glance 2023*. Paris: OECD Publishing, 2023. https://doi.org/10.1787/e13bef63-en.
OECD. *Employment Outlook 2015*. Paris: OECD Publishing, 2015. https://doi.org/10.1787/empl_outlook-2015-en.
OECD. *Government at a Glance, 2021*. Paris: OECD Publishing, 2021. https://doi.org/10.1787/a1439e6a-en.
OECD. *Growing Unequal? Income Distribution and Poverty in OECD Countries*. Paris: OECD Publishing, 2008. https://doi.org/10.1787/9789264044197-en.
OECD. "Income Distribution." OECD Social and Welfare Statistics, 2023. https://doi.org/10.1787/data-00654-en.
OECD. "LMP Interventions for the Long-Term Unemployed: An Initial Assessment." March 2019. https://www.oecd.org/els/emp/LMP%20interventions%20for%20LTU%20-%20initial%20assessment.pdf.
OECD. "Net Pension Replacement Rates." 2023. https://doi.org/10.1787/4b03f028-en.
OECD. *Pensions at a Glance 2015: OECD and G20 Indicators*. Paris: OECD Publishing, 2015. https://doi.org/10.1787/pension_glance-2015-en.
OECD. *Pensions at a Glance 2017: OECD and G20 Indicators*. Paris: OECD Publishing, 2017. https://doi.org/10.1787/pension_glance-2017-en.
OECD. "PH4.2 Social Rental Housing Stock." OECD Affordable Housing, March 2022. http://oe.cd/ahd.
OECD. "Public Expenditure and Participant Stocks on LMP." 2023. https://stats.oecd.org/index.aspx?DataSetCode=LMPEXP.
OECD. *Reviews of Pension Systems: Korea*. Paris: OECD Publishing, 2022. https://doi.org/10.1787/2f1643f9-en.

OECD. "Social Expenditure—Aggregated Data." OECD Social and Welfare Statistics, 2023. https://doi.org/10.1787/data-00166-en.
OECD. "Social Expenditure—Detailed Data." OECD Social and Welfare Statistics, 2023. https://stats.oecd.org/Index.aspx?DataSetCode=SOCX_DET.
OECD. "Social Expenditure Update 2019: Public Social Spending is High in Many OECD Countries." January 2019. https://www.oecd.org/els/soc/OECD2019-Social-Expenditure-Update.pdf.
OECD. "Social Spending." 2023. https://doi.org/10.1787/7497563b-en.
OECD. *Society at a Glance: Asia/Pacific 2022*. Paris: OECD Publishing, 2022. https://doi.org/10.1787/7ef894e5-en.
OECD. *Society at a Glance 2019*. Paris: OECD Publishing, 2019. https://doi.org/10.1787/soc_glance-2019-en.
OECD. "Suicide Rates." 2023. https://doi.org/10.1787/a82f3459-en.
OECD. *Towards Better Social and Employment Security in Korea*. Geneva: OECD Publishing, 2018. https://doi.org/10.1787/9789264288256-en.
OECD. *Working Better with Age: Japan*. Paris: OECD Publishing, 2018. https://doi.org/10.1787/9789264201996-en.
OECD. *Working Better with Age: Korea*. Geneva: OECD Publishing, 2018. https://doi.org/10.1787/9789264208261-en.
Ogawa, Naohiro. "Population Aging and Policy Options for a Sustainable Future: The Case of Japan." *Genus* 61, no. 3/4 (2005): 369–410. https://dx.doi.org/10.2307/29789282.
Oguchi, Noriyoshi. "Productivity Trends in Asia since 1980." *International Productivity Monitor* 10 (2005): 69–78. http://www.csls.ca/ipm/10/oguchi-e.pdf.
Oh, Byeong Cheol, Ji-Yoon Yeon, Hyo-Sang Lee, Doo Woong Lee, and Eun-Cheol Park. "Correlation between Private Education Costs and Parental Depression in South Korea." *BMC Public Health* 20 (2020): 972. https://doi.org/10.1186/s12889-020-09058-w.
Oikawa, Masato, Akira Kawamura, Cheolmin Kang, Zentaro Yamagata, and Haruko Noguchi. "Do Macroeconomic Shocks in the Local Labor Market Lead to Child Maltreatment and Death? Empirical Evidence from Japan." *Child Abuse & Neglect* 124 (2022): 105430. https://doi.org/10.1016/j.chiabu.2021.105430.
Oishi, Akiko S. "Child Support and the Poverty of Single-Mother Households in Japan." National Institute of Population and Social Security Research Paper Series No. 2013–E01, August 2013. http://www.ipss.go.jp/publication/j/DP/dp2013_e01.pdf
Okuyama, Makiko. "Child Abuse in Japan: Current Problems and Future Perspectives." *Japan Medical Association Journal* 49, no. 11–12 (2006): 370–74. https://www.researchgate.net/publication/267782468_Child_Abuse_in_Japan_Current_problems_and_future_perspectives.
Oppenheimer, Valerie Kincade. "A Theory of Marriage Timing." *American Journal of Sociology* 94, no. 3 (1988): 563–91. https://doi.org/10.1086/229030.
Oxfam Hong Kong. "Hong Kong Poverty Report: Poverty and Employment during the Pandemic." October 2022. https://www.oxfam.org.hk/tc/f/news_and_publication/85693/poverty%20report%202022%20%28with%20cover%29.pdf.
Pan, Jennifer. *Welfare for Autocrats: How Social Assistance in China Cares for its Rulers*. New York: Oxford University Press, 2020.
Panda, Ankit. "What's Behind Japan's Rise in Senior Citizen Crime?" *Japan Times*, November 25, 2016. https://www.japantimes.co.jp/opinion/2016/11/25/commentary/japan-commentary/whats-behind-japans-rise-senior-citizen-crime/#.XQfb6S3Myt8.

Park, Jun-hee. "Spending on Private Education Surpasses W26tr in 2022." *Korea Herald*, March 7, 2023. https://www.koreaherald.com/view.php?ud=20230307000508.
Park, Myung Hee, and Il Woo Paik. "Hankuk sa-gyo-yook sijang jeongae eui yeoksawha euimi" [The history of Korean private tutoring market development and its implications]. *Educational Research for Tomorrow* 29, no. 2 (2016): 23–50.
Park, Shin-Young. "The State and Housing Policy in Korea." In *Housing and the New Welfare State: Perspectives from East Asia and Europe*, edited by Richard Groves, Alan Murie, and Christopher Watson, 75–100. Aldershot, UK: Ashgate, 2007.
Paul, Karsten I., and Klaus Moser. "Unemployment Impairs Mental Health: Meta-analyses." *Journal of Vocational Behavior* 74, no. 3 (2009): 264–82. https://doi.org/10.1016/j.jvb.2009.01.001.
Pempel, T. J. *A Region of Regimes: Prosperity & Plunder in the Asia-Pacific*. Ithaca, NY: Cornell University Press, 2021.
Peña-Casas, Ramon, and Mia Latta. *Working Poor in the European Union*. Dublin: Office for Official Publications of the European Communities, 2004.
Peng, Ito, and Joseph Wong. "East Asia." In *The Oxford Handbook of the Welfare State*, edited by Francis G. Castles, Stephan Leibfried, Jane Lewis, Herbert Obinger, and Christopher Pierson, 656–70. New York: Oxford University Press, 2010.
Pensions Funds Online. "Pension System in Taiwan." 2023. https://www.pensionfundsonline.co.uk/content/country-profiles/taiwan/100.
Peterson, Lani. "The Science behind the Art of Storytelling." Harvard Business Publishing, November 14, 2017. https://www.harvardbusiness.org/the-science-behind-the-art-of-storytelling/.
Pfohl, Stephen J. "The 'Discovery' of Child Abuse." *Social Problems* 24, no. 3 (1977): 310–23. https://doi.org/10.2307/800083.
Phang, Hanam. "National Pension, Labour Market and Retirement in Korea: Institutional Mismatch and Policy Alternatives." In *Korea's Retirement Predicament*, edited by Thomas R. Klassen and Yunjeong Yang, 96–111. New York: Routledge, 2013.
Phillips, David Rosser, and Zhixin Feng. "Challenges for the Aging Family in the People's Republic of China." *Canadian Journal on Aging* 34, no. 3 (2015): 290–304. https://doi.org/10.1017/s0714980815000203.
Pignatti, Clemente, and Eva Van Belle. "Better Together: Active and Passive Labour Market Policies in Developed and Developing Economies." International Labour Office, Research Department Working Paper no. 37, December 2018. https://www.ilo.org/wcmsp5/groups/public/---dgreports/---inst/documents/publication/wcms_660003.pdf.
Plekhanov, Dmitriy. "Is China's Era of Cheap Labor Really Over?" *Diplomat*, December 13, 2017. https://thediplomat.com/2017/12/is-chinas-era-of-cheap-labor-really-over/.
Po-chien, Chen. "Impoverishment of Elderly People." *Taipei Times*, September 17, 2016. https://www.taipeitimes.com/News/editorials/archives/2016/09/17/2003655291.
"Poverty Worsening among South Korea's Aged People." *Nation*, July 8, 2012. https://www.nationthailand.com/perspective/30185727.
Prasad, Eswar S. "China's Growth Model: Choices and Consequences." In *Emerging Giants: China and India in the World Economy*, edited by Barry Eichengreen, Poonam Gupta, and Rajiv Kumar, 227–42. New York: Oxford University Press, 2010.

Pressman, Steven. "Cross-National Comparisons of Poverty and Income Inequality." In *The Economics of Inequality, Poverty, and Discrimination in the 21st Century*, edited by Robert S. Rycroft, 17–37. Santa Barbara, CA: ABC-CLIO, 2013.
"Prosecutors Seek 20-Year Sentence for Man Who Let 5-Year-Old Son Starve to Death." *Japan Today*, October 10, 2015. https://japantoday.com/category/crime/prosecutors-seek-20-year-sentence-for-man-who-let-5-year-old-son-starve-to-death.
Puschmann, Paul, and Arne Solli. "Household and Family during Urbanization and Industrialization: Efforts to Shed New Light on an Old Debate." *History of the Family* 19, no. 1 (2014): 1–12. https://doi.org/10.1080/1081602X.2013.871570.
Qiu, Stella, and Elias Glenn. "China Goes on Tech-Hiring Binge and Wages Soar, Closing Gap with Silicon Valley." *Reuters*, January 24, 2018. https://www.reuters.com/article/us-china-economy-tech-analysis/china-goes-on-tech-hiring-binge-and-wages-soar-closing-gap-with-silicon-valley-idUSKBN1FD37S.
Quail, Simon, Steve Lewis, and Wai-duen Lee. "What Are the Options to Improve Housing Affordability in Hong Kong?" EY, March 31, 2023. https://www.ey.com/en_cn/government-public-sector/what-are-the-options-to-improve-housing-affordability-in-hong-kong.
Radbill, Samuel X. "A History of Child Abuse and Infanticide." In *The Battered Child*, edited by Ray E. Helfer and C. Henry Kempe, 3–17. Chicago: University of Chicago Press, 1968.
Ramesh, M. *Social Policy in East and Southeast Asia: Education, Health, Housing and Income Maintenance*. New York: Routledge, 2004.
Rauhala, Emily. "He Was One of Millions of Chinese Seniors Growing Old Alone. So He Put Himself Up for Adoption." *Washington Post*, May 2, 2018. https://www.washingtonpost.com/world/asia_pacific/he-was-one-of-millions-of-chinese-seniors-growing-old-alone-so-he-put-himself-up-for-adoption/2018/05/01/53749264-3d6a-11e8-912d-16c9e9b37800_story.html.
Raymo, James M., Hyunjoon Park, Miho Iwasawa, and Yanfei Zhou. "Single Motherhood, Living Arrangements, and Time with Children in Japan" *Journal of Marriage and Family* 76 (2014): 843–61. https://doi.org/10.1111/jomf.12126.
Raymo, James M., Hyunjoon Park, Yu Xie, and Wei-jun Jean Yeung. "Marriage and Family in East Asia: Continuity and Change." *Annual Review of Sociology* 41 (2015): 471–92. https://doi.org/10.1146/annurev-soc-073014-112428.
"Record 219,000 Cases of Child Abuse Logged in Japan in Fiscal '22." *Japan Times*, September 7, 2023. https://www.japantimes.co.jp/news/2023/09/07/japan/child-abuse-cases-hit-record/.
Renaud, Bertrand, Kyung-Hwan Kim, and Man Cho. *Dynamics of Housing in East Asia*. Chichester, UK: John Wiley & Sons, 2016.
Republic of China. National Bureau of Statistics. "China Statistical Yearbook." 2017. http://www.stats.gov.cn/sj/ndsj/2017/indexeh.htm.
Republic of China. National Bureau of Statistics. "China Statistical Yearbook." 2018. http://www.stats.gov.cn/sj/ndsj/2018/indexeh.htm.
Republic of China. National Bureau of Statistics. "China Statistical Yearbook." 2022. http://www.stats.gov.cn/sj/ndsj/2022/indexeh.htm.
Republic of China. National Bureau of Statistics. "Main Data of the Seventh National Population Census." May 11, 2021. https://www.stats.gov.cn/english/PressRelease/202105/t20210510_1817185.html#:~:text=There%20were%20253.38%20million%20persons,190.64%20million%20persons%20in%20the.
Republic of Korea. Ministry of Health and Welfare. "Basic Livelihood Security Program: Benefit Recipients & Payment." 2017. https://www.mohw.go.kr/

menu.es?mid=a20308000000#:~:text=Benefit%20Recipients%20%26%20 Payment-,Basic%20Livelihood%20Security%20Program%3A%20Benefit%20 Recipients%20%26%20Payment,recipients%20and%2091%2C000%20 institutionalized%20recipients.

Republic of Singapore. Central Provident Fund Board. "Workfare Income Supplement." 2023. https://www.cpf.gov.sg/member/growing-your-savings/government-support/workfare-income-supplement.

Republic of Singapore. Department of Statistics. "eBook of Statistics." 2023. https://www.singstat.gov.sg/publications/reference/ebook.

Republic of Singapore. Department of Statistics. "Household Income." 2023. https://www.singstat.gov.sg/find-data/search-by-theme/households/household-income/latest-data.

Republic of Singapore. Department of Statistics. "Labour, Employment, Wages and Productivity." 2023. https://www.singstat.gov.sg/find-data/search-by-theme/economy/labour-employment-wages-and-productivity/latest-data.

Republic of Singapore. Ministry of Finance. "Income Growth, Inequality and Mobility Trends in Singapore." August 2015. https://www.mof.gov.sg/docs/default-source/default-document-library/news-and-publications/featured-reports/income-growth-distribution-and-mobility-trends-in-singapore.pdf.

Republic of Singapore. Ministry of Manpower. "Gross Monthly Income." 2023. https://stats.mom.gov.sg/Pages/Labour-Force-In-Singapore-2022.aspx.

Republic of Singapore. Ministry of Manpower. "Silver Support Scheme." 2023. https://www.mom.gov.sg/employment-practices/silver-support-scheme.

Republic of Singapore. Ministry of Social and Family Development. "ComCare Long Term Assistance." 2023. https://www.msf.gov.sg/what-we-do/comcare.

Republic of Singapore. Ministry of Trade & Industry. Department of Statistics. "Report on the Household Expenditure Survey 2017/18." July 2019. https://www.singstat.gov.sg/-/media/files/publications/households/hes201718.pdf.

Restrepo-Echavarria, Paulina, and Brian Reinbold. "Measuring Labor Share of the Asian Tigers." Federal Reserve Bank of St. Louis, January 11, 2018. https://www.stlouisfed.org/on-the-economy/2018/january/measuring-labor-share-asian-tigers.

Rodrik, Dani. *Has Globalization Gone Too Far?* Washington, DC: Institute for International Economics, 1997.

Rodrik, Dani. "Why Do More Open Economies Have Bigger Governments?" *Journal of Political Economy* 106, no. 5 (1998): 997–1032. https://doi.org/10.1086/250038.

Rosenbluth, Frances McCall, and Michael F. Thies. *Japan Transformed: Political Change and Economic Restructuring.* Princeton, NJ: Princeton University Press, 2010.

Ross, Michael. "Is Democracy Good for the Poor?" *American Journal of Political Science* 50, no. 4 (2006): 860–74. https://doi.org/10.1111/j.1540-5907.2006.00220.x.

Roxburgh, Helen. "China's Radical Plan to Limit the Populations of Beijing and Shanghai." *Guardian*, March 19, 2018. https://www.theguardian.com/cities/2018/mar/19/plan-big-city-disease-populations-fall-beijing-shanghai.

Rudlin, Pernille. "Retirement Systems in Japan—Under Revision But Lacking Clarity." Rudlin Consulting, August 2022. https://rudlinconsulting.com/retirement-age-in-japan/.

Saito, Jun. *Jimintō chōki seiken no seiji keizai gaku* [The political economy of the LDP regime]. Tokyo: Keisō Shobō, 2010.

Sakai, Seiji. *Kodomo gyakutai e no chōsen: Iryō, fukushi, shinri, shihō no renkei wo mezashite* [Tackling child abuse: Aiming toward linking the medical, welfare, psychology, and judiciary]. Tokyo: Seishin Shobō, 2013.

Samuels, Richard J. *Machiavelli's Children: Leaders and Their Legacies in Italy and Japan*. Ithaca, NY: Cornell University Press, 2003.
Sandberg, Joanne C., Jennifer W. Talton, Sara A. Quandt, Haiying Chen, Maria Weir, Walkiria R. Doumani, Arjun B. Chatterjee, and Thomas A. Arcury. "Association between Housing Quality and Individual Health Characteristics on Sleep Quality among Latino Farmworkers." *Journal of Immigrant and Minority Health* 16, no. 2 (2014): 265–72. https://doi.org/10.1007/s10903-012-9746-8.
Sang-Hun, Choe. "A Lonely End for South Koreans Who Cannot Afford to Live, or Die." *New York Times*, November 1, 2015. https://www.nytimes.com/2015/11/02/world/asia/a-lonely-end-for-south-koreans-who-cannot-afford-to-live-or-die.html.
Sano, Yoshie, and Saori Yasumoto. "Policy Responses to Population-Declining Society: Development and Challenges of Family Policies in Japan." In *Handbook of Family Policies Across the Globe*, edited by Mihaela Robila, 319–31. New York: Springer Science & Business Media, 2013.
Sassen, Saskia. *The Global City: New York, London, Tokyo*. Princeton, NJ: Princeton University Press, 2001.
Sawada, Izumi. "Yōikusha ga mentaru herusu mondai wo kakaeru gyakutai kazoku e no shien" [Aid for the caretakers from abusive families that have mental health issues]. In *Kodomo gyakutai to kazoku: "Kasanari au furi" to shakai teki shien* [Child abuse and the family: The "cumulative disadvantages" and societal support], edited by Matsumoto Ichirō, 78–92. Tokyo: Akaishi Shoten, 2013.
Schoppa, Leonard. "Globalization and the Squeeze on the Middle Class: Does Any Version of the Postwar Social Contract Meet the Challenge?" In *Social Contracts Under Stress: The Middle Classes of America, Europe, and Japan at the Turn of the Century*, edited by Olivier Zunz, Leonard Schoppa, and Nobuhiro Hiwatari, 319–44. New York: Russell Sage, 2002.
Schoppa, Leonard. *Race for the Exits: The Unraveling of Japan's System of Social Protection*. Ithaca, NY: Cornell University Press, 2006.
Schroder-Butterfill, Elisabeth, and Philip Kreager. "Actual and De Facto Childlessness in Old Age: Evidence and Implications from East Java, Indonesia." *Population and Development Review* 31, no. 1 (2005): 19–55. https://doi.org/10.1111/j.1728-4457.2005.00051.x.
Scruggs, Lyle, and James P. Allan. "Welfare-State Decommodification in 18 OECD Countries: A Replication and Revision." *Journal of European Social Policy* 16, no. 1 (2006): 55–72. https://doi.org/10.1177/0958928706059833.
Selya, Roger Mark. "Taiwan as a Service Economy." *Geoforum* 25, no. 3 (1994): 305–22. https://doi.org/10.1016/0016-7185(94)90033-7.
Seong, Hye Yeong. "Yeongeum poreom gyeo-ul-ho: Hanguk, Miguk, Ilbon roh-in eui gagu sobi jichul bigyo" [Pension forum winter edition: Comparing the expenditure level of the elderly household in Korea, United States, and Japan]. *National Pension Research Institute* 60 (2015): 49–55.
Setser, Brad W. "The IMF's China Problem." Council on Foreign Relations, September 28, 2017. https://www.cfr.org/blog/imfs-china-problem.
Shaw, Victor. "Urban Housing Reform in China." *Habitat International* 21, no. 2 (1997): 199–212. https://doi.org/10.1016/S0197-3975(96)00052-5.
Shepard, Wade. *Ghost Cities of China: The Story of Cities without People in the World's Most Populated Country*. London: Zed Books, 2015.
Shi, Shih-Jiunn. "Shifting Dynamics of the Welfare Politics in Taiwan: From Income Maintenance to Labour Protection." *Journal of Asian Public Policy* 5, no. 1 (2012): 82–96. dx.doi.org/10.1080/17516234.2012.662357.

Shi, Wei, Jie Chen, and Hongwei Wang. "Affordable Housing Policy in China: New Developments and New Challenges." *Habitat International* 54 (2016): 224–33. https://doi.org/10.1016/j.habitatint.2015.11.020.

Shimabukuro, Yumiko. "Democratization and the Development of Japan's Uneven Welfare State." PhD diss., MIT, 2012.

Shimabukuro, Yumiko, and Arvid Lukauskas. "Building an Inegalitarian Welfare State: The Impact of Dualistic Coordinated Capitalism & Elite-Made Democracy in Japan." Unpublished manuscript, September 1, 2023.

Shirahase, Sawako, and James M. Raymo. "Single Mothers and Poverty in Japan: The Role of Intergenerational Coresidence." *Social Forces* 93, no. 2 (2014): 545–69. https://doi.org/10.1093/sf/sou077.

Schoyen, Mi Ah, and Bjorn Hvinden. "Climate Change as a Challenge for European Welfare States." In *Handbook of European Social Policy*, edited by Patricia Kennett and Noemi Lendvai-Bainton, 371–85. Northampton, MA: Edward Elgar Publishing, 2017.

"The Secure v the Poor." *Economist*, February 12, 2015. https://www.economist.com/finance-and-economics/2015/02/12/the-secure-v-the-poor.

Siegel, Daniel J. *The Developing Mind: How Relationships and the Brain Interact to Shape Who We Are*. New York: Guilford Press, 2015.

"Singapore PM Promises Safety of Foreign Workers." *India TV News*, December 15, 2013. https://www.indiatvnews.com/news/world/singapore-pm-promises-safety-of-foreign-workers-15348.html/page/2.

"Singapore Ruling PAP Party Wins Elections, but Support Falls." *BBC News*, July 10, 2020. https://www.bbc.com/news/world-asia-53358650.

Sito, Peggy. "Hong Kong is Third Most Expensive Place for Building Costs, According to Global Survey." *South China Morning Post*, July 2, 2015. https://www.scmp.com/news/hong-kong/economy/article/1831469/hong-kong-third-most-expensive-place-building-costs-according.

Sito, Peggy, and Sandy Li. "How Hong Kong Land Policies Help Fuel City's Ever-Rising Property Prices." *South China Morning Post*, December 23, 2017. https://www.scmp.com/print/property/hong-kong-china/article/2125469/hong-kongs-politics-deter-options-alter-land-sales-policy.

Sito, Peggy, Denise Tsang, and Lam Ka-sing. "Developers' Cosy Ties with Politics May Explain Hong Kong's Biggest Woe: Widening Income Gap in the Least Affordable City on Earth." *South China Morning Post*, September 2, 2019. https://www.scmp.com/print/business/article/3025260/developers-cosy-ties-politics-may-explain-hong-kongs-biggest-woe-widening.

Siwei, Cheng, and Guo Yingzhe. "Provincial Pension Funds Face New Squeeze as Government Waives Contributions." *Caixin Global*, March 4, 2020. https://www.caixinglobal.com/2020-03-04/provincial-pension-funds-face-new-squeeze-as-government-waives-contributions-101524077.html.

Smith, Nicola. "Taiwan Is Suffering from a Massive Brain Drain and the Main Beneficiary is China." *Time*, August 21, 2017. https://time.com/4906162/taiwan-brain-drain-youth-china-jobs-economy/.

Social Security Administration. "Social Security Programs throughout the World: Asia and the Pacific, 2018." 2018. https://www.ssa.gov/policy/docs/progdesc/ssptw/2018-2019/asia/taiwan.html#:~:text=Old%2DAge%20Benefits,of%20coverage%2C%20whichever%20is%20greater.

So-kum Tang, Catherine. "The Rate of Physical Child Abuse in Chinese Families: A Community Survey in Hong Kong." *Child Abuse & Neglect* 22, no. 5 (1998): 381–91. https://doi.org/10.1016/S0145-2134(98)00010-6.

Solt, Frederick. "Measuring Income Inequality Across Countries and over Time: The Standardized World Income Inequality Database." *Social Science Quarterly* 101, no. 3 (2022): 1183–99. https://doi.org/10.1111/ssqu.12795.
Song, Byung Nak. *The Rise of the Korean Economy*. New York: Oxford University Press, 1997.
Song, Jesook. *South Koreans in the Debt Crisis*. Durham, NC: Duke University Press, 2009.
Sook, Seong. "Pension Reform Options in Korea." International Monetary Fund Seminar, January 2013. https://www.imf.org/external/np/seminars/eng/2013/oapfad/pdf/kim_ppr.pdf.
Spearly, James L., and Michael Lauderdale. "Community Characteristics and Ethnicity in the Prediction of Child Maltreatment Rates." *Child Abuse & Neglect* 7, no. 1 (1983): 91–105. https://doi.org/10.1016/0145-2134(83)90036-4.
Starr, Raymond H., Jr., and David A. Wolfe. *The Effects of Child Abuse and Neglect: Issues and Research*. New York: Guilford Press, 1991.
Statista. "Annual Net Migration from and to Taiwan from 1990 to 2022." August 2023. https://www.statista.com/statistics/1305502/taiwan-net-migration/.
Statista. "Degree of Urbanization in China from 1980 to 2022." August 2023. https://www.statista.com/statistics/270162/urbanization-in-china/.
Statista. "Number of Taiwanese People Living Overseas as of 2021, by Continent (in 1,000s)." August 2023. https://www.statista.com/statistics/632642/taiwan-population-distribution-overseas-by-continent/.
Statista. "Share of International Trade of Goods and Services in Nominal GDP in Taiwan in Selected Quarters from 4th Quarter 2018 to 4th Quarter 2022." August 2023. https://www.statista.com/statistics/1266254/taiwan-quarterly-trade-to-gdp-ratio/.
Steinberg, Laurence D., Ralph Catalano, and David Dooley. "Economic Antecedents of Child Abuse and Neglect." *Child Development* 52, no. 3 (1981): 975–85. https://doi.org/10.2307/1129102.
Steinfeld, Edward. *Forging Reform in China: The Fate of State-Owned Industry*. New York: Cambridge University Press, 1998.
Stevenson, Alexandra. "A High-End Property Collapse in Singapore." *New York Times*, February 17, 2015. https://www.nytimes.com/2015/02/18/realestate/a-high-end-property-collapse-in-singapore.html.
Sturgeon, Timothy, and Ji-Ren Lee. "Industry Co-Evolution: A Comparison of Taiwan and North American Electronics Contract Manufacturers." In *Global Taiwan: Building Competitive Strengths in a New International Economy*, edited by Richard K. Lester and Suzanne Berger, 33–75. New York: Routledge, 2005.
Sub, Kim Won, and Shih-Jiunn Shi. "Emergence of New Welfare States in East Asia? Domestic Social Changes and the Impact of 'Welfare Internationalism' in South Korea and Taiwan (1945–2012)." *International Journal of Social Quality* 3, no. 2 (2013): 106–24. https://doi.org/10.3167/IJSQ.2013.030206.
Sui, Cindy. "Changing Times Force Taiwan to Raise Welfare Spending." *BBC News*, April 24, 2013. https://www.bbc.com/news/business-22243977.
Sun, Fiona. "Hong Kong Government to Give Eligible Elderly Receiving Allowances an Extra HK$995 a Month from September 1." *South China Morning Post*, June 20, 2022. https://www.scmp.com/news/hong-kong/society/article/3182418/hong-kong-government-give-eligible-elderly-receiving?campaign=3182418&module=perpetual_scroll_0&pgtype=article.
Sung-jin, Choi. "Basic Pension Coming on July 1, But Tangled in Bureaucratic Complications." *Hankyoreh*, June 24, 2014. http://english.hani.co.kr/arti/english_edition/e_national/643837.html.

"Survey: Almost Half of Homes with One Parent Live in Poverty." *Asahi Shimbun*, July 5, 2023. https://www.asahi.com/ajw/articles/14949058.

Taiwan (ROC). Ministry of Education. "Education Statistical Indicators." 2019. https://english.moe.gov.tw/cp-76-19147-e5295-1.html.

Taiwan (ROC). Ministry of Foreign Affairs. "Taiwan.gov.tw: Economy." https://www.taiwan.gov.tw/content_7.php.

Taiwan (ROC). Ministry of Labor. "Insurance Benefits." August 2022. https://english.mol.gov.tw/21004/21015/21075/21081/21273/#:~:text=The%20unemployment%20benefits%20shall%20be,withdrawal%20from%20this%20insurance%20program.

Taiwan (ROC). Ministry of Labor. Bureau of Labor Insurance. "The New Labor Pension System is not the Old-Age Benefits of the Labor Insurance Program." August 2021. https://www.bli.gov.tw/en/0010373.html.

Taiwan (ROC). National Development Council. "Industry's Talent Shortages: The Current Situation and Policy Response." January 2019. https://www.ndc.gov.tw/en/Content_List.aspx?n=0229104B3512BB61.

Taiwan (ROC). National Development Council. "Taiwan Statistical Data Book 2019." National Development Council, May 2019. https://www.scy.moj.gov.tw/media/20240907/taiwanplusstatisticalplusdataplusbookplus2019.pdf?mediaDL=true.

Taiwan (ROC). National Development Council. Department of Human Resources Development. "Demographic Indicators." 2023. https://pop-proj.ndc.gov.tw/main_en.

Taiwan (ROC). National Development Council. Department of Human Resources Development. "Strengthening Population and Immigration Policies." 2023. https://www.ndc.gov.tw/EN/Content_List.aspx?n=6F69D4E5D624660A.

Taiwan (ROC). Statistical Bureau. "Average Monthly Earnings." 2023. https://eng.stat.gov.tw/lp.asp?ctNode=1615&CtUnit=765&BaseDSD=7&mp=5.

Taiwan (ROC). Statistical Bureau. "Earnings and Productivity, Labor Productivity by Value Added." 2023. https://eng.stat.gov.tw/lp.asp?ctNode=1615&CtUnit=765&BaseDSD=7&mp=5.

Taiwan (ROC). Statistical Bureau. "Labor Force." 2023. https://eng.stat.gov.tw/cl.aspx?n=2365.

Taiwan (ROC). Statistical Bureau. "Net Government Expenditures of All Levels." 2023. https://eng.stat.gov.tw/News_Content.aspx?n=4302&s=218308.

Taiwan (ROC). Statistical Bureau. "Social Protection Expenditure." 2023. https://eng.stat.gov.tw/cl.aspx?n=2383.

Takahashi, Shigehiro. *Boshi shinjū no jittai to kazoku kankei no kenkōka—Hoken fukushi gakuteki apurōchi ni yoru kenkyū* [The reality of mother–child suicides and the health improvement of family relations—An academic study based on the social insurance approach]. Tokyo: Kawashima Shoten, 1987.

Takenaka, Harukata. *Korona kiki no seiji—Abe seiken vs. chiji* [Politics under the COVID crisis—Abe government vs. mayors]. Tokyo: Chūkō Shinsho, 2020.

Takenaka Tetsuo, "Kodomo gyakutai wa ima" [Child abuse today]. In *Kodomo gyakutai to enjo* [Child abuse and support], edited by Takenaka Tetsuo, Hasegawa Masato, Asakura Keiichi, and Kita Kazunori, 1–16. Kyoto: Mineruva Shobō, 2002.

Tanaka, Chisato. "Two Girls' Deaths after Alleged Abuse Expose Shortcomings in Japan's Child-Protection Services." *Japan Times*, March 25, 2019. https://www.japantimes.co.jp/news/2019/03/25/reference/two-girls-deaths-alleged-abuse-expose-shortcomings-japans-child-protection-services/#.XSgD_i3Myt8.

Tang, Ailin, and Keith Bradhser. "A Billionaire's Fall Spotlights Child Sexual Abuse in China." *New York Times*, July 9, 2019. https://www.nytimes.com/2019/07/09/business/child-sexual-abuse-wang-zhenhua-seazen.html.

Tang, Frank. "China's State Pension Fund to Run Dry by 2035 as Workforce Shrinks Due to Effects of One-Child Policy, Says Study." *South China Morning Post*, April 12, 2019. https://www.scmp.com/economy/china-economy/article/3005759/chinas-state-pension-fund-run-dry-2035-workforce-shrinks-due.

Tang, Pui Yee Connie. "Taiwan's Housing Policy in the Context of East Asian Welfare Models." In *Housing and the New Welfare State: Perspectives from East Asia and Europe*, edited by Richard Groves, Alan Murie, and Christopher Watson, 159–82. Aldershot, UK: Ashgate, 2007.

Taylor, Adam. "The Human Suffering Caused by China's One-Child Policy." *Washington Post*, October 29, 2015. https://www.washingtonpost.com/news/worldviews/wp/2015/10/29/the-human-suffering-caused-by-chinas-one-child-policy/.

Teichler, Ulrich. "Higher Education and the World of Work: Conceptual Frameworks, Comparative Perspectives, Empirical Findings." In *Mass Higher Education Development in East Asia: Strategy, Quality and Challenges*, edited by Jung Cheol Shin, Gerard A. Postiglione, and Futao Huang, 269–88. New York: Springer, 2015.

Tejada, Carlos. "China Places Cap on Local Government Debt." *Wall Street Journal*, August 30, 2015. https://www.wsj.com/articles/china-places-cap-on-local-government-debt-1440928627.

Thorbecke, Willem, and Namesh Salike. "Understanding Foreign Direct Investment in East Asia." ADBI Working Paper Series No. 290, June 2011. https://www.adb.org/sites/default/files/publication/156145/adbi-wp290.pdf.

Tien-lin, Huang. "The Facts about Wage Stagnation." *Taipei Times*, December 13, 2012. http://www.taipeitimes.com/News/editorials/archives/2012/12/13/2003550016.

Tingting, Chen, and Lv Pu. "Safeguarding Children against Domestic Violence in China." Asia Foundation, March 1, 2017. https://asiafoundation.org/2017/03/01/safeguarding-children-domestic-violence-china/.

Tong, Lian, Qiong Yan, and Ichiro Kawachi. "The Factors Associated with Being Left-Behind Children in China: Multilevel Analysis with Nationally Representative Data." *PLoS One* 14, no. 11 (2019). https://doi.org/10.1371/journal.pone.0224205.

Trading Economics. "Taiwan Minimum Monthly Wage." 2023. https://tradingeconomics.com/taiwan/minimum-wages.

Tsai, Pan-Long, and Chao-Hsi Huang. "Openness, Growth and Poverty: The Case of Taiwan." *World Development* 35, no. 11 (2007): 1858–71. https://doi.org/10.1016/j.worlddev.2006.11.013.

Tsang, Donald. "Statement on 5 June 2002 by the Chief Secretary for Administration on Home Ownership Scheme Policy." CB (1) 2100/01–02(01). June 5, 2002. https://www.legco.gov.hk/yr01-02/english/panels/hg/papers/hg0705cb1-2100-1-e.pdf.

Tsou, Meng-Wen, Jin-Tan Liu, James K. Hammitt, and Ching-Fu Chang. "The Impact of Foreign Direct Investment in China on Employment Adjustments in Taiwan: Evidence from Matched Employer–Employee Data." *Japan and the World Economy* 25–26 (2013): 68–79. https://doi.org/10.1016/j.japwor.2013.01.007.

Tweed, David. "New Hong Kong Housing Policies Will Bring Focus, Carrie Lam Says." *Bloomberg*, June 30, 2018. https://www.bloomberg.com/news/articles/2018-07-01/new-hong-kong-housing-policies-will-bring-focus-carrie-lam-says.

Twenge, Jean M., and W. Keith Campbell. *The Narcissism Epidemic: Living in the Age of Entitlement*. New York: Simon and Schuster, 2009.
"29% of Chinese Fiscal Revenues Derived from Land Sales." *China Banking News*, January 21, 2019. http://www.chinabankingnews.com/2019/01/21/29-of-chinese-fiscal-revenues-derived-from-land-sales/.
UNCTAD. *World Investment Report 2023*. New York: United Nations Publications, 2023. https://unctad.org/system/files/official-document/wir2023_en.pdf.
UNICEF. "Fact Sheet: A Summary of the Rights under the Convention on the Rights of the Child." https://www.unicef.org/montenegro/en/media/1891/file/MNE-media-MNEpublication12.pdf.
United Nations. Department of Economic and Social Affairs. Population Division. "Can Pro-Natalist Policies Reverse the Fertility Decline in Taiwan Province of China?" United Nations Expert Group Meeting on Policy Responses to Low Fertility Policy Brief no. 17, November 2015. https://www.un.org/en/development/desa/population/events/pdf/expert/24/Policy_Briefs/PB_Taiwan.pdf.
United Nations. Department of Economic and Social Affairs. Population Division. "World Population Ageing." 2017. https://www.un.org/en/development/desa/population/publications/pdf/ageing/WPA2017_Report.pdf.
United Nations. Department of Economic and Social Affairs. Population Division. "World Population Prospects: The 2015 Revision, Key Findings and Advance Table." 2015. https://esa.un.org/unpd/wpp/publications/files/key_findings_wpp_2015.pdf.
United Nations. Department of Economic and Social Affairs. Population Division. "World Population Prospects: The 2017 Revision, Key Findings and Advance Table." June 2017. https://population.un.org/wpp/Publications/Files/WPP2017_KeyFindings.pdf.
United Nations. Department of Economic and Social Affairs. Population Division. "World Population Prospects." 2022. https://www.un.org/development/desa/pd/content/World-Population-Prospects-2022.
United Nations. Department of Economic and Social Affairs. Population Dynamics. "World Urbanization Prospects 2018: Country Profiles." 2018. https://population.un.org/wup/.
Urban Reform Institute and the Frontier Centre for Public Policy. "Demographia International Housing Affordability." 2023. http://www.demographia.com/.
U.S. Bureau of Labor Statistics. "Employed Full Time. Median Usual Weekly Real Earnings. Wage and Salary Workers. 16 Years and Over [LES1252881600Q]." FRED, Federal Reserve Bank of St. Louis, September 2023. https://fred.stlouisfed.org/series/LES1252881600Q.
Ventura, Luca. "Household Savings Rates 2021." *Global Finance*, January 25, 2021. https://www.gfmag.com/global-data/economic-data/916lqg-household-saving-rates.
Vere, James P. "Education, Development, and Wage Inequality: The Case of Taiwan." *Economic Development and Cultural Change* 53, no. 3 (2005): 711–35. https://doi.org/10.1086/427245.
Wada, Ichiro, and Ataru Igarashi. "The Social Costs of Child Abuse in Japan." *Children and Youth Services Review* 46 (2014): 72–77. https://doi.org/10.1016/j.childyouth.2014.08.002.
Wade, Robert. *Governing the Market: Economic Theory and the Role of Government in East Asia's Industrialization*. Princeton, NJ: Princeton University Press, 1990.
Wagatsuma, Hiroshi. "Child Abandonment and Infanticide: A Japanese Case." In *Child Abuse and Neglect: Cross-Cultural Perspectives*, edited by Jill E. Korbin, 120–38. Berkeley: University of California Press, 1981.

WageIndicator. "Minimum Wage Updated in Shanghai, China from 01 July 2023—July 03, 2023." 2023. https://wageindicator.org/salary/minimum-wage/minimum-wages-news/2023/minimum-wage-updated-in-shanghai-china-from-01-july-2023-july-03-2023#:~:text=July%2003%2C%202023-,Minimum%20Wage%20Updated%20in%20Shanghai%2C%20China%20from,July%202023%20%2D%20July%2003%2C%202023&text=Minimum%20wages%20have%20been%20revised,CN%C2%A524.00%20per%20hour.

Wang, Feng, Jingjing Lu, Lin Leesa, and Xudong Zhou. "Mental Health and Risk Behaviors of Children in Rural China with Different Patterns of Parental Migration: A Cross-Sectional Study." *Child and Adolescent Psychiatry and Mental Health* 13, no. 39 (2019). https://doi.org/10.1186/s13034-019-0298-8.

Wang, Hong-Zen. "Immigration Trends and Policy Changes in Taiwan." *Asian and Pacific Migration Journal* 20, no. 2 (2011): 169–94. https://doi.org/10.1177/011719681102000203.

Wang, Jeanette. "One in 4 Elderly Chinese Living Below Poverty Line, Landmark Study Finds." *South China Morning Post*, May 31, 2013. https://www.scmp.com/news/china/article/1250311/one-4-elderly-chinese-living-below-poverty-line-landmark-study-finds.

Wang, Le. "Economic Transition and College Premium in Urban China." *China Economic Review* 23, no. 2 (2012): 238–52. https://doi.org/10.1016/j.chieco.2011.11.001.

Wang, Xiao, and Richard Herd. "The System of Revenue Sharing and Fiscal Transfers in China." OECD Economics Department Working Papers No. 1030, February 2013. https://www.oecd-ilibrary.org/economics/the-system-of-revenue-sharing-and-fiscal-transfers-in-china_5k4bwnwtmx0r-en.

Wang, Ya Ping. "From Social Welfare to Support of Home Ownership: The Experience of China." In *Housing and the New Welfare State: Perspectives from East Asia and Europe*, edited by Richard Groves, Alan Murie, and Christopher Watson, 129–58. Aldershot, UK: Ashgate, 2007.

Wang, Ya Ping, and Alan Murie. "The New Affordable and Social Housing Provision System in China: Implications for Comparative Housing Studies." *International Journal of Housing Policy* 11, no. 3 (2011): 237–54. https://doi.org/10.1080/14616718.2011.599130.

Wang, Ya Ping, and Alan Murie. "The Process of Commercialization of Urban Housing in China." *Urban Studies* 33, no. 6 (1996): 971–89. https://doi.org/10.1080/00420989650011690.

Wang, Yaquiang, and Xin Dong. "Housing Policies for Rural Migrant Workers in China." In *Urban Inequality and Segregation in Europe and China*, edited by Gwilym Pryce, Ya Ping Wang, Yu Chen, Jingjing Shan, and Houkai Wei, 181–203. Springer, Cham, 2021.

Wee, Sui-Lee, and Steven Lee Myers. "China's Birthrate Hits Historic Low, in Looming Crisis for Beijing." *New York Times*, January 17, 2020. https://www.nytimes.com/2020/01/16/business/china-birth-rate-2019.html?action=click&module=Top%20Stories&pgtype=Homepage.

Wei, Katherine. "Taiwan Boosts Affordable Social Housing by Converting Hotels to Homes." *Straits Times*, January 11, 2022. https://www.straitstimes.com/asia/east-asia/taiwan-boosts-affordable-social-housing-by-converting-hotels-to-homes.

Wei Shi, Jie Chen, and Hongwei Wang. "Affordable Housing Policy in China: New Developments and New Challenges." *Habitat International* 54, part 3 (2016): 224-33. https://doi.org/10.1016/j.habitatint.2015.11.020.

Wei, Zongcai, and Rebecca L. H. Chiu. "Livability of Subsidized Housing Estates in Marketized China: An Institutional Interpretation." *Cities* 83 (2018): 108–17. https://doi.org/10.1016/j.cities.2018.06.013.

Weise, Elizabeth. "Taiwan's Problem? Too Many College Graduates, Too Few Machinists." *USA Today*, May 7, 2015. https://www.usatoday.com/story/tech/2015/05/07/taiwan-too-many-college-graduates/26945515/.

Wen-po, Chang. "Pay Raises Alone Cannot Solve Low Wages." *Taipei Times*, January 23, 2018. http://www.taipeitimes.com/News/editorials/archives/2018/01/23/2003686256.

Wen, Qiao. "Estimating Education and Labor Market Consequences of China's Higher Education Expansion." *Sustainability* 14 (2022): 1–25. https://doi.org/10.3390/su14137873.

Wendler, Sybil. *Once upon a Rooftop*. CAAM, June 8, 2011. https://caamedia.org/blog/2011/06/08/watch-once-upon-a-rooftop/.

Westbrook, Laura. "Coronavirus Crisis Exposes Harsh Existence of Hong Kong's Poorest Households." *South China Morning Post*, March 14, 2020. https://today.line.me/hk/v2/article/lO8mNL.

"Why Some Japanese Pensioners Want to Go to Jail." *BBC News*, January 31, 2019. https://www.bbc.com/news/stories-47033704.

Whyte, Martin King, Wang Feng, and Yong Cai. "Challenging Myths about China's One-Child Policy." *China Journal* 74 (2015): 144–59. https://doi.org/10.1086/681664.

Wilensky, Harold, and Charles N. Lebeaux. *Industrial Society and Social Welfare*. New York: Russell Sage Foundation, 1958.

Willis, Rebecca. "The Use of Composite Narratives to Present Interview Findings." *Qualitative Research* 19, no. 4 (2019): 471–80. https://doi.org/10.1177/1468794118787711.

Wills, Ken. "Seeking Balance: China Strives to Adapt Social Protection to the Needs of a Market Economy." *Finance and Development* 55, no. 4 (2018): 20–23. https://www.imf.org/en/Publications/fandd/issues/2018/12/social-protection-in-china-wills.

Wilson, Lindsay. "How Big Is a House? Average House Size by Country—2023." Shrink That Footprint, 2023. https://shrinkthatfootprint.com/how-big-is-a-house/.

Windgender, Philippe. "Intergovernmental Fiscal Reform in China." IMF Working Paper WP/18/88, April 2018. https://www.imf.org/en/Publications/WP/Issues/2018/04/13/Intergovernmental-Fiscal-Reform-in-China-45743.

Wong, Brian. "As Hong Kong Marks 25 Years of British Handover, Its 'Cage Homes' Remain a Stark Reminder of Its Inequities." *Time Magazine*, June 30, 2022. https://time.com/6191786/hong-kong-china-handover-cage-homes/#.

Wong, Corine S. M., W. C. Chan, Linda C. W. Lam, W. Y. Law, W. Y. Tang, T. Y. Wong, and Eric Y. H. Chen. "Living Environment and Psychological Distress in the General Population of Hong Kong." *Procedia Environmental Sciences* 36 (2016): 78–81. https://doi.org/10.1016/j.proenv.2016.09.016.

Wong, Hung. "Impact of Active Labour Market Policies and Statutory Minimum Wage on Welfare Recipients in Hong Kong." Paper presented at the 19th FISS International Research Seminar on "Challenges for Social Protection," Sigtuna, Sweden, June 19, 2012. https://www.researchgate.net/publication/237054632_Impact_of_Active_Labour_Market_Policies_and_Statutory_Minimum_Wage_on_Welfare_Recipients_in_Hong_Kong.

Wong, Joseph. *Healthy Democracies: Welfare Politics in Taiwan and South Korea*. Ithaca, NY: Cornell University Press, 2004.

Wong, Margaret Fung-Yee. "Multidisciplinary Response in Domestic Violence: How We Started and Where We Are Heading." In *Preventing Family Violence:*

A Multidisciplinary Approach, edited by Ko-Ling Chan, 315–36. Hong Kong: University of Hong Kong Press, 2012.

Wong, Richard. "Demography, Housing, and the Economic Future of Hong Kong." Presentation at the Hong Kong CSB Advanced Leadership Enhancement Programme for Directorate Officials, Hong Kong, December 1, 2017.

Wong, Richard. *Fixing Inequality in Hong Kong*. Hong Kong: Hong Kong University Press, 2017.

Wong, Richard. *Hong Kong Land for Hong Kong People: Fixing the Failures of Our Housing Policy*. Hong Kong: Hong Kong University Press, 2015.

Wong, Stan Hok-Wui. *Electoral Politics in Post-1997 Hong Kong: Protest, Patronage, and the Media*. Singapore: Springer, 2015.

Woo, Jung-en. *Race to the Swift: State and Finance in Korean Industrialization*. New York: Columbia University Press, 1991.

Woo-Cumings, Meredith, ed. *The Developmental State*. Ithaca, NY: Cornell University Press, 1999.

Wood, Joanne N., Sheyla P. Medina, Chris Feudtner, Xianqun Luan, Russell Localio, Evan S. Fieldston, and David M. Rubin. "Local Macroeconomic Trends and Hospital Admissions for Child Abuse, 2000–2009." *Pediatrics* 130, no. 2 (2012): e358. https://doi.org/10.1542/peds.2011-3755.

World Bank. *The East Asian Miracle: Economic Growth and Public Policy*. New York: Oxford University Press, 1993.

World Bank. "Fertility Rate, Total (Births Per Woman)." World Development Indicators, 2023. https://data.worldbank.org/indicator/SP.DYN.TFRT.IN.

World Bank. "GDP Growth (Annual %)." World Development Indicators, 2023. https://data.worldbank.org/indicator/NY.GDP.MKTP.KD.ZG?end=2017&start=1970.

World Bank. "Government Expenditure on Education, Total (% of GDP)." World Development Indicators, 2023. https://data.worldbank.org/indicator/SE.XPD.TOTL.GD.ZS?most_recent_value_desc=true.

World Bank. "Labor Force, Total." World Development Indicators, 2023. https://data.worldbank.org/indicator/SL.TLF.TOTL.IN.

World Bank. "Life Expectancy at Birth, Total (Years)." Databank/World Development Indicators, 2023. https://data.worldbank.org/indicator/SP.DYN.LE00.IN.

World Bank. *Live Long and Prosper: Aging in East Asia and Pacific*. Washington, DC: World Bank, 2016.

World Bank. "Population Estimates and Projections." Databank/World Development Indicators, 2023. https://databank.worldbank.org/reports.aspx?source=Health%20Nutrition%20and%20Population%20Statistics:%20Population%20estimates%20and%20projections.

World Bank. "Poverty and Inequality Platform." 2023. https://pip.worldbank.org/home.

World Bank. "Trade (% of GDP)." World Development Indicators, 2023. https://data.worldbank.org/indicator/NE.TRD.GNFS.ZS.

World Bank. "Urban Population Growth (Annual %)." World Development Indicators, 2023. https://data.worldbank.org/indicator/SP.URB.GROW?end=2017&start=1970.

World Population Review. "Fertility Rate by Country." 2023. http://worldpopulationreview.com/countries/total-fertility-rate/.

World Population Review. "Largest Metro Areas in the World." 2023. https://worldpopulationreview.com/world-city-rankings/largest-metro-areas-in-the-world.

Wu, Alice. "Be a Better Neighbor, Don't Ignore Signs of Child Abuse in Hong Kong." *South China Morning Post*, January 21, 2018. https://www.scmp.com/comment/insight-opinion/article/2129679/be-better-neighbour-dont-ignore-signs-child-abuse-hong-kong.

Wu, David Y. H. "Child Abuse in Taiwan." In *Child Abuse and Neglect: Cross-Cultural Perspectives*, edited by Jill E. Korbin, 139–65. Berkeley: University of California Press, 1981.

Wu, Fulong. "Housing and the State in China." In *International Encyclopedia of Housing and Home*, edited by Susan J. Smith, Maria Elsinga, Lorna Fox O'Mahony, Ong Seow Eng, Susan Wachter, and Chris Hamnett. Vol. 3, 323–29. Oxford, UK: Elsevier, 2012.

Wu, Weiping. "Sources of Migrant Housing Disadvantage in Urban China." *Environment and Planning A* 36 (2004): 1285–304. https://doi.org/10.1016/j.cities.2018.04.006.

Xia, Xin, Joe Xiang, Jianbo Shao, Gary A. Smith, Chuanhua Yu, Huiping Zhu, and Huiyun Xiang. "Characteristics and Trends of Hospitalized Pediatric Abuse Head Trauma in Wuhan, China 2002." *International Journal of Environmental Research and Public Health* 9, no. 11 (2012): 4187–96. https://doi.org/10.3390/ijerph9114187.

Xing, Chunbing, and Jianwei Xu. "Regional Variation of the Minimum Wages in China." *IZA Journal of Labor & Development* 5, no. 8 (2016). https://doi.org/10.1186/s40175-016-0054-x.

Xu, Hangtian, and Yiming Zhou. "Public Housing Provision and Housing Vacancies in Japan." *Journal of the Japanese and International Economies* 53 (2019): 101038. https://doi.org/10.1016/j.jjie.2019.101038.

Yahya, Yasmine. "Helping Low-Wage Workers in Singapore: What More Can Be Done?" *Straits Times*, June 24, 2018. https://www.straitstimes.com/singapore/manpower/helping-low-wage-workers-what-more-can-be-done.

Yamada, Kana, "Gyakutai de shōgai, kenmei ni ikiru tōzakaru oya, mimamoru shisetsu shokuin" [Disabled because of abuse, working hard to live amid parental withdrawal, facility staff provides care]. *Asahi Shimbun*, October 20, 2016.

Yamadera, Kaoru. *Dare mo boku wo miteinai: Naze 17sai no shōnen wa sofubo wo satsugai shita noka* [Nobody is watching me: Why did the 17-year-old murder his grandparents?]. Tokyo: Popurasha, 2017.

Yamamoto, Tomohiro. "AI Put 39% Need for Protective Custody of Girl Who Later Died." *Asahi Shimbun*, July 11, 2023. https://www.asahi.com/ajw/articles/14953857#:~:text=The%20prefectural%20government%20uses%20past,percent%20need%20for%20protective%20custody.

Yan, Fung Ping. "Public Housing in Hong Kong Past, Present and Future." 2006. http://www.cih.org.hk/event_speaker_dnload/events2006100801/Public%20Housing%20in%20Hong%20Kong%20-%20Paper%20to%20SAHF.pdf.

Yang, Jae-jin. "The Welfare State and Income Security for the Elderly in Korea." In *Korea's Retirement Predicament*, edited by Thomas R. Klassen and Yunjeong Yang, 39–52. New York: Routledge, 2013.

Yang, Jae-jin, ed., *The Small Welfare State: Rethinking Welfare in the US, Japan, and South Korea*. Northampton, MA: Edward Elgar Publishing, 2020.

Yang, Li. "Towards Equity and Sustainability? China's Pension System Reform Moves Center Stage." World Inequality Lab No. 2021/13, April 2021. https://wid.world/wp-content/uploads/2021/04/WorldInequalityLab_WP2021_13_China_PensionSystem.pdf.

Yang, Shi-Chang, Ying-Li Zhang, Dong-Jun Zhang, Li-Juan Shen, and Gui-Ying Yao. "Meta-Analysis of Incidence Rate of Child Abuse in China." *Chinese Journal of School Health* 9 (2014): 1346–48. http://www.cjsh.org.cn/en/article/id/zgxxws201409021.

Yang, Sonam. "Cane of Love: Parental Attitudes towards Corporal Punishment in Korea." *British Journal of Social Work* 39, no. 8 (2009): 1540–55. https://psycnet.apa.org/doi/10.1093/bjsw/bcn034.

Yang, Sophia. "Taiwan Ministry of Labor Unveils Average Starting Wage across Different Sectors." *Taiwan News*, June 19, 2022. https://www.taiwannews.com.tw/en/news/4574732.

Yang, Zan, Chengdong Yi, Wei Zhang, and Chun Zhang. "Affordability of Housing and Accessibility of Public Services: Evaluation of Housing Programs in Beijing." *Journal of Housing and the Built Environment* 29 (2014): 521–40. https://doi.org/10.1007/s10901-013-9363-4.

Yashiro, Naohiro. "Aging of the Population in Japan and its Implications to the Other Asian Countries." *Journal of Asian Economics* 8, no. 2 (1997): 245–61. https://doi.org/10.1016/S1049-0078(97)90019-1.

Yates, Darran. "The Stress of City Life." *Nature Reviews Neuroscience* 12 (2011): 430. https://doi.org/10.1038/nrn3079.

Ye, Junija. "Migrant Landscapes: A Spatial Analysis of South Asian Male Migrants in Singapore." In *Changing Landscapes of Singapore: Old Tensions, New Discoveries*, edited by Elaine Lyn-Ee Ho, Chih Yuan Woon, and Kamalini Ramadas, 142–57. Singapore: National University of Singapore Press, 2013.

Yen, Meng-Feng. "The Wage Premium and Market Structure: The Case of South Korea and Taiwan." Paper presented at the Agriculture and Applied Economics Association Annual Meeting, Washington, DC, August 4–6, 2013. https://ageconsearch.umn.edu/record/151292?ln=en.

Yi, Chin-Chun, and Wen-Yin Chien. "The Linkage between Work and Family: Female's Employment Patterns in Three Chinese Societies." *Journal of Comparative Family Studies* 33, no. 3 (2002): 451–74. https://doi.org/10.3138/jcfs.33.3.451.

Yon, Hwangbo. "Around One-Third of Young South Koreans Experience Working Poverty." *Hankyoreh*, March 5, 2017. http://english.hani.co.kr/arti/english_edition/e_business/785120.html.

Yuan, Ye, Judy Major-Girardin, and Steven Brown. "Storytelling Is Intrinsically Mentalistic: A Functional Magnetic Resonance Imaging Study of Narrative Production across Modalities." *Journal of Cognitive Neuroscience* 30, no. 9 (2018): 1298–314. https://doi.org/10.1162/jocn_a_01294.

Zaidi, Asghar. "Poverty Risks for Older People in EU Countries—An Update." European Centre for Social Welfare Policy and Research, Policy Brief, January 2010. http://pdc.ceu.hu/archive/00006118/01/1264603415_56681.pdf.

Zeng, Wen, Philip Rees, and Lili Xiang. "Do Residents of Affordable Housing Communities in China Suffer from Relative Accessibility Deprivation? A Case Study of Nanjing." *Cities* 90 (2019): 141–56. https://doi.org/10.1016/j.cities.2019.01.038.

Zhai, Fuhua, and Qin Gao. "Child Maltreatment Among Asian Americans: Characteristics and Explanatory Framework." *Child Maltreatment* 14, no. 2 (2009): 207–24. https://doi.org/10.1177/1077559508326286.

Zhang, Jun, and Xiaofeng Liu. "The Evolving Pattern of the Wage-Labor Productivity Nexus in China: Evidence from Manufacturing Firm-Level Data." *Economic Systems* 37, no. 3 (2013): 354–68. https://doi.org/10.1016/j.ecosys.2013.05.001.

Zhang, Junsen, Yaohui Zhao, Albert Park, and Xiaoqing Song. "Economic Returns to Schooling in Urban China, 1988 to 2001." *Journal of Comparative Economics* 33, no. 4 (2005): 730–52. https://doi.org/10.1016/j.jce.2005.05.008.

Zhang, Kane, and Lynn Xu. "Surging Child Sex Abuse Cases in China: Recent Efforts Are Just a Bandaid on a Festering Wound Caused by Communism, Say Experts." *Epoch Times*, July 18, 2023. https://www.theepochtimes.com/china/in-depth-surging-child-sex-abuse-cases-in-china-5385749?saved=0?welcomeuser=1.

Zhang, Lijia. "Left-Behind Children a Poignant Reminder of the Cost of China's Development." *South China Morning Post*, May 26, 2018. https://www.scmp.com/comment/insight-opinion/article/2147787/left-behind-children-poignant-reminder-cost-chinas.

Zhang, Longmei, Ray Brooks, Ding Ding, Haiyan Ing, Hui He, Jing Lu, and Rui Mano. "China's High Savings: Drivers, Prospects, and Policies." IMF Working Paper WP/18/277, December 2018. https://www.imf.org/en/Publications/WP/Issues/2018/12/11/Chinas-High-Savings-Drivers-Prospects-and-Policies-46437.

Zhang, Saijun, Qinying Ci, and Min Zhan. "Public Assistance in Urban and Rural China: A Tale of Two Stories." *International Journal of Social Welfare* 26 (2017): 303–13. https://doi.org/10.1111/ijsw.12248.

Zhao, Fang, Juha Erkki, Antero Hamalaienen, and Honglin L. Chen. "Child Protection in China: Changing Policies and Reactions from the Field of Social Work." *International Journal of Social Welfare* 26, no. 4 (2017): 329–39. https://doi.org/10.1111/ijsw.12268.

Zhao, Xue, Jian Chen, Ming-Chun Chen, Xiao-Ling Lv, Yu-Hong Jiang, and Ye-Huan Sun. "Left-Behind Children in Rural China Experience Higher Levels of Anxiety and Poorer Living Conditions." *Acta Paediatrica* 103, no. 6 (2014): 665–70. https://doi.org/10.1111/apa.12602.

Zhou, Jing, and Richard Ronald. "The Resurgence of Public Housing Provision in China: The Chongqing Programme." *Housing Studies* 32, no. 4 (2017): 428–48. https://doi.org/10.1080/02673037.2016.1210097.

Zhou, Marrian. "Factory Strikes Flare Up in China as Economic Woes Deepen." *Nikkei Asia*, August 28, 2023. https://asia.nikkei.com/Business/Business-trends/Factory-strikes-flare-up-in-China-as-economic-woes-deepen.

Zhou, Winni, and Kevin Yao. "China Audit Uncovers Misuse of Affordable Housing Funds." *Reuters*, August 17, 2015. https://www.reuters.com/article/china-economy-housing/china-audit-uncovers-misuse-of-affordable-housing-funds-idUSL3N10S2GO20150817.

Zhuang, Juzhong, and Li Shi. "Understanding Recent Trends in Income Inequality in the People's Republic of China." ADB Economics Working Paper Series No. 489, July 2016. https://www.adb.org/publications/understanding-recent-trends-income-inequality-prc.

Zielinski, David S. "Child Maltreatment and Adult Socioeconomic Well-Being." *Child Abuse & Neglect* 33, no. 10 (2009): 666–78. https://doi.org/10.1016/j.chiabu.2009.09.001.

Zou, Yonghua. "Contradictions in China's Affordable Housing Policy: Goals vs. Structure." *Habitat International* 41 (2014): 8–16. https://doi.org/10.1016/j.habitatint.2013.06.001.

Zuo, Mandy. "Single Mum in Legal Fight for China's Unmarried Mothers." *South China Morning Post*, September 14, 2019. https://www.scmp.com/news/china/society/article/3026761/single-mum-legal-fight-chinas-unmarried-mothers.

Index

Page numbers in *italics* refer to figures and tables.

Abe Shinzō, 96
active labor market policies (ALMPs), 3, 46, 93, 182; China, 155, 169, 184, 194, 242n96; coverage rates, 28, *29*; defined, 23; Hong Kong, 94, 221n82; Japan, 96; Singapore, 94–95, 181; South Korea, 56, 97; spending on, 24–25, *24–25*, *44*; Taiwan, 90–91
affordable housing crisis, 2–4, 11, 15, 124–49, 209n83; China, 155, 162, 173–77, 233n34, 244n129, 244n132, 245n144, 245nn137–39, 246n153; Hong Kong, 2–4, 37–38, 49, 124–44, 149, 183, 231n9; Japan, 146–47, 183; policy responses, 135–36; Singapore, 144–46, 181, 183, 245n137; South Korea, 38, 147–48; Taiwan, 148–49, 237nn101–2; United States, 129–30
age dependency ratio, 39, *39*, 41, 73, 161, 166; defined, 209n73
Asian Development Bank (ADB), 10, 105, 205n28, 205n30, 220n66, 249n30, 249n31
Asian financial crisis (1997–98), 36, 56, 74, 86, 91, 130, 138, 139, 143–45, 174
authoritarian regimes, 56, 66–67, 79, 153, 205n23, 248n29

Beijing, 34, 176–77
Beveridgean pension system, 62–63, 213n44
birth rates. *See* fertility rates, declining
Bismarckian welfare systems, 21, 62–64, 204n18, 213n43

Cameron, David, 191, 248n25
Campbell, Andrea, 9
Canada, 63, 204n18, 250n53
Center for Child Abuse Prevention (Tokyo, Japan), 110
Chan Sui-lam, 122
Chen Shui-bian, 79
Cheung Chiu-hung, Fernando, 123
Chiang Ching-kuo, 79
Chiang Kai-shek, 79
Child Abuse Prevention Association (Osaka, Japan), 109–10

child maltreatment, 2–4, 11, 15, 100–123, 183; China, 38–39, 47, 162, 170–73, 183, 242n103, 243nn105–6; COVID-19 and, 195; declining fertility rates and, 122; demographic trends and single parenthood, 43, 101–6, 112–16; economic costs of, 6–7, 108, 225n31; economic insecurity and, 33, 36; family structures and, 101, 110, 122, 123; Hong Kong, 47, 122–23, 132, 232n24; human capital development and, 16, 47; income inequality and, 111–12; Japan, 3, 6–7, 16, 36, 38, 43, 49, 100–119, *101*, 123, 225n31, 227n63, 228nn85–86; mental disorders and, 111, 226n50; poverty and, 111–12, 121, 122; rise in, 100, *101*, 106–7, 111; Singapore, 121–22; South Korea, 120, 228n79; Taiwan, 120–21, 230n114; unemployment and, 227n63; urbanization and, 38–39, 101, 110–11, 121, 171; Western countries, 109
China, 150–78; affordable housing crisis, 155, 162, 173–77, 233n34, 244n129, 244n132, 245n144, 245nn137–39, 246n153; age dependency ratio, 161, 239n45; ALMPs, 155, 169, 184, 194, 242n96; Basic Old Age Insurance (BOAI), 165–67, 241n65; Belt and Road Initiative, 153; child maltreatment, 38–39, 47, 162, 170–73, 183, 242n103, 243nn105–6; China Standards 2035, 153; climate change policy, 197; closed economy, 192, 248n28; Communist Party, 153–54, 169; COVID-19 policy, 196, 242n95; Cultural Revolution, 152, 168; Decision on Deepening the Urban Housing Reform, 174; economic growth, 1, 48, 150–53, 155, 156, 178, 237n9; economic transformation, 12, 150–53, 167–68, 173, 177–78, 202n3, 237n6; education expenditures, 31–32, *32*, 164, 184, 240n59; education wage premium, 85, 160, 168–69; Employer-Sponsored Annuity, 165; Employment First initiative, 169, 242n97; familial support system, 154, 156, 162–64; family structures, 162–63; Family Support Agreements, 156, 162; Family Violence Law, 171; fertility rates, 161, 163,

293

China (*continued*)
239nn42–43; foreign direct investment in, 152, 160, 208n52; foreign exchange reserves, 238n19; GDP per capita, 205n29; ghost cities, 177, 246n155; globalization and, 160; Great Leap Forward, 152; Hong Kong and, 93, 127–28, 138, 201n3; Household Responsibility System, 152; Housing Provident Fund, 174, 245n137; *hukou* (household registration system), 39, 154, 157–58, 166, 167, 170–72, 174, 178; human capital development, 156; income inequality, 18–19, 30, *30*, 85, 160, 169, 177, 203n11, 239n39; intergovernmental structure, 158–59; international trade, 207n52; "iron rice bowl" of benefits, 154; labor force growth, *40*; labor unrest, 242n95; Made in China 2025 initiative, 153; migrant workers, 166–67, 172, 174, 176–77, 241n72, 246n153; Minimum Living Standard Assurance (Dibao), 166; minimum wage, 169–70, 242n100; New Rural Pension program, 165; old age crisis, 47, 63, 69, 156, 161, 163–67, 182, 215n78, 240nn60–61, 246n3; old age security programs, 63; one-child policy, 161, 172, 210n94, 239n41; Open Door policy, 152, 160; outward FDI, 35; passive labor market policies (PLMPs), 169; pensions, 164–67; policy façade, 165, 169, 177; political economy, 153; poverty, 28, 151, 167–68, 207n42; productivist approach, 4–5, 7, 12, 22, 49–50, 150–51, 154–63, 165, 178; rural to urban migration, 157–62, 171–72, 239n47, 239n49, 243n112; single parents, 171, 243n110; skill-biased technical change, 35, 160; social assistance, 154–56; social insurance, 155–56, *193*; social protection coverage, *29*, 155; social protection spending, 24–25, *24–25*, 28, *28*, 43, 44, 155, 184, 185, *191*, *193*; social welfare policy, 15, 153–59; Taiwan and, 79–80, 83–84, 86–87, 201n3, 218n38; Taiwanese professionals in, 84; tax policy, 169; unemployment insurance, 169; Urban and Rural Residents Pension Scheme (URRPS), 165–67; urbanization, 12, 37, 38–39, 161–62, 171–72, 175; Urban Resident Pension scheme, 165; urban workers, benefits for, 154, 157–58, 165; wages, 34, 81, *81*, 87, 167–70, 182, 242n100; women in, 164, 166
climate change, 196–99
community support systems, 30–31, *31*, 68, 83, 111, 115, 162
Confucian tradition, 13, 61, 120, 150, 156, 162. *See also* familial support systems

corporations, welfare provision by, 4, 21, 30–31, *31*, 65
COVID-19 pandemic, 70, 189, 194–97, 199, 217n16, 218n38, 231n8, 242n95, 250n53
crime, 69, 108–9, 114, 119, 146, 225n28
Croll, Elizabeth, 155

decommodification, 187
democratization, 91, 92, 105, 180, 186–90, 198–99, 247n8, 248n18
demographic trends, 6, 33, 39–41, 186; child maltreatment and, 43, 101–6, 112–16; housing and, 134; labor market and, 98
Denmark, 19, *20*, 62, 204n18
Desmond, Matthew, 9
developmental state, 17, 55, 203n8
development policies, 4. *See also* productivism
Dillon, Nara, 154
disability, 23, 71, 90, 108, 118, 194, 205n30, 223n115, 225n31
disadvantaged groups: democracy and, 189; employment gap, 97, 223n115; social protection for, 5, 14, 27, 29, 45–46, 65, 73, 105, 135–36, 139, 155, 187. *See also* safety net programs
dynamic integrated social welfare analysis. *See* social welfare analysis

East Asia: economic growth and social welfare policy, 1–2, 4–5, 7–8, 11–12, 16–20, 27, 179–94, 198–99; "misery beneath the miracle" paradox, 2–4, 11–13, 178, 190, 198. *See also* affordable housing crisis; child maltreatment; China; Hong Kong; income inequality; Japan; Singapore; South Korea; Taiwan; wage stagnation
education, 1; private spending on, *32*, 32–33, 53–55, 119. *See also* human capital development
education wage premium, 85, 99, 182; China, 85, 160, 168–69; Hong Kong, 82, 93–94; Taiwan, 82, 217n14, 219n57; United States, 85, 89, 217n16
elderly population. *See* old age crisis
Esping-Anderson, Gøsta, 21, 22, 201n6
European countries, 109, 248n26, 248n29. *See also* OECD countries; *specific countries*

familial support systems, 4, 21, 30–31, *31*, 36, 38, 83, 154, 156, 162–64; education expenditures, *32*, 32–33, 53–55, 119. *See also* Confucian tradition

family structures: changes in, 6, 15, 33, 41–43, 51, 61, 113–14, 134, 186, 228n79; child maltreatment and, 101, 110, 122, 123. *See also* single parents
fertility rates, declining, 6, *39*, 39–42, 48; child maltreatment and, 122; China, 161, 163, 239nn42–43; economic insecurity and, 84–85; Singapore, 41; South Korea, 51, 59; Taiwan, 84–85, 89
filial piety, 156, 162
Finland, 19, 144, 204n18
foreign direct investment (FDI): in China, 152, 160, 208n52; outward from East Asian countries, 34–35
Foxconn (company), 74, 87
France, 18, 204n18

Gercik, Patricia, 9
Germany, 18, 21, 23, *24*, *30*, *31*, 62, 64, 115, *193*, 204n18
global cities, 34–35, 130, 207n51
globalization, 6, 27, 33–37, 98–99, 160, 186; economic insecurity and, 101, 111–12, 129; wage stagnation and, 75, 85–86, 90, 93, 124–25
Gough, Ian, 197, 250n51
Great Recession (2008), 86

Hacker, Jacob, 9
health care, 1, 187–88; government spending on, 4, 21, *25*
Holliday, Ian, 21
Hong Kong: affordable housing crisis, 2–4, 37–38, 49, 124–44, 149, 183, 231n9; ALMPs, 94, 221n82; cage or coffin homes, 29, 38, 71, 125–26, 131–32; child maltreatment, 47, 122–23, 132, 232n24; China and, 93, 127–28, 138, 201n3; Comprehensive Social Security Assistance (CSSA), 71, 94; COVID-19 and, 195; demographic trends, 134; Disability Allowance, 71; education expenditures, 31–32, *32*; education wage premium, 82, 93–94; family structures, 134; Fanling Golf Course, 234n56; Home Ownership Scheme (HOS), 137–39, 234n60; Home Purchase Loan Scheme (HPLS), 137; housing policy façade, 46–47, 136–44, 149, 177; housing types, *131*; immigration, 124, 133–34, 233n34; income inequality, 18, *18*, 30, *30*, 35, 38, 48, 93–94, 124, 129, 132–33, 232n25; labor force growth, 40, 209n74; land use policies, 134–35, 140–44, 233nn39–40, 234n56; Light Public Housing (LPH), 141–42; Long-Term Housing Strategy Steering Committee, 144; Mandatory Provident Fund, 71, 215n95; minimum wage, 94; Old Age Allowance, 71; old age crisis, 57, *57*, 69, 71–72, 126–27, 132, 182, 215n78, 233n27, 246n3; Old Age Living Allowance (OALA), 71; political and economic context, 43–45, 127–29, 143, 191–92, 203n7, 205n29, 235n69, 248n27; productivist approach, 21–22, 125, 136, 143; protests and unrest, 48, 83, 128, 133; public housing, 29, 125, 126, 130–32, 134–35, 137–42, 206n36, 234nn59–60; Public Sector Participation Scheme, 137; real estate developers, 136, 138–44, 176, 235n71; Sale of Flats to Sitting Tenants Scheme (SFSTS), 137; skill-biased technical change, 35, 36–37; social assistance, 25, 129; social insurance, 129, 184, *193*; social protection spending, 24–25, *24–25*, 43, *44*, 185, *191*, *193*, 206n36; Steering Committee on Land and Housing Supply, 141; Support for Self-Reliance (SFS), 94; Task Force on Public Housing Projects, 141; tax policy, 139, 143, 207n45, 235n62; Tenants Purchase Scheme (TPS), 138; Umbrella Movement, 83, 128, 133; urbanization, 37–38; wages, 34, 81, *81*, 93–94, 221n77; zoning laws, 136, 142, 235n66
Hong Kong Housing Authority (HKHA), 131, 137–38, 140
Hong Kong Housing Society (NGO), 139
housing. *See* affordable housing crisis
Hu Jintao, 175
human capital development, 5, 12, 17, 27, 31–33, 184; brain drain and, 84; child maltreatment and, 47; dualistic welfare systems and, 186; government spending on education, 4, 21, 31–33, *32*, 37, 51, 75, 92, 99, 184, 204n21, 207n49 (see also *specific countries*); healthcare spending, 4, 21, *25*, 207n49; migration and, 48, 84, 99
human development indicators, 5, 11, 27, 198

income, equitable distribution of, 1, 5, 11, 18–19, 27
income inequality, 82, 217n17; child maltreatment and, 111–12; China, 18–19, 30, *30*, 85, 160, 169, 177, 203n11, 239n39; climate change policy and, 197; Germany, 18, *30*;

INDEX

income inequality (*continued*)
globalization and skill-biased technical change, 34; Hong Kong, 18, *18*, 30, *30*, 35, 38, 48, 93–94, 124, 129, 132–33, 232n25; increasing, 11; Japan, *18*, 19, 26, 29–30, *30*; mental health impacts of, 36; OECD countries, *30*; Scandinavian countries, 19, *20*; Singapore, 18, *18*, 30, *30*, 35, 95; South Korea, 1–2, *18*, 18–19, 29, *30*, 189, 203n11; Sweden, *30*; Taiwan, *18*, 18–19, 29, *30*, 37, 82, 203n11, 217n17; United States, 18, *30*, 85
industrialization, 1–2, 8, 17, 19, 55, 80, 105, 151, 152, 157
International Labour Organization (ILO), 10, 24, 189, 193, 249n36
in-work poverty. *See* working poverty
Ireland, 185, 204n18

Japan: Abenomics, 96, 209n81; affordable housing crisis, 146–47, 183; age dependency ratio, 239n45; ALMPs, 96; Bismarckian system, 62; Child Abuse Prevention Law (CAPL), 110, 225n34, 226n43; childcare institutions, 229n101; child maltreatment, 3, 6–7, 16, 36, 38, 43, 49, 100–119, *101*, 123, 225n31, 227n63, 228nn85–86; child protection policy framework, 115–16, *116*; Child Rearing Allowance, 229n104; Children and Families Agency, 119; Child Welfare Law, 114, 226n44; child welfare policy façade, 46, 116–19, 123; corporal punishment, 110, 114, 224n14; COVID-19 and, 195; deficits, 43; democratization, 105, 186–87, 247n8; Dependent Children's Allowance, 118; education expenditures, 31–32, *32*, 100, 119, 184; family structures, 42–43, 115; human capital development, 119; income inequality, *18*, 19, 26, 29–30, *30*; labor force growth, 40, *40*, 48, 209n74; labor market policies, 27, 194; Law for Prevention of Child Abuse, 106–7; Liberal Democratic Party (LDP), 105; liberal welfare system, 7, 22–23, 50, 181, 185, 187, 198, 201n6, 204n19; Livelihood Protection, 69, 119; mental health problems, 47; minimum wage, 96; multimember-district single-nontransferable voting electoral system (MMD/SNTV), 105, 223n6; National Pension, 69; nonregular workers, 96; old age crisis, 57, 63, 64, 69–70, 182, 211n10, 215n78, 246n3; old age security programs, 63, 64, 69–70; outward FDI, 35; political and economic context, 43, 104–6, 192, 205n29; poverty, 25, 28, 36, 57, 112, 182, 207n42, 208n63, 211n10, 227n69, 246n3; privacy laws, 115; private welfare spending, 31, *31*; productivist approach, 22–23, 105–6, 116, 123, 201n6; retirement, mandatory, 70; social assistance, 25, 105–6, 112, 118–19, 184; social insurance, 105–6, 119, 184, 185, *193*; social protection coverage, *29*; social protection spending, 23–28, *24–25*, *28*, 43, *44*, 105–6, 119, 186–87, 190, *191*, 192, *193*, 205n30; suicides, 69, 112, 113; Supplementary Welfare Benefits for Mothers and Children, 118–19; tax policy, 207n45; unemployment insurance, 194; urbanization, 37; wages, 34, 81, *81*, 95–96; women in, 42; *zaibatsu* (industrial conglomerates), 105
Jones, Randall, 188

Keidanren (Japanese business lobby), 96
Kim, Yeon-Myung, 187, 247n13
Kitagawa, Johnny, 106
Korea. *See* South Korea
Korea Employers Federation, 67
Korean National Child Protection Agency (CPA), 120
Korean National Pension Research Institute, 57
Korean War, 55
Kuomintang (KMT), 79, 148

labor force: growth of, 39–40, *40*, 209n74; women in, 42, 72, 87, 164, 166
labor market policies, 3, 15, 74, 182, 194, 204n16. *See also* active labor market policies; passive labor market policies
labor movements, 13, 67, 95, 96, 98
Lam, Carrie, 139, 141
Latin America, 82
Lee Hsien Loong, 146
Lee Ka-chiu, John, 141
Leung Chun-ying, 139, 144
liberal welfare systems, 7, 21, 22, 204n18; Japan, 7, 22–23, 50, 181, 185, 187, 198, 201n6, 204n19; South Korea, 7, 50, 181, 185, 198; United States, 21, 185

Malaysia, 145, 236n81
Mao Zedong, 152, 157, 168
"McRefugees," 71, 126
mental health, 47, 196; child maltreatment and, 111, 226n50; income inequality and, 36; women and, 196–97
Mia, Kurihara, 106, 118
migration: China, 172, 174, 176–77, 241n72, 246n153; China, rural to urban, 157–62,

171–72, 239n47, 239n49, 243n112; to global cities, 207n51; Hong Kong, 124, 133–34, 233n34; Singapore, 40, 145–46, 236n81; Taiwan, 48, 84, 99
minimum wage, 182–83; China, 169–70, 242n100; Hong Kong, 94; Japan, 96; Singapore, 95, 98; South Korea, 97, 223nn110–11; Taiwan, 46, 48, 82–83, 90–92, 217n20
modernization, 20, 74
Montfort Care (organization), 122
Moon Jae-in, 66, 97, 148

Netherlands, 144, 204n18
Ng, Irene, 70
Noa, Kakehashi, 106
Norway, 19, 204n18

OECD countries, 7; education expenditures, 31–32, *32*; income inequality, *30*; labor market policies, 194; OECD-18 members, 206n31; old age crisis, 57–58, *57–58*, 182; pension systems, 63; private welfare spending, 31, *31*; social insurance, *193*; social protection, 23–25, *24–25*, *191*, *193*; social welfare systems, 190–94; statistics, 9–10, 249n31
old age crisis, 2–4, 11, 51–73, 182; caregivers, 42–43; China, 47, 63, 69, 156, 161, 163–67, 182, 215n78, 240nn60–61, 246n3; graying population, 40–41 (*see also* age dependency ratio); Hong Kong, 57, *57*, 69, 71–72, 126–27, 132, 182, 215n78, 233n27, 246n3; housing and, 135; Japan, 57, 63, 64, 69–70, 182, 211n10, 215n78, 246n3; OECD countries, 57–58, *57–58*, 182; Singapore, 69, 70–71, 182, 215n78, 246n3; South Korea, 2–4, 7, 15, 45, 47, 49, 51–69, *57–58*, 73, 98, 182, 188, 212n25, 212n26, 215n78, 246n3; Taiwan, 63, 69, 72–73, 182, 215n78, 246n3
Osaka, 146
outsourcing, 34

Pan, Jennifer, 166
Parasite (2019), 1, 147
Park Chung-hee, 56
Park Geun-hye, 68
passive labor market policies (PLMPs), 93, 182, 194, 220n66; China, 169; Taiwan, 90–91, 221n71
patronage, 26–27
Peng, Ito, 22, 184–85
pensions, 3, 41, 62–63, 213nn43–44; China, 164–67; government spending on, *25*; South Korea, 3, 15, 63–65, 188

policy façades, 179–81, 186, 194, 198–99; defined, 6, 12; impact of, 8; productivism and, 43–47. See also *specific countries*
policymakers, autonomy of, 17, 203n6
poverty, 28–30, *30*, 36, 45; China, 28, 151, 167–68, 207n42; declining, 5, 27; defined, 207n42; Hong Kong, 36, 38, 71, 93–94, 122, 132, 211n8, 232n26, 233n28; Japan, 25, 28, 36, 57, 112, 182, 207n42, 208n63, 211n10, 227n69, 246n3; OECD countries, old age poverty in, 57–58, *57–58*, 182; Singapore, 70–71, 182, 246n3; South Korea, 28, 36, 41, 51, 66, 207n42, 208n63; Taiwan, 37, 72, 74, 82–83, 90, 182, 246n3. See also working poverty
poverty line: OECD, 211n7; World Bank, 164, 207n42
private welfare solutions, 4–6, 15–16; compared to public welfare spending, 30–31, *31*; effectiveness of, 27. See also community support systems; corporations; familial support systems
productivism, 11–50, 179–81, 198; defined, 4–6, 21–23; dualistic welfare provision (targeted benefits), 14–15, 27–33, 45, 68, 96, 100–101, 186, 192; economic harms caused by, 6–7, 27, 47–49, 98; factors undermining viability of, 33–43; negative consequences of, 12–13, 27; political support for (vested interests), 6, 12, 27. See also policy façades
protests and unrest, 204n16; China, 242n95; Hong Kong, 48, 128; labor market policies and, 204n16; Taiwan, 48, 83–84, 217n25
public health policy, 194–98

Robin Hood paradox, 28–30, 100
Rodrik, Dani, 191
Roh Tae-woo, 147

safety net programs, 20, 24, 36, 186, 194; limited, 4, 21. See also social assistance
Saitō Riku, 117–18
Samuels, Dick, 9
SARS epidemic (2003), 36–37, 86, 130, 139, 145
Scandinavian countries, 19, *20*, 21
Seoul, 34, 51, 68, 147–48, 183
Setser, Brad, 178
Shanghai, 158, 176–77, 242n100, 245n138
Shenzhen, 177
Singapore, 201n5; affordable housing crisis, 144–46, 181, 183, 245n137; ALMPs, 94–95, 181; Big Love child protection center, 122; Central Provident Fund, 22, 70, 145, 235n77;

Singapore (*continued*)
  Central Provident Fund (CPF) Retirement Account, 70; child maltreatment, 121–22; Child Protective Service, 121; ComCare Long Term Assistance, 70–71; education expenditures, 31–32, *32*, 184; family planning policies, 210n94; fertility rates, 41; free trade policy, 203n7; GDP per capita, 205n29; Home Ownership Scheme, 145, 235n77; Housing Development Board (HDB), 70, 144–45; income inequality, 18, *18*, 30, *30*, 35, 95; migrant workers in, 40, 145–46, 236n81; minimum wage, 95, 98; National Trades Union Congress, 95; National Wages Council, 95; old age crisis, 69, 70–71, 182, 215n78, 246n3; old age security programs, 70–71; People's Action Party (PAP), 95, 222n93; poverty, 70–71, 182, 246n3; productivist approach, 21–22; Progressive Wage Model (PWM), 95, 182–83; Silver Support Scheme, 71; skill-biased technical change, 35; social assistance, 184; social insurance, *193*; social problems, 4; social protection coverage, *29*; social protection spending, 24–25, *24–25*, *28*, 43, *44*, 185, *193*; urbanization, 37; wages, 34, 81, *81*, 94–95, 222n86, 222n91; Worker's Party, 95, 222n93; Workfare Income Supplement, 95, 222n89
single parents, 43, 101–6, 112–16, 118–19, 171, 227n69, 229n104, 243n110
skill-biased technical change, 6, 16, 33–37, 98–99, 160, 186; economic insecurity and, 101, 111–12; wage stagnation and, 75, 85–86, 90, 93, 124–25
social assistance, 3, 15; China, 154–56; coverage rates, 28, *29*, 184, 185, 192–93; defined, 23; Hong Kong, 25, 129; Japan, 25, 105–6, 112, 118–19, 184; in productivist systems, 21; Singapore, 184; South Korea, 25, 56, 184, 185, 188; spending on, 24–25, *24–25*, 43–45, *44*; Taiwan, 80, 83, 217n22
social democratic welfare systems, 21, 204n18
social insurance, 3, 15, 20, 22, 184; China, 155–56, *193*; coverage rates, 28, *29*, 185; defined, 23; Hong Kong, 129, 184, *193*; Japan, 105–6, 119, 184, 185, *193*; OECD countries, *193*; Singapore, *193*; South Korea, 56, *193*; spending on, 24–25, *24–25*, 43–45, *44*; Taiwan, 80, 90–92, 184, 185, *193*; United States, *193*. *See also* pensions
social protection coverage, *29*
social protection spending, 1, 6, 11; categories of, 3, 23 (*see also* active labor market policies; social assistance; social insurance); data on, 9–10, 205n28, 205n30; economic development and, 7–8; levels of, 43–45, *44*; for poor and nonpoor recipients, 28, *28*; relative levels of, comparing East Asia and OECD (primarily Western) countries, 13, 23–27. *See also* policy façades; *specific countries*
social rights, 21
social welfare analysis, 20–23; capitalism and, 202n9; dynamic integrated approach, 3–8, 13–16, 179–83, 194–99; East-West comparison, 181, 190–94, 198–99, 246n1; micro/macro lens, 14–16; narratives used in, 8–9, 16; temporal dimension, 16. *See also* Bismarckian welfare systems; liberal welfare systems; social democratic welfare systems
Society for Community Organization, 140
Southeast Asia, 34–35, 87, 145–46, 236n81
South Korea: affordable housing crisis, 38, 147–48; age dependency ratio, 41, 239n45; ALMPs, 56, 97; Basic Livelihood Security Program (BLSP), 63, 66, 214n64; Basic Old Age Pension (BOAP), 63–66, 68; Candlelight Revolution (2016), 68; *chaebol* (industrial conglomerate), 55, 67, 211n3; child maltreatment, 120, 228n79; Child Welfare Act, 120; community support systems, 68; corporate benefits, 65; COVID-19 and, 195; democratization, 186–90; Earned Income Tax Credit (EITC), 66; economic growth, 51–52, 55–56, 66–68; education expenditures, public and private, 15, 31–32, *32*, 51, 53–55, 60, 212n26; Employment Success Package Programme, 97; family structures, 61; fertility rates, 51, 59; Government Employees Pension Service, 63; Green New Deal, 197; health care, 67, 187–88; income inequality, 1–2, *18*, 18–19, 29, *30*, 189, 203n11; *jeonse* system, 147, 236n92; labor force growth, *40*, 209n74; labor market policies, 19, 27, 194; liberal welfare system, 7, 50, 181, 185, 198; life expectancy, 51, 59; minimum wage, 97, 223nn110–11; National Pension Service (NPS), 63–65, 188; nonregular workers, 65, 97–98; old age crisis, 2–4, 7, 15, 45, 47, 49, 51–69, *57–58*, 73, 98, 182, 188, 212n25, 212n26, 215n78, 246n3; old age security programs, 62–66, 213n50; pension system, 3, 15, 63–65, 188; personal resources (household savings), 60–62, 212n23; political and economic context, 45, 55–56, 68, 191, 205n29, 211n6, 248n27; political economy of social protection, 66–68; poverty, 28, 36, 41, 51, 66, 207n42, 208n63;

private welfare spending, 31, *31*; productivist approach, 22; retirement, mandatory, 52–53, 61–62, 64, 67, 213n36; skill-biased technical change, 35, 51, 65; social assistance, 25, 56, 184, 185, 188; social insurance, 56, *193*; social protection coverage, *29*; social protection spending, 23–28, *24–25*, *28*, 43, *44*, 56, 180, 184, 187–89, *191*, *193*, 205n30; social security policy façade, 45, 52, 64, 73; suicides, 38, 47, 51, 54, 58–59, 68, 210n1; unemployment, 97–98, 194; urbanization, 37–38, 51, 60–61; wages, 34, 81, *81*, 97–98, 222n105; women in, 42, 97
Soviet Union, 150, 151
standards of living: declining, 4; improving, 1, 11, 19, 74
suicides, 195–96; Japan, 69, 112, 113; mother–child suicides *(boshi shinjū)*, 112, 113; South Korea, 38, 47, 51, 54, 58–59, 68, 210n1
supply chains, 34, 85, 152, 160
Sweden, 23, *24*, 30, *31*, 64, *193*, 204n18
Sze Lai-Shan, 140

Taipei, 34, 74, 83, 183, 237n102
Taiwan: affordable housing crisis, 148–49, 237nn101–2; ALMPs, 90–91; brain drain (emigration of high-skill workers), 48, 84, 99; child maltreatment, 120–21, 230n114; Child Welfare Act, 121; China and, 79–80, 83–84, 86–87, 201n3, 218n38; college-educated workers, 75–78, 80, 82, 83–84, 86, 88–89, 219n47, 219n57; community support services, 83; Democratic Progressive Party (DPP), 79, 86, 237n100; democratization, 91, 92, 186–87, 189–90; economic growth, 74, 79–80; education expenditures, 31–32, *32*, 88–89, 92–93, 99, 219n52; education wage premium, 82, 217n14, 219n57; Employment Insurance Act, 91; familial support systems, 83; fertility rates, 84–85, 89; foreign workers in, 87, 218n41; globalization and, 86; health care, 189; income inequality, *18*, 18–19, 29, *30*, 37, 82, 203n11, 217n17; labor force growth, *40*, 209n74; Labor Insurance or Labor Pension program, 72; labor market policies, 3, 90–93; labor market policy façade, 45–46, 90–93; Labour Insurance Act, 91; massification of tertiary education, 88–89, 92–93, 99, 182, 219n52; minimum wage, 46, 48, 82–83, 90–92, 217n20; National Pension, 72; offshoring, 86–87, 218n38; old age crisis, 63, 69, 72–73, 182, 215n78, 246n3; passive labor market policies (PLMPs), 90–91, 221n71; political and economic context, 45, 79–80, 87–88, 191–92, 205n29, 248n27; poverty, 37, 47, 72, 74, 82–83, 90, 182, 246n3; productivist approach, 14–15, 22, 75, 92–93; Protection of Children and Youth Welfare and Rights Act, 121; protests and unrest, 48, 83–84, 217n25; skill-biased technical change, 86; social assistance, 80, 83, 217n22; Social Assistance Act, 91; social insurance, 80, 90–92, 184, 185, *193*; social protection spending, 24–25, *24–25*, 43, *44*, 80, 180, 185, 189–90, *191*, *193*; Sunflower Movement, 83; unemployment, 81–82, 86, 90–91; urbanization, 37; wage stagnation, 2–4, 7, 34, 37, 45–46, 48–49, 74–93, *81*, 98, 99; women in, 42, 72, 87
Taiwan Fund for Children and Families, 83
Takashi, Masuzawa, 114
tax policies, 29–30, 207n45
Tetsuo, Takenaka, 109
Tokyo, 34, 35, 112, 130, 146
trade: free trade policies, 203n7; international, 34, 85, 207n52. *See also* globalization; supply chains
Tsang, Donald, 139
Tung Chee-hwa, 138

unemployment, 81–82, 97–98, 227n63
unemployment insurance, 5, 36, 90–91, 169, 194, 195, 220n66, 221n71
United Kingdom, 46, 62–63, 85, 185, 204n18, 213n38
United Nations Convention on the Rights of the Child, 109, 114, 170
United States, 84, 115, 204n18, 229n101, 248n28, 250n53; affordable housing crisis, 129–30; child maltreatment, 109; economic insecurity, 8, 190; education wage premium, 85, 217n16; income inequality, 18, *30*, 85; income support policies, 46; liberal welfare system, 21, 185; old age security programs, 62, 64; private welfare spending, 31, *31*; social insurance, *193*; social protection spending, 23, *24*, *193*, 194, 198; wages, 81
unrest. *See* protests and unrest
urbanization, 6, 15–16, 37–39, 186; child maltreatment and, 38–39, 101, 110–11, 121, 171; China, 12, 37, 38–39, 161–62, 171–72, 175; community assistance and, 111, 162; familial support services and, 33, 38; Hong Kong, 37–38; housing and, 135; Japan, 37; mental disorders and, 111; Singapore, 37; South Korea, 37–38, 51, 60–61; Taiwan, 37

wages: China, 34, 81, *81*, 87, 167–70, 182, 242n100; economic growth and, 182; high-skill workers, 37, 85–86; Hong Kong, 34, 81, *81*, 93–94, 221n77; increasing, 74; Japan, 34, 81, *81*, 95–96; labor movements and, 98; Singapore, 34, 81, *81*, 94–95, 222n86, 222n91; South Korea, 34, 81, *81*, 97–98, 222n105; United States, 81. *See also* education wage premium

wage stagnation, 4, 11, 34, 36, 75, *81*, 98–99, 182–83; causes of, 85–86; globalization and, 75, 85–86, 90, 93, 124–25; skill-biased technical change and, 75, 85–86, 90, 93, 124–25; Taiwan, 2–4, 7, 34, 37, 45–46, 48–49, 75–93, *81*, 82–89, 98, 99

Western countries, 7, 13. *See also* OECD countries; *specific countries*

women: in labor force, 42, 72, 87, 164, 166; mental health issues, 196–97. *See also* single parents

Wong, Joseph, 22, 91, 184–85, 187, 205n23

workers: high-skill, 34, 35, 37, 85–86; low-skill, 6, 34, 35, 37, 75, 85–86, 92, 98, 182; mid-skill, 34, 35; targeted social protection for, 4, 21 (*see also* productivism). *See also* skill-biased technical change; wages; wage stagnation

working poverty, 5; Europe, 221n80; Hong Kong, 93–94, 132, 233n28; Japan, 112; Taiwan, 82–83, 90. *See also* safety net programs

World Bank, 152, 204n21; *The East Asian Miracle,* 17, 207n49; poverty line, 164, 207n42

Xi Jinping, 161, 241n77

Yōko, Ishikura, 114
Yoon Suk-yeol, 66, 148, 223n118
Yua, Funato, 106

Studies of the Weatherhead East Asian Institute Columbia University

SELECTED TITLES

(Complete list at: weai.columbia.edu/content/publications)

In Search of Admiration and Respect: Chinese Cultural Diplomacy in the United States, 1875–1974, by Yanqiu Zheng. University of Michigan Press, 2024.

Perilous Wagers: Gambling, Dignity, and Day Laborers in Post-Fukushima Tokyo, by Klaus K. Y. Hammering. Cornell University Press, 2024.

The Chinese Computer: A Global History of the Information Age, by Thomas S. Mullaney. The MIT Press, 2024.

Beauty Matters: Modern Japanese Literature and the Question of Aesthetics, 1890–1930, by Anri Yasuda. Columbia University Press, 2024.

Revolutionary Becomings: Documentary Media in Twentieth-Century China, by Ying Qian. Columbia University Press, 2024.

Waiting for the Cool Moon: Anti-imperialist Struggles in the Heart of Japan's Empire, by Wendy Matsumura. Duke University Press, 2024.

Beauty Regimes: A History of Power and Modern Empire in the Philippines, 1898–1941, by Genevieve Clutario. Duke University Press, 2023.

Afterlives of Letters: The Transnational Origins of Modern Literature in China, Japan, and Korea, by Satoru Hashimoto. Columbia University Press, 2023.

Republican Vietnam, 1963–1975: War, Society, Diaspora, edited by Trinh M. Luu and Tuong Vu. University of Hawai`i Press, 2023.

Territorializing Manchuria: The Transnational Frontier and Literatures of East Asia, by Miya Xie. Harvard East Asian Monographs, 2023.

Takamure Itsue, Japanese Antiquity, and Matricultural Paradigms that Address the Crisis of Modernity: A Woman from the Land of Fire, by Yasuko Sato. Palgrave Macmillan, 2023.

Rejuvenating Communism: Youth Organizations and Elite Renewal in Post-Mao China, by Jérôme Doyon. University of Michigan Press, 2023.

From Japanese Empire to American Hegemony: Koreans and Okinawans in the Resettlement of Northeast Asia, by Matthew R. Augustine. University of Hawai`i Press, 2023.

Building a Republican Nation in Vietnam, 1920–1963, edited by Nu-Anh Tran and Tuong Vu. University of Hawai`i Press, 2022.

China Urbanizing: Impacts and Transitions, edited by Weiping Wu and Qin Gao. University of Pennsylvania Press, 2022.

Common Ground: Tibetan Buddhist Expansion and Qing China's Inner Asia, by Lan Wu. Columbia University Press, 2022.

Narratives of Civic Duty: How National Stories Shape Democracy in Asia, by Aram Hur. Cornell University Press, 2022.

The Concrete Plateau: Urban Tibetans and the Chinese Civilizing Machine, by Andrew Grant. Cornell University Press, 2022.

Confluence and Conflict: Reading Transwar Japanese Literature and Thought, by Brian Hurley. Harvard East Asian Monographs, 2022.

Inglorious, Illegal Bastards: Japan's Self-Defense Force During the Cold War, by Aaron Skabelund. Cornell University Press, 2022.
Madness in the Family: Women Care, and Illness in Japan, by H. Yumi Kim. Oxford University Press, 2022.
Uncertainty in the Empire of Routine: The Administrative Revolution of the Eighteenth-Century Qing State, by Maura Dykstra. Harvard University Press, 2022.
Outsourcing Repression: Everyday State Power in Contemporary China, by Lynette H. Ong. Oxford University Press, 2022.
Diasporic Cold Warriors: Nationalist China, Anticommunism, and the Philippine Chinese, 1930s–1970s, by Chien-Wen Kung. Cornell University Press, 2022.
Dream Super-Express: A Cultural History of the World's First Bullet Train, by Jessamyn Abel. Stanford University Press, 2022.
The Sound of Salvation: Voice, Gender, and the Sufi Mediascape in China, by Guangtian Ha. Columbia University Press, 2022.
Learning to Rule: Court Education and the Remaking of the Qing State, 1861–1912, by Daniel Barish. Columbia University Press, 2022.

www.ingramcontent.com/pod-product-compliance
Lightning Source LLC
Chambersburg PA
CBHW030523230426
43665CB00010B/745